THE BERKSHIRE HILLS

Mountain Road in The Berkshires   Courtesy of The Society
for The Preservation of New England Antiquities

THE BERKSHIRE HILLS

Compiled and Written by
*Members of the Federal Writers' Project of the
Works Progress Administration for Massachusetts*

*With a New Foreword by
Roger B. Linscott*

NORTHEASTERN UNIVERSITY PRESS

BOSTON

First Northeastern University Press edition 1987

First published in 1939 by The Berkshire Hills Conference, Inc. in the American Guide Series, with the editorial and research assistance of the Federal Works Agency, Works Projects Administration for the State of Massachusetts.

Library of Congress Cataloging-in-Publication Data

The Berkshire Hills.

Reprint. Originally published: 1st ed. New York: Funk & Wagnalls, 1939.
1. Berkshire County (Mass.)—Description and travel. I. Federal Writers' Project (Mass.)
II. Berkshire Hills Conference, Inc. III. Series: American guide series.
F72.B5B39 1987   917.44'0442   86-33333
ISBN 1-55553-012-5

Printed and bound by Edward Brothers, Inc., Lillington, North Carolina. The paper is Warren Old Style, an acid-free sheet.

MANUFACTURED IN THE UNITED STATES OF AMERICA

91   90   89   88   87   5   4   3   2   1

A NEW FOREWORD TO THE 1987 EDITION

In the nearly half-century since *The Berkshire Hills* was originally published, at least a dozen books dealing with the Berkshires have followed into print. Some have merited a place beside it, some have not. But as a lively yet comprehensive town-by-town guide to this special region and its people, this book remains unique. No wonder so many of us who cherish the area have worn out our original copies, and copies that occasionally turn up at used bookstores sell quickly at many times the original price.

In truth, the Berkshire County it describes is not quite the Berkshire County of today. For one thing, a number of landmarks have disappeared. Some, like Andrew Carnegie's hundred-room Shadowbrook "cottage" in Lenox, were destroyed by fire. Others, like the historic Peace Party House in the center of Pittsfield, fell prey to bulldozers and indifference. Industries traditionally linked to the region have disappeared as well. Most of the textile mills that once sustained Adams and North Adams have gone bankrupt or gone south. In Pittsfield, 1986 saw the end of an era when General Electric announced that it would phase out the local manufacture of power transformers—a product intimately identified with the Berkshires ever since electrical pioneer William Stanley used alternating current to light up the main street of Great Barrington a century earlier.

The changes in the countryside have been at least as dramatic as those in the towns. While agricultural technology has enabled Berkshire County's total milk production to remain constant for a half-century, the ratio of cows to people and farmers to non-farmers has dropped precipitously. In 1940, Berkshire County boasted more than three hundred dairy farms; today, fewer than sixty remain. True, this hasn't reduced the rural census figures: many Berkshire hilltowns whose populations steadily declined in the 150 years between the first U.S. census and World War II are now growing.

But their new residents are commuters or second-home buyers from the cities—countrymen by adoption, not by birth. Many a Yankee who once made a living by the plow or the ax is now making it by selling off an inheritance, ten or fifteen acres at a time—and at prices that would have been considered preposterous twenty years ago.

Another major change since 1940 has been an explosive growth in Berkshire tourism. Summer visitors have been coming to the Berkshires since the mid-nineteenth century, but in recent decades tourism has flourished. Of the seventy-odd great estates that defined the social life of Berkshire County at the turn of this century, few remain as private homes. But the money pumped into the county's economy by their millionaire owners in the Gilded Age is small change compared to the estimated $90 million spread about annually by skiers in the winter, foliage lovers in the fall, and, above all, culture seekers in the summer. The Berkshire Music Festival alone draws a third of a million people every July and August to the Boston Symphony's summer home at Tanglewood. It is supplemented by a panoply of musical and theatrical activities plus a satellite empire of hotels, motels, and restaurants, many of top caliber. There is local dispute whether tourism is the region's second or third biggest industry, but no dispute about that fact that it is the fastest-growing.

Yet, amid all the changes of a kaleidoscopic era, many things in the Berkshires remain very much the same, and these tend to be the things that count most. Not least is an unusually strong sense of identity among the region's inhabitants—a conviction that the county is something rather special and rather good. Common sense might suggest that pristine Egremont, charming, rural, with lots of well-heeled émigrés from Manhattan, has little in common with, say, North Adams, a decidedly blue-collar community forty miles to the north. But, in fact, the bond is still surprisingly strong. The country squire in Egremont and the second-generation mill hand in a North Adams double-decker both regard themselves as Berkshirites. Both feel an unusual degree of regional patriotism, and both believe that the area's biggest shortcoming is its inability to provide enough jobs to keep their sons and daughters from straying to other pastures.

This pride of place has deep roots. Berkshire County was settled a century later than the Connecticut River Valley, only fifty miles to the east, and when the first settlers did arrive, they came mainly up the Housatonic River Valley from Connecticut rather than from Massachusetts. This bred a sense of isolation from the authorities in Boston, together with a penchant for independence in matters both spiritual and temporal. At the Berkshire Jubilee of 1844, when some four thousand inhabitants and alumni of the area gathered in Pittsfield for a giant homecoming, the theme of enlightened provincialism was sounded by Mark Hopkins, revered president of Williams College. "Unlike most counties, Berkshire, having a peculiar geological formation, is a place by itself, separated from the rest of the world by natural boundaries. . . . Between us and our fellow-citizens of the eastern part of the state, there is a perceptible difference."

The passage of time and the construction of the Massachusetts Turnpike may have made this difference less perceptible, but it remains a part of the Berkshire state of mind. The distrust of state authority that provided fertile ground for the seditious seeds of Shays' Rebellion two hundred years ago is echoed today in the region's running war with "the Boston politicians," who are alleged to believe without exception that Massachusetts extends no farther west than the Connecticut River.

At the same time, this sense of regional identity unquestionably has made Berkshire citizens more conscious of their assets and more vigilant about protecting them. Since 1967, the Berkshire Natural Resources Council has been spreading the doctrines of conservation while providing a vehicle for placing private land in public trust for future generations. The thriving Berkshire County Historical Society, an outgrowth of the county's bicentennial celebration in 1961, now occupies Arrowhead, the house where Herman Melville wrote *Moby Dick*. Another nearby literary landmark, the Mount, in Lenox, where Edith Wharton lived and wrote for many years, has been similarly preserved for the public by private munificence. And, in perhaps the most ambitious restoration of all, the once-thriving Shaker colony in Hancock has been brought back to life as a living museum of Shaker life and crafts.

These are clearly positive aspects of the past fifty years in the Berkshires. The negative aspects of today would be the inevitable by-products of material "progress": more blacktop, more traffic, more commercialization, and, with it all, a certain loss of innocence, or, at least, of bucolic flavor. On balance, though, it is safe to say that most of those who know the region best— certainly those of us who live there by choice—still regard it as singularly blessed by nature and by man, handsome to look upon and nicely situated between the pressures of urban life and the intellectual isolation of true backcountry. In the pages of *The Berkshire Hills,* you will encounter a varied parade of illustrious Americans who came to the region as visitors, succumbed to its charms, and stayed to put down roots. They continue to do so today.

Roger B. Linscott

CONTENTS

ILLUSTRATIONS

INTRODUCTION

THE BERKSHIRE HILLS geographically are merely that portion of the great Appalachian chain which lies in western Massachusetts. But no hills amid which people have lived long can be considered merely as geography, nor even chiefly as geography. They color the life which goes on in their valleys and on their slopes, and that life in turn colors them. Before Wordsworth and his fellows made famous and romantic the hills and vales of northwestern England, the Lake Country had done something to the poets. Before the Berkshire Barrier—that high plateau which separates the Connecticut valley from the valleys of the Housatonic and Hoosac Rivers—was much more than a wilderness, a little boy grew up in Cummington and while still in his teens wrote "Thanatopsis" and "To a Wild Fowl." Bryant, to be sure, was not the first literary light in the Berkshires. Half a century earlier, while preacher to the Stockbridge Indians, Jonathan Edwards wrote *The Freedom of the Will*. But that great work, after all, contributed little to our appreciation of Nature, nor drew its inspiration from the local scene. Jonathan was too concerned with the next world to bother about this one.

William Cullen Bryant in verse, Catherine Sedgwick in fiction, were the first to make effective use of our local scene in literature and thus to draw attention to the local flavors and to color the future. Neither of them, to be sure, did so thoroughly efficient a job as Washington Irving at the same time did for the Catskills. Ninety-nine out of every one hundred Americans to this day see the Catskills as Irving colored them, and the fact that they aren't a bit like that any more doesn't trouble most of us merely because we don't go there. If Bryant had created as vivid a legend for the Berkshires as Irving did for those mountains which we can see from our Taconic divide, huddled blue against the west, I suppose we would resent the General Electric plant in Pittsfield, the Lenox villas, the cement highways, and all the other marks of the later nineteenth and this twentieth century. (Some of them, may I remark parenthetically, some of us *do* resent.) But no such overwhelming haze of legend was distilled around the Berkshires to remove them forever into a hushed and wistful past. What was built up, by action and reaction, by what our hills themselves imposed on their inhabitants and by what the inhabitants came to think and feel and write about them, may be described as a decorously passionate appreciation of the peculiar natural beauties of the scene and a desire on the part of most of our people to erect our dwellings, adorn our streets, and in general to conduct our community lives in keeping with our surroundings. We appreciate our birthright and we are proud of it (sometimes, I fear, a bit boastfully so), and we do our best, against all the pressure of commercial exploitation, to preserve it.

Not all the writers who have lived in the Berkshires appreciated them. Hawthorne did not, during the year and a half he lived in a tiny house in Lenox at the head of Stockbridge Bowl and looked southward over the same view which now enchants the visitors to our Music Shed. But he was a seaboard man—and hated cold weather. At the same time there lived in Lenox the famous Fanny Kemble, niece of the more famous Sarah Siddons, and she adored the Berkshires, with an enthusiasm surprising in a Briton. She knew that Hawthorne's view across the Bowl to the blue Dome of the Taconics was lovely with the same qualities of subdued ruggedness and romantic repose found in the Lake Country, and she admired our strong growing forests and the shadowed roads winding through them. Even Matthew Arnold, who spent two summers in Stockbridge in the late 1880's but who was not given to excessive admiration of things American, condescended to praise our wild flowers and to speak highly of the "noble" prospect from the spot where now stands the studio of the late Daniel Chester French, in Glendale. This is another vista which is closed by the Dome of the Taconics (Mount Everett), for all its lack of great elevation one of the most esthetically satisfying mountains in New England. So the English appreciated us if Hawthorne didn't. Not that it greatly mattered to us. We had admired the Dome years before Arnold ever gave it his approval. Thoreau had climbed Greylock. Henry Ward Beecher had made his summer home with us and added his appreciative essays to our store of place literature. Holmes had lived among us and celebrated our cattle shows in verse. We had begun to absorb the fashionable and wealthy without losing our local prides, and with their aid were fighting the good fight to keep our villages as neat and as tree-shaded and as quietly dignified as our landscape.

The first village improvement society in America was founded in Stockbridge—and still flourishes there. In the nineties Stockbridge was one town which did not yield to the trolley craze, but put the tracks down below the beautiful main street, out of sight. A little later, it put all its telephone and electric light wires under ground. And I think I am right in saying that there is not a billboard within the town limits. At any rate, the number is so small that it is negligible. All this wasn't accomplished by legislation but by public sentiment, by local pride, by what we like to think is the Berkshire spirit. It is not, of course, operative 100 per cent in our entire county, but we are constantly striving to make it so.

Our hills are not high, and with the exception of Greylock (the highest) and the Dome, they seldom make pronounced individual summits. They are long horizontals rising on the east to an extensive upland plateau which is still for the most part sparsely populated, covered with second-growth forest, and criss-crossed with old roads which invite exploration. These hills are well watered, and our mountain brooks are constantly breaking into waterfalls of unexpected charm—unexpected because the casual tourist may sometimes pass within a few hundred yards of them on the highway and never guess their existence. They tumble down through forests of yellow birch and maple and hemlock, over rocks dripping green with moss and maidenhair, or overhung with laurel and hobblebush. They are true wilderness gardens. We have orchid gardens in our swamps—to the positions of which I pray this guide book gives no clue! We have what we call cobbles, an old English term signifying an extensive outcropping of rock, in our case limestone. On these cobbles grow exquisite fern gardens of ebony and maidenhair spleenwort, of walking fern and purple cliff brake. We have miles of mountain and forest trails. In short, we in the Berkshires have quick escape from urbanity into comparative wilderness.

The wild and the cultivated are close companions in our country, and we are happy in the companionship. One of the prize gardens in Lenox is based around a giant boulder at the edge of woods, the crevices of the stone still verdant with forest ferns, and the view from the house terrace is not of formal flowerbeds, but of a distant mountain.

Almost every estate, in fact, strives to incorporate its particular view into the garden scheme, to make the enfolding Berkshire Hills forever a part of the domestic life pattern. That is what we think of our country.

And that is what we hope you will come to think of it if you visit the Berkshires. If that isn't what you are looking for, and you are insensible to the subtler differences of landscape appeal and ways of living, I'm not sure we want you at all. However, if you have purchased and perused a carefully prepared guide book, you surely are sensible to what makes one way of life, one portion even of New England different from another; or are curious to discover. You, we do want. We want you to see the Berkshires. We want you to stay long enough to explore and understand them. And if you do, we are pretty certain you will love them.

WALTER PRICHARD EATON

Twin Fires
Sheffield
June, 1939

THE BERKSHIRE HILLS

Chapter I

INDUSTRY PENETRATES THE HILLS

FLORIDA—Mass 2, sett. 1783, alt. 2180, pop. 405.

CLARKSBURG—Mass 8, sett. 1769, alt. 1000, pop. 1333.

NORTH ADAMS—Mass 2 and 8, sett. 1768, alt. 800, pop. 22,085.

Roads—Florida is on Mass 2, 130 miles from Boston (Mohawk Trail), 180 miles from New York City (US 7 through Pittsfield and Norwalk, Connecticut, then US 1), 50 miles from Troy, New York. (Mass 2 and NY 96) and 30 miles from Greenfield (Mass 2); North Adams is on the same route; Clarksburg is on Mass 8, through North Adams.

On February 9, 1875, at 4 o'clock in the afternoon, a steam engine covered with bunting hurled its first black puff of smoke into the Valley of the Hoosic. Out of Hoosac Tunnel, the second longest in the world at the time, had come three platform cars and a freight bearing 125 merrymakers whose excitement not even the thirty-four-minute trip through the smoke-filled "hole in the wall" could choke. This was the first official run from *FLORIDA*, in the Deerfield Valley, through the depths of Hoosac Mountain into the Valley of the Hoosic to North Adams. It had cost twenty-four years of labor, fifteen million dollars, and 195 lives to build a cavern four and three-quarters miles long.

A direct means of transportation from eastern Massachusetts to North Adams and the New York State line was first proposed in 1825. There was a wild idea about running a canal through the mountain. In 1828, a State Commission reported a railroad more feasible than a canal. Nothing was done, however, until '48, when the Troy and Greenfield Railroad Company was chartered to begin construction of a road from Greenfield to North Adams. Upon actually starting work three years later, Laommi Baldwin, the engineer who had made the first survey of the route, exclaimed with enthusiasm:

"It seems as if the finger of Providence had marked out this route from the east to the west."

"Too bad the same finger wasn't put through Hoosac Mountain," was a cynic's reply.

The cynic knew what he was talking about. For twenty-four years men dug and bored and drilled a passage through the depths of the range. Work was several times abandoned, only to be resumed when enough money was collected. For the first fourteen years, they worked with pickaxes, hand drills, and black blasting powder, for air drills and blasting dynamite had not been perfected. The black powder made a great racket and smoke, but dislodged only small fragments of rock. Hand drilling was slow and tedious. While one man held the drill and turned it, another whaled away with a sledge. Sometimes the hammer missed its mark, but there were always plenty of workmen eager for the "soft job" of holding the drill. Year after year they labored to the guttural humming of the driller's song made famous during the construction of the Union Pacific.

> Drill, ye Tarriers, drill,
> And its work all day,
> Without sugar in your tay,
> When you're working for the U.P. Railway.

All over the country doubting Thomases declared the tunnel would never be finished. Critics by the carload rose to denounce the work as a stupid and expensive folly. Among the rich, respectable, and powerful opponents was Francis Bird, Boston landowner and politician, whose pamphlet of 1868, *The Last Agony of the Great Bore,* accused Berkshire politicians of having "tunnel on the brain." Oliver Wendell Holmes observed that the millennium and the completion of the Hoosac Tunnel probably would occur simultaneously.

While public sentiment was sharply divided, a strong and reasoned plea for continuation was put forth in *Scribner's Magazine* by J. G. Holland, Berkshire historian.

The commercial intercourse of New England with the West has been greatly obstructed by this mountain barrier. . . . The people of New England did not, however, sit down behind their mountain wall and suck their thumbs. Close business relations with the great West were essential to their prosperity, and they determined to establish and maintain them. . . . If the mountain would not give way to Mahomet, Mahomet must go through the mountain. That is how the Hoosac Tunnel came to be built.

It is a clear announcement that New England does not intend to be left out in the cold.

Despite criticism and ridicule, the work went grimly on. At the very outset, a huge boring machine was erected near the eastern end of the proposed tunnel and great hopes were entertained for its ability to bore through the mountain. For ten feet it cut one smooth, half-moon-shaped hole—and stopped forever. Another machine was tried out at the western portal, but it didn't budge an inch. It took four years and half a million dollars to sink a central shaft 1,028 feet from the summit of the mountain into the maw of the earth. From this shaft men could cut their way to meet others working from both ends. Another shaft, 318 feet deep, was sunk on the North Adams side of the mountain.

Scenes around the shafts while work was going on were reminiscent of mining towns or camps in the far West. There were rows of small cabins, and cheap boardinghouses where the tunnel workers slept and ate. A mixture they were of many races and creeds, Irish and English, French-Canadians, Italians. Children poured in and out of the squalid houses where women, speaking foreign tongues, were busy with cooking and babies. Roughly dressed men, black with grime, went in and out of the diggings.

Report of death underground always brought a crowd of workmen's wives from Florida's shanty town to the pit head. After a while they got so used to disaster that there was no frenzy. When a limp body in earth-stained overalls and torn black shirt was carried out into the sunlight, a sobbing woman hid the eyes of her small boy in her skirt. The crowd melted away, other wives relieved that for one more day tragedy had passed them by. But in 1867 when fire broke out in the powerhouse of the central shaft and thirteen miners were trapped underground, the usual stoicism gave way to hysteria. In a bedlam of shrieks, curses, shrill whistles, a group of volunteers scrambled into the elevator car to descend the shaft and attempt a rescue. Above the tumult was heard the piercing cry of a child. "Pa! Ma says not to go down in the little house. You kill yourself!" Before the "little house" could even begin its perilous descent there was a muffled explosion underground. A burst of flame and a shower of rocks, bits of cloth and fragments of charred flesh.

While human moles burrowed their slow way into the mountain's heart, men of science worked in laboratories to perfect new equipment. Under the most favorable conditions, sixty feet a month was the best that could be done with hand drill and gunpowder. In 1865, after foreign-made drills had proved impracticable, an American air drill was introduced and used with success. In the same year, Professor George M. Mowbray tried out a new explosive called nitroglycerin, to replace the ineffectual black powder. Arthur Nobel had adapted nitroglycerin for ordinary excavation, but it was hair-trigger stuff. There was no known way to carry the "soup," as it was called, from place to place without danger of an explosion. It was said to be so sensitive that the scraping of a fiddle was enough to set it off. People thought it would blow up immediately if allowed to freeze. It took "Hell," so the story goes, to solve Professor Mowbray's problem.

Helton Swazey was the professor's assistant. When "Hell" was sober he was a mild young man, but when he got drunk, as often happened, he was a demon. One night, as he was helping the professor to close up shop, a hurry call came through from the east portal at Florida for some nitroglycerin. Swazey was taking his girl to a dance over that way, and he agreed to deliver the quart cans of "soup."

"You'd best not tell the young lady about it! She mightn't like it," the professor warned. "Not that there's any danger. We'll wrap the stuff in flannel and blankets, with a hot water bottle to keep it from freezing."

The night was bitter cold, and on the way Swazey often found it necessary to fortify himself from his liquor jug. Then the girl began to complain that she was freezing. When he obligingly pulled up the horse and fetched blankets and a hot water bottle, the girl thought him remarkably considerate. She was unaware that in the back of the sleigh there rode cans of nitroglycerin, uncovered now in the zero air.

At the hall, the party was in full swing. "Hell" and his girl hurried to join the dancers. Meanwhile the sleigh stood outside, the horse shivering under blankets. Before long Swazey began to feel his liquor and became so boisterous that the crowd pitched him out into a snowdrift to cool off. It was then that he remembered the packages in the sleigh. With an armful of cans he returned to the hall and faced his tormentors. Tunnel workers all, they knew nitroglycerin when they saw it. There was a stampede. As the door slammed on the last of the fleeing crowd, "Hell" broke loose! Crash! One of the cans hit the dance hall door. Another bounced off the red-hot stove. Chattering with rage, "Hell" hurled the nitroglycerin at various targets. At last his ammunition was exhausted, and he planked himself down beside the stove to sleep.

The word spread that Helton Swazey, dead drunk, was sound asleep among cans of frozen nitroglycerin which hadn't yet blown him up. At daylight Professor Mowbray appeared in the doorway. All around were evidences of the barrage. The professor was delighted. Obviously, the way to transport nitroglycerin was to freeze it. What could he do to show "Hell" his appreciation? Ah, yes, of course. He could buy him a drink!

With the new improvements, the digging on the Tunnel was speeded up. On Thanksgiving Day, 1873, twenty-two years after work was begun, the final blast broke away the last barrier of rock separating the Hoosac from the Deerfield Valley. The two gangs of workmen, forging toward each other from the east and the west, met so exactly that the error was only five-sixteenths of an inch. Freight trains went through the Tunnel as early as February, 1875; passenger trains not until the next fall.

Today the Tunnel operated by the Boston and Maine Railroad is equipped with double tracks, and electric locomotives are attached to the steam engines to draw trains through with a minimum of gas and smoke. For forty years after the Tunnel was completed, steam locomotives filled the cavern with smoke and cinders. Passengers who entered one end of the Tunnel looking like fashion models came out the other, gasping and choking, as black as southern field hands. In 1911 the Tunnel was electrified, and now modern air-conditioned cars keep their passengers immaculate.

Florida, a boom town when the Tunnel was being built, aspired to become a city when it was completed. In 1805, when the town was incorporated, there was talk of the United States purchasing the territory of Florida from Spain. The new village among the mountains chose the name of the flat, tropical region of palms and pelicans. Perhaps an overdeveloped sense of humor on the part of the town fathers contributed to the extraordinary choice. When the

Tunnel was completed, most of Florida's prosperity and population. drained out into the city of North Adams and the world beyond. Today the town has about 400 inhabitants, not half the number of workmen once employed on the "hole in the wall."

One day when the Tunnel was nearly finished, a newspaperman questioned an Irish workman:

"Do you think the Tunnel will be a financial success, Pat?"

"No, begorra, I don't that," replied Pat, "but 'twill be an ornament to society."

Pat was wrong. The ornament to society is the MOHAWK TRAIL, Mass 2, which winds over Hoosac Mountain on its way from Greenfield to North Adams. Completed in 1914 by the Massachusetts Highway Commission, the Mohawk Trail touches and crosses the old Trail blazed by the Indians. From earliest times, this path across the mountains was the natural route of travel from the Hudson Valley to the east. Bands of Indians on hunting and war expeditions went over it on their way into the Connecticut Valley. During the French and Indian Wars, the Canadian Mohawks filed along this path to prey on the scattered frontier villages of the English. It is for these warriors, rather than the Mohawks of New York, that the modern highway is named. Later, white men began to use the old Indian path: couriers sent by the Dutch from the Hudson Valley to warn the English settlers of imminent Indian attack, soldiers bound for Fort Massachusetts, hunters and scouts moving silently through the forest.

The soldiers and early settlers came on horseback, cutting their way through the wilderness. Gradually the trail was widened into a bridle path. White settlers brought ox carts and the path was again widened into the semblance of a road. No one knows when the first of these rude highways over the Hoosac Range was built, but in 1764 Samuel Rice of Charlemont petitioned the General Court of Massachusetts for a grant of land near the Deerfield River. In return, he promised to build a road over Hoosac Mountain—"the present one being dangerous, several creatures lost their lives thereon." In 1797, the State of Massachusetts ordered a new road built over the mountain, to be called the Second Massachusetts Turnpike. It extended from the western boundary of Charlemont, in Franklin County, to the western foot of the Hoosac Mountain in Adams, now North Adams.

The zigzagging course of Rice's road, which was surveyed for a county road in 1794, was possibly the same highway known as the Shunpike, because it was used by travelers who wished to dodge the toll on the Massachusetts Turnpike. During stagecoach days, the road over the mountain was the scene of many a holdup. Morris Carpenter, who drove the stage for years around the middle of the nineteenth century, often told of being held up by robbers, who "believed that there was a clear ten thousand in booty or ransom inside the stage." When they found only a few empty bottles, the bandits broke them over the passengers' heads in disgust and "bade them God-speed and a good doctor."

As late as 1848 the Indian Trail was still open and Williams College boys used to run up and down ahead of the lumbering coach. At the foot of the Trail was a sign reading, "Walk up, if you please." Another, at the summit, ominously challenged, "Ride down, if you dare." In 1893 the Indian Trail could still be traced, and even today there are short stretches hidden in the woods which are discernible, but most of it has been entirely obliterated. Where the county and state roads have not covered it, nature has. The modern Mohawk Trail touches the original Indian Trail at only two places, on Main Street in North Adams and at Western Summit, the western peak of the Hoosac range.

There have been many famous journeys over the trail. Perhaps the most picturesque was made by a band of Minutemen from Charlemont, who on the morning of the Battle of Bennington, August 16, 1777, started out to reinforce the patriot army, then fighting General Baum. The party traveled by "riding and tying," a custom followed by many New England pioneers when horses were so scarce their services had to be shared by two or more persons. One man would ride a horse to a certain spot and tie it. His companion, starting out on foot, would take the horse when he reached it. Meanwhile, the first rider, having dismounted, would take his turn on foot knowing that he would find the horse awaiting him up the road. Thus each man walked and each man rode; the horse had his rest and did his work.

The journey of the Charlemont Minutemen across the lofty rugged

range, down into the Hoosac Valley, through Williamstown and on
to Bennington, in less than a single day was quite a feat, for they
had to "ride and tie" over a distance of forty miles. Yet at the end
of the journey, they still had strength enough to chase the Hessians.

In 1850, many years after the Minutemen had raced over the mountain, Nathaniel Hawthorne rode from North Adams to Shelburne
Falls. In the *American Note-Books,* he has recorded his impression of
the mountain:

> The top of this Green [Hoosic] Mountain is a long ridge, marked on the
> county map as two thousand one hundred and sixty feet above the sea; on
> this summit is a valley, not very deep, but one or two miles wide . . . The
> scenery on the eastern side of the Green Mountain is incomparably more
> striking than on the western, where the long swells and ridges have a flat-
> ness of effect; and even Greylock heaves itself so gradually that it does
> not much strike the beholder. But on the eastern part, peaks one or two
> thousand feet high rush up on either bank of the river, in ranges, thrusting
> out their shoulders side by side. They are almost precipitous, clothed in
> woods, through which the naked rock pushes itself forth to view. Some-
> times the peak is bald, while the forest wraps the body of the hills, and
> the baldness gives it an indescribably stern effect. Sometimes the preci-
> pice rises with abruptness from the immediate side of the river; sometimes
> there is a cultivated valley on either side—with all the smoothness . . .
> of a farm near cities—this gentle picture strongly set off by the wild
> mountain frame . . . I have never driven through such romantic scenery,
> where there was such a variety and boldness of mountain shapes as this
> . . . mountains diversified the view with sunshine and shadow, and glory
> and gloom. . . .

Now lines of motorists speed up and down the mountainside and
around the curves at all times of the year. The Trail is passable even
in winter, although freak New England blizzards sometimes interfere for short periods.

The floods of September, 1938, tore with such fury at the eastern
side of the mountain that the Trail was blocked between Florida
and Charlemont and had to be closed through the winter of '38-'39.
The heavy precipitation of rain caused six or seven new landslides
on the Hoosacs, some of them plainly to be seen below Whitcomb
Summit—long, bold scars on the steep mountainsides fifty to a hundred feet wide and half a mile long. Earth, rocks, trees, and all surface
material thundered down into the Deerfield Valley.

The Tunnel, the Trail, and the Turnip are Florida's chief con-
tributions to the world. The Florida turnip is a hardy vegetable, which
accounts for its being the chief agricultural product of the region
today. Although in the mid-nineteenth century Florida raised a diversity of crops, there has been a steady decline in farming during the
past thirty years. State Reservations have absorbed much of the best
farm land—almost nine thousand of Florida's fifteen thousand acres
captured by the forest. In 1937 there were only thirty-five farms left
in the town.

Dr. Daniel Nelson, an early settler of Florida, arrived from Stafford, Connecticut, toward 1800, and established himself in the southeastern section. The land drew others from Connecticut, the Connecticut Valley, and eastern Massachusetts. In addition to tending the ills of
the community, Dr. Nelson later tended the toll-gate on the Massachusetts Turnpike. His successor as toll-keeper around this period was a
Mrs. Nelson, though tradition does not say whether she was related to
the doctor. The famous story of her kidnaping is recounted without
passion in Beers' *History of Berkshire County:*

A Colonel White, a great landholder, once owned the road over the
Deerfield River near the Hoosac Tunnel. Here he had a toll bridge, and a
most efficient employee in a Mrs. Nelson, who had a sharp eye for business. One very rainy night, just as the old lady was about to retire, a
young blade came rattling along in a chaise, and rushing out shoeless and
bareheaded, she stood on a board by the side of the gate to receive the
customary fee. Reaching down her brawny arm, the young Jehu, instead of
dropping his pence into her open palm, adroitly lifted the astonished
dame into the vehicle, and in spite of her expostulations, carried her to
the next tavern. Here he paid her lodging for the night, and gave her fifty
cents to pay her stage fare home in the morning.

Modern Florida consists of scattered farms along the mountains
and two small centers of settlement. Upper Town on the Mohawk
Trail has a white church visible for miles around, a town hall, and a
few houses and roadside stands. Lower Town, at the foot of Hoosac
Mountain near the Tunnel, was once East Portal Camp. Today it
is called Hoosac Tunnel. The descent to Lower Town from the
Mohawk Trail is one of the best trips in Berkshire. On the Trail from
Charlemont, up past the Drury garage, a dirt road turns east into

the Deerfield Valley, and curves downward in a long spiral descent
through thick woods and by swift little waterfalls.

The natural division of the town into separate sections has been
the cause of an outstanding feud that has fed Berkshire gossip for
more than a decade. When the land level of a town is fairly con-
sistent, it doesn't much matter where the town hall is located. But
when half of the town lies on a mountaintop two thousand feet in the
air, and the other half at the mountain's foot, location is everything,
especially in winter. That's what Florida people will tell you when
they mention the "Feud."

The two factions in Florida are the farming Mountaineers, who
live on the summit, and the Tunnelites in Lower Town, most of
them railroad and power plant employees. Before 1900, town meetings
were held in an old building high up on the mountain, easily accessible to the Mountaineers. Early in the new century, the State of
Massachusetts offered to give the town a piece of land near the Tunnel
entrance at the foot of the mountain. Florida accepted the gift with
alacrity and erected a combination schoolhouse and town hall. This
meant that the Mountaineers would have to travel six miles over
rutty mountain roads in order to cast their ballots. Until 1920 the
Mountaineers held the balance of power, and it did not much matter
if a few of them forgot to show up on election day. With the passage
of the Nineteenth Amendment, however, the majority went to the
Tunnelites and their ladies. Their majority gone, the Mountaineers
determined somehow to maintain the upper hand. A single vote
might decide an issue. Before the next election day, men tramped
miles around the snowy mountain tops coaxing neighbors to be on
hand to vote.

One zero day in 1922, the band of Mountaineers braved a snow
and sleet storm to creep down the slippery mountain road into the
valley, only to find the Town Hall locked. A mistake in date or some
such explanation was offered by the Tunnelites. The Mountaineers
held an indignation meeting in the general store, and then started
the slow, painful crawl up the frozen mountain road. Anger kept
them warmer on the return journey. By the time the mountaintop
was reached, the "Feud" was full-grown.

The Mountaineers began a fight for their "legal rights" at once.
They demanded a new town hall on the summit. Several town meet-

ings were held, without any decision being reached. Finally a loyal Mountaineer donated a tract of land for the new building, and the young people of the mountaintop raised enough money by dances and parties to erect the building. Not that the young Mountaineers were especially civic-minded. They admitted they wanted a place to dance.

This did not end the feud by any means. In 1923 the Tunnelites ignored the town meeting in the new mountain building and held their own at Hoosac Tunnel. Matters became so tangled that the law had to step in. The case was taken to the Superior Court, where the meeting held by the Mountaineers was declared illegal. Finally the General Court of Massachusetts officially ruled out both meetings, and set the first Monday in February, 1924, for a new assembly to be held in the Mountain Town Hall. The meeting lasted two days and was more like a street fight than anything else. Mountaineers and Tunnelites slapped and kicked and bit each other with gusto. When a recess was called, the Tunnelites refused to eat the baked bean luncheon prepared by the Mountain women. The Mountaineers took charge the first day, electing their own officers and passing their own measures. The second day they refused to have any part in the proceedings. Some of them remained at home, because they were indifferent or because they were suffering from too many bruises. Thereupon the Tunnelites had a Roman holiday. They rescinded all the votes of the previous day and passed an article that the town would pay the $2,500 bill for all the litigation which had been going on.

As a climax the State had to intervene once more. Financial matters were straightened out and Florida residents began to see the situation in its real light. The Feud still sputters occasionally, but there is little fire in it. Both town halls are recognized. Elections are now held at the one on the mountain, and the business meeting, at which articles in the town warrant are read, is held the following day at the schoolhouse in the valley. At the 1938 election, everything was harmonious.

Although a large part of Florida's area is covered by State Forests, only MOHAWK TRAIL STATE FOREST in the eastern section has been developed for recreation. MOHAWK PARK borders the Mohawk Trail before it climbs out of Charlemont on a long ascent to the top of Hoosac Mountain. The Park is well equipped with facilities for picnicking, has a ski tow and a Sky Trail.

In the Park there is a STATUE OF A MOHAWK INDIAN erected by the Society of Red Men of America as a tribute to the tribe. The figure stands with arms upraised in salutation to the rising sun. Below the Indian is a WISHING-WELL, also erected by the Red Men, where you may wish your cares away in icy, refreshing water.

At the point where Mass 2 crosses the Cold River Bridge, a dirt road turns left, if you are ascending the Trail, for a side trip into SAVOY STATE FOREST, a tract shared by the towns of Savoy, Florida, North Adams, and Adams. The forest, whose only recreational section in Florida is NORTH POND, has an area of over ten thousand acres, including a game preserve and the lovely cascade of TANNERY FALLS, both in Savoy.

A mere corner of the MONROE STATE FOREST occupies the extreme northeastern tip of the town of Florida. Visitors to the RAY-CROFT LOOKOUT, an observation platform built by the Civilian Conservation Corps on the barren edge of a mountain, declare the view of the Deerfield River, 1000 feet below, is unsurpassed in eastern Berkshire. To the south appears a beautiful, high waterfall leaping from a ledge of white rock in a deep ravine between hills where SMITH BROOK pours down through the woods. On Fife Brook, further south, not visible from the Lookout, is a cascade known as TWIN FALLS, not more than fifteen minutes' walk up-stream from Hoosac Tunnel Station.

Through one end of the State Forest, a six-strand high-tension power line carries 650,000 volts of electricity over the mountains from the Deerfield River power stations to the Hoosac Valley communities. Once these wires, burdened with ice and sleet, were cleared by an engineer at one of the power plants through the use of a unique and previously untried method. The circuit at the receiving end on a set of three wires was closed and extra voltage and amperage "shot" into the wires until they reached a temperature of about 40 degrees Fahrenheit, which melted the frozen sleet and ice. Then the other set of wires was similarly treated. The success of the operation led to its general use wherever power lines are exposed to low temperatures.

About a mile and a half past the village of Florida, on Mass 2, rises WHITCOMB SUMMIT, 2,110 feet high. Its sixty-five-foot observation tower overlooks four states: to the east, Mt. Monadnock in New Hampshire; north, the Green Mountains of Vermont; west and south, Mt. Greylock and the Berkshires, and on clear days, the mountains of New York State.

When Hawthorne visited the "homely tavern kept by P. Witt" on Whitcomb Summit, he was entertained by an itinerant showman bearing a dilapidated diorama, typical of Berkshire amusements a hundred years ago.

"We left our horse in the shed," he writes; "entering a little unpainted bar-room, we heard a voice in a strange, outlandish accent, exclaiming Diorama. It was an old man, with a full, gray-bearded countenance, and Mr. Leach exclaimed, 'Ah, here's the old Dutchman'—though, by the way, he is a German and travels the country with this diorama in a wagon . . . We looked through the glass orifice of his machine, while he exhibited a succession of the worst scratches and daubings that can be imagined. There were views of cities and edifices in Europe, and Napoleon's battles and Nelson's sea-fights, in the midst of which would be seen a gigantic, brown hairy hand (the Hand of Destiny) pointing at the principal points of the conflicts . . ."

Of a number of well-stocked ponds and streams in Florida, DEER-FIELD RIVER is the best known. Since the Deerfield River rises and ebbs whenever its gates are opened and shut, anglers find it a hard stream to wade.

Thousands of people drive over the Mohawk Trail through Florida every year, thousands more catch a glimpse of the settlement of Hoosac Tunnel before their trains disappear in the mountain, but few of these travelers know the name of the town through which they are passing. The future may change this. Outsiders have discovered the State Forests, the picnic groves and the trout streams, and skiers have found that the snow on the Florida heights comes earlier and stays longer than on most Berkshire slopes. A new army may invade Florida, bent on pleasure rather than on a "job" as were their predecessors, the Tunnel workers. For the present the town depends on the Tunnel, the Trail, and the Turnip.

The Mohawk Trail, on its descent from Florida to North Adams, makes a wide reverse curve known as HAIRPIN TURN, really part of the little town of Clarksburg, which stretches out a finger of land at just the right angle to claim its share of the famous highway. From the wooden OBSERVATION TOWER, at the head of the hairpin, there is a magnificent view overlooking the township of Clarksburg and a panorama of North Adams, northern Berkshire, and southern Vermont, with Greylock and the Taconics forming the western sky-line. Nathaniel Hawthorne looked down on the village in 1838 and noted, "The rush of the stream comes up the hill somewhat like the sound of a city." They were prophetic words.

The Mohawk Trail dips sharply along the wooded mountainside as it passes into the crowded textile section of North Adams. Three miles from Hairpin Turn, in the outskirts of North Adams, Mass 2 meets Mass 8, the road between mountains through Clarksburg to Vermont. In this vicinity Hawthorne visited a kiln that inspired his story *Ethan Brand,* the tale of a lime-burner obsessed by an "unpardonable sin" only to be atoned for by casting himself into the burning lime. The lime quarry, long since abandoned, would be difficult to locate today without much scrambling among ledges and cliffs.

About three-tenths of a mile north on Mass 8, a narrow road leads left across Hudson Brook and up along the bank of the stream to a marble quarry and mill. Behind the mill and high above an excavation made into the white rock, is the NATURAL BRIDGE, one of two such bridges of stone in the East. To reach it, walk through the quarry and ascend a long flight of steps at the side. The sight of the curiously narrow, deep gorge and the strange shapes engraved in the rock from top to bottom makes it worth running the gauntlet of dynamiters and jack-hammer operators (who are careful to warn visitors when a blast is to be blown) in order to explore the bridge formed by water cutting through the roof of a subterranean cave.

Early legend has it that Seth Hudson of Fort Massachusetts found the caves and the bridge when he narrowly escaped a plunge into the gorge as he went hot-foot after a deer. He explored the caverns and saw the mighty arch of marble high above his head. Man of action that he was, he left no record, but after a visit to the bridge the dependable Nathaniel Hawthorne observed:

The fissure is very irregular, so as not to be describable in words and scarcely to be painted—jutting buttresses, moss-grown, impending crags, with tall trees growing on their verge, nodding over the head of the

observer at the bottom of the chasm, and rooted, as it were, in air . . .
The marble crags are overspread with a concretion which makes them
look as gray as granite, except where the continual flow of water keeps
them of a snowy whiteness.

Over 150 years ago, there were remnants of a beaver dam just
below the gorge of the Natural Bridge. A locality near here was once
known as BEAVER or "The Beaver" and later as "Beaver Mills,"
and even now Beaver Street carries Mass 8 into Clarksburg. The
constant toil of the little animals, together with the flood-wood which
accumulated against their growing barrier, raised a dam of such great
height that the water flowed back and obliterated the falls. There
are plain evidences that it must at some period have washed the
whole surface and worn the stone away into fissures, chasms, and
basins. Geologists insist that water alone worked the miracle. The
thriving settlement of "Beaver," snugly ensconced between the hills,
was in its original state a wild, sequestered locality, scarcely approach-
able on foot by either fisherman or hunter.

To enter the town of *CLARKSBURG* proper, continue north
along Mass 8. One of the smallest towns in Berkshire, Clarksburg is
one of the few where population has grown during the past century.
The increase is largely due to the presence of the STRONG-HEWAT
COMPANY, whose "Virgin Wool" plant employs over four hundred
men. More than a century ago, four mills were operating in the town,
all of them located along the northern branch of the Hoosic River
in BRIGGSVILLE. Three of the mills liquidated, leaving the Briggs
Woolen Mill the only survivor. In 1898, this plant was purchased by
the Strong-Hewat Company, new machinery was installed, and the
mills enlarged.

Briggsville and Red Mill are two small centers along the highway. Crowded between the river and the steep hillsides is a single
main street of well-kept mill tenements. Neatly curtained windows
brighten the appearance of the freshly painted houses, and the new-
mowed lawns before them are colorful with well-tended gardens.
R. A. J. Hewat, who came from Scotland seeking his fortune, preferred to recruit his employees from his birthplace, and today twenty
per cent of the population are of Scottish descent.

Clarksburg was settled in 1769 by Captain Matthew Ketchum from
Long Island and Nicholas Clark and his brothers from Rhode Island.

Thirty years later some of the petitioners for the incorporation of the town wanted it named "Hudson" in honor of Henry Hudson, a famous Vermont hunter who was supposed to have felled the first tree in the territory of the town. Hudson had come to Clarksburg two or three months before the Ketchums and the Clarks. But the Clarks were numerous and outvoted all others in favor of naming the town after themselves.

Much of Clarksburg's territory was originally known as "Bullock's Grant." In surveying the land for his grant, Colonel William Bullock laid his northern line about a mile south of the northern line of the Massachusetts Colony. Doubtless he was afraid he might get over the border into the State of Vermont. This land, or "gore," has since become a part of the town.

Early settlers were Baptists, although it was not long before the Methodists outnumbered them. Congregationalists were few; in 1829 there was but a single member of the sect within the village precincts. The first church, erected in 1783, was a log building with a bark roof, built on the state line in order that both Clarksburg and Stamford, Vermont, Baptists might share the same minister. The settlers farmed and cut lumber during the first fifty years of the town's existence, sending great quantities of hemlock and spruce down river to Adams and Williamstown. In the mid-nineteenth century grist mills, sawmills, lime kilns, a woolen and a carding mill, and a number of powder mills all used the valuable water power furnished by several large brooks flowing into the northern and southern branches of the Hoosic.

Though the wild landscape of the town is as impressive as any forest scene in New England, almost no one sees it, for less than half the area can be reached by road. The western side, fully one-third of the town's land, is covered by a State Forest, at present developed for its timber rather than for its scenic and recreational value. The eastern part of the town is on a steep slope rising more than a thousand feet above the valley. Between the two heights, in the southeast corner of the level valley, lies Briggsville.

The small town has no church, no lawyer, and no physician. There is no summer or tourist trade, for the community has done nothing to make known its really fine resources. Local people feel that their fate lies with the mills of Briggsville; let future residents develop the wild lands of the township. Back among the hills and narrow valleys live descendants of the old Yankee stock, still making a fair living from the land. They find a ready market for their dairy and garden products in North Adams, but they have not yet peddled the beauty of their surroundings.

Entering *NORTH ADAMS* proper, Mass 2 curves left by the St. Francis Catholic Church and parochial school. The low buildings which crowd close by are reminiscent of the old French cities of Canada, where the ancestors of many North Adams families once lived.

Main Street is the business district of North Adams—mid-Victorian blocks, small drygoods stores, taverns, colorful fruit stands and markets, and ten-cent stores. French and Irish names appear on the windows of the office buildings, designating lawyers, doctors, beauty salons, real estate and insurance agencies. There is a constant hum of noise and a confusion of tongues: French-Canadian, Italian, nasal Yankee, and the upper New York twang characteristic of northern Berkshire. North Adams is nervous with the energy of twentieth-century America. No city of twenty-five thousand people in New England has a greater variety of retail establishments; merchants must stock goods for workers of different nationalities and notions, and for a large farming population whose lean pocketbooks force their owners to "close buying."

North Adams was originally part of East Hoosuck township, laid out in 1762. Berkshire natives are used to the various ways of spelling Hoosic, and will explain without so much as the bat of an eyelash that the Hoosic River flows through the Hoosac Valley at the foot of the Hoosac Mountain Range through which the Hoosac Tunnel runs; but the Hoosic River becomes the Hoosick River when it flows into New York State where the town is called Hoosick Falls. The original towns in the area, predecessors of Adams, North Adams, and Williamstown, were called East and West Hoosick, East and West Hoosuck, and East and West Hoosac, apparently depending on the idiosyncrasies of eighteenth-century spelling. It is all very confusing to anyone who wishes to spell Hoosic, for to be certain one must know whether the reference is to a mountain, a river, or a town. The origin of the name is simpler; in the Indian language it means "a stony place."

In 1778 East Hoosuck became the town of Adams. South Village, on the more fertile land, grew rapidly, but pioneers were slow in coming into the "north village" of Slab City. Though as early as 1747, John Perry, a Fort Massachusetts soldier, had reared a little house in the northern wilderness, for years only a few people came to live there. Once the land was cleared, the abundant water power began gradually to attract settlers.

In the "Slab City" days of North Adams the pine forest was so dense that the pioneers had to chop their way through to establish a settlement. For years huge trees stood along the streets of the town, one giant stump remaining in the middle of Main Street until 1858.

In 1793 Joseph Darby set up a trip-hammer to pound out scythes and saws. Six years later, Dickinson and Brown erected a forge for making wrought iron from native ore, and by 1804 they were turning out a grade good enough to sell at $140 a ton. Within half a century the small grist mills and forges were replaced by textile plants, brickyards, marble quarries, and metal-working shops.

"There are several factories in different parts of North Adams, along the banks of a stream," wrote Hawthorne in his notebook, "a wild, highland rivulet . . . It is strange to see such a rough and untamed stream as it looks to be so subdued to the purposes of man, and making cotton and woolens, sawing boards and marbles, and giving employment to so many men and girls. And there is a sort of picturesqueness in finding these factories, supremely artificial establishments, in the midst of such wild scenery. For now the stream will be flowing through a rude forest, with the trees erect and dark, as when the Indians fished there . . . And then, taking a turn in the road, behold these factories, and their range of boardinghouses, with the girls looking out of the windows."

Long on water power, North Adams was short on capital. Lack of transportation facilities retarded industrial growth, until citizens finally raised $31,000 to help finance a continuation of the Western Railroad. After the State had taken over and finished the job of boring through from the Deerfield Valley into the Hoosac Valley, North Adams had the advantage of two railroad lines, and in 1875 the town began to boom. Besides water power, it now had direct contact with large retail centers. There was always plenty of pure spring water for various dyeing processes. Labor alone was lacking, though not for long. Released from railroad jobs, French-Canadian and Irish workmen swarmed into the town, bringing their relatives and friends. In 1878 North Adams was incorporated as a town separate from Adams, and was on its way to becoming a bustling industrial community.

In his book, *From the Hub to the Hudson,* Washington Gladden has left a picture of North Adams as it appeared to him in 1866:

North Adams was, indeed, a good sample of a New England democracy. All its traditions were of an uncompromising radicalism. If there were aristocratic elements in the population of many New England towns, Adams boasted none of these things. It was Sam Adams, and not John, whose name she borrowed when her organization was set up. There were no old families who claimed homage on the score of birth or breeding. There were a few men to whom the war brought large and rapid gains; the cotton and woolen mills and the print works were in the high tide of prosperity, and several of these wealthy manufacturers were building for themselves fine houses; but nothing had yet occurred to disturb the sense of equality which characterized all social relations. I have attended an evening party in one of those new fine houses at which were present not only capitalists and merchants and professional people, but working mechanics and clerks and operatives in the mill of which the host was the owner. That class consciousness which some of our industrial leaders have would have been wholly inconceivable to the people of this New England town forty years ago . . .

Although textile finishing finally became the major industry, the city never has depended solely on one type of manufacturing. Shoes, textile machinery, electrical goods, rugs, brushes, boxes, bricks, biscuits, iron, brass, and aluminum castings are among the varied products of North Adams.

Worse than any economic slump that ever hit North Adams have been the furious floods which periodically visit the city in its narrow gulch. In 1785 the mills were ruined by the so-called Parker's Flood of which a contemporary said, "Noah's flood is the only one that ever equaled it." After the great deluge of 1869, an optimistic historian commented, "Now, it does not seem as if further danger need be expected, as the timber on the watershed has been so cut off that many springs and feeder brooks are now dried up and the river is much smaller than in olden times." Of course he spoke too soon, for the very act of stripping the hills and valleys of their trees was to make "bigger and better floods" possible in the future.

Within the past twelve years there have been three disasters, in '27, '36, and '38. The flood of 1938 began at 5 p.m. on September 21 when a brook broke through a culvert on River Street and covered the thoroughfare. Within the next half hour other small streams broke out of their banks, and two branches of the Hoosic River tore loose, hurling tons of water through the center of North Adams. High winds felled poles and wires and plunged the city into darkness. By midnight one entire street had vanished as if it never had existed. Landslides rumbled down steep banks near the center of town, blocked roads, clogged storm sewers and drains, undermined buildings.

The flood crest went eighteen inches higher than in 1927 on the South branch of the Hoosic River and was several inches higher than any previous mark on the North branch. North Adams was cut off by washouts on the highway at Cold River bridge in Savoy and at Green River bridge in Williamstown. The city, deprived of railroad communications, was without water, electricity, telephone and gas service, and the damage was estimated at more than a million dollars. Public clamor arose for a comprehensive program of flood control in the Hoosac Valley.

In the past, when North Adams made up its mind, something was likely to be accomplished. It happened that way in 1894 when the General Court voted to establish a new normal school, and North Adams wanted it located there. The town went so far as to add $50,000 to the State appropriation, and got the school. The marble and yellow brick buildings of the TEACHERS COLLEGE lie on Church Street, which goes south out of the center. Church Street runs into Mass 8, which continues across the Hoosic River and the Pittsfield-North Adams branch of the Boston and Albany Railroad, passing on the way MEADOWBROOK ARENA, the principal recreation establishment for dances, prize-fights, roller-skating, and other indoor amusements.

You can return to the center by a new-cut straight road, the Curran Memorial Highway, which connects with Mass 8. A hillside marker near the start of the road tells of the old church once here. Near where the road runs past a steep hill, a trail climbs at an angle up into the pines to one of the two caves within the limits of the city. It is known as RICHMOND CAVE after the family that originally owned a farm here. Within, a large chamber made of mixed sandstone, limestone, schist, and quartz has a floor of rubble; at one end a tiny waterfall splashes down a fallen rock. For some years the Ravenscrag cave, atop the jagged peak that shows directly beneath Greylock's summit, was believed to have a "bottomless pool," but recently explorers, armed with flashlights, ropes, and plummets, have discovered that the water is exactly six inches deep. The small, winding difficult passages make the dark cavern a safe haven for bats.

Some of the early settlers who cut down the giant trees of "Slab City" were men of mighty frame and strength. Among them was Josiah Holbrook, the fearless, who captured single-handed a baker's dozen of Hessians at the Battle of Bennington. He surprised his captives while they were drinking at a spring, and reported his achievement to General Stark with simplicity;

"Gin'rel, I jest surrounded them, sir."

Josiah was one of those who joined Shays' forces during the Rebellion. After the defeat of the movement and his return home a party of four troopers tried in vain to arrest him. No one would have dared to tackle Josh single-handed. He was finally captured by a company surrounding his house in the night, breaking in the door, and seizing and binding him in bed. He submitted, gave up all his arms, took the oath of allegiance to the Commonwealth, and was released. It was a standing joke among the inhabitants of North Adams that his whisper could be distinctly heard by everybody when he was out of doors; when he spoke his voice resounded to the top of Hoosac Mountain.

A runaway boy, Allen Wilson, escaping from the cruelty of a hard-fisted farmer to whom he was bound out, drifted into North Adams in the late 1840's and began work as a cabinet-maker. He met Miss Brooks of Williamstown, an industrious seamstress whose swift needle flying back and forth as she worked gave him the idea for a sewing machine. In 1851, after numerous trials and failures, Wilson secured a patent on his machine with a small sum given him by a North Adams friend. Other local capitalists considered Wilson an eccentric fellow on the verge of insanity. With sixty cents in his pocket and a model of his sewing machine in a cloth bag he left for Pittsfield. Here he again took up a trade, in spare time trying to interest someone in his machine. He failed, shook the dust of Pittsfield from his feet, and went to Bridgeport. There he met a man named Wheeler who mortgaged his property for nine hundred dollars and became a joint partner with Wilson. Together they started the manufacture of the Wheeler-Wilson sewing machine, whose shares soared until they paid higher dividends than any other stock in the United States. Wilson returned prosperous to North Adams, and in 1866 erected the Wilson House on Main Street, the most imposing hotel and business block of its day in Berkshire County. It was destroyed in a spectacular fire.

The first Irishman to settle in North Adams in the 1850's was Michael Ryan, a genial, whole-souled emigrant. He is pictured in an account written in 1901 as clad in corduroy trousers coming just below the knees, thick stockings, his vest cut low at the neck, and a jaunty hat on his head. One fair but cold day in October, Michael returned from a tramp into the hills with a rattlesnake wrapped in his handkerchief, and thrust in his vest to keep warm. "The pore little bird, it is cowld, it is," he exclaimed to a Yankee neighbor who encountered him. Michael had never seen a snake in St. Patrick's Ireland.

C. T. Sampson was not a "Berkshire Borner." He originally came from Stamford, Vermont, "a real old-fashioned white-birch Yankee." Arriving in North Adams around mid-century, he apprenticed himself to a shoemaker, and by peddling footwear through the countryside managed to get together money enough to start a small factory of his own. When, in the late '60's, workmen in his North Adams factory went on strike and joined a labor organization known as the "Knights of St. Crispin," Sampson sent an agent to California to buy up a trainload of Chinamen. The day the Chinese arrived in North Adams, an angry crowd was at the depot to meet them. So were Sampson and an armed constable. The strikers threatened violence if the yellow-skinned "heathens" set foot on the ground, and the Chinese workmen were thoroughly frightened. Finally the crowd allowed them passage and they reached the factory unmolested. "These pig-tailed, calico-frocked, wooden-shod invaders made a spectacle which nobody wanted to miss even long enough to stoop for a brickbat," said Washington Gladden, a minister in North Adams.

Sampson's factory loft was filled with wooden bunks for the Chinese, and native cooks provided food within the walls. Most of the Orientals stayed close to their work. They knew nothing of the shoe trade, even the simplest processes. To teach them took several months, during which factory output dropped way down.

The Chinese later boarded with private families, joined local churches, and became an accepted part of the community. One of them, Sam Sing, who came as an interpreter, left the factory to open a grocery store. Lue Gim Gong became a notable horticulturist, moved to the South, and there worked so successfully developing new types of citrus fruits that his memory is honored throughout Florida. In the 1870's, machinery introduced into the shoe factories to carry out the process of bottoming shoes forced the Chinese out of their jobs. Many had already left North Adams, some returning to California, others, who had saved their money, going back to China. Of the hundred-odd who once lived in North Adams, not one is left today.

The importation of the Chinese caused a furore in Massachusetts, and Wendell Phillips, in his article in the *National Standard Magazine* for August 1870, summed up general opinion. After stating that men of all races and nations should be welcomed on American soil, he continued:

But such immigration to be safe and helpful must be spontaneous. It must be the result of individual will obeying the laws of industry, and the tendencies of the age. Immigration of labor is an unmixed good. Importation of human freight is an unmixed evil.

That dollar now left after all the bills are paid on Saturday night, means education, independence, self-respect, manhood . . . The importation of Chinese labor seeks to take that dollar from our workingmen.

North Adams has been fertile soil for a crop of inventors. Among those of greatest fame was the late Frank J. Sprague, who received his early education in North Adams. At the Philadelphia Electrical Exposition of 1884 the Sprague electric motors were exhibited for the first time, creating a sensation. The Sprague Electric Railway and Motor Company was organized and the electric lighting industry greatly stimulated.

Mr. Sprague was awarded the gold medal at the Paris Exposition in 1889 for electric railway development, the Elliot Cresson medal at Franklin Institute in 1904 for the multi-unit system, the grand prize for "invention and development in electric railways" at the St. Louis Exposition in 1904, the Edison gold medal for "meritorious achievement in electric science, engineering and art" in 1910, and the Franklin medal in 1921 for "fundamental inventions and achievements in electrical engineering." On his seventy-fifth birthday in 1934 he was hailed as the "Father of Electric Traction."

Opposite the Hunter Machine Company on Pearl Street in the rear of a brick block is the establishment of "Billy" Barber, inventor and single-handed manufacturer of his own "porcupine boiler." A Yankee, self-made and self-taught in his trade, William B. Barber remains an unusual type in the modern world. A tall, lanky, stoop-shouldered man nearing sixty, with an aquiline countenance, a piercing eye and a ready flow of technical language concerning heating, power, electricity, hydraulics, and things mechanical, he is often called in conference by highly educated engineers, contractors, and industrialists to solve by his native genius some problem which has puzzled experts.

Once when an electric motor generator stalled in a large plant in North Adams and could not be started by company engineers, the owner sent for Barber. Within ten minutes Billy had the motor running and the mill could operate again.

"Send me a bill," said the pleased owner in an off-hand way.

Barber's bill sent the next day read as follows:

One gadget .... $ .60
Time 1.25
Brains 23.15
Total $25.00

As Mass 2 traverses more open country on the western outskirts of North Adams, a modern road, offically opened to motorists in the summer of 1937, though not entirely completed even yet (1939), turns off to the top of Mount Greylock. The opening of this route, approached from North Adams by way of Mass 2, has shortened the distance from the city to the summit of the mountain by ten or twelve miles. The Notch Road turns south from Mass 2 to ascend the side of the mountain in gradual slope, following in part the course of the old stagecoach line.

The NEW NOTCH ROAD, as it is called, was begun in 1932 by the Civilian Conservation Corps. Some of it was cut through Greylock schist with dynamite and jackhammers. Work was spread out over several years because of the impossibility of carrying on in winter when deep snow and heavy frost, chill mists and high winds make the upper stretches an Arctic region. The road ascends through a thick growth of beech, maple, elm, and birch trees into thick spruce. Even in midsummer the forest is so dense that the light is dim in the center, where the ground is literally carpeted with seedlings. From the road vistas have been cut out to permit a striking view into the Notch and farther up into the Hopper on the Williamstown side. In the winter time, skiers whizz down the long slope of the road.

Notch Brook tumbles down alongside and sometimes under the highway. On the dashing mountain stream, in heavily wooded country, are THE CASCADES—waterfalls in the shade of dense evergreens. Beyond lie The Notch and Bellows Pipe, steep ravines rising up to the sheer slopes of Mt. Greylock.

The mountains are farther away and the houses less frequent as you move toward the North Adams-Williamstown line and a REPLICA OF OLD FORT MASSACHUSETTS, the parent of both Adams and North Adams. Fort Massachusetts dates from 1745, when it was built as the westernmost of a chain of four forts. Besides guarding against French and Indian war parties, the fort was meant to discourage Dutch settlers who paddled up the Hoosic River from the Hudson to claim land in Berkshire County.

The tragic consequences of the raid upon the fort in 1746 are recorded by Henry Trumbull in his elaborately titled *History of the Discovery of America, of the Landing of Our Forefathers, and of Their Most Remarkable Engagements with the Indians in New England* (1825).

Aug. 20. An army of about 9000 French and Indians, under command of Gen. DeVaudreuil, made an attack on Fort Massachusetts. The fort was commanded by Colonel Hawks, who, unfortunately, was not in a situation to defend it against such a force, having but 37 persons, men, women, and children, in the fort; and being miserably provided with ammunition. With great fortitude he defended it for 28 hours and had not his ammunition failed it is probable he never would have given up the fort. He was finally necessitated to capitulate; and he offered such articles as were accepted by DeVaudreuil. . . . Colonel Hawks lost but one man in the siege. Gen. DeVaudreuil, according to the best accounts the prisoners could obtain, lost 45, who were either killed outright, or died of their wounds.

The fort was burned to the ground. For a few hours the French flag floated above the ruins, the first and only time that French conquest was so marked in this State.

The following year the fort was rebuilt and in August of 1748 it was again assaulted by a force of several hundred French and Indians. The attack failed and the enemy, driven off, took themselves down the trail, carrying their dead and wounded with them. During the next few years Fort Massachusetts continued to be garrisoned by a small company, but about 1760 it was finally abandoned. The West Hoosac fort at Williamstown had become more convenient for those who had taken up lots in that vicinity.

CHAPTER II

TRADITIONS THAT MARCH ON

WILLIAMSTOWN—Mass 2 and US 7, sett. 1749, alt. 603, pop. 4,272.
Roads—Mass 2 leads directly from North Adams.

"TICKETS," flashed an advertisement in the *Columbian Centinel* for
June 16, 1790, "in the Eighth Class of Williamstown Free-School Lottery, which positively commences drawing on Monday next, and
will be completed the next morning, may be had of NATHAN
BOND, No. 31, Cornhill, where the prizes will be paid on demand."

Ten days later the lucky winners of the Williamstown Lottery
were announced:

"The fortunate Adventurers are required to call, as soon as convenient, for their money, as the Managers (who live at a great distance from this town) intend to close the business of the Lottery, as
soon as possible."

The holder of Ticket 2209 carried off the five hundred dollars
top-money. He and his numerous companions, the fortunate (and
unfortunate) Adventurers, might be called co-founders of one of
the most illustrious institutions in the Berkshires—Williams College.

Its original founder was Ephraim Williams, Jr., colonel in the
service of the Massachusetts provincial government. With a party of
three surveyors he had appeared in the Valley of the Hoosic in the
fall of 1739, commissioned by the Governor and Council to lay out
two townships at the headwaters of the Hoosic. Here was an excellent site for a military outpost. A natural passage east and west, the
valley had been a favorite trail for French and Indian raiders attack-
ing English settlements. Conscious of its strategic value, leaders in
Boston had taken alarm at the inroads of enterprising Dutchmen,
who were steadily encroaching from northern New York. Colonel
Williams' survey was never completed, however, because his group
was continually harassed by "sundry gentlemen from Albany." (The
colonies of Massachusetts and New York were not to settle their

boundary disputes until after the Revolution.) In 1749, a decade after Williams' attempt, another group finally succeeded in laying out the towns of East and West Hoosuck.

Although his surveying was a failure, Williams never forgot the natural resources and beauty of the region. When West Hoosuck was established as a township he purchased two lots for himself and planned to make a home in the valley; only the colonies' demand for his military services during the Revolution kept him from following his pioneer intent.

Williams, born in Newton in 1715, was a colorful figure in the early history of Massachusetts. An adventurous and scholarly youth, he left his native hearth to seek his fortune in foreign parts.

For several years in early life he followed the sea, but by the persuasion of his father relinquished the business. In his several voyages to Europe he visited England, Spain and Holland; acquired graceful manners and a considerable stock of useful knowledge. . . .

The "stock of knowledge" stood him in good stead when he took up soldiering. Rising quickly in rank, he was commissioned a Colonel in 1742 and placed in charge of Fort Shirley; later he was transferred to Fort Massachusetts, the westernmost outpost. When the French and Indian War broke out anew in 1754, the military authorities put him in command of the Hampshire Regiment and ordered him to join the siege of Crown Point on Lake Champlain.

While on his way to the battlefield, Williams stopped at Albany and on the night of July 22, 1755, wrote a last testament:

It is my will and pleasure and desire that the remaining part of Lands not yet disposed of shall be sold at the discretion of my Executors within five years after an established peace, and the interest of all the money and also the interest of my money arising by my bonds and notes shall be appropriated towards the support and maintenance of a Free School (in a township west of Fort Massachusetts commonly called the West Township) forever, provided the s^d Township fall within the jurisdiction of the provinces of the Massachusetts Bay and provided also that the Governor and General Court give the s^d Township the name of Williamstown.

On the eighth day of the following September, Colonel Williams was killed at the Battle of Lake George, but it was many years before the provisions in his will were carried out.

By June 21, 1765, West Hoosuck had a sufficiently large group of settlers to be incorporated as *WILLIAMSTOWN*. At the first town meeting, there were recorded "59 taxable polls, 57 oxen, 75 cows, and 85 sheep." Colonial recruits in the French and Indian wars had gazed upon the broad, fertile valley encircled by hills on their marches to meet the enemy; veterans, they had returned to establish homes.

The peaceful growth of the town was interrupted by the Revolution and sporadic Indian raids. During the campaigns at Bennington and New York, the new outpost served as a base of operations. On his way to Ticonderoga, Benedict Arnold stopped here to enlist volunteers for the Colonial army. Bread and beans for the soldiers at Bennington were baked in the home of Nehemiah Smedley while shots from the battlefield echoed through Williamstown.

In the early years of the nineteenth century this was a prosperous agricultural community. Wide fields produced an abundance of rye, barley, and wheat, and farmers did well at dairying. Life in Williamstown, though self-sufficient, was also isolated. The Berkshires were an almost complete barrier to penetration from the east. Communication was slow and dangerous, for the stagecoach service between Boston and Albany over the hazardous mountain roads was irregular. The mails were expensive and slow. Until 1876 and the coming of the railroad to North Adams the isolation was unbroken.

There were abortive attempts to establish manufactories about the middle of the century. A potato starch factory was erected in 1833 and a cotton mill some years earlier. As in the other Berkshire towns, the industrial flurry soon attracted strangers. A few French-Canadian families drifted down into the cotton mills, where a considerable number of English and Welsh operatives were already employed. With the railroad there sprang up a community of lusty, fun-loving Irish.

In most ways Williamstown of the 1850's was a typical New England town. Its distinctive possession was a college raised "in the shadow of a mountain."

Nearly forty years passed after the death of Colonel Williams before his dream of a free school was realized. Although the Revolution and the general insecurity of the times were obstacles, the primary cause of delay was a stipulation in Williams' will that the school

had to be located within the Massachusetts Bay Colony. To determine whether Williamstown was going to end up in Massachusetts
or New York the boundary dispute had to be settled, and this did
not happen until 1787. Raising enough money for the maintenance
of a free school was an equally thorny problem, for despite honest
management, the Williams estate after three decades amounted to
only ten thousand dollars—too meager a sum to establish even an
unpretentious institution.

By 1790, however, more than a £1200 profit had been realized
from the lottery advertised in the *Centinel,* and the first building,
West College, was erected in 1791. Within a year the trustees felt the
need for expansion and once again a plea was made to the Legislature setting forth the "laudable wish" to see

Massachusetts the Athens of the United States of America to which young
gentlemen from any part of the Union may resort for instruction in all
branches of useful and polite Literature.

Williams College was formally chartered on June 22, 1793. After
bestowing its spiritual benediction, the Legislature appropriated £300
annually for four years. And to this were added numerous con-
tributions from the townspeople.

Eighteen gangling farm youths and two teachers began the college
in October, 1793, under a direct and simple curriculum devised by
Dr. Ebenezer Fitch, the first president. He arranged the course of
instruction as follows:

> Freshmen —English, Latin, Greek, French.
> Sophomores—Geography, Arithmetic, Rhetoric, Logic, Algebra.
> Juniors   —Higher Mathematics, Natural Philosophy, Astron-
>   omy, Chemistry.
> Seniors   —History, Ethics, Physics, Theology, Natural Law,
>   Civil Polity.

It was an imposing but a deceptive list, for courses were sketchy,
teaching was dry and unimaginative, and the instructors generally
not much advanced over the ignorant youths whom they were direct-
ing. During the early years keeping discipline was a continuous
faculty problem. The harassed teachers acted as instructors, police

officers, and judges. Devotion to study was counterbalanced by love of roistering. Smoking, gambling, and considerable drinking forced the trustees to institute a drastic system of punishments for various breaches of behavior. Fines were made to fit the crime, as a contemporary list of penalties shows:

Absence from classes	1 penny
Late for prayer	3 pennies
Employing a barber or hairdresser on the Lord's Day	2 shillings
Drunkenness	3 shillings
Hunting and fishing without leave	1 shilling
Every spot of ink on a book	1 shilling
Turning down the leaf of a book	1 shilling

Not all the students' leisure hours were, to be sure, spent in impious debauch, for theological societies abounded. In 1817 the debating society engaged in bitter controversy over such vital matters of the day as "Liberty of the Press," "Theaters," "Divorce," and "The Education of Girls."

In 1815, toward the end of President Fitch's term, Williams went into a decline. Student registration fell off and college finances were in a sorry state. Williamstown was considered too distant from centers of population for a college, and claims were put in by Stockbridge, Northampton, Greenfield, and Amherst. Dr. Moore, president of Williams from 1815 to 1821, wished to see the school in a more fortunate location and thought it should be removed to Amherst, the seat of an already flourishing academy. Nine of the dozen trustees agreed with him, but the little group who clung to Williamstown won out. Necessary funds to continue operation were gathered largely through the efforts of the Reverend Doctor Edward Griffin, appointed in place of Moore. He raised twenty-five thousand dollars in addition to the eighteen thousand dollars which the inhabitants of the town had already pledged toward the support of the college. New life was infused into a dying institution, and Williams was never again to suffer so acute a crisis.

Though Williams never sought to establish official relations with any church, constant preoccupation with religion was the outstanding interest of students during the first decades of the nineteenth century.

Teachers were ordained ministers, a majority of the books in the college library were theological, and the home life of the student was bathed in a spirit of piety.

The American Foreign Missionary movement and indirectly the United Brethren Church in the United States owe their origin to Williams College students. It all began during the height of a thunderstorm one August afternoon in 1806, when a group of young men, under the direction of Samuel John Mills, Jr., held a prayer meeting. In a letter written to a friend, Bryam Greene, one of the five students who took part, described the dramatic scene:

> That prayer meeting becomes interesting to the Christian community because it was then and there proposed to send the Gospel to the pagans of Asia and to the disciples of Mohammed . . . Mills proposed to send the Gospel to that dark and heathen land, and said that we could do it if we would.

> "Come," said Mills. "Let us make it the subject of prayer, under this haystack." . . . We all prayed . . . Mills made the last prayer. . . . He prayed that God would strike down the arm with the red artillery of heaven, that should be raised against the Cross.

Mills went to Africa, founded a mission, and died at sea on his way home. The site of the prayer meeting is marked by the HAYSTACK MONUMENT amid the evergreens in Mission Park.

Despite close relations between church and school, science held a high place in the college curriculum. In 1811 Chester Dewey began his meteorological investigations at Williams. Amos Eaton inaugurated laboratory instruction in chemistry and physics in 1819, some years before the famed Liebeg in Germany and Thomson and Lord Kelvin in Scotland. The first field expedition in the history of American education was sent out from Williams under the guidance of Professor Albert Hopkins, one of the pioneer exponents of geological and botanical field trips for undergraduates. One still hears about the day in 1835 when Professor "Al" Hopkins invited a party of students to accompany him to the quartzite ledges on East Mountain. After they had gone too far to back down, the canny professor produced crowbars which, he told them, were to be used in the construction of a novel building. Egged on by curiosity and tongue-lashed by their erudite overseer, the victims began to pry, dig, and tumble down great blocks of stone. In this manner was laid the cornerstone of the Hopkins Astronomical Observatory, the second of its kind in America.

Scholarship at Williams required brawn as well as brain, for one had to possess warm blood and bulging muscles to withstand the rigors of Williamstown winters. The Berkshire saying that "the best products of the county were ice and men" seemed true. Most of the student body was self-sustaining. They wore simple homespun, and lived for the most part on bread, milk, and cheese. Many were the days when students listened to early morning lectures, their attention divided between the needs of the brain and the desires of the stomach.

The Williams working day began at half-past five in summer and at six in winter. At the first warning bell a student hopped out of bed into the ice-cold, pitch darkness. If the oil in his small lamp had not frozen during the night, he lighted it; the fire had to be started in the potbellied stove, and water drawn from the common well. At six came a second bell, a prelude to morning services. The chapel rarely had a fire, and the benches were hard. A professor would read from the Bible and then offer prayer. If the student at times turned a slightly frozen ear from lofty thoughts of Heaven to inviting reflections on a warm Hell, who is to blame him?

Life had its brighter side. For the religious, there was a theological society; for the literary, there was the college magazine, *The Adelphi;* for the few who sought to shine in the social firmament, fraternities were formed in 1832. Debating and temperance societies kept some students active. And always there was the refuge of the Berkshires with its tree-mantled hills, its deep valleys and streams.

In his *Recollections* Washington Gladden has left a vivid picture of the town and the college at the mid-century:

Williams College in 1856 was an institution of modest pretensions. Its faculty consisted of but nine members, all of them full professors, and the four classes averaged less than sixty each. . . . The curriculum was perfectly rigid; all the work was required; the only electives were in the junior year, when we were permitted to choose between French and German. The classes were not divided, the instructional force did not admit of that; the whole class met, three times a day, in the recitation room; naturally a student became pretty well acquainted with all his classmates. . . .

College life in that time was very simple . . . My board, in a club, the first term, cost me two dollars and thirty cents a week . . . The entire expense of my college course, for the three years, including clothing, was less than nine hundred dollars.

Commencement in August was the culmination of these years of work and play. In describing his own graduation, Gladden wrote:

It drew to the village all the people of the countryside, and there were booths for gingerbread and root beer, and sellers of whips and toy balloons, and the usual assortment of fakirs. Few of the hundreds of country people who flocked to the show paid much attention to the graduation exercises; the occasion simply supplied them with an out-of-door holiday. . . .

Out of a total of fifty or sixty, from thirty to thirty-five men presented original orations. The speaking began in the village church about nine o'clock in the morning and continued until noon; after an intermission of two hours for dinner, the floodgates of oratory were reopened, and it was after four o'clock before the valedictorian made his final bow to the applauding crowd.

The most momentous event in the development of the College during the nineteenth century was the appointment of Mark Hopkins as president in 1836. He was a true "Berkshire Borner" from Stockbridge. Precocious as a child, he found that family circumstances made formal education dependent upon his own efforts. In 1820, when he was eighteen, he taught school in Virginia to earn money enough to go to Williams. Within ten years he had not only graduated from Williams, but had an M.D. degree from the Berkshire Medical College in Pittsfield. From 1830 to 1836 he taught Philosophy and Rhetoric at Williams and served as assistant to the president. In the midst of these heavy labors, in 1833, he was ordained a minister.

Hopkins, who served as president of Williams from 1836 to 1872, was an imposing figure in the lecture room. His tall frame slightly stooped above his great breadth of shoulder, his massive head with white sparse locks brushed forward over its gray dome, his long high-bridge aquiline nose, his piercing gray eyes beneath their bushy brows, his wide firm mouth ready to break into a smile—a figure of superb majesty combined with ready geniality.

Personal relations between professors and students were officially encouraged during the Hopkins era. Book-knowledge was of secondary interest. Quoted frequently is his precept, "Accept only that which is the product of your own reason and intelligence."

Revolutionary teaching, indeed, for the times! All the orthodox looked askance when he championed the laboratory and the experimental method of education. In order to illustrate his lectures in Anatomy and Physiology, he needed a life-sized figure that would open up and show its internal workings. This cost six hundred dollars—a lot of money in those days. Promptly Hopkins set out carrying the dummy in the back of his sleigh, giving lectures in little Berkshire villages to pay for it; and as he jogged over the country roads, he looked for all the world as if he were taking a corpse to ride. James A. Garfield summed up the opinions of Williams men when he declared, "A pine bench, with Mark Hopkins at one end of it and me at the other, is a good enough college for me."

Williams owes to Hopkins a system of general examinations given for sophomores, not unlike the Honors Examinations now used at the College and at a number of other American universities.

When Hopkins left in 1872, Williams was "a place of intellectual power, refined taste and moral excellence." After this, a period of decline for the College again set in. A number of faculty members left for other positions, and the science courses, which had been such a vital part of the Williams curriculum, were weakened. Vigor was not regained until a decade later.

Before the Civil War, two Negro servants played as important a role in the intimate history of the college as the presidents. "Aunt Hagar" Thompson, a former slave and a famed cook, served for years in the household of Doctor Griffin, the third president. A witty, talkative woman, she was the power behind the presidential chair. Many a rebellious student owed the continuation of his college work to the persuasive pleading of Hagar as she waited on table. After leaving the Griffin service, she served as laundress for the college until her death at the reputed age of 105 years.

"Aunt Dinah" was another Williams "mammy." A foundling left at the Williamstown Tavern, she grew up with the college, and never acquired a last name. No Williams functions were complete without Aunt Dinah, clad in all her finery. She treated the deans and doctors as equals, and only once did she come off second best—

when she went to a class-day exercise with her dress on wrong-side-out.

The town also had its quota of "characters," whose fame extended to the College Campus. There was Bill Pratt, known throughout the region as the "Sawbuck Philosopher." A gangling, loose-jointed sawyer with protruding teeth, Bill was a spell-binding speech-maker. He managed to combine his official duties as woodcutter with the unofficial one of "town drunk." To the youth of the day, he was a sort of patron saint. Sometimes they called him "Bill of the Multiple Trousers" because of his habit of wearing three pairs of pants at one and the same time, in the depths of winter or on the hottest summer days.

Then there was Abe Bunter, Bill's business rival and arch enemy. Abe was a cider maker. Possessed of a Gargantuan thirst, he had a wide reputation for drinking two gallons of his spirits to every one that he sold. His favorite pastime was butting his head like an enraged bull against the handiest door, fence, or post whenever Bill Pratt's virtues were extolled.

Bill Pratt and Abe were among the champion hunters of the town—no easy honor, as hunting was one of the chief sports of the boys and men of Williamstown in the mid-nineteenth century. The woods were still full of deer and smaller game, and the numerous brooks and streams provided good fishing. Trapping the wily woodchuck kept many a farm boy out in the fields until long after the summer sun had set behind the Taconics. In winter the tedium of the short gray days and long nights was relieved by coasting, skating, and sleighrides.

During the second half of the nineteenth century, this simple, self-sufficient life began to change. New currents and manners made themselves felt in Williamstown. Summer colonists, attracted by the culture and learning of the College, established homes. New buildings adorned the widening campus. New homes, smarter and more elaborate than any Williamstown had ever seen, were built. Fewer farmers tilled the fields on the outskirts. New roads leading into the town were surveyed. The Hoosac Tunnel, completed in 1875, made travel swift and easy from Boston to the West. Sidewalks were laid. Street lights were erected to add a metropolitan touch to the one main street. In 1885 the town fathers numbered among local assets

3600 people, 624 houses, 575 horses, 1210 cows, and 2054 sheep; the tax rate was $1.50 per $1000. Williamstown had gone a long way in a century.

Any attempt to industrialize Williamstown was a feeble gesture at best. Today, only a small wire goods factory, a small cord mill, and a ginger ale factory remain. The famous SAND SPRING supplies water for the ginger ale. The spring is a thousand feet above sea level in the northeast corner of the town, near the old Indian North Trail. Indians enjoyed the warm, soft water which welled up, not through limestone, but filtered by volcanic deposits, sand, and gravel. By 1800 a log bathhouse had been built beside the spring, and in 1850 the first curative claims were made for it. For about sixty years the spot was used for a hotel where patients came to "take the waters;" later it became a sanitarium. In recent years, the bottled water and the ginger ale have proved more profitable. Through the Berkshires, Sand Springs Ginger Ale is favored over all "foreign" brands.

Extensive MOUNT HOPE FARM, in South Williamstown on Mass 43, is owned and operated by Mr. and Mrs. E. Parmalee Prentice, daughter and son-in-law of John D. Rockefeller. There are people who, upon hearing mention of Williamstown, think of Mount Hope Farm rather than of the College. Mount Hope is famous as the home of scientifically produced larger and better eggs. The farm has developed a brand-new type of cattle called the American Dairy Cow; agricultural research conducted here has received awards both in this country and abroad. Visitors are welcome on any day except Sunday, and if notice is sent in advance, they will be met by employees and driven to the farm.

Famous though Mount Hope Farm is in certain circles, it is Williams College that still dominates the town, for more than one-half of the townspeople derive their livelihoods from service, in some form or other, to the college. The union of town and gown is complete.

Relations between the townspeople and the students have not always been so friendly and amiable as they are today. Stories are still told of cows taken from barns during the night and marooned in the upper reaches of West College. Angry farmers missing hogs or goats from their flocks went instinctively to the college, where they found the animals entertaining students in one of the class-rooms.

In 1881, with the accession of Franklin Carter to the presidency, Williams took on new vitality. Endowments flowed in, the faculty was enlarged, and new buildings constructed. Seniors were the first to change from a rigid curriculum to elective courses, and by 1911 this freedom extended to all classes. The honor system was first used during the spring of 1896.

By the end of the century Williams could list outstanding graduates: Amos Eaton, naturalist; William Cullen Bryant, poet; Stephen Field, a justice of the United States Supreme Court; James A. Garfield, President of the United States; Arthur Latham Perry, in his time the foremost American political economist and free trader, and his son Bliss Perry, teacher, author, editor-in-chief of the *Atlantic Monthly,* and professor of English at Harvard.

Williams kept pace with the new educational problems of the twentieth century. Harry A. Garfield, son of President Garfield, gave up a successful business career to become president of the college from which he had been graduated. In 1912 an unusual idea was launched at Williams. For some years, President Garfield had planned a series of round-table discussions in which the best brains of the world might participate. The courses offered to a selected group of advanced students and teachers would, he hoped, be an influence on education throughout the United States. Fulfillment of the plan, accepted by the trustees of the college in 1913, was delayed by the War. President Garfield finally persuaded Bernard M. Baruch to underwrite the project, which as the "Institute of Politics" held its first summer session at Williamstown in 1921. A group of world authorities under the leadership of James Bryce and Elihu Root conducted discussions. The Institute met with immediate favor, and its scope and attendance were enlarged during the succeeding years until it reached a high point in 1926 with an enrollment of more than three hundred. In 1935, '37, and '39, the National Conference of Jews and Christians held an "Institute of Human Relations" at Williamstown.

William Tyler Dennett, a Williams graduate, was elected as successor to Dr. Garfield in 1934. He abolished the student council and inter-fraternity board, revised the curriculum, and made chapel attendance optional, rather than compulsory as it had been. Dr. James

Phinney Baxter III succeeded Dennett in 1937. Dr. Baxter, an alumnus of Williams, as was his father, announced in his inaugural address that he was in complete agreement with the educational aim of his predecessor, and in favor of increased freedom and responsibility for the students.

The Williams that opened in 1793, with one building, two faculty members and eighteen students, has undergone vast expansion. Today the college has an endowment of more than seven million dollars, a library of more than a hundred and fifty thousand volumes, over a hundred members on its faculty, and a student enrollment of eight hundred and fifty-seven. The college grounds cover more than two hundred and fifty acres of land with sixty lecture and classroom buildings, dormitories, and faculty dwellings.

An impression of harmony, despite a variety of architectural styles, makes itself felt on the Williams campus, where buildings are set on wide lawns and among fine old trees. THOMPSON MEMORIAL CHAPEL is probably the most impressive unit. In this great, gray stone Gothic structure lies the body of Ephraim Williams. GRIFFIN and HOPKINS HALLS, named for former presidents of the college, flank the church. Behind the chapel is STETSON HALL, housing behind its red brick façade the Williams College Library and the famous Alfred Clark Chapin Library of Rare Books. Among the Chapin treasures is a set of the first four folios of Shakespeare, Columbus' letter announcing the discovery of the New World, Queen Elizabeth's autographed copy of Cranmer's Bible dated 1561, and a large collection of incunabula.

Across from the Chapel, EAST COLLEGE, CURRIER, FAYER-WEATHER, and BERKSHIRE HALLS form a generous-sized quadrangle with the squat stone HOPKINS OBSERVATORY in the background. LAWRENCE HALL, the English Georgian building to the right of East College, is the art museum where Greek, Etruscan, Peruvian, and Mayan pottery, Egyptian and Assyrian reliefs, potteries and flints, and Japanese ivories and ceramics are on display.

Next to the President's House on the north side of Main Street is the CONGREGATIONAL CHURCH, which used to be the College Chapel as well as the town church. Its slim spire, shining white paint, and graceful outline make it one of the most attractive churches in Berkshire.

Lining Main Street are college buildings, fraternity houses, and old homes. The fraternity houses vary, lavish twentieth-century show places next to mellow houses with history written on every hinge and doorstep. Back of Chapin Hall on the campus is the VAN RENS-SELAER HOUSE, now the headquarters of Sigma Phi Fraternity, formerly the home of Stephen Van Rensselaer, last of the Dutch patroons, projector of the Erie Canal, and founder of Rensselaer Polytechnic Institute. When the house was about to be demolished in Albany, the College brought it here.

Where Mass 2 and US 7 turn toward Troy at the western end of the Common, a large gray stone MEMORIAL BOULDER has been placed on the site of the blockhouse of 1756. This was the civic center of the infant West Hoosuck settlement, now Williamstown. In the autumn of 1752, some sixteen proprietors lived in West Hoosuck. When war with the French and Indians broke out anew after a short period of truce, eleven of these proprietors, feeling a bit uneasy, petitioned the General Court for a haven nearer than Fort Massachusetts, which was too far east to be of much help. Fort Hoosac was built, a flimsy affair of mortised logs defended by a scant handful of yeomen with muzzle-loading, smoothbore guns. It was the sole refuge for the women and children. Here a memorial has been raised to "the memory of the original settlers of West Hoosac who endured the perils and the appalling loneliness of the wilderness in heroic defense of this barrier town."

One of these early settlers was Colonel Benjamin Simonds, the only English captive of the many taken to Canada from Fort Massachusetts who returned to settle in Hoosuck. Colonel Simonds built the RIVER BEND TAVERN which stands just across the wide, new bridge on the road toward Bennington (US 7), where the Hoosic makes a wide sweep along Simonds Road. The tavern has in its cellar a great stone oven, fully large enough to hide a dozen men or more. Beans and bread were baked here for the Revolutionary soldiers and sent to Bennington posthaste.

Opposite the River Bend Tavern is the old WELL SWEEP HOUSE, with the date 1770 on the front corner. In this little white clapboarded dwelling Colonel Simonds passed the last ten years of his life. The old well with its long sweep supplied water for the neighborhood. In his declining years the Colonel liked to sit in the front doorway of his Well Sweep home, rigged out in his regimental coat, knickerbocker trousers, frilled shirt, and continental hat, greeting anyone who passed by.

Among the first occupants of West Hoosuck Blockhouse was Captain Nehemiah Smedley, an original homesteader of Williamstown and one of the builders of the first meetinghouse. Between 1770 and 1777 he raised the large farmhouse called the GREEN RIVER MANSION, which stands back a bit on the road leading to North Adams (Mass 2) about half a mile from the center of Williamstown. It is three stories in height, and broadly clapboarded. The mansion was famous for its huge stone oven which could accommodate many dozen loaves of bread, countless batches of rye bread, and johnnycake enough for a regiment.

One of the visitors to Captain Nehemiah's cellar kitchen was Benedict Arnold, as his bill of expenses rendered the government shows:

> The Honorable Provincial Congress of Massachusetts Bay
> To B. Arnold, Dr.
> Disbursements from Cambridge to Ticonderoga, 1775
> May 6—To ferrage at Deerfield, 1s.6d.; breakfast 2s.2d.
> . . . . .
> . . . . .
> To dinner and lodging, 4s.10d.; paid Nehemiah Smedley 60s.

Certainly 60s. is a great deal for a meal—more than could have been eaten either by Arnold or his companion. Did he pay Captain Nehemiah, an officer in the militia and one of the most prominent and influential men thereabouts, the extra £3 to enlist men for him? This seems likely, for Arnold was in a hurry to collect troops, hopeful of becoming the sole commander of the Green Mountain Boys whom the Connecticut Committee of War had equipped. He could not foresee that Ethan Allen would be in command at the surrender of Ticonderoga.

Of the other houses perhaps the oldest is the PROPRIETORS' HOUSE, where the first town meeting in Williamstown was held in 1753. A small, white cottage with neat green trim, it stands on Buckley Street about a half mile from the junction of Mass 2 and US 7 near the Hemlock Brook bridge.

Less than a quarter of a mile from the junction of Mass 2 and Mass 43 is another great-grandfather dwelling, the "TOWNER" or "WELCH" HOUSE (64 Water Street), built in the early 1770's. The light-brown, shingled structure has been in the Welch family for seventy-two years. Prior to that a jeweler occupied it, and his forge, built into the wall, still remains. The TOWN HALL, formerly the Methodist Church, is now used in summer as a theater by the Williamstown Players.

Thoreau's comment aptly fits Williams:

It were as well to be educated in the shadow of a mountain as in more classic shade. Some will remember, no doubt, not only that they went to college, but that they went to the mountain.

As mountains go, the Berkshires are not lofty, not even Greylock, 3,505 feet and the highest point in the State. But Greylock and the Berkshires, especially around Williamstown, have a charm not found in many of the great mountains of the world. Of the stories and legends about Old Greylock, the one about the "Specter" is most popular.

Thirty years ago, at the end of the summer season, a Berkshire man was bringing down the piano from the little recreation house atop the mountain. Suddenly he saw himself, his horse and wagon and the piano standing upright, outlined in monstrous design against the sky. Unable to decide whether he had quaffed too much from the "cup that cheers," he is said to have fled in haste from the mountainside to the minister, and taken the pledge at once.

The phenomenon of a gigantic shadow of an object reflected in a cloud is so well known as to have a German name, the *Brockengespenst* (Specter of the Brocken) from Brocken, the highest peak of the Hartz Mountains. As Greylockgespenst would be a bit unwieldy for Berkshire, here it is simply called the Specter. C. H. Towne tells more about it in his *Autumn Loitering*.

The GREYLOCK RESERVATION offers great variety in recreation—trails for ambitious hill climbers, swift mountain brooks for ardent fishermen, glimpses of deer and bears in the birch, hemlock, and pine forests, and ski trails and snowshoe paths in winter. But the mere sightseer has his own pleasures. He may go by car from North Adams up the Notch Road or, when this is closed in winter, the best route is south, along US 7 to the New Ashford Road, which leads into Rockwell Road and so up to the TOWER ON GREY-LOCK. Here is a view overlooking the entire valley. The heavy foliage in summer, the richly shaded leaf-change in the fall, even the bleakness when winter comes, each has its special attraction. It was from a high point on the mountain that Hawthorne saw

a view of Williamstown at the distance of a few miles—two or three, perhaps—a white village and steeple, in a gradual hollow, with high mountainous swells heaving themselves up, like immense, subsiding waves, far and wide around it. On these high mountain-waves rested the white summer clouds, or they rested as still in the air above; and they were formed into such fantastic shapes that they gave the strongest possible impression of being confounded or intermixed with the sky. It was like a day-dream to look at it; and the students ought to be day-dreamers, all of them.

CHAPTER III

OIL LAMPS AND BALLOTS

NEW ASHFORD—US 7, sett. 1762, alt. 1350, pop. 94.

HANCOCK—Mass 143, sett. 1767, alt. 1020, pop. 408.

LANESBOROUGH—US 7, sett. about 1753, alt. 1210, pop. 1237.

Roads—US 7 leads directly from Williamstown to New Ashford; Lanesborough is on the same route.

At Brodie Mountain Road, south of New Ashford, branch right to Mass 43, then left to Hancock Center.

FIVE times in twenty years the mountain village of *NEW ASHFORD* has made the front page of newspapers from Maine to California. Even the foreign journals have recognized New Ashford. Spaniard and Japanese, Frenchman and Russian, each soundlessly mouthing the outlandish name, have read how New Ashford, Massachusetts, cast its twenty-five or thirty votes for President of the United States. From 1916 to 1932 the Berkshire community was first in the nation to have its presidential choice recorded, and in the columns of the press led all the cities and towns of the country.

This feat of high-pressure publicity was planned by two newspapermen from the city of Pittsfield. In 1912 Carey S. Hayward, city editor of the *Pittsfield Journal,* and Dennis J. Haylon, managing editor of the *Berkshire Evening Eagle,* conceived a way to bring fame to New Ashford and to all Berkshire County. The town fathers approved the scheme, but unfortunately the election warrant calling for the polls to open at· 10 a.m. had already been posted. Nothing could be done; for four more years the little town had to endure obscurity.

National press associations, approached in 1916, met the Haylon-Hayward plan for Berkshire publicity with raised eyebrows. Even the now defunct *Pittsfield Daily News,* Hayward's paper, which had absorbed the *Journal,* rejected the idea. But the *Eagle* was persuaded to cooperate and the support of many citizens of Pittsfield was enlisted. Then in the flush of enthusiasm Haylon approached the Associated Press.

"It can't be done. And if it could, what of it?" was the response.

That year New Ashford's polls opened at 6 a.m. and were scheduled to close by 10 a.m. at the latest. Twenty-two out of the twenty-three voters were willingly driven "city style" to the schoolhouse. Despite their cooperation, however, the polls closed at exactly ten; not that it required four hours to assemble the town's voters, but because one individualist, whom "fate tried to conceal by naming him Smith," felt that if the law decreed that the polls should be open until ten in the morning then it was a violation to close before that time. He entered the school at 9:55 and, as soon as his vote was cast, the townspeople fretted until the officials frantically tallied sixteen votes for Hughes to Wilson's seven. The press cars stood by with throbbing engines, ready to race to the nearest telephone, three miles away in Lanesborough. At last the automobiles, donated by Pittsfield enthusiasts, roared away from the schoolhouse over the rutty country roads. New Ashford, despite Mr. Smith, had made the front page.

In 1920 other small towns entered the competition; excitement ran high. Would obstinate Mr. Smith insist on standing on his rights? Everyone expected him to deposit his vote at the very last minute, unruffled by the glares and mutterings of his fellow townsmen. To the surprise of all, he was the first to cast his ballot when the polls opened, and even graciously consented to pose for the grinning cameramen. At his side stood shy Miss Phoebe Jordan, nearing seventy, the first woman to vote in New Ashford after the passage of the woman's suffrage bill. The record vote—twenty-eight for Harding and Coolidge, six for Cox and Roosevelt—was totaled by half past seven. New Ashford again had scored a smashing victory over rival towns.

In 1922, the path to fame was made easier. A new concrete highway (US 7), continued from Lanesborough into New Ashford, provided the town with the first hard-surfaced road in its history. People could get to the polls much more quickly, and New Ashford hit its stride in 1924, tallying Coolidge's twenty votes and Davis' four by 6:53 in the morning. Four years later, twenty-seven minutes were slashed off the record and a short-wave radio set was installed in the schoolhouse to flash out New Ashford's verdict: Hoover, twenty-eight votes; Al Smith, three.

The neighboring hilltop town of Peru was considered a serious contender for first honors in 1932, but New Ashford rushed in ahead by two hours, with twenty-four votes for Hoover and eight for Roosevelt. An exotic touch was added by Gregory Makaroff, a naturalized Russian, who hoofed it along the concrete highway with a sign "Good luck to Roosevelt!" on his back.

Then came the fateful year 1936. New Ashford had gone in heavily for modern improvements—two telephones now, a pay-station at Benjamin Boyce's filling station right in the center of town, and another at the home of Forrest C. White, one of the selectmen. The seven voters of Millsfield, New Hampshire, had been tipped off that their newly formed town might become first in the nation, if only they were willing to go to bed later than usual. Massachusetts law, less flexible than New Hampshire statute, forbids opening the polls before 5:45 a.m.; at 12:01 a.m. the citizens of Millsfield dropped all seven ballots in the box and New Ashford lost its place in the morning papers of the nation.

The townspeople of New Ashford were unaware that a plot was on foot to deprive them of their moment of fame. Long before sunrise on this short November day a crowd of some 250 "furriners" assembled about the small weatherworn building that for a century and a half has served New Ashford as schoolhouse and town hall. Some were curiosity-seekers eager to edge into the limelight; others were newspaper men out on a "color story." Photographers, with cameras and flash bulbs ready, jostled good-naturedly in the vantage points before the schoolhouse, with its sagging shingled roof and squat chimney. The scarred doors, hooked open, revealed a scene of absorbed anticipation: booths and tables crowded the fifteen-by-eighteen-foot floor space; an official, seated importantly, was tapping his teeth with a pencil; other officials bustled about on weighty errands.

For more than an hour lights had been winking in the windows and lanterns had been bobbing in the yards of hill farms. Women were giving the older girls last-minute directions for the care of the babies, and every member of each family had some chore, from the toddlers underfoot trying to help, to the boys serious with their responsibility of feeding the stock and milking the cows. Men tried to crank the cold engine of the Model T without splitting the seams of their Sunday jackets. Then proudly erect on the worn cushions of the family car, jouncing over the steep stony roads, the voters of New Ashford started out to do their civic duty.

Almost everyone was early enough for some discussion of agricultural matters, a little neighborly gossip, and a few glances at the "furriners" who were frankly staring. Someone sniggered as a photographer took a flashlight picture of an old lady in a rusty black coat and ancient bonnet. She did not smile and only blinked rapidly as the light exploded in her face. When these preliminaries were over, an official, watch in hand, nodded his head and the voters filed into the hall. By six everyone present had dropped a ballot in the box. But they couldn't begin the count. Mrs. William Rainey from 'way over in the foothills of Greylock on the edge of the wilderness, had signified her intention to vote. But she had not appeared, to the great concern of the townspeople clustered together, anxiously watching the road. There was still time, for by law the polls had to remain open until ten. They knew that Mrs. Rainey had to walk miles from her lonely home. Perhaps one of her children was sick, or the cow had calved. After what seemed an interminable wait, someone espied her coming down the mountain road, her coat billowing out behind her in the wind. A cheer arose as she came into full view, ran the last few paces, shoved aside two heifers that had strayed from a nearby pasture, and stumbled up the steps into the schoolhouse.

But she was too late. The returns from Millsfield, New Hampshire, were already in. The lady from the hills arrived less than twenty minutes after the polls opened. The culprit, if any, was the Massachusetts law, which believes that the voter should have his night's sleep before going to the polls.

"It is so quiet and peaceful in New Ashford that you can hear a feather drop from the breast of a bird," wrote Josh Billings back in the 1850's. He knew, because he had been born only a few miles away in Lanesborough. Twenty-five years ago, you could still hear a feather drop in New Ashford, and today, provided you abandon the main highway, you will discover the peace of the hills. Even the mansion houses along the fringes of Greylock have settled down into the tranquillity of the thousands of forested acres that surround them.

Mountain brooks dash over schist ledges to empty into the swift Green River and find their way to the Hoosic at Williamstown; the woodland runways of the wild deer pass close by the doors of the village; and raccoons whistle their shrill startling notes from the ledges that enclose the narrow valley.

The original settlers of New Ashford came from Rhode Island, Connecticut, and eastern Massachusetts. As early as 1762 several Baptists and Methodists built their homes along the steep mountainsides, where there is scarcely enough level ground for a "cow to get a footing." They chose this inaccessible spot rather than the lowlands to avoid the valley mist which, they believed, brought fever. Moreover, Indians could too easily ambush a valley farm. On the heights, then, they built a fort and houses and began to clear their tilted fields. For many years rotting ash logs, once part of the defense of the settlers against Indian arrows, indicated the location of Ashfort, as the town was then called. Today the site of the fort, marked by a monument, lies within the Greylock Reservation near the crossing of the old stagecoach road from New Ashford and the Rockwell Road to Greylock.

As Indian hostilities diminished and the fear of fever waned, New Ashford residents ventured into the valley, staked their lots, and laid plans for a new and permanent settlement. Without railroad or main highway until the twentieth century, New Ashford grew to maturity in the silence of the hills.

So solitary a spot appealed to a British deserter who joined the Americans during the Revolution. In an effort to break all links with the past, he adopted the name of Robert Twentymen. "A dinner for Twentymen," was the order sent on ahead to the landlord of a certain tavern whither Robert Twentymen was journeying one day. And a dinner for twenty men was brought steaming from the great kitchen as Twentymen's knock sounded at the door. Though the landlord's anger mounted higher and higher, Twentymen indignantly refused to pay for the nineteen extra dinners which he had never requested.

During its more active days around 1822 the town began to quarry its blue and white marble deposits, but by 1845 transportation from the quarry to the railroads cost too much to make business profitable. The sawmills and charcoal kilns have likewise long been idle, and residents of the town have steadily decreased in number. Along the highway (US 7), which closely follows the course of the old road built in 1841, connecting Pittsfield with Williamstown, there are cabin camps, roadside stands, and summer cafés. Nine bridges carry the modern highway across the loops and coils of the meandering Green River. While they do "a bit of fishing" or "go out after a deer," Berkshire visitors board and lodge in New Ashford. Hikers and amateur naturalists come in increasing numbers. The tourist season no longer ends with the falling leaves, for the smooth, steep slopes of New Ashford's mountainsides attract hundreds of skiers.

About one mile south of the center of town, on US 7, is RED BAT CAVE, named by the late Cortlandt Field Bishop, world traveler. In 1918 he and a group of scientists explored the cave, then called Baker Cave, and discovered black bats with red heads hibernating there. It may have been used during the Revolution as a refuge by Tories who knew that they would receive little quarter from Berkshire patriots if they were found. It is now equipped with electric lights and ladders for exploring its depths, and during the summer months is open to the public. And the town lives up to its electrically lighted cave, for since November, 1931, the Pittsfield Electric Company has had nineteen customers in New Ashford. But tourists, telephones, twentieth-century trappings have hardly altered the mountain village. Folks raised in the serene shadow of the hills don't easily change their ways.

Beyond New Ashford, in a secluded valley among the Taconics, lies *HANCOCK*. A glance at the map reveals a sprawling township. Houses and farms are scattered down a narrow valley seven miles long, following the course of the branches of the Green and Kinderhook rivers.

About 1767 Hancock was described as a "long, ungainly town, so badly located that the inhabitants of one end can not reach the other end without going out of town, and mostly out of the county and State; it is hemmed in by steep mountains on both sides, so steep that one can not climb out without spoiling the knees of his pantaloons, or go back without spoiling their seat."

This timely witticism of the town's Representative in the General Court, Samuel Hand, saved Hancock from an increase in valuation and taxes when assessments in other towns were raised.

Hancock was originally called Jericho, probably because of the mountains that hem it in. The town was incorporated in 1776 for an interesting reason, as the record shows:

Whereas it has been represented to this Honorable Court that the inhabitants of a place called Jericho, in the county of Berkshire, have been taxed for several years past, and have met with difficulties in assessing and collecting the same and likewise are liable for many other inconveniences for want of being incorporated into a township. Be it therefore enacted by the Council and House of Representatives in General Court assembled and by the authority of the same that the said Plantation . . . containing about 20,000 acres of land, be and hereby is enacted into a town by the name of Hancock . . . and be it further enacted that Asa Douglass, Esq., be and hereby is directed and impowered to issue his warrant, directed to some principal inhabitant within this town, requiring him to warn the inhabitants of said town, having a free hold therein to the value of forty shillings per annum, or other estate to the value of forty pounds, to meet at such time and place in said town, as shall be therein described, to choose all such officers as are or shall be required by law to manage the affairs of said town, etc., July 2d, 1776.

Although Hancock is New Ashford's nearest neighbor on the west, there is no direct road between the two towns. The Brodie Mountain Road from Lanesborough leads off US 7 to the west just past the New Ashford-Lanesborough town line, and winding sharply over the mountain between dark hillsides, descends in a long, slow grade into Hancock Center.

The Potter Mountain Road from Pittsfield is an alternate route, though dangerously muddy in wet weather. It offers a drive through a thickly forested region with mountain scenery. Many prefer a third route, Mass 43, which goes out of South Williamstown.

This route turns off at the four corners in South Williamstown, where a sign points the way to "Hancock and Stephentown," along a macadam road leading into a broad green valley between the Taconics. From the valley floor rolling fields sweep gently upward east and west till lowland and highland are blended in the sky. In contrast to this natural beauty are the small, dingy, nondescript houses along the roadside, their front yards littered like junkyards with rusty farm implements. For a five-mile stretch there are no electric transmission lines, no telephone wires. The traveler will pass a hillside boulder marking the five hundred acres of the EDWARD HOWE FORBUSH MEMORIAL WILD LIFE SANCTUARY. Nearby is a little cemetery surrounded by a fancy iron grill fence, gnarled old trees, and a clump of somber firs. So clear is the air that you can hear the singing brook as it rushes to join the Hoosic, and the sharp rhythm of an axe biting into standing timber.

The valley narrows in the dark bulk of the mountains, and houses more numerous and pretentious mark the existence of HANCOCK CENTER, once a prosperous town with flocks of sheep grazing on the steep slopes, a flourishing textile industry, grist mills, tanneries, quarries, and sawmills. In 1790 the town had a population of 1211. Hancock is a ghost town now, with a gaunt, forlorn appearance. The population has shrunk to 408, and the houses are shabby and worn; only an occasional wagon or automobile passes down the main street; perhaps a woman will appear briefly to shake a rug or to call a child. But the town remembers the old days when the paint was bright on the houses and life moved faster.

Traditions and tales from the past are Hancock's chief contribution to the history of Berkshire. Her glory was at its peak during the years when the "Berkshire Boys" marched up the long valley to Bennington, and Tories received short shrift from the patriots.

A loyal Tory of Hancock, Richard Jackson, was accused of high treason against the Colonies when he was captured on his way to join the British near Bennington. Making no pretense of being other than a Royalist, ready to fight for his king, he was taken to the jail at Great Barrington to await trial in Springfield. The jail was dilapidated and the guard lax, so that any prisoner could have escaped with ease. But Jackson's integrity was beyond question. Local tradition has it that he appealed to the sheriff.

"Let me go free that I may work and earn something."

"But—but—" stammered the sheriff, who respected Jackson, though he felt that this request was a little unorthodox.

"Have no fear, Sheriff, I shall come back at night," and he added grimly, "When it's time for me to be hanged, I'll be there."

Morning after morning Jackson was let out, did his day's work, and was safely locked up again at night. Finally in May it became the sheriff's duty to take him to Springfield. But seeing that his jailer was loath to leave his plowing and planting, Jackson suggested that he make the trip alone.

The sheriff, accustomed by this time to his prisoner's unusual requests, agreed, and his charge set off alone to trudge miles through the woods to his trial and execution, for there was no apparent hope of acquittal. In the woods of Tyringham he was overtaken by the Hon. Mr. Edwards, who was on his way to a meeting of the Executive Council in Boston.

"Whither are you bound?" asked Edwards. "To Springfield, sir, to be tried for my life," was the calm rejoinder.

Without disclosing his own identity, Edwards soon learned his companion's story. Pondering, he went on to Boston, while Jackson stopped in Springfield, was duly tried, and condemned to death. Meantime, the Executive Council, which at that time exercised power of release over those condemned to death, was listening to petitions for pardon. After all these had been read, Edwards asked the Council if a pardon was not to be granted to Mr. Jackson of Hancock. Earnestly addressing the assembly, Edwards told the story of Jackson's loyalty not only to his king, but to the laws and regulations of the Colony in so far as they implied no disloyalty to his English sovereign. The members of the Council hesitated, scarcely believing their ears, but when the story was proved true, they unanimously agreed that such a man as Jackson ought not to be sent to the gallows. An unconditional pardon was immediately made out and the loyal Tory returned to his family and farm in Hancock.

The early town records of Hancock lead one to wonder what kind of reception awaited Jackson after he cheated the noose. The town was militantly patriotic in Revolutionary times. Her sons served their country valiantly and as a rule Royalists received little tolerance from the Town Fathers, as witness the record of September, 1777:

Voted that Mr. Benjamin Baker be, and hereby is, appointed to procure such evidence as may be had against all persons charged by the inhabitants of this town as being enimically disposed towards this or any of the United States, and lay evidence before the court . . . That Timothy Walker is not a suitable person to serve this town in the capacity of selectman . . . That Christopher Kinyon shall not serve this town in the capacity of committee man hereafter . . . That six persons . . . are by this vote ordered to be kept confined in Hampton jail . . .

Those people who were judged unfit for public office, one infers, had Tory leanings. Others were disposed of in the following manner:

"Voted the eleven persons above named shall not be suffered to dwell nor remain in town."

At the Battle of Bennington the "Berkshire Boys" fired their muskets with such enthusiasm that anxious wives in Hancock could hear the roar. The wife and daughter of Lieutenant James Smith of Hancock scrambled up to the high northern summit of what is now called Potter Mountain. All day long they listened to the far-off reports of guns and cannon as Britishers and Yankees gave each other ball for ball. A little earlier on that historic day (August 16, 1777), fighting Parson Allen of Pittsfield, at the head of the Berkshire troops from that section, had met General Stark with the words:

"We, the people of Berkshire, have frequently been called upon to fight, but have never been led against the enemy. We have now resolved, if you will not let us fight, never to turn out again."

They had their chance that day. Mrs. Smith, perched precariously on the ledge, wiped her eyes again and again as her daughter repeated: "Ma, that's Pa's gun for sure! Ma, can't you hear it?" As night approached Mrs. Smith suddenly "felt a presentiment."

"Molly, I do believe your father's coming home tonight!" she exclaimed. "We'd better go home and put the kettle on and get the supper, for Jamie'll soon be here." Sure enough, the soldier greeted his delighted family at supper time; a night's furlough had been granted him after the victory at Bennington.

In early colonial days the town of Hancock embraced a section of Lebanon, New York, once famous for its Warm Springs. To enjoy its medicinal properties, men and women took turns bathing in it on alternate days. A high fence insured privacy from "Peeping Toms." Let the warrant drawn up by the town fathers tell the rest of the story:

That whereas a complaint is preferred . . . to inform this meeting of some dishonorable conduct of a number of animals said to be in Human Shape, who being so lost to every principle of Modesty and every Sentiment of Humanity, Good order and decency as to tair off the Raillings which surround the Bath, to peak in and climb up look over etc., at a time when the Female Sex are Bathing therein, it is Resolved that Lieutenant Ephraim Bowman be . . . requested to Erect and Set up at the Most Suitable place near Said Pool, at the expense of this town, a Sufficient Whipping Post for the Immediate punishment of all such Sordid Miscreants who dare in future to be found Guilty of Such Shameful Misconduct . . .

There is no further record of "Peeping Toms" in Hancock.

Care for the morals of the community also appeared in the ordinance that "There shall be no horse-racing in this town." The order did not apply, it seems, to the famous Berkshire horse, "Old Ti," and his fearless rider, Asa Douglass, one of the first settlers of Hancock and the town's representative in the General Court. Douglass offered his services as a spy for the colonists. Pretending to be a farmer in search of lost cattle, he penetrated right into the midst of the enemy at Fort Ticonderoga. After studying the fortifications and estimating the enemy's man-power, Douglass crept stealthily to the outskirts of the camp, mounted his horse, and started for home. But his movements so aroused suspicion that a soldier shouted: "A spy! The old farmer is a spy!"

Douglass gave "Old Ti" free rein and implored him, "Race as you never raced before! Get me home to the Berkshires and I swear I'll never put a saddle on your back again!" The sturdy young horse galloped up hill and down dale, outdistancing the pursuit. Some say that Asa was true to his impulsive promise, and that the horse lived to a peaceful old age in the pasture. Others insist that his master saddled him once more, when he rode at the head of his company to the capture of Fort Ticonderoga in May, 1775.

Settlers of the southern part of Hancock, who built homes on and near Lebanon Mountain, became Shakers and established their own meetinghouse and village. The community was small at first, consisting of Israel Talcott and the Goodriches—Daniel, Nathan, David, Ezekiel, Hezekiah, and Jeremiah. These seven formed the nucleus of the faith's second community.

Mother Ann Lee with eight followers from Manchester, England, propagated the faith. In 1779 the sect, one of the first of almost two hundred communistic societies attempted in the country, settled New Lebanon, New York. Two years later, the founder, who claimed immortality and called herself "Ann the Word," started proselytizing in New England. The Shakers, who were pacifists, had arrived in America at an ill-chosen time, and their persecution and imprisonment were ended only when Governor Clinton intervened in their behalf. Besides their advocacy of peace, the Shakers held to three cardinal principles: confession, celibacy, and community of interest. Their converts announced, "The worldly goods which we possessed are no longer our own," before they were admitted to the society to practise the virtues of faith, hope, honesty, continence, innocence, simplicity, meekness, humility, prudence, patience, thankfulness, and charity. This abundance of virtue could be achieved, they believed, by duty to God, duty to man, practical peace, simplicity of language, right use of prosperity, and the celibate life.

No road leads over the mountain heights from Hancock Center to the Shaker community. The main highway (US 7) to Pittsfield and then the road to Albany (US 20) will take the visitor there. When the sect first settled, in the 1790's, there were only a few families, but they spread their doctrines so successfully that they eventually owned some 5000 acres of land and the large community came to be known as SHAKER VILLAGE. A picturesque feature of the settlement is a circular stone barn erected in 1826. Its circumference is 276 feet, and all the stalls face the outer walls. The spacious upper floor is so arranged that ten wagons may be driven around it, nose to tailboard, at one time.

Only a remnant of the once prosperous Shaker family remains today, but they still conduct a small school, under State supervision. Now and then, a gentle-faced Shaker lady in bonnet, sober gown, and antiquated cape is seen on the streets of Pittsfield, although the elders of the sect have not appeared there for some years. They keep their houses freshly painted, lawns trimmed, and paths carefully marked; within their old brick dormitory they guard their precious antiques. A small store sells handicraft work to passersby during the spring and summer, but otherwise there is a loneliness in the moribund community.

From the time of its settlement Hancock itself was a Baptist town and most of its inhabitants still adhere to the Baptist faith. The first meetinghouse of 1772, in which fifteen members foregathered with their pastor, Elder Clark Rogers from Rhode Island, was built of logs. The present building was erected in 1850.

The Shaker village and Hancock town grow ever weaker, while the forest with renewed vigor marches forward over fields once laboriously cleared. It may be that mountains and trout streams, ski slopes, and hiking trails will bring new blood to revitalize the dying Berkshire town. More than half of the Pittsfield State Forest is in Hancock. From Pittsfield by the Berry Pond Circuit Road or by a foot-trail through the forest from Hancock one reaches the well-stocked fishing waters of BERRY POND, the highest body of water in the county and an idyllic setting for picnic excursions.

If the town is eventually abandoned, the tourist of the future may pass only a few heaps of timbers on a woodland trail. Already the gay Hancock Fair has been given up. No longer is there a proud display of prize cattle, a showing of dahlias remarkable for size and color, a line of jellies anxiously appraised by rival housewives. No more do people gather to feast under the big tent or to admire and sample homely breads and cakes.

Up the long hill from Hancock Center the road leads over Brodie Mountain to *LANESBOROUGH,* the third and largest of the group of mountain villages. Compared with New Ashford's population of ninety-four and Hancock's 408, Lanesborough with 1237 seems almost a metropolis, though beside Pittsfield and North Adams, Lanesborough is a drowsy village. Set upon two hills north of Pittsfield, it stands halfway between the silence of the mountains and the bustle of the city, and has taken on something of the character of both—a New England village on the edge of the torrent of traffic which rushes constantly north and south along US 7. Streams of trucks crawling up the grades and rushing down prove that all Berkshire is not somnolent. Modern industry, supplying food and raiment to the outside world, rumbles past quiet hermitages. Today traffic only rushes through Lanesborough; in the '80's it stopped there.

During the nineteenth century Lanesborough was a prosperous mining and manufacturing town. In 1822 it boasted five hotels, three tanneries, two hatters, five shoe shops, three tailor shops, a harness maker, five blacksmith shops, two cloth dressing and carding factories, two wagon makers and repairers, a grinding mill, five sawmills, and one shop for making spinning wheels.

Then iron was discovered. In 1847 the Briggs Iron Company was formed to manufacture soft iron. When J. L. Colby took over the company in 1864, the manufacture of car-wheel iron was begun. The property covered four or five hundred acres of woodland, and two hundred men were employed. In 1885 new owners changed the name of the company to the Lanesborough Iron Works.

Of even greater importance were the marble quarries which by 1840 supplied the chief product of trade. The marble was of the purest white or of interestingly variegated color. In 1842 and 1843 the industry supplied the rest of the country with more than two hundred thousand dollars' worth of its valuable stone.

Lanesborough sand was used for the manufacture of glass by the Berkshire Glass Company. And a host of lesser industries thrived: brick ovens, lime kilns, sawmills, and grist mills.

When the absence of railroad connections made Lanesborough's industries less lucrative, change was inevitable. Having relinquished its own manufactures, Lanesborough now houses industrial workers from neighboring towns. Men from the factories and stores of Pittsfield settle there with their families, but they come, not to work, but to live.

Originally Richfield and later New Framingham, the town adopted its present name at the time of incorporation by an act of the General Court, June 20, 1765. Tradition has it that a Mr. Lane of England promised the community a bell if they would take his name, but the bell was never produced. It is also possible that the name may be connected with James Lane, Viscount Lanesborough in the Irish Peerage, or with the town of Lanesborough in Ireland upon the Shannon River, or derive from the "fact that its six miles square adjoining south on Indian Town (Stockbridge) on the Housatonic River" lay along a winding lane. The name may even have been a tribute to the beautiful Countess of Lanesborough, court favorite, and friend of the Royal Governor of Massachusetts.

Lanesborough has its share of famous men and local celebrities in the persons of Josh Billings, Jonathan Smith, "a plain man," as he said, Reuben Humphreyville, and Woodbridge Little, the caveman Tory. They are remembered, while industrial Lanesborough has now lapsed into oblivion.

In the 1830's Reuben Humphreyville of Lanesborough and Darius Mead of Pittsfield furnished central Berkshire with its music for dances and other festivities. Humphreyville, who was a famous old-time master of the bow and strings, was totally blind, while Mead had but one eye, so that it was said that he and his musical partner "had but a single eye between them." Mead played second violin, and Humphreyville, besides being first violinist, had the important duty of "calling off." Before a dance began, when the sets were ready for the music, Humphreyville would cry out "All right, Reuben!" The phrase became a catchword that still lives in local lore. So acute of hearing was Humphreyville, without whose presence no dancing party was a success, that if anybody was out of place in the "sets," even in the one most distant from him, he would dress the bunglers down. In every hotel and house which he had once visited, he would move about with great freedom and ease, hang up his garments, and take his place on the dance-hall platform and at the dining table with skill astonishing in a sightless man.

During a dance in the old Eagle Hotel in Dalton, Mead, who had a diamond in the end of his fiddle bow, cut the names, "Capt. A. S. Chamberlain, Reuben Humphreyville and Darius Mead," on a small old-fashioned glass pane. One morning the window pane was missing; the putty had been removed from the sash by some one who was bound to become possessor of the signatures on the pane by fair means or foul.

Josh Billings was a different sort of entertainer. His home was on CONSTITUTION HILL, a neatly rounded elevation about two-thirds of a mile from the present Post Office. Although born Henry Wheeler Shaw, son of a local dignitary, as a young man he was hard pressed to make a living. After a varied career which carried him to all parts of the country and into all sorts of occupations from farmer to steamboat captain, Shaw settled down as an auctioneer. In 1858 he was inspired by Artemus Ward, another "crackerbox philosopher" of the time, to use phonetic spelling. Or perhaps he may once have had a glimpse of early Lanesborough town records, of which this is a sample:

"Voted, the scool hows should be 28 ft. long, 24 ft. wid and 9 ft. stod."

When his *Essa on a Muel* appeared, he signed the piece "Josh Billings." From that moment and for the next twenty-five years, he was famous all over England and America as a humorous writer and lecturer.

Berkshire folk, along with the rest of the country, enjoyed his homely wit and peculiar spelling. They said he must have missed his fishing when he was down in the city, and it pleased them that he remembered the trout pools in New Ashford township. They were proud when landlord "Tot" Mallory, who kept the one hotel in town, whispered abroad that Josh was "stoppin' off a spell" with him. Almost every summer for years, Mallory's little hostelry in the shadow of Greylock brightened in the reflected glory of its distinguished visitor. Josh Billings had "come back, b'gosh, t' get a good mess o' fish!"

This small-town wit had an original blend of nonsense and horse sense. He was called the "queerest and wisest" of humorists of his day, and he made a place for himself in American literature as one who was as typically New England as pie for breakfast. Lanesborough became known as the home town of a celebrity—Lanesborough, where Josh Billings stole apples and raffled off a small boy's treasures, where he trudged over the hills and wisecracked on his way to church!

"Nobody really luvs to be cheated, but it doz seem as tho everyone was anxious to see how near they could cum to it."

"The man who is as kind and courteous to his office boy as he is to a millionaire, is a gentleman."

"2 sta is 2 win."

These were typical sayings. The last was written in black crayon on the wall of a Pittsfield newspaper office when the editor was having hard sledding and was thinking of closing up shop. With "2 sta is 2 win" staring down at him, he had no alternative; he stayed and coincidentally won.

A friend once asked the humorist, "How fast does sound travel?"

"Wal, it depends a lot on the noise in point," Billings drawled. "Now, the sound of a dinner bell, for instance, travels a half mile a second, while an invitashun to get up in the mornin', I have known to be three-quarters of an hour goin' up two pair of stairs—and then not hev strength enough to be heard."

Lanesborough cherished Josh Billings as much for the memory of his childhood pranks as for the philosophical puns and witticisms of his later years. There was the time Josh put the cow in the cupola of the Pontoosuc Mill in Pittsfield. How he got her there was a mystery never solved. The men who had to get her out swore the Devil must have been his accomplice.

The old SHAW HOUSE stands near picnic grounds and often

it must have been rocked to its foundations by the antics of the
talented mischief-makers within. The road leading to the Shaws' is
called Silver Street, because of the legend that counterfeiters once
made silver pieces in a cave on the west side of the hill. Other houses
along the village street were occupied by the Shaw family at one
time and another, but the dwelling on Constitution Hill seems to
have the aura of Josh Billings about it.

JOSH BILLINGS' GRAVE is marked with a rough granite
boulder in the old cemetery in Lanesborough Center. In a recessed
rectangle, with letters simulating rude twigs, the name stands out in
bold relief:

JOSH BILLINGS

On the top in polished ovals can be read the more conventional inscription:

HENRY WHEELER SHAW
Born April 21, 1818. Died Oct. 14, 1885
ZILPHA BRADFORD, HIS WIFE
1821–1901

Constitution Hill received its name from Jonathan Smith, who
lived there in 1788. He made himself famous by a single speech when
the Massachusetts Convention assembled to consider whether they
should or should not adopt the Federal Constitution. After hours of
argument and highflown oratory, Jonathan Smith of Lanesborough
rose to his feet. "I am a plain man and get my living by the plow."
Plain John Smith knew what he thought and wasn't afraid to
speak out.

I am not used to speak in public, but I beg your leave to say a few
words . . . I have lived in a part of the country where I have known the
worth of good government by the want of it . . . The Constitution, I
found, was a cure for these disorders. It was just such a thing as we
wanted. I got a copy of it and read it over and over . . . I did not go to
any lawyer to ask his opinions; we have no lawyer in our town, and we
do well enough without . . .

Brother farmers, let us suppose a case now . . . Suppose two or three
of you have been at the pains to break up a piece of rough land, and sow it

with wheat; would you let it lie waste, because you could not agree what sort of a fence to make? Would it not be better to put up a fence that did not please everyone's fancy, rather than not fence it at all, or keep disputing about it until wild beasts came and devoured it . . . I say take things in time, gather fruit when it is ripe. There is a time to sow and time to reap. We sowed our seed when we sent men to the Federal Convention; now it is the harvest—now is the time to reap the fruit of our labor, and if we don't do it now, I am afraid that we never shall have another opportunity. . . .

There was another Lanesborough man who wasn't afraid to say what he thought, although he considered it his privilege to change his mind. Before the Revolution broke out, Woodbridge Little settled in Lanesborough to practice law. In wartime he refused to keep his Tory sympathies to himself. As a result the Committee of Safety advertised for him in the *Hartford Courant* as a "Wanted Man." Little fled to a marble cave in Lanesborough. This "Diamond Cave at the base of the Taconics," as it was then called, is today northwest from the village center, along a narrow, rutty road not too good for low-slung cars; it lies beyond the abandoned ore beds where formerly there was a mining settlement. The tiny village has vanished, save for a few piles of stones, a grassy mound of earth, and a rotted bridge. Only the marble cave is left, under the north shoulder of Laurel Hill, concealed from casual inspection by underbrush. In "COON HOLLOW CAVE," as Lanesborough now calls it, Woodbridge Little existed for many days and nights. His food was brought by friends and neighbors, for aside from his Tory sentiments he was a popular man. Later, he completely changed his convictions, emerged from the cave, and enlisted on the side of the Colonists to fight at Bennington in Lieutenant Hubbard's company.

There are more accessible caves in the limestone and marble terrain outside Lanesborough. Off US 7 in the northern section of the town is DISAPPEARING BROOK, where visitors can watch a stream vanish underground and reappear four times within a mile. Mysterious caverns and passageways have been discovered in the surrounding countryside—one of them a tunnel of white marble some 140 feet in length. The tunnel opens from an abandoned quarry which once supplied marble of a superior grade for the Capitol at Washington.

Near the caves, in the wastelands of the quarry, is BROWN'S
BOULDER, with an inscription to recall the Brown-Barker romance.
Although she was a village belle, Susan Barker never married, but
not for lack of chances. At the age of eighty, she saw no reason for
abandoning comfortable spinsterhood to wed Captain Brown. This
seventy-year-old swain, who had waited patiently for many years,
suddenly became insistent, and so Miss Susie handed him his "walking
papers." The captain, despondent and perhaps a little vengeful, retired
to the pasture with a mason's chisel and for the attention of the
Almighty and such others as might be interested scratched these lines:

CAPT. JOHN M. BROWN, BORN AT STAFFORD'S HILL,
OCT. 1, 1809, CHESHIRE, MASS.
INSCRIBED UPON THIS ROCK, APRIL 2, 1879.
MAY GOD BLESS SUSAN AND ALL OF HER BAREN
LAND AND WHEN SHE GITS TO HEAVEN I HOPE SHE
FINDS A MAN.

In this same northern section of the town, close by the spot where
Rockwell Road leads off US 7 to Greylock, stands the old brown
BRADLEY HOUSE, known for the last century and a half as "British Headquarters." When Burgoyne's soldiers were marching through
the Berkshires after their defeat at the Battle of Saratoga (1777), they
stopped for a night in Lanesborough and the quartermaster of a
Hessian regiment was billeted at the house. Deciding to pay a call
on some Tory ladies, he took the precaution to hide in the great brick
oven of his billet a bag of gold entrusted to him. When he returned,
the bag had vanished, and not a single coin has ever turned up,
even to this day.

A part of Cheshire was once included in Lanesborough. An electric
railway between Lanesborough and Cheshire ran along what is now
the macadam road out of Lanesborough Center over the hill past
the red-brick Baptist Church. The hill forms the dividing line between
the Housatonic and the Hoosac Valleys. From its top, the Indian
Pontoosuck Trail led out of the Housatonic Valley to join the Mohawk Trail in North Adams. The road runs toward Greylock, the
mountain looming in full view for the greater part of the way.

Besides caves and underground passageways Lanesborough has

another geological curiosity. About a mile west of US 7, on a country road that follows the north shore of Pontoosuc Lake, is BALANCE ROCK PARK, where the amazing Balance Rock occupies a prominent position among other curious boulders deposited by the glaciers of prehistoric times. Some of the most prominent have been called Split Rock, Cross Rock, and Elephant Rock. An Indian legend explains these errant boulders in the hillside pasture as the playthings of an Iroquois champion who tossed them there to show some Mahican youths how to play quoits. Beyond the park, POTTER MOUNTAIN, shared by Lanesborough and Hancock, keeps westerly guard over the town. A steep road between its twin peaks crosses close to the site of the lonely farmhouse owned by the Potters who gave the mountain its name. The highest peak is 2400 feet above sea level and the southern summit is now a part of the Pittsfield State Forest. From its high-flung crest the hills of New York roll away to the west; on a clear day, the Battle Monument in old Bennington is visible through binoculars; and the shadowed Housatonic Valley stretches out on the east toward Pittsfield.

Chapter IV

METROPOLIS IN THE HEART
OF THE BERKSHIRES

PITTSFIELD—US 20, US 7, Mass 8, Mass 9, sett. 1752, alt. 1038, pop. 47,516.
Roads—US 7 runs from Lanesborough to Pittsfield.

ONE fine fall evening a genial landlord coined a phrase that best suits this shire town of the westernmost reaches of Massachusetts. Standing on the broad flagstone step that led to the principal tavern of the little village of Pontoosuc, one day to be called Pittsfield, mine host flung a greeting into the night:

"Welcome! Welcome, traveler! Welcome to the Heart of the Berkshires!"

To assimilate the atmosphere of *PITTSFIELD* most successfully, or, better yet, to identify the city's past with its present, you will do well to seek the roots of Pittsfield life in CITY HALL PARK. Journeying into the town on any of the main highways, you come directly to the central green or "oval," formed at the junction of the four main streets—the compass-named thoroughfares, North, South, East, and West Streets. Here Pittsfield tells its story in bronze and stone.

There is the tale of Isabel Walton and the Old Elm, since replaced by a SUN DIAL. Savage Indian captors had bound Isabel at the foot of the Old Elm, and timber lay heaped about her ready for lighting. The band of redskins was on a triumphal journey home from a scalp and captive-grabbing orgy in the Connecticut Valley, and the fair Isabel was unquestionably an encumbrance to the expedition. But just as the fire was to be struck, a young and, of course, handsome French lieutenant, Pierre Lanaudinière by name, swooped down from St. Francis, a French fort bordering the Colonies, and saved the trembling victim's life. He took her off with him to Montreal, where they were married.

William Brattle House in Pittsfield   *Courtesy of The Society for The Preservation of New England Antiquities*

Interior of Bulfinch Church (First Church of Pittsfield)
Courtesy of The Society for The Preservation of New England

Just why this Frenchman leaped from his charger at such an opportune instant and dashed away with Isabel without bearing off her father too (who, it is recorded, was among the captives) is not for posterity to ask. Let it be content with the thought of Isabel safely ensconced in her Canadian home, learning her hero's language, patiently darning his socks, and perhaps thinking occasionally of the Old Elm.

Because of marauding bands of Indians during the French and Indian wars—savages who were in nowise related to the friendly Stockbridge Indians of the county—settlement of Pontoosuc plantation and the rest of western Massachusetts was long delayed. In 1736 Colonel Jacob Wendell, ancestor of the poet Oliver Wendell Holmes, had paid the town of Boston £1320 for a tract of land six miles square in the heart of the Berkshires. But it was not until 1752 that a brave man—throwing aside discretion and casting off the fear of the Indians which possessed pioneers in the wake of the Connecticut River atrocities—came riding from the east of Pontoosuc.

It was Solomon Deming who first hacked his way through the dark forests from Wethersfield, Connecticut, to establish his rooftree in the Berkshire wilderness. And with him came Sarah, his wife, transporting the utensils of her former home into this wild, albeit beautiful, territory, where fierce men and beasts waited for her destruction.

Some distance east of the Old Elm the man chose a place for his house, after first ascertaining that the Indians whose wigwams dotted the burned-out clearing in the nearby woods were of a friendly disposition. These redskins were Mahicans, whose brethren were singing hymns and offering Christian prayers at the Indian mission in Stockbridge.

Today, if you drive out from the Park along East Street, branching to the right on Elm, you will come to an old white frame house (847 Elm Street). Attached to this house, which is known as Wells' Tavern, is a COPY OF SOLOMON DEMING'S CABIN. It contains some of the original timber hewn by the axe of the first pioneer. Within the rude shelter made from these timbers, Dorothy Deming, the first white child in Pontoosuc, was born.

Later in the same year, Nathaniel Fairfield and his young bride bumped over the mountains from Westfield, Connecticut, traveling

in an ox cart and taking three days for the journey. Following soon
after, Charles Goodrich brought the first cart and team of horses
into the plantation, cutting his way for miles through the thick woods

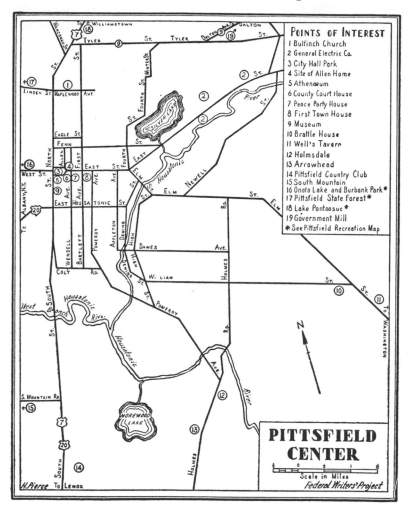

from the same town of Wethersfield. Some of the early settlers built
their homes near the center, others out toward the east, near where
the Boston and Albany Railroad now thunders over the Housatonic

River. Fort Anson was erected on the small hill south of West Street at the southern end of Onota Lake, the shining "Big Sea Water" of the Mahicans. Serving a double purpose as fort and tavern, it became the gathering place for settlers, friendly Indians, and passing soldiers, and a block house for refuge and defense when plundering bands of Mohawks came skulking over the Long Trail.

After the Demings and Fairfields came William Brattle, who hewed out the corner posts for a most imposing dwelling. The over-hanging stories of the BRATTLE HOUSE are to be seen not far from Well's Tavern, near the junction of William and Elm Streets, just as they were when Brattle laid his timber upon a foundation of rough field stone. The boards of the house are said to have been cut entirely from a single primeval giant growing on the homestead lands. It is a great roomy red clapboarded dwelling set on a knoll among old trees.

By September, 1753, there were enough settlers in the area to hold a meeting and talk of incorporation. Aroused by the need for a permanent civic center and a real church, the settlers of Pontoosuc chose a site on the high plot of land where the Old Elm stood. The lot was cleared of trees and underbrush to make way for the little church, but by some chance the Old Elm remained unscathed.

Pittsfield was named for the statesman William Pitt, its natal day coinciding with that same April day in 1761 when Berkshire and Hampshire became separate counties. Meantime the frame of a church was erected; rather a gaunt, lonely frame, since for some seven or eight years the building itself was not completed. Nevertheless, services were held there and the settlers spake their Ayes and Nays at town meetings, until in 1770 it was "accepted as it stood," being thirty-five by forty-five feet, two stories high, belfry-less and without ornamentation.

In 1764 the Reverend Thomas Allen, who was to play a dominant part in the early life of the town, settled as the first minister. The residents of the tiny village were beginning to talk of "laying out streets," as befitted the new dignity of their community. It was agreed that Captain Charles Goodrich, the highway surveyor, would soon start measuring off paths on which people could walk. Carefully drawing the lines of East Street around the Old Elm, he left it standing there at the side of the church. Among all those determined New England surveyors who "much preferred to climb a hill instead of going round," luck had it that there was one man willing to deviate from the straight pathway.

Under the spreading branches of the Old Elm soldiers were mustered in and mustered out. They met here in anxious groups, muttered excitedly, and marched off to fight the French and the Indians. They gathered again at the news from Concord and Lexington and, in response to the call, "To Arms! To Arms!" marched off to meet the British, with "Fighting Parson Allen" riding in a gig at their head.

Later Allen accompanied the "Berkshire Boys" to the Battle of Bennington. His prayer is said to have inspired the soldiers, and some of the success of the day is credited to his vigorous appeal that "the God of armies will teach their hand to war and their fingers to fight."

When in 1790 a new church was needed to replace the old frame on the high mound, one Colonel Charles Bulfinch of Boston was engaged to design the building. But alas and alack, plans for the edifice called for it to rise upon the site of the Old Elm tree.

Axemen arrived and began to gauge the proper spot for the first blow . . .

"Wait! Ah, good gentlemen, wait!"

Deftly pushing the men aside, Lucretia Williams thrust herself between the sturdy trunk of the Elm and the men's bloodthirsty axes. "Don't cut it down!" she pleaded, "Oh, if only . . ."

At that moment good husband John Chandler Williams, possibly anticipating his Lucretia's "if only," appeared on the scene and after sufficient inquiry swapped the town a square of his own front yard for the ground on which the Elm stood.

Services in the BULFINCH CHURCH (1793) were suspended in 1851 and the building itself was dragged away from its home in City Hall Park to the corner of North Street and Maplewood Avenue. You can still distinguish the charm and dignity of line and proportion characteristic of a Bulfinch building, although the old church now looks as if a strong wind would tear it apart. Colonel Bulfinch, it will be recalled, designed Faneuil Hall and the State House at Boston and the Capitol at Washington. A building that was a Bulfinch was a building to be proud of. Mulberry tones in the handmade bricks; Georgian touches and the use of solid San Domingo mahogany; and the graceful steeples so typical of the Colonel's style.

John Chandler Williams, husband of the brave Lucretia (history calls her "doughty"), was something of a personage in Pittsfield during the halcyon days of the Elm's hardy middle-age. The son of a well-known Bedford family of depleted means, young John came to the Berkshires to seek his fortune. Appointed deputy sheriff of Pittsfield at the age of eighteen, he gave up his job to enter Harvard College. A studious, hardworking man, he wrote at one time that during the course of fourteen years he had been absent from public worship but two half days. As a result of his virtuous ways, perhaps, he came to be a lawyer and a property owner in Pittsfield—a substantial businessman who established himself and his Lucretia in a gambrel-roofed mansion erected by Colonel James Easton on the southwest corner of East Street and what is now Wendell Avenue, the site of the present COUNTY COURT HOUSE. First known as the "Williams' Long House," in later years it was called "Peace Party House."

Today, the old PEACE PARTY HOUSE is located on the southeast corner of East Street and Wendell Avenue, where it was moved intact in 1869. Many memories cluster around the old house; memories of strong-minded Lucretia, who to the end of her days professed loyalty to the English King and spoke of the Revolution as "the Rebellion;" memories of that eventful evening in 1783 when, with much dancing and singing and shouts of "Hurrah! Hurrah! God save the Colonies and General Washington!" the signing of the Peace Treaty with Great Britain (the Treaty of Paris) was celebrated.

There were great platters of goose and turkey that night, and half an ox, roasted to a turn. Rum, punch, wine, and cider flowed so freely that the Yankees who gathered from the towns round about might as well have been signing the treaty themselves, to see them carry on. Ladies came from far and near, mounted on their pillions. There were speeches and more speeches, rousing songs and cheers as the liquor flowed free and fast, and in the center of this brilliant gathering was Lucretia, daughter of Israel Williams, noted Tory, and wife of John Williams, ardent Patriot.

In 1864 they ultimately had to cut the Old Elm down. It had been struck by lightning. Struck more than once, too. It began to bend over toward the ground and folks were afraid it might fall on someone and kill him. And so the men came and axes began to ring. Contemporaries have described the scene; people weeping and holding out their hands for a chip or a twig of the tree they'd all grown up under.

Herman Melville, who lived in Pittsfield during the last years of the scarred elm, described the tree in his portrait of Captain Ahab in *Moby Dick*.

Threading its way out from among his gray hairs, and continuing straight down on either side his face . . . you saw a slender . . . mark, lividly whitish. It resembled that perpendicular seam sometimes made in the straight lofty trunk of a great tree, when the upper lightning tearingly darts down it, and without wrenching a single twig, pulls and grooves out the bark, from top to bottom, ere running off into the soil, leaving the tree still greenly alive, but branded . . .

It was to be expected that Crazy Sue Dunham, the Berkshire wandering hag, would somehow get involved with the Old Elm. On one occasion, as a group of school girls were passing along the village green, Sue darted out from under the shade of the tree. Mysteriously she bade each of them kneel on the ground before the Elm, first instructing them to deposit their lunch pails in a pile at their backs. She was going away for a few moments, she assured them, but on her return she would conduct some sort of a "service" for their benefit. The moments sped by. She did not return. The girls' knees grew weak but they waited, entranced by the thought that they were to be initiated in some mystic rite of which "Crazy Sue" was high priestess. If they waited long enough, would they hear voices and see strange sights? Hearing no voices, neither Sue's nor any other, the girls finally arose. By this time their legs wabbled absurdly. Suddenly one of them shrieked, "Girls! Oh, girls, where are our dinner pails?" The dinner pails had vanished, and Sue was nowhere to be seen. Another account relates that when the girls discovered Sue in the act of stealing the dinner pails she piously exclaimed, "Children, the Good Book says that you should watch as well as pray."

The second house east of the Peace Party House is the FIRST TOWN HOUSE, erected in 1766, which, like so many of Pittsfield's old houses, has been moved from its original site. Back in 1825, General Lafayette popped his head out of one of the upper windows and delivered an address to the populace assembled below. Later, the building served as a schoolhouse. Greatly remodeled and changed, it is now a private residence.

Diagonally across East Street from Peace Party House is a brick business block with a tablet on its front to indicate the SITE OF PARSON THOMAS ALLEN'S HOME. From 1764, when the Parson came to Pittsfield as its first minister, until 1914, a member of the Allen family always lived there. "Fighting Parson Allen" ruled Pittsfield with a religious hand for almost half a century, fired a musket at the Battle of Bennington, acted as army chaplain during the Revolution, gave money without stint to the impoverished colonies, and left scions who made their mark in Pittsfield and Berkshire.

On the north side of the Park, between the Congregational and Episcopal Churches, stands the yellow brick CITY HALL, built in 1832.

From 1823 to 1868 Pittsfield was the seat of a medical school called the Berkshire or the Pittsfield Medical College. On January 14, 1823, the school was given both a charter and a grant of $5000 by the General Court of Massachusetts, despite much opposition, especially on the part of Harvard College. When first organized there was some dismay among the inhabitants of Berkshire County because no legal provision had been made by which medical students could obtain cadavers for dissection. Forays into neighboring cemeteries constantly roused Pittsfield folk, and there was a horrified outcry whenever a new grave was violated. In his *American Notebook* Hawthorne made the macabre observation:

It is the custom in this part of the country—and perhaps extensively in the interior of New England—to bury the dead first in a charnel-house, or common tomb; where they remain till decay has so far progressed as to secure them from the resurrectionists. They are then reburied, with certain ceremonies, in their own peculiar graves.

The "resurrectionists," those who robbed graves to get cadavers for dissection, plied their gruesome trade until in 1830 more stringent laws put an end to the practice.

Lectures were first delivered in a section of the old Pittsfield Hotel, in whose stable on a corner of Parson Allen's lot a laboratory was opened in 1824. As years passed, the college expanded into several

buildings and the Pittsfield Hotel was converted into a dormitory.
In 1868, when the college was finally closed, the building was purchased by the city for ordinary school purposes.

During the forty-five years of its existence, 1138 students graduated from Berkshire Medical College. It never was properly self-
supporting and seemed always on the verge of being abandoned,
but it played an important part in furnishing Berkshire with well-
trained physicians.

Next to the County Court House is the BERKSHIRE ATHE-
NAEUM, a reminder of the era when American architecture was
dominated by the Victorian Gothic movement. In 1871, the Athenaeum
trustees were incorporated "for the purpose of establishing and main-
taining in the town of Pittsfield an institution to aid in promoting
education, culture, and refinement." A library, reading-room, lectures,
museums and cabinets of art and of historical and natural curiosities
were put at public disposal.

Around the corner on South Street is the MUSEUM OF NATU-
RAL HISTORY AND ART, a gift of Zenas Crane, the papermaker.
The building is on the site of Easton's Tavern, in which the Battle
of Ticonderoga was planned. Among the treasures of Americana,
one is delighted to see the famous old "one-hoss shay" which belonged
to Jacob Wendell, great-grandfather of the poet, Oliver Wendell
Holmes, who wrote so amusingly of the vehicle in *The Deacon's
Masterpiece*. Expecting to find but a heap of dust, one is rather surprised to see the old chaise in pretty fair condition, although Holmes
told us:

> What do you think the parson found,
>   When he got up and stared around?
> The poor old chaise in a heap or mound,
>   As if it had been to the mill and ground!

Alas for legend, the desk (also in the Natural History Building)
whereon Nathaniel Hawthorne wrote *The House of the Seven Gables*
shows no holes worn by the author's elbows. Nor do the two sledges
used by Peary on his trip to the North Pole bear teeth marks where
his hungry dogs are supposed to have "chawed" at the sides.

Oliver Wendell Holmes in 1849 built a house at Canoe Meadows,
part of the Wendell family acreage. Here he spent his vacations till

1856. In his *Autocrat of the Breakfast Table,* he writes of his Pittsfield years as "seven blessed summers . . . which stand out in memory
like the seven gold candlesticks in the beautiful dream of the holy
dreamer."

The part of Canoe Meadows surrounding the Holmes estate is
out East Street from City Hall Park, then right on Pomeroy Avenue.
Just beyond the confluence of Pomeroy Avenue and Holmes Road is
HOLMESDALE, as the place is now called.

At the Berkshire Jubilee, 1844, the doctor described his home at
Canoe Meadows as a "mansion . . . surrounded by a beautiful meadow,
through which the winding river made its way in a thousand graceful curves." The brown house and windmill are standing much as
Dr. Holmes left them, but they are almost completely screened from
the road by trees. Holmes once said:

I have one pleasant remembrance about my old place . . . that I, in
a sense, created it. The trees about are all of my planting. How much
better I have deserved the gratitude of posterity than the imbecile who
only accomplished a single extra blade of grass.

Across the road from Holmesdale is a hill, once the poet's favorite
writing nook, now the site of a girls' school. Here he could gaze upon
the scene which he described in his poem, "The Ploughman," written
for the agricultural fair of 1849.

About a mile beyond Holmesdale at the top of a hill is the house
where Herman Melville lived from 1850 to 1863. A spacious gambrel-
roofed farmhouse with a tremendous chimney, ARROWHEAD looks
toward Greylock twenty miles away. As Melville wrote in his *Piazza
Tales,*

The house is old. Seventy years since it was built . . . Whoever built
the house builded better than he knew or else Orion in the zenith flashed
down his Damocles sword to him some starry night and said, "Build
there;" for how else could it have entered the builder's mind that upon
the clearing being made, such a purple prospect would be his? Nothing
less than Greylock with all his hills around him like Charlemagne among
his peers appears before me.

Melville was in many respects the counterpart of Hawthorne.
The "dark, mysterious elements" in the two young authors made a

bond between them while they were in Berkshire—Melville at Pittsfield, and Hawthorne at Tanglewood, near the boundary of Lenox and Stockbridge. Melville, the shy, unassuming man whose perplexities were misunderstood by the complacent Victorian generation in which he lived, had sought the answer to his quests in a life of adventure and danger. Lost in a valley of the Marquesa Islands of the South Pacific when only a boy—Tahiti and Hawaii when these islands were little known—cannibals—fights—escapes. He knew terror and brutality and despair.

After his adventures at sea Melville returned to Boston in 1844, wrote *Typee,* a volume of travel and romance, and found himself a "hero over night." The South Sea beauties, now commonplaces of the movies, were first made known to the reading public in his book. Melville was twenty-six at the time. Five years later, he removed to Pittsfield, but there life was rarely free of domestic tribulation. Money was never plentiful, his wife was a failure at housekeeping, and several relatives who lived with him put an extra strain on the family pocketbook. While bound to the duty of providing for his household, Melville's mind constantly turned back to his years of wandering. He began, as he told Hawthorne, "patching and tinkering around in all directions" in order to recapture the spell of those days. Nostalgic passages abound—"The first peep of a strange house rising beyond the trees is for all the world like spying, in the Barbary coast, an unknown sail." Melville never for a moment forgot his beloved sea. "The blown down" of dandelions gone to seed seemed to him "wafted like spray," and the haze over the Berkshires was "just the purple of the billows."

My Chimney and I, Piazza Tales, and *October Mountain* were written in this period. Here he wrote the most famous of all his works and possibly the most important American novel, *Moby Dick.* It made him a celebrity and freed him for a short time from constant drudgery. But his conservative, "proper" Victorian generation had so little interest in his later works, labeled "obscure," that at the time of his death, the newspapers of the country had to dig deep into their files to find out just who he was. Unlike Dr. Holmes, one of the leading spirits in Pittsfield's social life, Melville was content to rusticate on his farm. Holmes seems to have attended all the parties, dances, and picnics that were given, for he was gay and fond of company—a contrast to Melville, who was happy to sit "Canute-like, watching the long ground swells roll the slanting grain and little wavelets of the grass ripple over the low piazza as they beach . . ."

During the years that Holmes and Melville were in Pittsfield, the Berkshires were a center for many of the leading personages of the day. Catherine Sedgwick, the author, and Fanny Kemble, the actress, were living in Lenox and Hawthorne at Stockbridge. The poet Longfellow first came to Pittsfield "a-wooing bent" to court Frances Appleton, who lived with her grandfather, Thomas Gold, in a home that has recently been razed. During Longfellow's honeymoon here in 1843, the poet noticed at the head of a broad flight of stairs an old clock which inspired a poem, finally written in 1845—

> Somewhat back from the village street
> Stands the old-fashioned country-seat.
> Across its antique portico
> Tall poplar-trees their shadows throw;
> And from its station in the hall
> An ancient timepiece says to all,—
> > "Forever—never!
> > Never—forever!"

The Gold-Appleton mansion was thereafter known as the "House of the Old Clock."

In 1849 Longfellow spent many months in Pittsfield writing his novel *Kavanagh,* which, like Holmes's *Elsie Venner,* vaguely reflects contemporary life in the town. The Longfellows stopped at historic BROAD HALL, which may be reached by continuing southward from Arrowhead, by way of Holmes Road, through pine woods to the main highway. Turn sharply to the right onto the highway (US 7 and US 20) leading northward to the Park. About two miles beyond the turn is the handsome Dutch Colonial mansion of the PITTS-FIELD COUNTRY CLUB. Broad Hall, as it was called at the height of its fame, was built in 1781 by Henry Van Schaack, formerly post-master of the city of Albany and a prominent business man there. During the lifetime of the first owner the house had many distin-guished visitors—John Jay, Fisher Ames, Bushrod Washington, Oliver Wolcott, Stephen Van Rensselaer. In 1775 Van Schaack had with-drawn from public office and declared himself a royalist. He had decided that the contest with the mother country "was carried on with too much acrimony" and that "the Congress of 1774 had left no back door open for reconciliation." His attitude caused the Committee of Correspondence in Albany to ask him to withdraw to some place in Massachusetts or Connecticut. He tried Richmond and Stockbridge only to be refused, but finally found refuge in Pittsfield. From here he watched affairs in the colonies with great interest, holding aloof from the strife. A sincere lover of America, he was nevertheless firm in his belief that it was ill-advised for the colonies to withdraw from England. After the war his act of banishment was revoked and General Schuyler invited him to return to New York. Instead he became a citizen of Massachusetts, telling his brother:

So perfectly am I satisfied with the manners, customs and laws of the Commonwealth that I would not exchange them for any other I know in the world. Beggar and vagrant we are strangers to, as well as overbearing, purse proud scoundrel . . . Murder, robberies and burglaries are scarcely heard of in this country . . . If any of your friends wish to migrate . . . you may assure them land is good and cheap in Berkshire . . . I have never lived among a more civil and obliging people . . . A purse hung up in the public streets would be as safe from our inhabitants as it used to be in King Alfred's time . . .

In the Van Schaack house the first domestic rag carpet manufactured in the Berkshires is said to have been produced by a group of Shakers, under the direction of Mrs. Van Schaack. It was later sent to Alexander Hamilton, Secretary of the Treasury, and was "immediately placed in the committee room of the House of Representatives among the collection of specimens of American manufacture transmitted to the Treasury from several of the states."

Elkanah Watson, the sheep-fancier, was the next resident of Broad Hall; he lived there from 1807 until 1816, when he returned to Albany and sold the house to Major Thomas Melville, uncle of Herman Melville. Thomas Melville was a polished, suave man of the world with something of the beau about him; his wife, a lovely, vivacious French woman. Young Herman Melville, who occasionally visited his uncle's home, was fascinated by the famous literary men of the time who moved along the massive staircase of Broad Hall and through its spacious rooms.

There was Nathaniel Hawthorne, reserved and shy, he with "the smell of beeches and hemlocks" upon him and the "broad prairies" in his soul. And there was Longfellow, tall and lank, peering out at the blossoming countryside; stooping to pat the moss at his feet; standing in rapture before the tiny lakelet called Morewood Lake, and jotting down in his notebook "Tear of Heaven." Charles Sumner was a frequent visitor to Broad Hall, and it was probably due to his influence that its ample cellar became one of the depots for the "Underground Railroad" of the fleeing Negro slaves. Among its apple and potato bins there were vaults and passageways where trembling human flesh lay in concealment.

SOUTH MOUNTAIN lies south along the highway (US 7 and US 20) from Broad Hall, and here on the Coolidge estate the Berkshire Festival of Chamber Music gives its summer concerts by famous string ensembles. The magnificent enterprise is almost entirely the accomplishment of Mrs. Elizabeth Sprague Coolidge, whose part in it has been inadequately described as adding to "the fine art of the composer and the fine art of the performer, the fine art of paying the bill." If you want a good view of Pittsfield and its environs, go up to the summit of South Mountain. From here the whole city lies at your feet—rows of small houses, church spires among the trees, the tall General Electric chimneys, the sparkle of lakes, and in the distance on all sides—the mountains.

Pittsfield is now, as it has been for many years, a "Saturday city," for on that day out-of-towners mingle with out-of-staters to suggest a thickly populated metropolis. In the '90's, on a Saturday afternoon or evening, a stranger in town would have seen rows of horses tied to the wooden railings encircling the Park. Even today, there appears an occasional ancient buggy, a "Democrat" wagon, or a phaeton hauled by a moth-eaten mare. In the back of the phaeton a market basket and the inevitable vinegar jug jostle dangerously against the iron weight used for tethering in some back alley or side street. When horse and wagon are secure, the driver and his lady, in all the finery of the '90's, make their weekly round of the "red front" stores and the "big city" markets.

Such anachronisms are, to be sure, becoming less frequent every year. Modern fashion has penetrated the forests, crept along the narrow roads, and reached the outlying hamlets and remote farmhouses. Nowadays the younger generation comes in from the hills for Saturday shopping in the latest summer suits and print dresses, driving newly-painted second-hand cars. The young girl from far back in the hills will be dressed in a sun-back frock, sheer hosiery, and bright-colored sandals. Only the lady from one of the pretentious estates in Lenox is likely to appear in flat heels, cotton stockings, and a knitted dress.

On circus day in Pittsfield you will see the rare picture of a genuine hill-billy Berkshire family. This one day in the year the hill dwellers descend into town to congregate on street corners and wait for the free parade. They are all there—from squalling infants in arms and small boys uncomfortable in tight shoes to housewives in homemade garments, unrecognizable as to style or year of make. Many a group has its bearded grandfather who needs only a scythe to complete the illusion that he is Father Time in person.

Circus day is part of the social life that Pittsfield offers to its suburban neighbors. Just as the city's Saturday shopping day is not exclusively its own, so its whole social and cultural life is open to the surrounding region. Residents of nearby towns and visitors to Berkshire attend the city concerts together, subscribe to lectures and musical courses, become members of up-to-the-minute clubs, and join the various political and charitable groups. The American Institute of Electrical Engineers, Pittsfield Section, sponsors a popular-priced lecture course during the winter months. A Women's Club, with a large membership and a progressive program, a branch of the League of Women Voters, a Garden Club, and similar organizations appeal to many tastes. The Pittsfield Town Players, an amateur group organized in 1920, produce excellent drama in the winter season, not only in the city but in neighboring communities. The Berkshire Musical Association, the Pittsfield Symphony Orchestra, and the Stanley Club Junior Symphony Orchestra, whose members are under eighteen, contribute high service to the musical life of the community. The Pittsfield Community Concerts Association brings three artists of national musical reputation to town every winter. And throughout America, Pittsfield is known for the South Mountain concerts of the Berkshire Festival of Chamber Music.

Twenty-three years ago Edward Boltwood, Pittsfield historian, described the beginning of a change that was to transform Pittsfield from an inconspicuous, inland town to a modern industrial city:

> Pittsfield is no longer the quiet, dullish, somewhat dingy village that some of us remember it, standing with Yankee reserve in the midst of fine scenery, where it seemed a little out of place. It has become of late years a bustling, ambitious . . . town . . . with fine public buildings, parks and fountains and an abundance of "carriage people." The streets and squares look less like a New England village than like the fast-growing cities of the West.

The entire complexion of the city was altered by the establishment in 1907 of the huge GENERAL ELECTRIC COMPANY, northeast of the Park past Silver Lake. As soon as it opened, the city's early isolation was shattered by the new needs and technique of industry. The development attracted capital, which in turn greatly expanded the city's trade and commerce. A building boom resulted and census figures multiplied. In the first ten years of the twentieth century, the population jumped forty-seven per cent, an increase in the State second only to that of New Bedford. Pittsfield took a century and a half to acquire a population of 25,000 and then almost doubled the number in less than thirty years.

As a natural consequence, Pittsfield has large segments, not of "Berkshire Borners," but of newcomers mingling with the older Yankee and Irish stocks. Today, Pittsfield is a compound of Italians, French, Poles, and Germans, with some Jews, Armenians, Greeks, Lithuanians, and Negroes. Each group retains to some extent its own religious and social customs, though the leveling influence of common interest has drawn them together.

Pittsfield has been called "The City of Artisans." The metal trades attracted a group of skilled workmen earlier in the history of the town. Their presence, in fact, was a good reason for the establishment here of the General Electric Company, manufacturers of machinery for the transmission and distribution of electricity. And the rather favorable economic position of thousands of trained workers has had its effect upon the appearance of the city. Pittsfield's streets are broad and clean, and the houses, most of them single-family dwellings, are neatly set among lawns and gardens. The large number of public buildings gives the visitor an impression of a thriving city, for Pitts-field has indeed become the "Metropolis of the Berkshires."

The General Electric Company located a plant in Pittsfield because of earlier efforts of William Stanley, of Berkshire stock himself, in making alternating current commercially possible by inventing the electric transformer. Four years after Stanley had given light to stores in Great Barrington he organized the Stanley Electric Manufacturing Company (1890) to produce the machines necessary for the operation of alternating current. As 1500 power stations in the country used such a system at the time, and only two other companies, the Westinghouse and the Thomson-Houston Electric Companies, were competitors in the field, the success of the Stanley Company was immediate. It was absorbed by the General Electric Company in 1907 and the Pittsfield Works were thus created. Today the General Electric plant produces electrical devices ranging from transformers as big as a six-room house to tiny light switches, bridge boards, and flat-iron handles. Transformers are still the chief product, and here Pittsfield leads the country. The production of midget transformers with a maximum capacity of 2000 volts and of leviathans of 220,000 volts is one of the routine problems of the company.

The High Voltage Laboratory in Pittsfield is one of the most fully equipped in the world. In it discoveries have been made which vastly expanded the uses and control of electricity. It was here that a Jovian flash of ten thousand volts was stepped up from period to period by such electrical wizards as Dr. Charles P. Steinmetz, F. W. Peek, and their successors. In 1921 the generation and transmission of electricity in excess of a million volts was dramatically demonstrated in this laboratory; less than two decades later, in an inconspicuous section of the plant, Karl B. McEachron with perfect control now shatters targets with ten times that power. The most awesome feature of this research is the "artificial lightning," a jump of electric current between two or more high steel towers unconnected by wire. But the man-made lightning and huge transformers are not the only attractions of the plant. The new million-dollar Plastics Department, where finished parts for radios, refrigerators, and oil heating units are manufactured from raw materials, is one of the largest of its kind.

Since its organization the General Electric Company has increased its employment to the present force of over 4000 people, more than one-third of all workers in the city. Many of them live in Morningside, a residential section along the northern and eastern border of the works. But the company, though dominant in the industrial picture in Pittsfield, has not altogether usurped the place of other manufacturing concerns.

The textile industry in Pittsfield dates from 1800. In that year Arthur Scholfield, a young Englishman who had worked as a clothier in Yorkshire, came to the Berkshire town from Byfield near Newburyport. The manufacture of cloth in America was then primitive in method. Carding, spinning, and weaving were done on crude machines at home, and even the finishing processes, performed by professional clothiers, were at best imperfect jobs. Scholfield undertook to improve these methods by the introduction of machines used in England.

The nature of the new machinery was a carefully guarded British secret. To get some of the parts out of the country, Scholfield hid them in piles of bedding which went unexamined to America. In 1801 a modest advertisement appeared in the *Pittsfield Sun.*

Arthur Scholfield respectfully informs the inhabitants of Pittsfield and neighboring towns that he has a carding machine half a mile west of the meeting-house where they may have wool carded into rolls for 12½ cents per pound . . .

Housewives were at first reluctant to entrust their wool to the hands of the young stranger, but their doubts were stilled after the first brave souls who tried the new machine were rewarded with fine, strong cloth.

While Scholfield was perfecting his textile machines, Elkanah Watson came to live in Pittsfield, bringing with him Merino sheep prized for their excellent wool. Three years later, in 1810, he organized the Pittsfield Agricultural Fair, held in the Park. It was the first of its kind in Berkshire County and probably the first "country fair" in America. People came from near and far on that eventful day. Hours before sun-up, old-fashioned "Democrat" wagons jogged over the bumpy country roads on their way to the cattle show, bringing their passengers to see huge, thick-necked oxen, their yokes hung with dahlias and sunflowers, lead off the Great Cattle Cavalcade. The paramount attraction, however, was sturdy Merinos of the

Transhumante breed imported by Jonathan Allen, shipping magnate of the day. He had brought them from Lisbon, where the American consul, in a tidy bit of private business for himself, was dealing in goods confiscated from the Count of Monaco, a member of the Spanish Junta, when he was driven from Spain by French invaders and had taken refuge in Portugal. Merinos became the nucleus of vast flocks which supplied the woolen mills of Berkshire for generations.

The importation of sheep with heavier wool and machinery of greater efficiency furthered industry, but not as much as did the Embargo and the War of 1812. Imports cut off, demands for clothing and army supplies for American use were so great that Pittsfield definitely established itself as a textile center. Fresh impetus was given the new industrial development in the 1840's by railroad connections between Pittsfield and New York and Boston. At the time of the Civil War, the city was an industrial center of national importance.

For a long time textiles were the principal products of industry; shoes and paper rated second and third. High-grade stationery is still made by the Eaton Paper Company, successors of the old firm of Eaton, Crane and Pike. The GOVERNMENT MILL on Dalton Avenue (Mass 9 and Mass 8) produces banknote paper at a plant which, though located within the limits of Pittsfield, actually belongs to Crane & Company of Dalton. This industry is advanced by the international business of E. D. Jones & Sons Company, makers of machinery for the manufacture of paper. Besides these major businesses, recent years have seen sundry small enterprises established in the city: factories for making ladies' handbags, buttons and silk products, textile machinery, hospital appliances, and automobile gauges.

Recreation, fast growing in importance in the whole Berkshire area, promises to develop into another major occupation in Pittsfield. As far back as the '80's and '90's, Pittsfield was attracting a large summer population from a wealthy leisure class. Luxurious Victorian houses, set among spreading lawns and equipped with stables and conservatories, were a common sight in those days. People who did not own property patronized hotels built on the Saratoga plan with long verandas and high-ceilinged rooms. These "carriage people" rode about the quiet streets in shining victorias and runabouts.

Today the pace and appearance of the city have altered. Many of the mansions have been absorbed by realty developments and others have been turned into rooming houses or tourist homes, and their stables converted into garages. The few that have escaped such a transformation remain meek reminders of quiet, yet faintly glamorous days when the character of Pittsfield's summer business was less transient. Modern successors to the "carriage people" drive about the city in swift automobiles coming from everywhere, bound for everywhere. They ride in Model T's without spare tires and they come in limousines driven by liveried chauffeurs. Traffic surveys taken at the main junctions in the city show that the week-ends of summer and autumn bring cars from nearly every state in the Union and from most of the Canadian provinces. During the week they come in dribbles, but by the end of the week they flow in an unbroken stream, for, despite industrial developments, Pittsfield has in its vicinity many natural beauties. The fine lakes north and west of town are the natural center of the large playground area of Berkshire County.

Of the six lakes within the city limits of Pittsfield, the largest is LAKE ONOTA, lying in an upland basin toward the northwest. Tradition tells that Lake Onota, the "Lake of the White Deer," was the favorite haunt of a pure white doe, an omen of such good fortune to all Indians in the valley that no arrow was drawn against her. "So long as the snow-white doe comes to drink at Onota," ran the proverb, "so long famine shall not blight the Indian harvest nor pestilence come nigh the Indian's lodge, nor foeman lay waste his country." During the French and Indian Wars, Montalbert, a young French officer, conceived the idea of shooting the doe and carrying its gleaming pelt back to Canada. Who knew but that his feat might finally reach the attention of the French Court at Versailles and become an added feather in the young officer's cap? A corrupt Indian guide named Wondo agreed to show him the doe's customary drinking place. The pretty creature appeared, drank, and, startled by a sudden movement in the bushes, raised her dainty head. She received a fatal shot. Montalbert, greatly rejoicing, started for Montreal with the prize. The moon rose an angry red over Lake Onota. The Indians, who had crept to the shore to watch their beloved doe drink of the sparkling waters, shook their heads and silently disappeared. They knew that the white doe of Onota who had brought

prosperity and contentment to the Valley Indians was with the Great
Father of Many Waters and that somehow He would avenge her
death.

Wondo, who had so ignominiously betrayed the Mahicans' beautiful mascot, was artfully seduced by fire water, confessed his guilt,
and was duly punished. Montalbert met his death as he bore the
white doe's lifeless pelt over the Long Trail to Canada. As for the
tribe itself, its numbers diminished, its prosperity vanished, and
slowly its people wasted away.

The lake can be reached from the center by turning west from
West Street onto Onota Street and north on Lakeway Drive along
the shore to the 133 deeply-wooded acres of BURBANK PARK. Here
are some of the finest canoe birches in all Berkshire. This land was
given to the city by heirs of Abraham Burbank, a gentleman who
"came to town with five dollars, a hammer and a saw, and proceeded
to build it into a city." He amassed a considerable fortune, some say
by salvaging crooked nails and straightening them out. When he
died in 1887, he tried to give the city about two-thirds of the buildings
he had erected, but Pittsfield, fearing that the gift would force it
into the real estate business, chose Burbank Park with its canoe birches
instead. That Mr. Burbank was an honest man there can be no doubt,
for his promissory note scribbled on a shingle was honored at any
of the banks.

Although Onota is the largest of the Pittsfield lakes, to many PON-
TOOSUC is the most beautiful—Pontoosuc of the topaz waters. To
reach Pontoosuc from Burbank Park, continue on the Drive to Peck's
Road, turn left and continue past the end of the lake. At Hancock
Street turn right to the public park. This road joins North Street
(US 7) at the south end of Pontoosuc.

It is said that even today the ghostly voices of Moon-keek and
Shoon-keek, hapless lovers whom a jealous intruder brought to death,
may be heard at night along the lake shore whispering the love words
of their tribe.

PONTOOSUC LAKE PARK was once known as Honasada, after
the title bestowed upon Colonel William Williams by the Indians.
From a parking place beside the road leading to the lake, there is a
superb view through the dark columns of the pines—those white
pines which are one of Pittsfield's glories. It is difficult to conceive

that this area was once a street-railway amusement park with driving horses and the gaudy attractions of the noisy carnivals that were the rage of small towns.

Today Pontoosuc Lake is surrounded by hundreds of cottages. It has its bathing beach and its picnic grounds, and a summer population of some three or four thousand. On the east shore is CAMP MERRILL, where the local Y.M.C.A. has a fine picnic grove of its own, cabins, and a canoe club. The BLUE ANCHOR BOAT CLUB sets a modest membership fee, and across the lake from it is the GOLF COURSE at Hodecker's Grove where old Peter Hodecker— over ninety but still going strong—plays golf on his former ancestral acres.

A wag named Keiler, owning property adjacent to the lake, once tried to make a sale of Pontoosuc—winter-bound as the lake was at the time—to a New York gentleman who mistook its snow-covered level expanse for highly desirable land set in a singularly attractive locality amid the encircling hills. The deed of sale was drawn up, but for some reason or other the transaction was never consummated. Possibly the would-be purchaser tried to see just how deep he would have to dig in order to place his cellar. The lake was called "Joe Keiler's Farm" for many a day.

The drive (US 7) running along Pontoosuc's eastern shore offers one of the best views in all Berkshire. Straight ahead is the round top of Constitution Hill; on the west stand Honwee, Tower, and Potter Mountains, their peaks rising above the open slopes where steep ski trails plunge precipitously into the PITTSFIELD STATE FOREST. The Forest, covering 3850 acres, lies partly in Hancock and partly in Lanesborough.

The hilly territory in days gone by was the favorite haunt of Herman Melville, who used to wander high above the road to the summit of Honwee Mountain to visit Berry Pond. In the spring, the woods around this little pond are pink with mountain laurel; in June come the red and white azaleas; and in September, the deep red glow of the sumac. Melville wrote of spots in the forest:

It has been a most glowing and Byzantine day—the heavens reflecting the hues of the October apples in the orchard—nay the heavens themselves looking so ripe and ruddy that it must be harvest—You should

see the maples—you should see the perennial pines—the red blazings of
the one contrasting with the painted green of the others and the wide
flushings of the autumn—I tell you that sunrises and sunsets grow side
by side in these woods and momentarily moult in the falling leaves . . .

A celebrated "petition" written in 1856 by a noted local wag,
Horace Taylor, shows with what ardor Pittsfield imbues its sons:

To the Honorable Senate and House of Representatives:
  For Great and Weighty Reasons, We, the undersigned, inhabitants of
the Commonwealth of Massachusetts, would respectfully represent that
the State House should be removed from Boston to Pittsfield, for the
following reasons, to wit:
  The latter place being the most accessible from all points of the Commonwealth, it being the terminus of four Railroads, one from the East,
one from the West, one from the North, and one from the South, is
delightfully situated in the valley of the Lanesborough pond, and stands
at the head of the navigable waters of the Housatonic, being but 175 miles
from New York, 3500 from London, 2 from Bobtown, and 2½ from
Pontoosuc, where there is a woolen factory in good running order, supporting four or five of the most respectable families in Western Massachusetts.
  Pittsfield is conceded to be the most healthy place in North America,
there having been but a single case of genuine Asiatic cholera there for
the last five years! The people of Pittsfield are exceedingly modest, and of
great hospitality, but patrons of temperance; their gas is excellent, and
their wine not wanting in age—it has a peculiar pungency and flavor,
well adapted to respectable revelry and legislative banquets; and zephyrs
sweep their hillsides, and the wild robin and the school girl sing in the
valleys. Whereupon, we pray our humble request may be granted, and
that Pittsfield be the capital of our great and ancient Commonwealth,
from and after 1856.

Oliver Wendell Holmes, on the other hand, balked at even the
ordinary institutions of a metropolitan center, let alone a state capital.

  It seems too bad to take away its charming rural characteristics, but
such a beautiful healthful central situation could not resist its destiny
and you must have a mayor, I suppose, and a common council, and a lot
of aldermen. But you can never lose sight of Greylock nor turn the course
of the Housatonic.

CHAPTER V

HAY AND SUMMER PEOPLE

RICHMOND—Mass 41, sett. 1760, alt. 1107, pop. 628.

WEST STOCKBRIDGE—Mass 41 and 102, sett. 1766, alt. 744, pop. 1138.

Roads—US 20 west from Pittsfield intersects with Mass 41, which runs south to Richmond and West Stockbridge.

RICHMOND and West Stockbridge lie along a rolling valley between the Lenox-West Stockbridge range on the east and the Taconics on the west; but more than a mere mountain range now separates them from the Lenox and Stockbridge of which they were once a part. Lenox and Stockbridge have put on airs; Richmond and West Stockbridge have remained farming towns, though in no sense are they backward communities. Fields are fenced in, barns and silos painted, cattle well-bred and well-fed. Agriculture still pays dividends, in cash money and independence, to hard-working, scientific farmers. Of course, the summer people have come, bought farms, and run them right, too; fixed up old houses that were going to rack and ruin. Quite a few stay the year round or come back to Richmond or West Stockbridge to vote. The newcomers have taken the towns as they found them and have not tried to make them into replicas of their home cities. "Our principal crops? Wal, reckon they're hay and summer people," the natives say.

To reach *RICHMOND* from Pittsfield, go south from City Hall Park along South Street to West Housatonic Street (US 20) and turn right. About four miles west of the Park, near the site of the Lebanon Shaker settlement, turn left on Mass 41 into the Richmond Valley. The road runs through farming country, criss-crossed by streams. In the distance on both sides stretch wooded mountains, dominated to the west by Perry's Peak. Now and again you will see rows of curious rocks, like a train of cars, cutting across the valley and up the slopes of the hills. These are the RICHMOND BOULDER TRAINS—made famous by Charles Lyell in his *Antiquity of Man*—

which the glacier that descended over New England from the fields of Labrador chiseled from the mountaintops.

The whole face of the primitive landscape was scarred by moving ice. It scooped out lakes and river beds, carved mountains into new shapes. On the surface of the ice or buried in its depths were borne colossal boulders, hewn from the mountainsides and carried miles away from the parent ledges. When at last the Ice Age ended, the melting glacier left along its course the rocks of the Richmond Boulder Trains.

In the township there are seven trains, each torn from a different ledge. Some of the boulders rode the ice current to ridges higher than the peaks from which they came. The longest train extends for nine miles and measures five hundred feet at its widest point. The other six are shorter and less regular, with gaps where the glacier was checked by the tough schist rocks beneath. The boulders vary in size from small fragments of schist and limestone to giants twenty-five feet in circumference and thirty feet high, weighing twenty tons or more. They differ sharply from the underlying ledge both in type and form. They are rounded like the waterworn stones of a river bed, and many show deep scratches where they were dragged over the rock bottom.

One train crosses Mass 41 about two miles south of the Pittsfield-Richmond town line, opposite the cemetery. Another, also on the main road, extends southeasterly from the Congregational Church. The longest train crosses the same highway two miles north of the Richmond Railroad station, continuing across the Richmond Valley, over the Lenox Range, and into the Lenox-Stockbridge Valley.

Eons after the rough-shod wheels of the Boulder Trains ground to a halt in Richmond's pastures, the first white settlers came to the region. In 1760 Captain Micah Mudge and Ichabod Wood of Connecticut established themselves in the rocky area called Yokuntown and Mt. Ephraim, after the two Indian sachems who sold it. Chief Ephraim probably acquired his Biblical name from Colonel Ephraim Williams, prominent Stockbridge resident. Chief Yokun, it is known, added Timothy to his name in honor of Timothy Woodbridge, who had converted Yokun's Indian family to Christianity.

Later the tract was divided into the townships of Lenox and Richmond. In the verse of an esteemed local poetess:

> Richmond and Lenox at first were just one
> But a long, lazy mountain runs through the town
> Later the township, which seemed too widespread,
> Divided itself, and then hist'ry read:

> Jonathan Hinsdale came up the valley;
> Hartford he left, in a new world to sally.
> Two centuries back and in "sixty seven"
> Several new homes raised their chimneys toward Heaven.

The two pioneer settlers built houses on Mt. Ephraim not far from the site of the present Congregational Church in Richmond. They were followed by the Sherrills, Piersons and Chapins, who according to another verse of the jingle soon "completed their mansions." In 1765 Mt. Ephraim was incorporated as the town of Richmond, named for Charles Lennox, Duke of Richmond, defender of Colonial rights. As the settlers were weak on spelling, for twenty years the new name was written Richmont instead of Richmond. In 1767, the eastern valley withdrew to become the independent town of Lenox, and the boundaries were laid out to include the whole of each land owner's fields in one town or the other. As a result, the lines zigzag like a flight of stairs.

Among the families whose land remained in Richmond was that of Nathan Cogswell, a blacksmith who lived to marry four wives; three now lie buried in the town, the fourth in New Lebanon, New York. John Cogswell and his family had come to this country on Sir Walter Raleigh's ill-fated *Angel Gabriel,* which was storm-wrecked on our shores. Six Cogswell children reached safety, and one of them became the great-great-great grandmother of Ralph Waldo Emerson. Oliver Wendell Holmes also traced his ancestry to this line.

Twenty-five years ago the section of Richmond around the railroad station was called "Wall Street" because of the number of rich people, generally brokers and members of the Stock Exchange, who lived there during the summer. The depression has changed the picture somewhat, but there are still a goodly number of wealthy business men who have kept up their summer homes. Richmond's

rural surroundings, excellent train service, and easy access to Pittsfield and Albany are rare advantages. Some houses are still occupied
by natives of the town, some by descendants of early settlers who have
returned to Richmond to live, and others by "city people" from New
York, who have restored early dwellings.

About a mile from the Pittsfield line is the PARMALEE HOUSE,
a two-and-a-half story frame structure with an overhanging second
story. It was built by Deacon Silas Parmalee in 1763. This oldest
house in Richmond once contained a secret passage leading to a stone
vault, a place of refuge in case of Indian attack.

Among the old houses in the town is the PIERSON PLACE,
built about 1800, on the right of Mass 41, two miles from the
Pittsfield-Richmond town line. It is a large, white clapboarded structure pierced by huge brick chimneys and surrounded by landscaped
lawns and stately elm trees. When the Pierson family lived here in
the first part of the nineteenth century, they owned acres of rich farm
land, many head of cattle, and a tannery.

It was probably in this house that another Parmalee, Captain
Moses, welcomed a meeting of blacksmiths on Tuesday, November
24, 1795, at one o'clock. The blacksmiths of the Berkshire regions
wanted to organize for higher wages. Along with the rest of the
country, the people of Berkshire felt the economic distress which
followed the conclusion of the Revolution. We get an inkling of the
situation from the following account in the *Western Star,* a weekly
paper printed in Stockbridge:

At a late meeting of the Blacksmiths—after taking into confidence the
present high prices of the necessities of life, and the advanced price of
stock, it was agreed that the price of their labor must be enhanced, in
order to enable them to support themselves and families by their occupation. They have therefore determined to charge in future 8d. where they
heretofore charged but 6d. and so on in that proportion. To convince
the publick of the reasonableness of their conduct, they here subjoin an
account of former and present prices.

	Former Prices	Present Prices
Wheat	4s. 6d.	10s.
Rye	3s.	5s.
Corn	2s. 6d.	4s.
Beef	16s. 8d.	25s.

Beyond the Pierson house, near the junction of the old Pittsfield Road and Mass 41, stands KENMORE, built in 1792 by Henry Sherrill, ancestor of the present Episcopal Bishop of Eastern Massachusetts. A large yellow house trimmed with white, it has an impressive Palladian window above the front door. Down the Pittsfield Road, the fifth house on the left is the OLD DWIGHT HOUSE, another property belonging to the Sherrills. Mary Sherrill received it from her father, one of the town's early settlers, on her marriage to the Reverend Edwin Welles Dwight, Congregational minister in Richmond. Raymond Buell, President of the Foreign Policy Association, now lives in the house and calls it "Goodwood."

About a mile beyond the Boston and Albany Railroad bridge, at a junction of four roads, stand two venerable structures. The one on the right is the old TRADING POST, built during the early nineteenth century and now owned by Roland Perry, New York portrait painter. It is a weather-beaten, rambling sort of place, set back on a well-shaded lawn. Opposite is the weather-beaten STEVENS TAVERN, a famous hostelry in stagecoach days.

About a mile straight ahead on the Pittsfield Road is one of the few brick houses in the town, built in 1820 by William Nichols. It remained in the Nichols family until a few years ago but is now owned by Albert Sterner of New York. The front hall is decorated with murals of flowers and rural scenes by the owner, a well-known artist and illustrator, noted for his paintings in the Yale University Library. The STERNER HOUSE, on a high hill, commands one of the broadest views in the town.

Back on Mass 41, nearer the town center, is another old SHERRILL HOUSE, built by Samuel Sherrill about 1763. Occupied by successive generations of the family for 171 years without a new deed being drawn up, it now belongs to Mrs. Mary L. Sherrill, widow of the last male owner. These houses are private, not open to visitors.

"Next door" in Richmond may easily mean a mile away, for the town has no central common. The houses, unusual in view of the New England tradition of a precise pattern around a "village green," look as if they had been scattered haphazardly over the landscape. The prim old white church and town hall stand by themselves on an isolated hill; the general store, a garage, and two or three small houses cluster on Mass 41 by the railroad station. The rest of the town is spread out thinly over the valley.

Richmond is an old town and has its portion of legends and stories. Many of these are about "Old Nogard," said to have been one of the first tramps in Berkshire. He never told much about his past, but is supposed to have been a camp follower of the British Army during the Revolution. "Old Nog," as he was popularly called, held the belief that any man who did a hard day's work committed a misdemeanor. Williamstown to Lenox was his "beat," but his headquarters were in Pittsfield and Richmond. In order to get money to buy whisky, he caught fish and kidnaped stray cats whose skins he sold. All the housewives hid their pets whenever he appeared in the neighborhood, for if fishing was not good and Nog was out of his favorite beverage, he stalked the pussies. Once, while fishing in Richmond, he pulled out a large catfish. He hurled the fish into the water, exclaiming with disgust, "When I go catting, I go catting, and when I go fishing, I go fishing." On another occasion he was caught fishing on Sunday and haled into court. He defended himself by pleading, "I wa'nt fishing, just trying to drown a fish worm."

Another picturesque Richmond character was countryman Waddams, who opened a store in the 1880's on the Canaan Road. He wore a stovepipe hat during his waking hours, and kept many of his cash accounts on it with white chalk. Waddams' idiosyncrasies amused the whole township. William H. Sherrill, former County Commissioner, lifelong resident, and one of the oldest citizens in town, takes delight in telling of an official encounter he had with Waddams. One day Waddams asked Mr. Sherrill to come to his farm so that the Commissioner could see the carcass of a sheep which had been killed, supposedly by a pack of dogs. Much impressed by the petitioner's display of grief and indignation over the dead sheep, Commissioner Sherrill hastily valued the animal at a price the county would by law repay. A week later the Commissioner was again asked to come to Waddams' farm, only to be led to another field to inspect another sheep killed by dogs. The carcass looked strangely familiar, and Sherrill requested that a shovel and an axe be brought to the field. When the hired man came with the tools, he was set to work digging a pit, while the official himself cut up the carcass with the axe. Waddams, watching with melancholy aspect, sadly protested, "Now William, that is no way to treat me! Don't you realize that you are depriving me of my only means to earn an honest living?"

Iron mining, an important industry in Richmond for many years, was started by Gates Petee and Company in 1827. When an interest in the properties was sold to George and John Coffing in 1850, the new owners changed the name to the Richmond Iron Works. At first the ore went by saddlebag to a forge in Glendale down the valley, but after a while they did their smelting at the RICHMOND FURNACE, erected beside the highway just south of the railroad station. The high-grade iron was so durable that it was soon in demand for special purposes. During the Civil War, the output of Richmond furnaces was used in manufacturing the "Rodman" guns with which the *Monitor* attacked the *Merrimac,* first ironclad vessel of the War. Iron for super-heaters, high-pressure castings, ammonia castings, chilled rolls, steam cylinders, and car wheels came out of the Richmond mines. For nearly forty years during the latter part of the nineteenth century, the Pennsylvania Railroad used Richmond iron for making "chilled" car-wheel mixtures. Richmond boasts that no wreck was ever caused by an imperfect wheel made of its iron.

Nearly three miles of track were laid in the underground corridors of the Richmond Iron Works, and there was an average yearly output at the beginning of the twentieth century of ten to twelve thousand tons of ore. Though a half-million tons are presumably still underground, the high price of charcoal and the competition of western and southern companies made mining so unprofitable that in 1924 the Richmond mines were closed. Now the shafts are filled with water and all the buildings, except one office, have been razed.

When the mine was thriving, a large settlement with its own post-office, general store, and railroad station grew up around the Furnace. From fifty to a hundred men were employed at the mine—Irishmen, Scotchmen, Englishmen, and Yankees. One brick house of this old Furnace settlement is called the FLOWER HOUSE because of its unusual panel, painted by Zorton Denemuth of New York. The decorative design shows hollyhocks, pond lilies, a birch tree, and a boy watching a sunset.

Continuing south from Richmond, Mass 41 gradually descends through a narrowing river valley to enter *WEST STOCKBRIDGE,* whose history may be read in its buildings. Square white houses, dignified and well-kept, are monuments of a prosperous nineteenth century. They mingle with frame buildings, faced with flat boards grooved to resemble mortar joints, and small houses, relics of mining and quarrying days when colonies of Italian and Irish laborers lived here. The Irish came with the railroad building of the 1830's and 1840's and remained to work in the quarries and lime works, which also attracted the Italians after the middle of the century.

Three lime plants are still in operation, but it is considered unlikely that they will ever expand their business. Prominent citizens who have been engaged in the quarrying industry in the past see little hope of recapturing an industrial boom. Rather they have turned their backs on the old type of enterprise, and look forward to a new way of earning a livelihood. They hope to develop West Stockbridge into a "home town for city folks" who find in Berkshire something recreative that cities cannot give. Already many of the homes in West Stockbridge have been purchased and restored by the newcomers. On one road, eighteen houses have been sold within the past five years by a single real estate man.

As part of the development program for the town, a road from West Stockbridge to the New York State Line is being constructed to connect with New York City and the Canadian highways, in the hope that it will divert tourists into the hills of Berkshire. Plans are also under way to widen Mass 41, which runs south from Pittsfield and Richmond, and Mass 102 going east to Stockbridge. By use of the new roads, traffic going north and south through Berkshire can avoid the more heavily traveled US 7 and 20.

The OLD STONE MILL on lower Main Street, at the junction of Mass 41 and Mass 102, was built in 1830, during the period when West Stockbridge was a leading marble town. The Boynton family owned the largest quarry at the time and built the mill for sawing marble blocks. For more than forty years the best-equipped and most modern marble sawmill in Western Massachusetts, it was operated until the marble industry was abandoned. In later years, the mill was used to grind emery, and then as a storage house. In 1929 Benjamin Eggleston, New York artist, came to West Stockbridge looking for a summer home, and turned the old mill into a studio. It afterwards became one of the tea rooms in a chain established through Berkshire.

The old mill building has stone walls twenty-six inches thick on three sides, and a back wall ten inches thicker. The hand-hewn girders were put in when the building was constructed. Now the race-way is sealed and the water turned back of the mill.

The marble deposits that underlie West Stockbridge were discovered by chance when a farmer going out to fetch his cows stumbled on an open vein. Another farmer turned his ankle in a woodchuck's hole and found iron ore. As soon as news of the finds was spread, everyone went prospecting. Other ore beds and marble veins were discovered, and a dozen or more quarries were opened, whereupon the farmers decided to farm less and quarry more.

From 1824 to 1860 West Stockbridge was a marble town of such importance that thousands of dollars were invested in the enterprise. The stone ranged in color from pure white to a dark bluish tint resembling granite. Although its texture varied, much of it was sufficiently high-grade to be used in parts of the State House in Boston, the City Hall in New York, and Girard College in Philadelphia. The surface veins were thin, however, and once they were exhausted, the underlying rock lay too deep to be quarried profitably.

In the boom days of the two important industries it was hard to get the marble to the nearest shipping point at Hudson, New York. Between West Stockbridge and Hudson lay thirty-five miles of road hardly better than a lumber trail. Sometimes it took five span of oxen to haul a single slab of marble over this distance. After reaching the Hudson River, iron and marble were easily carried to New York in barges and from there shipped to the four corners of the earth.

As transportation difficulties increased, the need for a feeder line to join the Hudson and Berkshire Railroad at State Line became apparent, but its financing was made difficult by an early prejudice against railroads. The farmers said horses and cows would be frightened by the noise of the locomotives, and, moreover, should trains displace horses, there'd be no market for oats and hay. But the day was saved by the Hudson and Berkshire Railroad, which supplied construction, superintendence, and money. The West Stockbridge line was organized and chartered on April 26, 1838, and by August 10 the three-mile road to State Line was opened.

With a clash, rattle, and cloud of smoke the first train in western

Massachusetts arrived at the West Stockbridge station, eastern terminal of the railroad. The 25th of September, 1838, was a big day in the town. The flimsy matchboard coaches were filled with passengers, and numerous friends greeted the train with shouts and cheers as it finished its precarious journey. This was the culmination of ten years of never-ceasing work with opposition at every turn, especially from the county's horse-raisers, who wished to devise a system of canals with horse-drawn barges.

As if to justify the contentions of the new road's enemies, the heat of summer expanded the rails and the snow in winter often blocked the line for weeks or months. As snow plows were unheard of, all the work of cleaning the line had to be done by hand. The ice was broken from the rails by flangers, pulled by two men and guided by a third. The severity of Berkshire winters was so great that often the rails were broken.

Oil lamps furnished lighting facilities and wood stoves the heat. Wood stations, replenished by farmers under contract, were erected about every fifteen miles along the line, and often when the trains stopped to refuel, the passengers left the cars to explore the environs.

The line operated until 1854, when the Western Railroad bought it out for a hundred and fifty thousand dollars. During its sixteen years of existence the most serious accident occurred when the train, leaving the West Stockbridge switching yards, ran into a cow, and the concussion hurled the engine into a neighbor's front yard. At the time of the crash, the train was dashing along at the rate of eighteen miles an hour!

The OLD ROUNDHOUSE, located by a townsman as "7 telephone poles from the junction of Mass 41 and the railroad crossing near the West Stockbridge depot," dates from 1838. It was built at the same time as the railroad to house the little wood-burning engine that labored furiously on its trek across the mountains. Today only the turntable pit and crumbling stone walls remain.

Early engines were small and did not require any turntables, but when larger locomotives came into use, an annex had to be erected on the front of the building. The train crew, in putting the engine into its stall, would back the tender into the enginehouse and then uncouple it, switch it to another parallel track by hand, and back the

Stockbridge Bowl in Stockbridge   Courtesy of The Society
for The Preservation of New England Antiquities

Lower Mill in Stockbridge   *Courtesy of The Society for The Preservation of New England Antiquities*

engine in next to the tender. If the piston rods straightened out to their full length, the engine sometimes could not start its morning run. Then a farmer named Robinson who lived on the Kniffin farm nearby would lend his yoke of oxen to the trainmen. The animals, hitched to the engine, would get it moving by a strong pull. Often when the engine would refuse to function just as the train was made up and ready to start, the crew would have to rush after Mr. Robinson and his yoke of oxen.

From the beginning, the trains on the old Hudson and Berkshire line had their difficulties in moving freight and passengers. Ore carts had to be pushed ahead of the little engines from the low point of the railroad up to the ore beds, halfway to State Line. There the brakes would be set by hand and the engine would back down. After loading, the cars coasted down to the main track controlled only in part by the brakemen, for the hand-operated brakes didn't always work. With the loaded cars coupled on, the train would then back into West Stockbridge, where other freight, express, and passengers were taken aboard for the hazardous trip to Hudson, New York. There was some danger and little comfort in riding one of these early trains, for the passage was slow and the tracks never safe. Heavy wooden timbers were laid down as ties with pieces of planking from two to three inches thick spiked to them. Strips of iron were fastened to the planks for rails, but often the spikes worked loose. Pieces of the iron rail would then curl up beneath the train and penetrate the floor boards in a "snake head," as old railroad men called it. From time to time such a loosened rail would spit a passenger right in his seat. Despite these perils, both passenger traffic and freight traffic were heavy, for this was the quickest means of getting from central and lower Berkshire to Albany and other ports on the Hudson River.

To the West Stockbridge terminal people came from all parts of western Massachusetts by all modes of travel—on horseback, by stagecoach, and often by oxen, to board the puffing, noisy monster or to ship or receive mail, freight, and express. Coal for all Berkshire was received at West Stockbridge and distributed by teams and oxen to the towns of the region. Jason Clapp ran a line of elegant coaches from Pittsfield to connect with the cars at West Stockbridge, and continued to do so until the opening of the Western Railroad.

STATE LINE, once the junction of the Hudson and Berkshire and the West Stockbridge railroads, is now on the main line of the Boston and Albany Railroad and on a ten-mile branch of the Berkshire division of the New York, New Haven and Hartford. The hard-surfaced road which swings west off Mass 41, at the war memorial just north of West Stockbridge, enters State Line from the north.

An ancient tavern, the STATE LINE HOUSE, is now being demolished to make room for a new highway. For a long time everyone supposed it to be on the New York-Massachusetts boundary, until an error in the survey was discovered. As this placed the house about twenty feet east of the line, an ell extending over the new boundary was built to maintain the tradition. The situation was most convenient, especially when there was a liquor raid in one state, for the bar, purposely mounted on casters, needed only to be wheeled to the side of the house farthest from the raiding party. Somehow raids by both states seem never to have been scheduled at the same time.

Returning from State Line to Mass 41, watch out for a signboard marked WEST CENTER on a road to the right, for this was the original settlement in West Stockbridge. Lambert Burghardt, one of the first settlers, came up from Egremont in 1766 and built his house at the Center, near the present site of the Congregational Church. Joseph Bryant settled in the extreme northwestern corner near State Line. Some say his was the first house within the town boundaries; certainly his land deed is dated two months earlier than Burghardt's.

The territory was the site of a Stockbridge Indian town called Qua-pau-kuk, which in 1724 was conveyed to white settlers by the Konkapot treaty, still to be read in the *Book of Records of the Lower Housatonic Proprietary.*

Know all Men by these presents that we, Conkepot Poneyote Partarwake . . . Waenenocow . . . Cauconaughfeet Nonamcaunet . . . Sunkhunk . . . Tartakim . . . Cancannap . . . Mauchewaufeet John VanGilder . . . all of Housatonack for & in consideration of a valuable sum . . . Four Hundred and Sixty Pounds Three Barrels of Sider & thirty quarts of Rum . . . have given, granted, bargained, sold, aliened, conveyed & confirmed . . . unto Col. John Stoddard Capt. John Ashley, Capt. Henry Dwight & Capt. Luke Hitchcock . . . a certain Tract of land lying upon Housatonack River . . . we ye sd Indians are ye true, sole, & lawful owners of ye aforegranted premises . . . this 25th day of April, in ye tenth year of his Majisty's rign and in ye year of one thousand seven hundred & twenty four:

Signed, sealed & deld
in presence of us
Conreat Borghghart
Benjamin Smith
John Gun Jun
Samuel Bartlett

The section ceded by the Indians was called Queensborough, perhaps to complement the land to the west, which had been named King's District. In 1771, residents began a campaign to free themselves from the mother town of Stockbridge. Elijah Williams, one of the leading residents, addressed a revealing letter to Colonel William Williams, representative to the Massachusetts General Court, regarding the change.

Sir: We now have a petition in the General Court to have the west part of Stockbridge set off and made a district, which I suppose, will meet with no opposition. We have called the place Queensborough, sh'd be glad to have it retain that name if it is agreeable to his Excellency. I forgot to desire Squire Woodbridge to mention it to the Governor, and had I thought of it, I suppose he would have been too negligent to have done anything about it. I would therefor now beg favor of you, sir, to request his Excellency to call the place Queensborough if it is agreeable to him. I am sir, with respect to your very humble servant.

ELIJAH WILLIAMS
Queensborough, June 4, 1771

Squire Woodbridge was the Stockbridge representative to the General Court. In 1774 the Court gave the territory which lay within the western boundary of Stockbridge the right to incorporate separately under the name of West Stockbridge.

On the West Center road is the old SILVERNAIL HOUSE, built in 1810, the second dwelling to occupy this site. The first house was described by Frederick Tobey, town historian, as "a modest wooden frame building not far removed from a log cabin." Elijah Slosson, a relative of Mother Ann Lee, founder of the Shakers, erected this first dwelling about 1775. Here Mother Ann visited at a time when she was trying to convert Eliphet Slosson, Elijah's son, to Shakerism.

Eliphet was betrothed to a pretty girl in the neighborhood, and stead-fastly refused to embrace the Shaker doctrine of celibacy. Finally Mother Ann feigned defeat, and to show her good will invited the young couple to the Shaker settlement in Lebanon, New York, for a wedding dinner. Within a few months, the two were married and crossed the mountains to Lebanon for the feast. Evidently Mother Ann had laid her plan well, for before the meal was finished, the bride and groom decided to live in the settlement in Shaker fashion as brother and sister. The bride lived on to the age of ninety-four in the West Pittsfield Shaker Colony, while her husband stayed in Lebanon.

The old house that now stands on the Slosson site has been re-stored to its original beauty, and the surrounding broad acres of fertile farm land brought again to productivity. The house is set back from the road with lilac bushes and old elms around it. There is a magnificent view here of distant Mt. Greylock to the north, the wooded side of Lenox Mountain, and the line of the Hoosacs far to the east.

The Shakers were not the only sect to seek converts in West Stockbridge, for in 1839 a missionary entered the community and organized a Mormon society with thirty members. The sect seems to have found its Berkshire neighbors uncongenial. In 1841 most of the converts joined the Mormon migration to Nauvoo on the Mississippi River, and the rest pressed on with a group of Mormons who settled Salt Lake City.

A less organized but spectacular religious movement was initiated by a religious fanatic named Reed, who appeared at about the same time as the Mormons. Believing that the Lord wished him to atone for his sins, this prophet decided to offer up a pig on an altar near the summit of Stockbridge Mountain. With a frightened youth to assist him in driving and carrying the pig, Reed climbed the mountainside to a spot where there were several large rocks resembling a sacrificial table. The pig was tied on a pinnacle of wood, but at the first touch of the flame, it rolled off and fled down the mountain, squealing frantically. The terrified helper was close at its heels, for between curses and holy ardor, Reed shouted that a human sacrifice would do. It is said on the best authority that the youth ran so fast that he overtook and passed the pig.

Nearly a century has passed since West Center was a thriving community. Only a few scattered farm houses and barns and the old CONGREGATIONAL CHURCH (1788) remain. There are many more elaborate churches in Berkshire, but none more graceful than this old building. Simple and well proportioned, it stands with the Taconics at its back, old lilac trees nestling by its side, and a crumbling stone wall ranging across the front.

Back of the Congregational Church rises TOM BALL MOUNTAIN. On its rocky summit many years ago, another fleeing man, one Benjamin Johns, sought refuge from his wife's clacking tongue. Benjamin was a pious Methodist, one of the first in the section, and he took his religion hard. His life became a round of prayer and Bible-reading. Such sanctity was too much for his wife. She nagged him to feed the stock when he wanted to pray; she ordered him out into the fields when he had settled down with the Good Book. Home was no longer his castle nor even his sanctuary. He decided to seek a spot where he could commune with God at his pleasure. The place nearest God and farthest from his wife was the top of Tom Ball Mountain, and here, so they say, Benjamin prayed in peace to the end of his days.

In West Stockbridge you will hear a Berkshire version of the murdered traveler story, variations of which occur all over New England. On a night when a violent storm was raging, with plenty of thunder and rain, an unknown traveler from New York State stopped at a West Stockbridge tavern for supper. After he had paid his bill from a large roll of money, inquired the way to Stockbridge, and departed "on the edge of the evening," he was never seen alive again. There were other strangers in the inn that night, two "evil-looking" men, who cast covetous eyes at the bank roll. But there seemed no cause for alarm until in the spring the melting snow surrendered the body of the traveler. The spot is on Mass 102 about a mile south from the junction of that highway and Mass 41 on the road to Stockbridge. Near a small ravine by a brook on the right of the road, near the town, is his burial place, or so it is said. The melancholy tale is recorded by William Cullen Bryant in "The Murdered Traveler."

> When Spring to woods and wastes around
> Brought bloom and joy again

The murdered traveler's bones were found
Far down a mountain glen.

They little knew, who loved him so,
The fearful death he met,
When shouting o'er the dessert snow,
Unarmed and hard beset. . . .

Nor how, when strangers found his bones,
They dressed the hasty bier,
And marked his grave with nameless stones
Unmoistened by a tear.

Fruitless attempts have been made to identify the murdered traveler of West Stockbridge. Quite a few local families would like to have him as an ancestor—a companion, perchance, for the skeleton in the closet.

Chapter VI

MIDAS TOUCHES THE HILLS

STOCKBRIDGE—US 7, and Mass 102 and 183, sett. 1736, alt. 829, pop. 1921.
LENOX—US 7 and 20, Mass 183, sett. 1750, alt. 1210, pop. 2706.
Roads—Mass 102 goes direct from West Stockbridge to Stockbridge; from there to Lenox the direct route between centers is US 7, but Mass 102 west to Mass 183 and then north is a nearer way to Stockbridge Bowl.

THE Lenox and Stockbridge region is Berkshire in its best dress suit and evening gown. Here you drive past luxurious estates and a sculptured landscape. Here are all the habiliments of great wealth and power. This is Berkshire, the sophisticate, in contrast to old New England in Berkshire, where simplicity and the old order hold sway.

Miles of tailored hedges and smooth roads enclose spacious lawns and flower-filled gardens, the handiwork of landscape architects who know how to add the fitting human touch to a natural setting of great beauty. So concealed are the mansions in their deliberate isolation that only an occasional roof and chimney are visible above the green tops of the trees.

Long before the coming of the English gardeners, Indians roamed these heavy forests and pushed their canoes up the Housatonic. The local tribe was a remote connection of the Mahicans of whom Cooper wrote in his *Leatherstocking Tales;* the name is variously spelled, as Mohegan or Mahican or Mohican, but all are a corruption of Mukhekaneew, "the people of the ever-flowing waters." The plague of 1616-1617 wiped out all but a few of the tribesmen who had once ranged far and wide from New York into the upper Housatonic Valley. The Mahicans, as they were commonly called in Berkshire, were members of the powerful Algonquin branch of American Indians, and it seems fairly certain that some of the Stockbridge group were Algonquin migrants from Manhattan Island. The Algonquin tribes were for the most part friendly to white men, and they appeared willing to accept the Christian religion.

Mahicans roamed the Berkshire Hills until the first settlement by the whites in *STOCKBRIDGE* in 1736. At least that is the orthodox date, although it is true that a certain Dutchman named Van Valkenburg had for years before then occupied a tiny cabin at the base of Monument Mountain, where he bartered frequently and nefariously with the Indians, trading trinkets and whisky for furs and food.

In 1734 the Reverend Samuel Hopkins of West Springfield became interested in the "neglected" natives of Berkshire and began to advocate the erection of a mission for their "redemption." Together with the Reverend Stephen Williams, the "Boy Captive" of Longmeadow, he went to visit the Mahicans and talked with Konkapot and Umpachenee, the chiefs of the tribe, pointing out to them the need of their people for the white man's teaching.

The Mahicans hesitated, not sure that they wanted white teachers to show them the light. Umpachenee, more suspicious than the rest of his tribe, was quick to ask: "What is the cause of the sudden favor shown my tribesmen? . . . If we should permit the whites to become co-proprietors of our land, will not our children be imperiled?" But Chief Konkapot, whose innate nobility saw only good in the proposal, persuaded his people to accept the white man's mission and to welcome him as a friend and brother.

The General Court of Massachusetts granted a tract of land for the purpose of establishing the Indian mission, with lots set apart for four white families. The Reverend Mr. Hopkins was appointed the first Indian missionary, but his was only a nominal title. In 1734 John Sergeant, young tutor at Yale, became the first resident missionary at Stockbridge. Shortly, he obtained Timothy Woodbridge as substitute teacher and went back to Yale. The following year an ecclesiastical council of ministers and laymen, including such notables as the Governor and his council, assembled at Deerfield, and there, in the presence of numerous Indians, Sergeant was solemnly ordained and embarked upon his life's work.

A year later Governor Belcher invited Sergeant and a delegation of Mahicans to come to Boston to effect a transfer of Stockbridge land to the whites. Needless to say, the Indians got the short end of the stick, for they agreed to exchange a bale of pelts and fifty-two square miles of land for a church. The Governor promised that the new church would be built immediately, to replace the first rude shelter erected by the Mahicans under the guidance of John Sergeant.

Carefully preserved in the files of the Stockbridge Library is a copy of a letter written by the minister in 1743 to a friend in Boston. After nine years' toil among the Indians, John Sergeant still held to his dream of "redeeming" his brothers.

What I propose in general is to take such a Method in the Education of our Indians as shall in the most effectual manner change their whole Habit of thinking and acting; and raise them, as far as possible, into the Conditions of a civil, industrious, and polish'd People; while at the same Time the Principles of Vertue and Piety shall be carefully instilled into their Minds in a Way that will make the most lasting Impression; and withal to introduce the English Language among them instead of their own imperfect and barbarous Dialect.

For sixteen years John Sergeant lived among the Indians, slept in their wigwams before they built his house, shared their venison and edible roots, and conversed with them in their own language. He helped them to incorporate an Indian township, to construct houses like those of the white men, to cultivate the land, and to worship God in their own little church. So great was the fame of the Stockbridge Mission that Indians from New York and Connecticut were drawn to enjoy its benefits.

When the first great leader of the Stockbridge Mission passed on. other men, equally able and sincere, succeeded him—Jonathan Edwards, the great Puritan divine, Stephen West, John Kirkland, and John Sergeant, Jr. The Indians showed definite signs of becoming properly civilized according to the standards of their teachers. They went to church, they tilled the soil, and some of them held public office along with the whites in the government of the town.

But despite the good men who came to teach them, and despite their own efforts to adapt themselves to the new civilization, the Indians were driven from the land of their fathers. John Sergeant's work was lost. War took its toll—war at the white man's elbow, for these Indians were always loyal, faithful to their white friends even when only the shell of friendship remained on the side of the whites and the core was eaten away by cupidity.

With touching humility the Indians presented on June 21, 1775, a petition that temperance might be preserved among them.

We, whose names are hereunto subscribed, being soldiers enlisted to serve in the provincial army during summer, beg leave to lay this request before you. We, in our more serious hours, reflect with shame upon our aptness to drink spirituous liquors to excess when we are under temptation; by which foolish conduct, when we are guilty of it, we render ourselves unfit for usefulness and service to our fellowmen and also disagreeable to those that have anything to do with us.

We are sensible that we injure ourselves more than anybody else. When we get a taste we must some of us with shame say that sometimes no interest of our own will prevent us from procuring more till we get too much. We therefore desire you would, in your wisdom, do something during our residence there that we may get so much as will be good for us and no more.

The petition is signed by various Bills, Johns and Samuels, bearing the colorful surnames of Wauyumpskeynunnaunt, Auhheckhubinauhoot, and Naunaupretaunkey.

Thumbed again, the Proprietors' Record Book yields numerous entries more ominous for the future of the Indian:

Voted that T. Woddbridge Esq. make sale for the payment of the just debts of the Indian proprietors . . . all tracts of land lying . . .

Voted that 100 acres of land belonging to the Indian props. of Stockbridge be sold for the payment of a debt of £40 to one Moses Parson of Windsor.

At meeting of May 1766—voted to Wm. Goodrich in consideration of his having his ox killed, 50 acres of land.

One hundred acres, fifty acres—all Indian land taken away for this reason and for that. It must have been comparatively easy to get property away from the Indians through legal machinations. An old Berkshire historian attributes the loss of their heritage to "the Indians' preference for the shining coin to possessions which involved constant and uncongenial labor, leaving it probable that finally by far the most valuable lands of the town became the property of their shrewder brethren of the paler race."

The tragic day came when the sons and grandsons of Konkapot awoke to the fact that they were no longer wanted, though their land and their property were. In 1783 there was one last council fire—a few murmured protests and threats—and then they agreed, one by one, to leave the land of their fathers and to seek the reservation and hunting ground of the Oneidas in New York. Under the sorrowful supervision of John Sergeant, Jr., the Stockbridge Indians made their unhappy trek to New York; within five years the migration was completed. So ended John Sergeant's mission. Not with bloodshed, not with curses.

In the southwestern part of the town on a grassy plateau from which one may get a clear view of the Housatonic Valley and Monument Mountain, is the old BURIAL PLACE OF THE STOCKBRIDGE INDIANS. On a tall monolith of native stone is graven a belated tribute:

THE ANCIENT BURIAL PLACE

OF THE

STOCKBRIDGE INDIANS

1734

THE FRIENDS OF OUR FATHERS

Descendants of the town's pioneer white settlers dedicated this memorial to the original red settlers in 1877. A noble gesture, but it cannot obliterate the memory of what happened to a people who, when the settlers of Stockbridge were sorely pressed, sent the following message of devotion to the Massachusetts Legislature:

Our ways of fighting are not your ways. We cannot train as your soldiers do, but only show us where your enemies are. That is all we want to know.

As the center of an experiment in Indian mission work, Stockbridge from its earliest days had a character all its own. John Sergeant, Jonathan Edwards, Stephen West, and John Sergeant, Jr., were the leaders of the town. But men of worldly position and wealth also came to live here and formed a powerful clique, intent upon accumulating fortunes by defrauding the red men and the Colonial government of money given for the conversion and education of the savages. One historian comments that

The town was an inviting place for all those schemers who make up Indian "rings" and grow rich off the Indian's necessities, and more than

once the righteous Edwards burned with holy anger against their iniqui-
tous doings.

In the autumn of the first year of Edwards' service the "ring" did
everything in its power to have the minister dismissed. He fought
back successfully.

From its settlement, Stockbridge attracted many visitors because
of the interest in the Indian Mission and the men who conducted it.
When Judge Theodore Sedgwick moved his family from Sheffield to
Stockbridge in 1785, the town began its life as a resort community.
A brilliant lawyer and a firm patriot, Judge Sedgwick was one of the
most prominent men in New England. His presence in Stockbridge
had a marked effect on the town's destiny. As Catherine Sedgwick, his
daughter, wrote years later:

My father's public station and frequent residences in town gave him
a very extensive acquaintance, and his affectionate temper warmed acquaintance into friendship. There were then no steamers, no railroads, and
a stage route through our valley but once a week. Gentlemen made their
journeys in private carriages, and, as a matter of course, put up at their
friends' homes. My father's home was a general depot and when I remember how often the great gate swung open for the entrance of traveling
vehicles, the old mansion seems to me to have resembled much more a
hostelry of the olden time than the quiet house it now is. My father's
hospitality was unbounded.

In the early nineteenth century, Stockbridge was on the main
route of the stagecoach line between Boston and Albany, and eight
coaches a day, four each way, made regular stops. During these
years, Daniel Webster, Martin Van Buren, Harrison Gray Otis, and
other notables stopped in the town to visit the Sedgwicks or to
enjoy the hospitality of the Red Lion Inn and the Stockbridge House.

The removal of the Charles Sedgwicks to Lenox in 1821 and Catherine's departure did not by any means end Stockbridge's era of prominence. Men and women who had visited the town were drawn by
the quiet country life, the superb scenery, and the congenial company. By the 1860's, men began building country homes, which were
as a rule to be occupied only part of the year—usually in the autumn
when the foliage was most brilliant.

But Stockbridge has never become simply the showplace of the wealthy; it still retains the right to be called an "aristocratic town" rather than merely a rich one. Descendants of the first families have kept ancestral homes here, even into the third and fourth generations; Dudley Field, a grandnephew of David Dudley Field, William Ellery Sedgwick of the famous Sedgwick family, Henry W. Dwight, whose forebear was the early settler, General Joseph Dwight, all make Stockbridge more or less a permanent home. Other people of distinction established homes in the town, among them Norman H. Davis, diplomat, Daniel Chester French, the famous sculptor, and Owen Johnson, novelist and statesman.

Stockbridge never took to large-scale industry. Only in the century from 1750 to 1850 were woolens, chairs, and paper produced in limited quantities, and hats and hand-wrought nails in sizable lots. Though foundries and machine shops also operated during a part of the century, no organized manufacturing or heavy industry exists in Stockbridge today. A few Stockbridge people work at a sawmill just over the Lee town line, others find employment in the textile and paper mills in Great Barrington and Lee, and a few commute to Pittsfield to work in the General Electric Company.

The immaculate appearance of Stockbridge is not a matter of accident nor of recent planning and care. For over eighty years the town has gloried in the achievements of a local improvement society—the Laurel Hill Association—organized originally in 1853, the first village improvement society in the United States. On LAUREL HILL, a slight height at the east end of Main Street where once the Indians met in grand council, is a rostrum in memory of Henry D. Sedgwick. Through the decades the Association, a model for the rest of the country, has planted thousands of trees and miles of hedges; public taste has been educated into preserving the beauty of the town.

The Common is the natural center of interest, and grouped around it are stately reminders of Stockbridge's history.

The present CONGREGATIONAL CHURCH, set far back from the Common amid tall Norway spruces, was built in 1824. It is a handsome modified Georgian structure of red brick, mellowed by the elements, and its original small-paned windows and dark green shutters have fortunately been preserved. Long balconies surround the three sides of the interior, while the fourth side holds the fine walnut

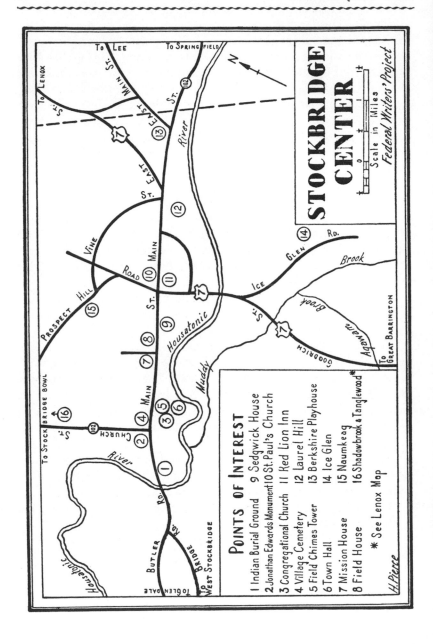

POINTS OF INTEREST

1 Indian Burial Ground   9 Sedgwick House
2 Jonathan Edwards Monument 10 St. Paul's Church
3 Congregational Church 11 Red Lion Inn
4 Village Cemetery   12 Laurel Hill
5 Field Chimes Tower   13 Berkshire Playhouse
6 Town Hall   14 Ice Glen
7 Mission House   15 Naumkeag
8 Field House   16 Shadowbrook & Tanglewood

                         * See Lenox Map

pulpit, used for the first time in the second structure and later rebuilt by David Dudley Field. Marble plaques on either side of the pulpit recall the first three missionaries to the Indians, John Sergeant, Jonathan Edwards, and Stephen West.

The large, square TOWN HALL is not the original structure. Around the earliest building on this site dramatic events took place about 150 years ago. One February dawn in 1787, the ragged debt-ridden followers of Daniel Shays, most of them from over the border in New York State, rounded up nearly fifty of the "Berkshire gentry," rich and powerful Stockbridge citizens. During the six months that the southern Berkshire towns were controlled by Shays' men, these "silk stockings" were frequently terrorized by mobs of fellow townspeople. On the occasion of the kidnaping of the fifty "silk stockings," the farmers swooped down during the absence of the Stockbridge militia and dragged the aristocrats off to Great Barrington. Before the day was over, the rebels had been defeated on an Egremont backroad, and the humiliated Stockbridge men returned home. Solomon Gleason, the village schoolmaster, had been killed, but doubtless the Shays men would have been better pleased if the victim had been Judge Theodore Sedgwick, who some time before had led an expedition which had taken eighty-five rebel prisoners.

The Judge was absent from Stockbridge the day the "Insurrectionists" came to town. Invading his home, they found only black Mum Bet, a former slave who had made herself a member of the Sedgwick family. Warned that the marauders might search the house, she had hidden all valuable papers and possessions before the rebels appeared on the doorstep. Armed with a kitchen shovel and with a countenance that boded no good, she met the troop of farmer-soldiers at the door and slowly escorted them through the house. They were amused, yet a little in awe of this black-faced hell-cat. Upstairs in the chambers, her tongue was as busy as her brain. In her own little bedroom, taking her seat on top of a chest—which, in fact, contained the family silver at the moment—she supervised the room's search. "Now better take a look in dis pore ole nigger's clo'se chest," she urged the searchers, adding sarcastically, "seein' as you-all are such gen'lemans."

"Aw, let the old nigger alone," expostulated a soldier, "there ain't anything here except her tongue—and that ain't worth takin'."

Nevertheless, Mum Bet's tongue saved the Sedgwick silver.

Elizabeth Freeman was her real name, and before becoming a servant in the Sedgwick family she had been a slave in the home of Colonel Ashley of Sheffield. One day as she tried to shield her sister from a shovel-blow, aimed by their mistress in a fit of passion, she received a cruel bruise on her arm. Mum Bet left the Ashley household and neither commands nor entreaties could move her to return. Colonel Ashley resorted to the law to recover possession of his property. The trial took place in Great Barrington and the outraged slave was ably defended by Judge Theodore Sedgwick.

At the time of Mum Bet's emancipation the Constitution of Massachusetts had just been adopted. The Massachusetts Bill of Rights, which stated that "all men are born free and equal," had its first practical application when Judge Sedgwick won Mum Bet's freedom. She is believed to have been the first slave in Massachusetts legally set at liberty.

Side by side in the old VILLAGE CEMETERY across from the Common lie both the early settlers and the famous people of later years. Here are buried Cyrus W. Field and his father; Joseph H. Choate, brilliant lawyer and one-time Ambassador to the Court of St. James; John Sergeant and the innumerable Goodriches, Sergeants, and Sedgwicks of Stockbridge history. The grave of Captain John Konkapot, chief sachem of the aboriginal Housatonic or Stockbridge Indians, is in the extreme southwestern corner. There is a story, perhaps legendary, that the original headstone bore an inscription reading

HERE LIES CAPTAIN JOHN KONKAPOT.
GOD, BE AS GOOD TO HIM AS HE WOULD BE TO YOU
IF HE WERE GOD AND YOU WERE JOHN KONKAPOT.

Also insistent on past memories is the FIELD CHIME TOWER, erected by the eminent lawyer, David Dudley Field. The Tower commemorates the site of the Indian mission church. Mr. Field's father, the well-known minister, spent the years from 1819 to 1837 preaching in Stockbridge, although originally he had come to stay only a few weeks. After a fourteen-year pastorate at Haddam, Connecticut, he returned here in 1851 to spend his remaining years editing one of the best of the Berkshire county histories. His son, David Dudley, Junior, won a reputation through his work in effecting legal reform; another son, Stephen, was renowned as a member of the United States Supreme Court. Henry Field followed in his father's footsteps, becoming a preacher and later editor of a religious weekly. Only recently one of his descendants, Rachel Field, has portrayed this least-known of the famous Field brothers in her novel, *All This, and Heaven Too*. Miss Field's book gives the best description we have of Stockbridge in the mid-nineteenth century.

Cyrus West Field was the most illustrious of this family, for he it was who founded the Atlantic Cable Company. In 1856 the American continent was connected with Newfoundland by a submarine cable. When two years later a cable was laid between Newfoundland and Ireland, Queen Victoria sent the first message to the President —James Buchanan—on August 16, 1858. And after the Queen's message the Field family, gathered together in Stockbridge, received a message from Cyrus: "The cable is laid!"

"The cable is laid!" shouted school children running down Stockbridge streets, rejoicing not alone in the cable (which to some of them had a vague meaning) but in the fact that school had let out early. Bells were rung. Guns were fired. Cyrus Field, who used to take part in amateur theatricals at Stockbridge Academy when he was a youngster, had become a hero on a worldwide stage! The United States Congress voted him a gold medal and the thanks of the Nation, while the Prime Minister of England declared that if Field had not been a citizen of another country he would have received the highest honors within the power of the British Crown.

The Field Chime Tower, sometimes called "the Children's Chimes," was erected in 1878 on the site of the old Indian meeting-house. David Dudley Field, Junior, later added a clock and the chime of bells which at six on summer evenings send out their peal from the seventy-five-foot tower.

Another reminder of the great men of the past is the JONATHAN EDWARDS MONUMENT, diagonally opposite the Chime Tower. In 1751 the Reverend Jonathan Edwards of Northampton settled here, to be paid for his ministry partly in money and partly in firewood. The Indians supplied him with eighty loads of wood and the whites with twenty, indicative of the Indian majority at the time. In 1758, when Edwards left his charge, there were only eighteen white families. He had come to Stockbridge at a time when his spirits were very low, for after twenty-three years of indefatigable labor, his previous congregation had forced him out because of his severe theological beliefs. His doctrines, though they had aroused great opposition, were in part responsible for New England's most stirring religious epoch, the "Great Awakening." Almost an exile in Stockbridge, he devoted his six years here to continuation of the missionary work begun by Sergeant and to the composition, in the solitude of his study, of the great philosophical treatise that preserves his fame, *An Inquiry into the Freedom of the Will.*

Like many a brilliant student, Edwards was very absent-minded and anecdotes have grown up about his failing. At one time, riding on horseback, he took a path leading through a pasture, where he met a lad who respectfully lifted his hat and opened the gate. The great man, who never lacked courtesy, thanked him, asked whose son he was, and then rode on. When he returned not long after, the lad was still there; the same proceedings were repeated and the same question asked. Unappreciative of his interrogator's peculiarity, the boy answered with surprise—"Why, sir, I am the same man's son I was fifteen minutes ago."

In the general vicinity of the junction of US 7 and Mass 102, in the center of town, are other treasured memorials of the past in Stockbridge. Most impressive in an historical sense is the MISSION HOUSE (*open summer 10-12.30; 2-6; Sun. 2-6; winter 2-4 and by appoint.; adm. 25¢*), a third of a mile east of the Common. With the help of his Indian friends, Parson Sergeant built it on the hill in 1739. When Miss Mabel Choate determined to restore it in memory of her father and mother, it was brought down to the center, piece by piece, and set up as nearly as possible in its original condition. Now an old-fashioned garden of flowers, small vegetable plots, and beds of striped grass give it a Colonial setting. Behind the house the original well-sweep stands silhouetted above its well-head. The silvery gray clapboarded house, with its exquisite doorway brought overland from the Connecticut Valley, is one of the gems of Berkshire architecture. The two-story frame structure forms a pleasing mass. Though it departs from the usual habit of unit composition, its various parts are of the same period. Particularly conspicuous are the chimneys, oddly placed below the ridge line on the rear slope of the roof, and the elaborate paneled doorway accenting an otherwise severe façade.

The "Connecticut Valley" entrance derives from Wren and his followers by way of a baroque interpretation of motifs and details.

The house, furnished after much research, delights enthusiasts of the American antique. Rare pieces of furniture include a dole with slats for circulation of air, an oak chest brought over by John Choate almost three hundred years ago, crewel work in bird and flower designs, and the silver used in the Mission in 1739. This communion set had gone as far afield as Red Spring, Wisconsin, where some members of the Stockbridge Indian tribe lived after the dispersal. A few years ago their descendants gave it to Stockbridge.

Edwards probably did not live here and the study shown to visitors as his was not the scene of the composition of his famous essay on free will. The stern Calvinist's own Stockbridge home stood till 1900. In lamenting its destruction, a local antiquarian writes:

Few towns in America can boast two such Meccas for all literary pilgrims as the house where Hawthorne wrote his *House of the Seven Gables* in 1851, and the house where Jonathan Edwards wrote the *Freedom of the Will* a hundred years earlier—yet the former was burned down, and the latter torn down.

Close beside the Mission House is the FIELD HOUSE, home of the Reverend David Field and his illustrious family.

Perhaps the most famous home on Main Street is SEDGWICK HOUSE, belonging to a family so numerous and so influential in Stockbridge and Berkshire history that Longfellow remarked on visiting here that even the crickets sing "Sedgwick, Sedgwick, Sedgwick." Judge Theodore and his daughter Catherine were the most famous of the clan. Honors came to the renowned "Kate" in the early 1820's. Born in Stockbridge, she published her first book, *A New England Tale,* in 1822. The novel, written with didactic purpose, "to lend a helping hand to some of the humble and unnoticed virtues," made such a sensation that she was hailed not only as the first American woman writer of note, but also as one of the foremost writers of the day. At that time, when she was thirty-three, Washington Irving was just being heard of, Cooper was in the throes of his *Leatherstocking Tales,* Nathaniel Hawthorne was a youth of eighteen years, and Harriet Beecher Stowe was not yet in her teens. For a quarter of a century, until the appearance of *Uncle Tom's Cabin,* Kate Sedgwick's novels were best sellers. She has been described as "heretic, moralist, Christian, all in one," but she explained herself far more simply when she wrote in her autobiography, "A habit of doing our own thinking has always dominated our clan." Miss Sedgwick's revolt against Calvinism aroused the orthodox of her day. It was equally characteristic of her that she resented foreign criticism, notably in the coarse exaggerations of Mrs. Trollope, English writer of travel books, who had declared that all the bigotry in America was concentrated upon the Berkshire hills.

At no great distance from the Sedgwick House, there is a natural beauty spot, ICE GLEN, described by Timothy Dwight in his *Travels* as a "tremendous geologic convulsion." It is a deep gorge in a wilderness of growth where ice stays all through the summer. In this Berkshire jungle wandered Crazy Bet, a heroine of Kate Sedgwick's New England sketches. The author's great-niece, Nathalie Sedgwick Colby, herself a novelist, tells in her autobiography, *Remembering,* of the Ice Glen parade, an autumn event of her girlhood. In October, at the time of leaf change, a huge bonfire was made, after a torchlight procession of maskers in all sorts of costumes had trooped to the Glen. Social distinctions were forgotten in this Berkshire Saturnalia. The Glen is reached by the first road south of town, off US 7 past the railroad bridge.

Back at the village center, near the junction of the highways, are two other notable links with the past. The RED LION INN, which replaced a 1774 tavern of the same name, contains the Plumb collection of Colonial china, pewter, and furniture. The Inn is now owned by a prominent Stockbridge citizen, Mr. Allen Treadway, a member of the United States Congress. Across the street is ST. PAUL'S CHURCH, whose first structure, built in 1834, was the second oldest Episcopal church in Berkshire. The present building, designed by McKim, has an interior richly supplied with numerous works of art: a baptistry by Saint-Gaudens, a reproduction of Luca della Robbia's "Singing Boys," a La Farge stained-glass window, and a Florentine pulpit. The clock was a gift of G. P. R. James, the once popular historical novelist who was for two years a resident of Stockbridge. The chancel furniture was given by Mrs. Franklin Delano, grandmother of President Franklin Delano Roosevelt.

The modern villas that now occupy Indian lands are in sharp contrast to the austerity of the old Mission House, as witness the estates on Prospect Hill. The road of that name runs out of Stockbridge Center beside St. Paul's Church. NAUMKEAG, the third estate on the left, was the home of Joseph H. Choate, lawyer and diplomat. It is now owned by his daughter, who restored the Mission House. A curiously Oriental and exotic touch is provided by a pagoda in an ornate setting of landscaped gardens and lawn. A marble pedestal and the "sacred rock" from Peiping, China, are said to date from the Ming Dynasty four or five hundred years ago.

Choate's brilliance and wit attracted to his home celebrities from all over the world. Matthew Arnold, over from England on a visit, once caused considerable consternation among the serene folk of Stockbridge. Like so many illustrious citizens, Mr. Choate was an enthusiastic and wily fisherman. Naturally he wanted to show his friend from England what an extraordinary catch might be taken from Stockbridge streams. Before Mr. Arnold could try the sport, however, he had to purchase a fishing license costing one dollar. No sooner had the permit been issued than a caucus of fishermen was held in the town hall; fifteen years had been spent in cultivating bass in Berkshire waters and it did not seem right that for a paltry fee a British subject should be allowed to take the choice catch.

"Thunderation! That Britisher'll get all our fish!"

"Humph! He won't have to work very hard, that's sure. Why, he's a regular doggone perambulating rainbow! Black bass've got a natural failing for gaudy colors, you know."

"By gollies, you're right! Recollect that day Henry Dean wore his crimson chest protector out to Garfield Hole? He caught nineteen bass in about an hour!"

"Yeah. And he took a red-headed boy along, for good measure."

For a moment the hall was quiet. Each fisherman was conjuring up the image of Matthew Arnold, the Britisher, wearing his flamboyant Scotch cap, his vermilion neckpiece, and his gold-colored hose. With such a colorful costume to charm the fish—yes, and add to this rainbow presence on the lake, the almost inhuman fishing skill of Joseph Choate!—the unsophisticated bass around Stockbridge would have no chance at all.

"All I can see," finally vouched an earnest member of the gathering, "is that we'll have to set up a counter irritant—something like painting Sayles' barn bright blue and his boathouse yellow?"

"Sure, 'n then invite a Sunday school picnic to play games along the lake's banks!"

It was a good suggestion. The caucus, however, refused to pay for paint, and in the end no protective measures were taken against Matthew Arnold as a potential menace to Berkshire's prize black bass. At half-past seven the following morning the streets of Stockbridge were crowded. The spectators watched as the fishing party's paraphernalia, including three quarts of worms, were loaded onto a wagon.

Suddenly a cheer broke from the throats of the watchers. Nonchalantly Arnold came into view and with the sight of him, clad in corduroy, gray flannels, and a meek cap, hearts and spirits were revived. The Britisher himself had taken "protective measures!"

The day was not auspicious for the fishermen. When he left Stockbridge not long after, Arnold is quoted as saying, "If the American idea of fun is for three men to broil nine straight hours in a flat-bottomed boat for the sake of three small pumpkin seeds and one perch, I regret my own lack of power to appreciate it." Evidently there were compensations for this experience, for on his return he wrote his daughter, then in America:

You cannot think how often Stockbridge and its landscape come into my mind. None of the cities could attach me, not even Boston, but I could get fond of Stockbridge . . .

Many people have grown fond of Stockbridge; not only of its landscape, but of its gusto for arts and letters. There is even a summer dramatic season in the old Casino, a handsome structure designed by McKim. It once stood on the present site of the Mission House, but in 1927 the Three Arts Society moved the building east of the High School, on Main Street, and converted it into the BERKSHIRE PLAYHOUSE. Since the opening of the theater the following year, some of the most famous players in America have appeared upon its stage. Playing nightly, with a Wednesday matinee, for nine or ten weeks each season, the Playhouse had up to 1938 presented some three hundred actors and actresses in more than a hundred plays. Guest stars have included Ina Claire, Ethel Barrymore, Walter Connolly,

Katharine Cornell, Katharine Hepburn, Claude Rains, Donald Meek, Jane Wyatt, Sylvia Field, and Henry Hull.

The Playhouse features an Art Exhibit during late summer or early fall. Prizes are awarded for the best landscape, portrait, pastel, and etching. Early in the twentieth century this region caught the imagination of artists—among them Daniel Chester French, Frederic Crowninshield, Walter Nettleton, Lydia Field Emmet, and Marie Kobbe—and they initiated the exhibition.

The music center lies out in the other end of town, on the edge of Lenox. Take Main Street (Mass 102) west to Mass 183, and turn right. Close to the town line in INTERLAKEN is one of the large outlying estates, which attracts unusual public interest. It was created as a show place by Dan R. Hanna, son of President McKinley's close friend and political adviser, Mark Hanna. Each July the Lenox Horse Show is held here; a two-day exhibition, dating from the '90's, it brings a fashionable sporting set from many states. The Lenox Dog Show is another well-established institution which makes use of Interlaken, but its entries are largely from local kennels. The Bit and Bridle Club has privately owned trails here.

Crystal-clear Mahkeenac Lake lies off to the right of the road, not far beyond Interlaken. The Indian name, meaning the "Great Water," displeased Miss Sedgwick because it would not fit easily into poetry. Her suggestion of the name STOCKBRIDGE BOWL has been generally accepted.

On the high ground overlooking the Bowl, on the left-hand side of Mass 183, is "SHADOWBROOK COTTAGE," a large house which takes its name from Hawthorne's *Wonder Book*. Only a corner of the estate is in Stockbridge. When the "Cottage" was built (1892-1894), it was the largest private residence in America. Its hundred rooms cover an acre of floor space; the wide main staircase would accommodate a coach and four, and the dining room a hundred guests. Such palatial grandeur cost its builder, Anson Phelps Stokes, half a million dollars. Later Mrs. Cornelius Vanderbilt lived at "Shadowbrook," and sold it to Andrew Carnegie, who died here in 1919. A sprawling English Gothic structure with scarlet roof and gray stone exterior, this thousand-acre estate is outmatched in Berkshire only by the Tytus Palace in Tyringham and the enormous caravansary of Barrington House in Great Barrington. At present the Jesuit order owns the estate, using it to house Saint Stanislaus School for Novitiates.

On the northern shore of the Bowl once stood a little red cottage, where harassed Nathaniel Hawthorne came in 1850 with his family. He had been recently saddened by the death of his mother, and was embarrassed because the new Whig President, Zachary Taylor, had dismissed him from his post in the Salem Custom House. Brooding over what he considered the treachery of former friends, he was morose and unsociable, writing from his Berkshire retreat, "Here I feel remote and quite beyond companionship." His children, however, enjoyed themselves thoroughly. Years later his son Julian wrote:

> To us children, the succession of summer, autumn, winter and spring was like the coming of four delightful playmates, one after the other, and we knew not which we loved the best. Our father and mother were our playmates, too, without whom the others would have lost their charm . . . The great thing for us in winter was the coasting. We had a sled big enough to hold my father with us children on his back . . . After the coasting we would come glowing in, and after our snow-besprinkled jackets and tippets had been taken off, we would eat a big supper and go happy to bed . . . And then another day of glorious pleasure!

Hawthorne developed a most intimate companionship with Herman Melville, who was then living a few miles north in Pittsfield at his "Arrowhead" farm. Hawthorne had just written *The Scarlet Letter,* which Melville reviewed sympathetically in the *New York Literary World*. Hawthorne appreciated the review, but at first neither wished to presume on what he had said or done. Later they became friends as a result of a rainstorm. While walking together they were forced to take shelter in a recess on the west side of Monument Mountain; there, safe from the rain, they talked themselves into friendship. When Melville used to approach "Red Shanty," as Hawthorne called his Tanglewood cottage, a shout would go up "Here comes Typee!" the pet name the family had given Melville. During the summers of 1849 and 1850, the huge Arrowhead barn in Pittsfield often sheltered the two men, reclining on hay, deep in conversation.

While Melville was writing *Moby Dick,* he would often walk over to Tanglewood from Pittsfield and tell the Hawthorne children hair-raising stories of naked savages, evil-smelling whale ships, and "summer isles of Eden."

"Did Mr. Melville leave his black club here?" Mrs. Hawthorne once asked her husband after Melville had taken his leave.

"What club?"

"Oh, the one he was laying about with when he told us the story of how the captain cleared the deck of the savages," replied Mrs. Hawthorne with a twinkle.

Julian pondered and looked for the club. Nor did he at that time understand his father's answer: "That club is like Macbeth's dagger."

Despite Melville's powers as a teller of tales, Julian admits that in later years he could recall "much more substantially" Luther Butler, the milkman. "He and my father," he writes, "were great friends and never gave each other any trouble. We drank his milk and he never read my father's books."

Just before leaving Berkshire, Hawthorne ended his *The Snow Image and Other Tales,* dating the preface "Lenox, Nov. 1, 1851." Neither he nor Mrs. Hawthorne considered themselves residents of Stockbridge; entries in the *American Notebook* are made under "Lenox" and letters written as from there. Tanglewood was nearer the Lenox post office than it was to Stockbridge Center. A recent Lenox chronicler says:

Hawthorne and all who built villas in this part of the town have been solely identified with Lenox life. Technically it is true that Hawthorne's home was in Stockbridge; the novelist could flip a stone over the line into Lenox, wrote "Lenox" in his notebooks, went to the Lenox post office daily for his mail, and was identified in every way with Lenox.

In the serenity of this place Hawthorne wrote his *House of Seven Gables, Wonder Book,* and *Tanglewood Tales,* but he never fully accepted the Berkshires as home. At one time in a spirit of dire pessimism he wrote: "I hate Berkshire with my whole soul and would joyfully see its mountains laid flat."

A few visitors may come to TANGLEWOOD to see where Hawthorne lived and wrote, but it is the Symphonic Festival that really brings Berkshire people out. The idea of creating an American music festival was suggested by the famous Salzburg concerts. The first concert, conducted by the late Dr. Henry Hadley, composer and conductor, was held August, 1934, on Dan Hanna's Stockbridge estate,

Interlaken. The New York Philharmonic Symphony Orchestra gave three concerts before an audience of about two thousand people.

In 1935 the Berkshire Festival Society was incorporated, and two years later the permanence of its program was assured when Mrs. Gorham Brooks of Boston presented Tanglewood, her family estate, for the Festival's future home. The Boston Symphony Orchestra, under Serge Koussevitzky, agreed to play at six concerts. A large tent, holding five thousand people, was provided, crowds poured into Lenox and Stockbridge from every point of the compass, and the music was broadcast over a national hookup with Olin Downes as commentator.

During the 1937 concerts, a storm climaxed by a cloudburst dramatically interrupted an all-Wagner program. Conflict with the weather crystallized an idea to provide a music shed as protection from sun and rain. Within a few months more than eighty thousand dollars were collected for the needed improvement, itself a triumph of engineering and architectural invention. The shed, constructed of three hundred odd tons of steel, has a roof of two-inch planks and an exterior of a sound-deadening composition. The main auditorium holds almost six thousand people and three thousand more may sit in the colonnade.

LENOX itself was described in the early nineteenth century as "a bare and ugly little village dismally bleak and uncouth." This was before Midas had touched the hills and lowlands with his golden wand, and people of wealth and fashion had found their way here to build elaborate villas on great estates.

It was in 1750 that Jonathan Hinsdale, the first settler, built his house at the foot of what is now called Court House Hill in Lenox Center. He wasn't far ahead of Messrs. Cooper, Stephens, and Dickinson, who, somewhat later in the same year, also became "first settlers." Other pioneers followed from Connecticut and southern Berkshire to take up land in the little community that was named Yokuntown after Chief Yokun, a Stockbridge Indian. A rough Indian path was the plantation's only connection with the outside world. This trail wound up through deep forests from Sheffield along the Housatonic River, through Great Barrington, and, passing into Stockbridge, ended at Yokuntown.

Yokuntown only once experienced the disaster of an Indian raid. A band of Schagticokes from the Hudson River Valley, bent on revenging the death of one of their tribesmen, penetrated western Berkshire as far as the new white settlement, spreading terror in their path. Houses were burned, a woman was shot and another rescued just as she was about to be scalped. The panic-stricken settlers fled to Stockbridge, but soon returned to put up new homes on their half-cleared fields. There were no more raids, and the only Indian trouble henceforth experienced was over acquisition of land.

In 1762, when the provincial government proposed to sell at auction ten townships in the eastern section of "Indian lands," the Stockbridge Mahicans registered so threatening a protest that on the day of the sale it was deemed wise to grant £1,000 from the public treasury "providing said Indians shall release all claims to any lands in the province to which they pretend a title." In the end the Indians were paid the unusually high price of £1,700 for the tract which included Yokuntown and Mt. Ephraim, and Lenox was separated from its western neighbor, Richmond. In 1767 the town was incorporated and named for Charles Lennox, Duke of Richmond, a friend of the Colonies.

During the Revolution, Lenox was Tory-infested, according to petitions sent to the General Court regarding a

Large Number of Persons who not long since were apprehended in said County as Dangerous Persons, they had a fair & impartial Trial before a Special Court of the General Sessions of the Peace & a very respectable Jury for that Purpose, were found guilty after a lengthy, deliberate and expensive Trial, of such base, Wicked & inimical Conduct that their residence any longer with us, was judged to be Dangerous . . . The Court upon the verdict of the Jury ordered Edward Martindale & Elisha Martindale, John Burgheadt, 3d, Gideon Smith and James Taylor to be conducted to the Board of War . . . Now while we were solacing ourselves, that Justice had taken Place & that the Sentence would soon be put in execution . . . behold a number of these Persons made their Appearance in this County . . . some of them are guilty of braking open Continental Stores and Stealing large quantitys of goods, & attempting to justify their Conduct by saying we had taken the same Goods from their King.

An almost fatal yet successful attempt was made to convert the Tory, Gideon Smith, and force him to take the oath of allegiance to the Continental Congress. He was strung up twice by the local Committee of Safety until, choking and half dead, he consented to take the oath. Smith then hid in a cave at the base of October Mountain near the present New Lenox. His wife and children walked back and forth before his hiding place so that he might glance at them through the opening of the cave. TORY CAVE, as it is called, is merely a cleft in the rocks in which, it is true, a man might sit, but it must have been larger and better roofed when Smith used it as a refuge.

At the dawn of the nineteenth century, Lenox was a flourishing community with an iron foundry, marble quarry, hearthstone mill, and glass factory. As the county population gradually shifted to the north and Lenox was near the center of the area, its leading citizens, puffed with civic pride, petitioned in 1782 to have it replace Great Barrington as shire town. Despite vigorous opposition from Pittsfield, in 1787 Lenox was awarded the plum. By 1816 the present dignified, white county COURT HOUSE (now the Lenox Library) was completed in the center of the village.

With the arrival of the court, a new bustle came to the growing town. An old newspaper, under the heading "Lenox in Court Week," gives an idea of activity in town about a hundred years ago.

The goddess has occupied her throne here for more than a week past, and our village has abounded with judges and jurors, lawyers and litigants, prosecutors and prosecuted. To us who live in the country the occasion is quite imposing. It presents us with a vast variety of characters: young attorneys in the bustle of new-found business and the older ones assuming more and more the dignified gravity of the bench; waiting jurymen chatting in little clusters by the wayside; worrying clients complaining of sleepless nights; witnesses of all orders, sizes, sexes and ages; spectators trading horses in the street, and politicians smoking over government affairs in the bar-room. Our boarding-houses have long tables lined on both sides with earnest applicants, and all expect more business. Messages are sent and errands done between one end of the county and the other, business accounts are settled, plans laid; caucuses, conventions and singing-schools agreed upon; newspapers subscribed for, and distant matters in general arranged for the ensuing winter.

The Court House remained a center of Berkshire life until 1868, when Pittsfield became the county seat.

Charles Sedgwick, son of Judge Theodore Sedgwick of Stockbridge, is credited with "discovering" Lenox. He moved there in 1821,
and his famous sister, Catherine, soon came to live with him. Almost
immediately their home became the gathering place of the literati of
the day. In 1837 the first visitor from a distance, a New Orleans
woman, built a house there. By 1846 the rich and powerful Samuel
Ward, American agent of Baring Brothers, London bankers, gave his
cachet to the town by building "Highwood," a palatial estate.

The sylvan retreat began to change into a resort where society spent
its summers and autumns to await the opening of the winter season
back in the cities. First the newcomers bought cottages, then they
bought land and more land. On their newly acquired acres they built
magnificent estates, like regal palaces, each vying with his neighbor
to own the more beautiful dwelling. Thus Continental architecture
crowded out the simplicity of the old Colonial styles. The town was
a facsimile of Newport—an inland Newport where blue mountains
were the equivalent of sand and rolling surf. Gone completely was
the little Calvinist settlement that had been Lenox.

To name the famous people in the town during the last half of the
nineteenth century would be like reading from pages of the Social
Register. There were Harrimans, Stuyvesants, Aspinwalls, Crockers,
Adamses, Biddles, Vanderbilts, Sloanes, and many others. A gay social
round replaced the old informal life.

Wherever you go in the town, whatever route you take in entering
it, you will see romantic villas and pretentious mansions. Set far
back from the public thoroughfares, these houses are like enchanted
palaces about which, as though in mockery to the curious, hedges
have grown high and close. There is perfection of landscape on every
side, but the dominating motif of it all is to conceal.

These "enchanted palaces" have, in the true fairy-tale tradition,
turned into white elephants today, awaiting the magic touch of a
buyer. Not long ago in Lenox, as in all America, the more rooms
there were in a house, the merrier. Now the trains of servants are
gone and the rooms are getting dusty. For modern life calls for high-
powered, compact dwellings, not sprawling, many-roomed mansions.
With the passing of the heads of many of the old families, houses
and gates have been closed and barred. One after another the grand
residences are being struck off to buyers who want them for dairy

farms and hotels or else to cut up their grounds into a number of lots and sell them to prosperous business men and industrial executives seeking refuge from nearby noisier towns.

Because Lenox is spread out over a broad area and because there are so many ways by which to enter the town, better start your ramble around the town from Lenox Center, at the CURTIS HOTEL on US 7 and 20. Since 1773 there has been a hostelry on this site. The Curtis House, built in 1834, replaced the Berkshire Coffee House. The pleasant hostelry with its wide verandas and old-fashioned rooms was a rendezvous of county judges and lawyers who came to toast their shins at the open fires and talk over their latest cases before court opened.

Near the middle of the century Fanny Kemble, the actress-authoress, used to sojourn at Curtis's before she bought her own home in Lenox. One day while waiting for her spachcook to be served (a dish of which she was extremely fond) she turned upon a man standing near the office desk with the words:

"You should remove your hat. Gentlemen always remove their hats in my presence."

"But I'm not a gentleman, ma'am," protested the man, "I'm a butcher."

Fanny Kemble, of course, was pleased with such a reply, and she and the butcher became great friends from then on. That was the sort of person Fanny was.

For the traveler who puckers his forehead at the name of Fanny Kemble, it may be well to explain here and now just who this remarkable woman was who has left such a train of reminiscences in Lenox. That is, if anyone can explain Fanny. Born into a family of English actors and actresses, she was destined to become a brilliant success in the world of the theater. Her American début came in 1832. Two years later, after a blaze of glory in which she was the idol of the day, she married Pierce Butler, scion of a distinguished and wealthy Southern family and joint heir to a Georgia plantation and a host of slaves.

Some of the best, most authentic pictures of slavery as an institution in the deep South during pre-Civil War days have been left by Fanny Kemble in her notebooks written during the seven years of her married life. Eventually Pierce Butler divorced his wife, and

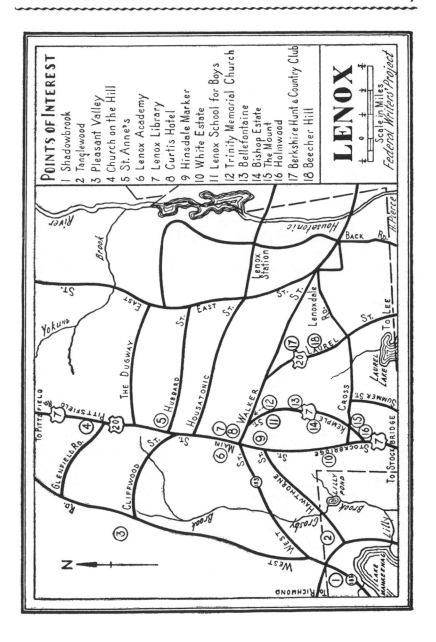

POINTS OF INTEREST

1 Shadowbrook
2 Tanglewood
3 Pleasant Valley
4 Church on the Hill
5 St. Anne's
6 Lenox Academy
7 Lenox Library
8 Curtis Hotel
9 Hinsdale Marker
10 White Estate
11 Lenox School for Boys
12 Trinity Memorial Church
13 Bellefontaine
14 Bishop Estate
15 The Mount
16 Holmwood
17 Berkshire Hunt & Country Club
18 Beecher Hill

LENOX

Scale in Miles
Federal Writers' Project

Fanny, brooding and lonely, found a sanctuary in Lenox, where her dear friends Catherine and Charles Sedgwick lived. Before long her personality, her sympathies, and above all her courageous spirit, made her the center of the literary group then living in Lenox. Statesmen admired her, in particular Charles Sumner, who renewed a pleasant friendship with her in 1844 while he was in this region for a few weeks. Longfellow, many times a visitor here, shared Sumner's admiration and wrote a sonnet in praise of her readings. Her intellectual genius is attested by Sumner's statement that the brilliance of her conversation made him feel "inferior."

Next to the Curtis House is an admirable old building with hand-hewn columns and graceful doors. For over half a century it was the Court House, but when Pittsfield became the shire town in 1868, the building was abandoned. Now it is the LENOX LIBRARY, one of the few Berkshire structures excelling in architectural design. Isaac Damon, champion of the Greek revival, planned the building with a simple, rectangular form, a facing of the heavy orders, and a well-studded, round, open cupola. In 1873, Mrs. Augustus Schermerhorn gave the building to the town, to be known as the Charles Sedgwick Library.

The square white building across the road, a little beyond the Library, is the old LENOX ACADEMY, founded in 1803. From it were graduated such men as Mark Hopkins, Julius Rockwell, Charles Sedgwick, and Anson Jones, the second president of the Texas Republic. The school closed its doors in 1910.

Among tall trees at the junction of the two main routes of travel (US 7 and 20) is TRINITY MEMORIAL CHURCH, whose attractive modern structure was dedicated by President Arthur in 1888. The Episcopalian Society was formed as early as 1793, though the first church was not built until 1816.

The first observance of the Saviour's natal day in Berkshire is said to have been at a Christmas party given by the Episcopalians of the town to the smaller fry, the Congregationalists, the Baptists, and the Presbyterians, for the furthering of better social relations. It was a grand red-and-green gathering where everybody had fun and where, after a banquet, there was dancing that was both sedate and risqué, including, as it did, the very proper square dances of the day, the *almost proper* mazurka (very modern, a recent importation from

Poland), the *not-so-proper* schottische and two-step polka, of late popularized in America by the Marquis de Lafayette, and the *frankly improper,* highly seductive new dance called the waltz.

Beyond the church on Kemble Street, a group of yellow clap-boarded buildings on the slope of the hill faces the distant mountains. In 1926 the Episcopal Church opened here the LENOX SCHOOL FOR BOYS; about seventy-five students are enrolled. Mrs. Charles Sedgwick's exclusive school for young ladies, a well-known institution from 1828-64, was nearby. Catherine Sedgwick lived here, and both Charlotte Cushman, the actress, and Harriet Hosmer, the sculptress, attended the school as pupils.

About half a mile beyond on the left side of Kemble Street are the ornate gates and high grillwork of BELLEFONTAINE, Giraud Foster's magnificent estate. A little distance south on the opposite side of the road is the BISHOP ESTATE, where in 1851 Fanny Kemble bought a house which she named "The Perch." Here she spent many years between her stage tours and her trips abroad. Near the en-trance to the estate and just within the grounds is a little marker half-circled by trees, designating the site of the Kemble cottage. The owners of the property, David W. Bishop and his son Cortlandt Field Bishop, startled the populace—both human and equine—in the late '90's by roaring through the streets in a motorized tricycle imported from Paris. When the smoke blew away, Mr. Bishop found himself involved in a lawsuit. A speed limit, enacted "solely to restrain Mr. Bishop," read:

No vehicle propelled by any motive power other than horses, mules, donkeys, cattle or hogs shall be allowed to pass over any of the streets or public ways of the Town of Lenox at a rate of speed more than six (6) miles per hour, or to use any portion of said street or ways except the right-hand portion of the traveled part of said streets or ways within six feet of the ditch.

It is said that the by-law of which this regulation was a part has never been repealed. Present-day motorists may well be wary.

Cortlandt Field Bishop was cut from the same piece of cloth as his father, and the cloth was far from Quaker gray. All ways of travel intrigued him. Bishop himself was no back number at manipulating divers machines. In 1923 he got out of France and into the United

States with a tractor-automobile which had been developed secretly by the French Army for use in the Sahara. He used it in Lenox to plow snow and carry mail.

Not far beyond the Bishop estate a winding drive leads from Kemble Street to the entrance of THE MOUNT, formerly the villa of the American novelist, Mrs. Edith Wharton. The house, in a setting of smooth lawns and formal gardens, is a copy of "Belton," a famous early Georgian manor in Lincolnshire. The setting of her popular story, *Ethan Frome,* is said to be somewhere in the Stockbridge countryside—an allegation not undisputed. The Anglo-American novelist, Henry James, was one of many famous visitors at "The Mount," where to the end of her life Mrs. Wharton spent such time as she could.

The neighboring place is HOLMWOOD, which Mrs. Margaret Emerson has recently sold to the Fox Hollow School for Girls. Formerly it was the home of George Westinghouse, the electrical magnate. In 1887 Mrs. Westinghouse was advised by her physician to live in the Berkshires. She and her husband spent the summer of that year in Lenox, and were so charmed with their place that later they bought several farms, creating the extensive estate then called Erskine Park. Mr. Westinghouse set up a power station to provide lights for the house and stables. Electric lights, rare at this time, were usually hung on the gas fixtures with no attempt to conceal the wires. Mrs. Westinghouse suggested a special molding for the fixtures at the joining of ceiling and wall, thus toning down the brilliance of the light but still giving sufficient illumination for ordinary use. At first her husband opposed the idea, but finally agreed to try it out, and Erskine Park with its 1500 indirect lights attracted such attention that the idea was quickly copied.

Turning back toward town on Stockbridge Street, when Kemble Street brings you to it at the Fox Hollow School sign, not far beyond the WHITE ESTATE you will find a small MARKER beside the road in memory of Jonathan Hinsdale, the first white man to settle in Lenox. The marker explicitly states that "his grave is in the churchyard on the hill." Although his long, last home is on the heights, he built his house, contrary to the custom of most of the Berkshire pioneers, in the valley.

The Hinsdale Marker is only a short distance from Mass 183.

If you'd like a drive into the woods, go left on this highway, and swing north on West Road, which leads past Lenox Mountain, on whose lower slopes is the PLEASANT VALLEY SANCTUARY. Since 1929, by the generosity of some Lenox residents, this tract has been set aside as a safe retreat for Berkshire bird and plant life. An inviting little cottage opens its doors to guests to provide rest and food. Cool walks lure the traveler through the woods, where there are miles of hiking trails, trout streams, and sequestered wild gardens with now and then a rare plant or flower to delight the finder. Furniture and various articles illustrative of early Berkshire life and of industries in the county are exhibited in the OLD BARN, which is also a museum of natural history. In the forest are good snowshoe paths, and an extension of the Sky Line Trail offers the skier connection with the Bosquets Ski Run in Pittsfield. To the south another ski trail goes down to the Beartown Mountain State Forest.

There are still other things to be seen in Lenox, and you'll want to return from the Sanctuary over Cliffwood Road, which will take you to US 20 and 7. The interesting structure at the foot of the hill, north of the center of Lenox, is ST. ANN'S CATHOLIC CHURCH, which has on one side a lovely grotto sacred to Our Lady of Lourdes. Rocks from the River Jordan, the Sea of Galilee, Lourdes, and Ireland have been brought together to form a shrine.

One of the finest examples of Berkshire Colonial architecture is the CHURCH ON THE HILL, dedicated in 1805 as the successor to the first religious edifice in the town. It dominates the scene almost as much as do the surrounding hills. When Fanny Kemble arrived in Lenox years ago, she offered to give a "reading" for the poor, only to be told, "We have no poor." Instead of giving alms to the non-existent needy, Fanny Kemble, out of the proceeds of a single night's performance, gave a clock for the tower of this church. The building has not been in use during the past half century except in the months from May to November, since it is still heated, as in the early days, only by two sheet-iron stoves and lighted by kerosene lamps. Undoubtedly the most memorable address ever heard from the old pulpit was the fire and brimstone sermon of Dr. Samuel Shepard, preached in 1806, when Ephraim Wheeler, who had been convicted of a capital offense, was taken from the jail to the church on a bob-sled and forced to listen to a vivid description of his probable fate in the next world.

If you are headed for Lee when you leave Lenox, there are alternate routes to choose between. From the Center, Housatonic Street will take you east through Lenox Station, at the foot of October Mountain, through Lenoxdale, past scenery that is perhaps as good as Berkshire offers, and into the adjacent town. The road is excellent, the natural beauties superior to those along the other route, US 20.

The national highway, if that be your choice, runs over Walker Street from the Center. Beyond the point where Walker Street leaves US 20 is BEECHER HILL, named in memory of the popular minister, Henry Ward Beecher, who had a farm here. He bought it, so he said, for a place "to lie down upon." The charm of Lenox and the beauty of his own bit of land so impressed him that he wrote *Star Papers* to expound the glories of the Berkshires. "I can see," he wrote, "sixty miles by simply rolling an eyeball."

It was on Beecher Hill that John Sloane, a wealthy carpet manufacturer, later built his rambling and lordly structure, "Wyndhurst," now one of the buildings of the CRANWELL SCHOOL FOR BOYS, opening in September, 1939, under the direction of the Jesuit Order.

On the southern edge of the Club grounds, Cross Road runs to LENOXDALE, a mile and a half southeast of Lenox. Years ago Lenox Furnace, as it was then called, was bent on being an industrial center; it had textile and paper mills, and, according to local boasts, the largest glass factory under a single roof. Even in the eighteenth century, the sand from this part of the Berkshires was especially valued. The "Glass Works Grant" of 1757, consisting of 1500 acres just south of Lenox Furnace, was given by the General Court to promote glass-making at Germantown, near Boston. Only the great pit from which the sand for glass manufacture was taken remains, for there has been no glass factory at Lenoxdale since 1880. Iron was worked here from 1780 to 1860. Shortly after the mines were abandoned, in November, 1862, the subterranean galleries and corridors, honeycombing the main street of Lenox, yawned open to swallow a house up to the second story.

Two small units of a Lee paper concern and the plant of a tobacco company are the sole survivors of a once lively industrial settlement. Lenoxdale, and to a lesser degree LENOX STATION, a half-mile or so east, have always been more closely related to Lee, both in personality and appearance, than to the town of which they are actually a part. The settlements hardly fit into the picture of the aristocratic, almost baronial Lenox with its mansions and estates.

Despite depressions, social changes, and the passing of many of the old families, Lenox, like a proud dowager, moves amid her luxurious surroundings, and carries on her sober revels in this "autumnal resort of fashion." Just as a hundred years ago, so today is Lenox admired with the ardor of Fanny Kemble when she praised

a landscape that combines every variety of beauty—valleys in the hollows of which lie small lakes glittering like sapphires; uplands, clothed with green fields and orchards and studded with every variety of forest tree; the woods—some wild, some tangled and all but impenetrable, others clear of underbrush, shady, cool, moss-carpeted and sun-checkered; noble masses of granite rocks, great shafts of marble, clear mountain brooks; and a full, free, flowing sparkling river.

Chapter VII

BREAD OUT OF STONES AND PAPER

LEE—US 20, sett. 1760, alt. 888, pop. 4178.
Roads—US 20, southeast from Lenox, runs directly to Lee Center.

LEE, compared to Berkshire's orchid towns next door, Stockbridge and Lenox, is quiet and unostentatious. There isn't anything stylish about the town; the streets are narrow, the trim houses modest, and the people occupied with the everyday job of earning a living in the paper mills and the marble quarry.

Cape Cod and Connecticut Yankees were the first settlers, sturdy, independent folk determined to make a home in the wilderness for their families of ten or a dozen. In the 1840's the railroad brought the Irish, speaking an English dialect new to the town, men quick to laugh and to defend themselves, always willing to work. Last of all, in the second half of the century, arrived the Italians, artisans who knew how to slice and carve marble, and to conquer antagonism aroused by a foreign tongue and Old World customs.

Though today Lee wears the self-assured air that comes with a long tradition, actually for thirty years after Great Barrington, Sheffield, and Egremont had been settled and for twenty years after the founding of Tyringham, Stockbridge, and New Marlborough the territory lay untouched. Isaac Davis, from over Tyringham way, gets the credit of founding the town in 1760. For ten years, few followed him. By 1770 John Winegar, a German, knew of only thirteen families in the region. But as more and more hamlets began to grow up in Berkshire, amazing tales drifted back to the Atlantic seaboard. There were people in Connecticut who had already grown discontented with the stony acres that had fallen to their lot. Not everyone on Cape Cod wished to risk a berth in Davy Jones' locker, and farming the sand dunes was a fool's occupation. When battles at sea during the Revolutionary War made shipping and fishing poor business, residents of Sandwich and Barnstable began to push west through the wilderness.

In the vanguard of these newcomers was Captain Joseph Crocker, riding on horseback with his aged mother on a pillion behind him, and the rest of the family trundling along in an oxcart. Captain "Joe" had learned to spin a yarn with the best of them during his dog watches at sea, and though his tales wouldn't always hold water, they held attention. Eager ears were turned to the fabulous stories about the Housatonic River Valley sent home by Captain Joe and his friends. Along its banks, so the tale went, the sod was so rich it dripped grease if you hung it in the sun. The hogs fattened so fast in the pastures, they ran around squealing "Kill me! Kill me!" The children grew so tanned and sturdy that the settlers mistook their own offspring for Indian youngsters strayed from the few remaining tribes —all peaceful, of course. Part of the story must be buncombe, but the other half had to be Gospel truth. Even Joe Crocker's imagination wasn't *that* good.

Gullible Cape Codders were taken in. At first they plodded over a blazed trail through the forest, the hard way. Then came the snow, eight feet of it. To Cape people, for whom the Atlantic had always been a friend, this strange, white drifted ocean was cold and threatening. Shivering around camp fires, they fashioned snowshoes and pushed on toward the hills. Later they sent their household goods by water from the Cape to Hudson, New York, and thence overland in Berkshire.

The Cape settlement centered along Cape Street in East Lee. The settlers built their one-room log houses on the hillsides overlooking Jacob's Ladder between Springfield and Pittsfield. In the South Lee area, and over to the west, were other pioneers, among them Reuben Pixley, for whom Pixley Mountain was named. The memory of William Ingersoll, one of the most important men in the early settlement, endures in the patriarchal inscription on his tombstone:

> Sacred to the memory of
> William Ingersoll
> Who was one of the first
> Settlers of this town and one
> of the first, who in 1780 were
> formed into a Church in this

place. Satisfied with living
and rejoicing in hope of Glory
he died, Aug. 10, 1815,
Aged 91 years and 4 mos.,
leaving behind him, in this
dying world, 149 descendants.

In an epitaph, Jesse Bradley, who came in 1773 from New Haven, Connecticut, described himself with Biblical exactitude, as

. . . the son of Daniel Bradley,
who was the son of Daniel Bradley,
who was the son of Abraham Bradley,
who was the son of William Bradley,
who was one of the first
settlers in New Haven in 1637.

The Footes of Lee were powers in the community. According to persistent story, Nathaniel Foote concealed young Charles the Second of England in an oak, to hide him away from pursuers—as in the Old Primer couplet:

The Royal Oak it was the tree
That saved his Royal Majesty.

The grateful king is said to have rewarded his benefactor with a tract of land in the Massachusetts Bay Province which included the whole territory of Lee. The Foote coat-of-arms depicts King Charles being awkwardly assisted into the oak by Nathaniel, who turns an apprehensive eye toward heaven. Unfortunately for this apparent confirmation of legend, Nathaniel Foote had migrated to Watertown before September, 1634, when Charles the Second was only four years old. He died when King Charles was about fourteen years of age, and the Battle of Worcester, after which Charles was secreted, was fought when Foote had been dead fully seven years. Nathaniel Foote, moreover, was a Puritan, and if he had been in England at the time, and alive, he would have been on Cromwell's side. It's too bad; they enjoy the story in Berkshire.

Very early the Dutch from New York settled in Lee, as the names Freese, Houck, Van Deusen, and Van Tassel in early town records bear witness. At Cornhill, a farm owned by one of these Dutch residents, Martin Van Buren used to visit as a small boy.

Lee, the twenty-first town incorporated in the county, was named in 1777 in honor of Major General Charles Lee of the Revolutionary Army, in his time almost as famous a soldier as Washington. The town had previously been called by various names, among them "Hoplands," because of the wild hops along Hop Brook.

The first town meeting was held in 1777 at Peter Wilcox's cabin in the center of the community, now the site of the CARNEGIE MEMORIAL LIBRARY. On that December morning, there were twenty offices to fill and twenty-five men to fill them. Three years later the meeting had to adjourn to Peter's barn to accommodate the growing number of citizens. Still later, the tavern was pressed into service, and, after that, town business was transacted in the meeting-house.

Lee Center was then a cluster of wooden houses around the little frame church. The town pound, thirty feet square, and the whipping post, six feet high, with a crosspiece the height of a man's arm, stood opposite. Not far off was the town well, with its wooden bucket on a heavy chain, a meeting-place for the community.

During the Revolution, Lee lived up to the reputation of its soldier namesake. Not yet an incorporated township during the earliest days of the conflict, it sent men and supplies in excess of its quota to the service of the Colonies. Josiah Bradley of Lee was only fourteen years old when he went off with Colonel Brown and his "six-footers" to the Battle of Fort Stanwix. In the confusion of the defeat, Josiah was chased for several miles by an Indian. At length, unable to run further, the boy turned and fired his gun in the general direction of his pursuer. The Indian fell. Josh sped on, but he was confronted with a problem of ethics. The Ten Commandments charged "Thou shalt not kill," but a soldier was bound to kill as many of the enemy as he could. All his days Josiah was haunted by the Indian whose life he had taken.

Hard on the heels of the Revolution came Shays' Rebellion. The Berkshire farmers, oppressed by heavy taxes, hard times, and the almost worthless post-Revolutionary currency, understood better than the "city folks" in Boston the real purpose of Daniel Shays' uprising. Lee was in particularly hard straits. In the winter of 1787, a battle more comic than tragic took place between the Shaysites and the government troops under General Patterson, drawn up on a hill in East Lee. Uniformed troops these, with polished rifles and menacing cannon. Opposite, across Greenwater Brook, were lined up the ragged and hungry rebels. They had only a few old-fashioned muskets, little ammunition, and no cannon. But someone had an inspiration. "Bring out Mother Perry's yarn-beam," he cried; "we'll make it look like a cannon to scare the sheep across the way." Quickly the ponderous piece of weaving machinery, looking remarkably like a cannon, was mounted on a pair of ox-cart wheels. A ramrod and other military gadgets were flourished for the benefit of the enemy. Peter Wilcox roared the order, "Fire," and a blazing tarred rope was brandished like a fuse. Before the flames could damage Mother Perry's property, General Patterson's troops were in flight. In a twinkling, the hill they had occupied was bare.

During the rebellion Peter Wilcox, Jr., and Nathaniel Austin were caught by the government troops and charged with treason. Condemned to death, they were locked up in the county jail to await execution. Meantime their wives were permitted to bring them food and comforts. When the two ladies, seemingly bent with sorrow, had left the jail one day, the guard discovered that his prisoners were women in men's clothing. Wilcox and Austin in disguise had gotten safely out of the way. Wilcox hid in a cave in the side of Ferncliff, overlooking the village square, until his subsequent pardon. To this day the place is known as PETER'S CAVE.

"We have been very Shaysy here," said a member of the Congregational Church to the new pastor, Dr. Alvan Hyde, when he came in 1792, "and you'll have to be as wise as a serpent to keep peace among us."

The despair and bitterness that incited Shays' Rebellion gradually faded, as an improved system of finance and government brought new hope. Lee was an agricultural town, dependent on its pastures and fields for a living. Though the soil seemed fertile to the Cape Codders, who had been transplanted from barren sand-dunes, the bottom lands were limited and the earth far from easy to till because of the huge stones lying around.

Quarrying was already an established industry when, in 1852, Charles Heebner of Philadelphia bought a farm in Lee. The gentleman from afar was not troubled by the stone slabs in his field; in fact, he bought the farm because of them, knowing the "stones" were really marble of a high quality. In many places moss and forest growths had covered up the veins. Opening a thriving quarry in the town, Heebner sold marble for building material. A single contract for the enlargement of the Capitol in Washington ran to almost a million dollars. The Pittsfield and Stockbridge Railroad, put through Lee in 1850, provided excellent transportation facilities.

From this time on, Lee was busy with its marble quarries. Though Lee marble is gray-veined and without a fine grain, it is unusually hard and admirably suitable for building purposes. According to the United States Bureau of Standards, Lee marble is the hardest quarried in the country. It sustains a pressure of 30,000 pounds to the square inch, 8,000 pounds greater than most American marble and 7,000 pounds more than Italian stone. In the first twelve years of operating his quarry, the wily Philadelphian took half a million cubic feet of marble from the place. By 1860 several marble quarries in the town were booming. Great blocks of marble were shipped out daily to Boston, New York, Philadelphia, and the West. For a quarter of a century, Lee held its place as the "Marble Town" of Massachusetts.

Out of the deep, white-walled, white-floored pits descending into the earth of Lee's pasture lands came headstones for the graves of American soldiers in the Arlington National Cemetery. Over 9,000 of these lustrous stones have been erected, all of uniform size. Hundreds more have been shipped by the United States Government throughout the world to mark the graves of American soldiers, sailors, and marines who have been buried on foreign soil. Parts of the Capitol in Washington, Grant's Tomb and St. Patrick's Cathedral in New York, the Los Angeles Armory, the Baltimore Court House, and the City Hall in Philadelphia were built from Lee's treasure.

Lee paused to adorn itself with a few municipal buildings made of its own marble. Among them is HYDE SCHOOL, off the main road. President Franklin Roosevelt's father, by the way, attended a school conducted in the mid-nineteenth century by Alexander Hyde, son of the town's most famous minister. The PUBLIC LIBRARY, the Fire Station, both on US 20, and an occasional business block with marble ornamentation are other examples. But you will remember that the shoemaker's children went barefoot, and, similarly, Lee is a town of wooden houses.

The mid-nineteenth century was the heyday of quarrying. Skilled workers were in demand in those days and could be found only in Italy. Italian marble cutters, imported from the old country, urged relatives and friends to come to Lee. Today, the Italian-Americans form one-fifth of Lee's population of 4,178. They live, for the most part, in three distinct Italian colonies, where they have preserved many of their native customs. "Little Italy" is in South Lee, just beyond the junction of US 20 and Mass 102. Canal Street, near the Lee Marble Company, is inhabited by Italian quarry workers, and even Dublin Street is now entirely Italian.

The very name of Dublin Street recalls the days when the Housatonic Railroad was pushed through by Irish labor. Irishmen, too, had been employed in the dangerous powder mills of South Lee, set up to supply the needs of the War of 1812. Although the enterprise added to the industrial development of the town, numerous explosions made the citizens decide that life was more important than wealth. Like the pottery and ironworks, the horse farms, and the carriage factory, the powder mills were abandoned. Lee settled down to its quarries and paper.

In recent years the marble industry has declined until today the Lee Marble Company is the sole surviving plant. There is still hard gray-veined stone far down under the town, but it is too costly and difficult to get out. The LEE QUARRY is probably the only one in Massachusetts taking out marble at the present time. To reach the quarry, which lies across the Housatonic River from Lee Center, turn west from the Park on West Park Street, go over the river, then turn left on a dirt road paralleling the railroad tracks. Visitors are allowed to watch the various processes of mining, cutting, and polishing.

The old marble pits in Lee are deep and filled with water. From the Philadelphia Hole, closed after thirty years of operation, came almost two million cubic feet of marble for Girard College and the City Hall in Philadelphia. Today the pit is a swimming hole for town youngsters.

Once all the work was done by hand. Now marble pits are opened by a channeling machine which does the work of twenty men. The floor is then cut into slabs of from six to thirty tons each. A derrick lifts the monster blocks to the surface and loads them on a flat car drawn by a bellowing little steam locomotive, to be carted off to the sawmill. Giant saws—plain, toothless steel bands in frames, that work under a stream of water—cut the blocks into specified sizes. A huge two-piece steel disc, kept drenched in water, performs the first rough-polishing operation. In a second polishing, the marble is honed with six carborundum blocks set in a spinning steel disc. Discs of compressed felt, whirling upon the marble blocks, finish the job.

Just beyond the quarry are the buildings of the LEE LIME COR-PORATION, established in 1885 by Martin and Michael Deeley. Using cast-off stone from the quarry, this company has furnished lime for building, agricultural, and chemical purposes throughout the eastern part of the United States. Lime from Lee was used in the construction of Radio City and the Port Authority Building in New York and the Albany and Boston Post Offices.

Along with marble and lime, Lee developed paper mills, fed on the great forests around the village. The Housatonic River has always offered good sites and abundant water power, and by 1806 factory wheels began to spin. Textiles, carriages, and machinery have been turned out, but paper surpassed them all.

Local conditions were ideal for paper making. Besides ample water power, there was clean, pure air—of vital importance before air-conditioning—and men with capital were ready to put up money. In 1806 Samuel Church built the first paper mill in South Lee. It was the second in the county, for Zenas Crane had erected one in Dalton five years before. Rag paper was the only sort then known, and all manufacture was by hand. The rags were first washed, allowed to stand in tubs of water for a few days, then pounded into a pulp fine enough to spread evenly on a wire sieve. The sieve was used to dip up the pulp, sheet by sheet. It required twenty mortars to reduce one hundred pounds of rags to pulp in one day. Hand labor was about eight times slower than modern machinery.

In 1819 Luman Church erected a second paper mill. Three years later, Samuel Church's pioneer concern in South Lee was sold to Owen and Hurlbut, and converted into a factory for the production of fine writing paper. Four men and six women with one engine and one vat turned out ten reams of letter paper and foolscap in a day. The hand-made sheets were left in a rough state, since no finishing

apparatus had been introduced; the edges of the reams were un-
trimmed and the quires unstamped. Metallic pens had not yet been
invented, and the roughness of the paper did not interfere with the
use of the quill. By 1850 Hurlbut's mill had thirteen engines, running on a day and night schedule. One hundred and sixty hands
were employed in producing four hundred reams of finished letter
paper daily.

In 1826, after the Laflin brothers had built the town's third paper
mill, they gave the *New York Daily Tribune* its start by granting to
Horace Greeley three months' credit on the paper stock he needed.
Subsequent orders from the highly successful newspaper justified the
Laflin venture, but sometimes the brothers were more adventurous
than wise. Once they joined with some clever fellow who had developed a material that looked like Leghorn straw, then much in
vogue for the smart "Navarino bonnets." The imitations sold for $5
apiece, much less than a genuine Leghorn. The business soared while
such millinery was new, but with the first showers came sadness to
the hat buyers and the end of the Navarino boom for the Laflins.

Until well into the nineteenth century, the original hand-processes
of paper-making had been only slightly improved. Inventions were
made, of course, from time to time. Rags were reduced to pulp not
by hand beating but by water-wheel machinery. The beating machine,
or Hollander, named from the country of its origin, was invented in
1690 but not used in the United States until the late eighteenth century.
In 1799 Louis Robert patented a machine for making paper in a
continuous sheet rather than in single small sheets as in the hand
mold. His machine was improved by the Fourdrinier Brothers in
1807 and is named for them. The first model was a crude affair. The
beaten pulp was thrown in a continuous stream across an endless
wire cloth stretched in a horizontal position, and carried toward rollers
which squeezed out excess water. The wet paper was then wound
on a wooden roller, and taken out as soon as sufficient paper had
been made.

The application of power in the second quarter of the nineteenth
century and the gradual introduction of machines brought about revolutionary changes in the industry. The Hollander and the Fourdrinier
processes were improved again and again. Berkshire manufacturers
were soon able to produce a quality of machine-made paper far

superior to the best foreign hand-made goods. By the middle of the century all the mills in Lee, even the old single vat ones, had been equipped with Hollanders, Fourdriniers, and power engines. In 1857, the zenith of production, there were twenty-five mills in Lee, manufacturing two million dollars' worth of paper yearly. The Civil War stimulated production and brought even greater prosperity to the town. Lee manufactured more paper than any other community in the United States.

During the Civil War, Federal authorities discovered that one of the Lee mills was making paper watermarked "C.S.A." One Mr. Linn, who manufactured bank-note paper, was summoned before the District Court in Boston to interpret the letters, which might mean Confederate States of America. Mr. Linn was either very ingenious or a great patriot. According to his story, he was carrying out orders given him by a group of Union sympathizers, who planned to flood the South with quantities of counterfeit Confederate bills. The value of Southern currency would thus be destroyed and the war would be over. The case was postponed to the next sitting of the court and apparently never was tried. Mr. Linn disappeared and the truth of his story remains a mystery.

The most dramatic episode in the history of paper-making in the United States occurred at the Smith-Platner mills in Lee on March 8, 1867—the first practical demonstration in America of the process of manufacturing paper from wood pulp instead of rags. Carried out under the direction of Frederick Wurtzbach, machine- and cabinet-maker from the Hartz Mountains in Germany, the trial was an immediate success.

By 1878 the Smith Mills were the undisputed leaders of the paper industry in Lee. At one time the *New York Herald* used a thousand dollars' worth of Smith pulp paper a day. One week of January, 1885, the company received orders for seven hundred tons of paper. On another day, James Gordon Bennett sent a hurry call for a thousand tons, and got it.

Fine writing stationery, coarse wrapping papers, paper-collar material, flat cap paper for bank and writing books, blotting and absorbent paper—out of Lee has come a varied contribution to paper-making in America. The Eaton-Dikeman Company, organized in 1891, was the first blotting-paper mill established in the State. As the manufacture of electrical equipment progressed, the demand for saturation papers for making Bakelite grew, and Eaton-Dikeman was one of the first to enter the new field.

In 1892 the Smith Mills, ever on the alert, began manufacturing fine-grade tissue papers. In 1913 they added the production of India paper, commonly used in fine Bibles and until then made only in England. During the World War, the cigarette paper mills in France were faced with a shortage of labor. Taking over throughout the war period, the Smith Company produced one-half of all the cigarette paper in the United States. Business boomed, plants were remodeled, and new equipment was installed.

Later years were not so good to Lee. The great Berkshire forests of spruce, poplar, and hemlock gradually gave out. Unlike Dalton, where rag pulp is still primarily used, Lee depended entirely on wood pulp. The extensive woodlands of Michigan, Minnesota, Wisconsin, and the far West drew paper manufacturers away from the East. It was too costly to import wood from the West. One after another, the paper mills bordering the Housatonic and every stream and brook in Lee ceased operation. Many were absorbed by larger companies, others just abandoned. All but three paper mills departed or closed— the Smith Mills, since 1933 owned and operated by the British-American Tobacco Company, the Hurlbut Paper Mills in South Lee, purchased in 1930 by the American Writing Paper Corporation, and the Mountain Mill in East Lee.

During the prosperous years of the paper and marble industries, around the Civil War period, Lee enjoyed a building boom. New houses were constructed by the mill and quarry owners. The Park in the center of town was leveled off, planted with trees, and encircled by a stout wooden fence. One wintry night in 1857 the church, built in 1800, was destroyed by fire, and within a year a more elaborate structure took its place. The CONGREGATIONAL CHURCH (1858) still stands at the head of the Park, stately and dignified, with its slender steeple visible for miles around. The walls and ceilings are decorated with colorful fresco work of the baroque type, painted by an itinerant German whose name has long been lost. The German appeared in town shortly after the church was finished. He got a job decorating the walls of the old Masonic Lodge, and its members were so delighted with his painting that they suggested he be assigned to dress up the new church.

The church is built of wood, instead of the Lee marble one might expect. But, strangely enough, native stone, beautiful in grain and color, was used in a monument on the HIGHFIELD FARM in South Lee. The memorial is not by way of tribute to an early settler, to the discoverer of the marble quarries, or to any citizen of note. The inscription reads:

> Here lies Highfield Colantha Mooie
> A
> Holstein-Friesian
> Cow
> Who held the
> World Record
> For Lifetime
> Milk Production
> Born, Lived and Died
> On This Farm
> 1919–1937

In her eighteen years at the Highfield Farm in South Lee, Colantha Mooie produced enough milk to flood the town. Her lifetime output totaled 205,928.5 pounds.

Lee's industries are fewer but bigger now, and it is still a busy place. Here and there along its shaded streets rows of houses with steep roofs and wooden lace decoration retain something of the appearance of the Victorian era—of the days when Lee's "paper families" rode in phaetons and carryalls, drawn along the streets of the town by high-bred horses. The two- and three-story business blocks are a little dingy, but still in good condition. They line Main Street, where a double row of cars is parked at 45-degree angles against the high granite curbs. No need to worry about speeding down Main Street in Lee; there isn't room.

For all the compact appearance of the Center, Lee is one of the most sprawling towns in Berkshire. EAST LEE, two miles to the east on US 20, which runs over Jacob's Ladder and on to Springfield, is one of the oldest settled areas. In 1868 the thriving mill settlement here was almost completely demolished when the dam at Mud Pond Reservoir burst, sending tons of water hurtling down the narrow ravine of the brook. Today East Lee is a somnolent village of old houses and an old-fashioned inn set on the sidehills.

The hamlet is the locale of a sentimental ballad written by Kate Putnam Osgood, "Driving Home the Cows." In the true melodramatic, Victorian style, the poem tells the story of a farmer boy, actually Charles Gates of East Lee, who went to the Civil War without previous notice or acclaim. One day he drove the cows to pasture, and did not come back. Many months later, the father set out to do his evening chores, as the poem relates:

> The summer days grew cold and late,
>   He went for the cows, when the work was done;
> But down the lane, as he opened the gate,
>   He saw them coming, one by one,—
>
> Brindle, Ebony, Speckle and Bess,
>   Shaking their horns in the evening wind,
> Cropping the buttercups out of the grass,
>   But who was it following close behind?
>
> Loosely swung in the idle air
>   The empty sleeve of army blue;
> All worn and pale from the crisping hair
>   Looked out a face that the father knew.
>
> The great tears sprang to their meeting eyes;
>   For the heart must speak when the lips are dumb;
> And under the silent evening skies
>   Together they followed the cattle home.

From East Lee is said to have come the phrase "pot luck" as applied to a delectable New England boiled dinner. A town historian, the Reverend L. S. Rowland, speaks of it as

. . . the most satisfying dish for the men who spent long hours in outside labor. It is interesting to note that corned beef and cabbage is not as generally supposed, a dish brought from Ireland by early immigrants. They did not arrive here until about 1850 and "pot luck" was well-known in 1791, in the town of Lee which was settled by Cape Cod people mostly.

This homely dish is still a favorite in Lee. In 1938 the Corned Beef and Cabbage Club was organized in the town for the purpose of "sociability and the enjoyment of good food." The founder has moved away, but if you should lift the lid of the iron pot bubbling on many a range in Lee, you'd sniff the appetizing smell of "pot luck."

South Lee, the first area settled in the town, lies on Mass 102, which joins US 20 just east of the Housatonic. The DAVIS HOUSE, oldest in the township, is a frame dwelling built in 1760 by Isaac Davis, the pioneer. It stands across the old COVERED BRIDGE as you enter the village. The 120-foot bridge is more than a century old and one of the few antiques of the highway in Berkshire County. After weathering years of spring freshets, its beams are still stout enough to support any six-ton load.

Halfway down the main street of South Lee, with the Housatonic at its back door, stands the POST ROAD HOUSE, an old tavern erected in the early nineteenth century. Open to visitors during the summer months, the old house contains the original decorations and furniture and an authentic antique bar.

Rising against the sky to the southeast, behind the Post Road House, Bear Mountain shadows the village. Until his death in 1905 it was the home of Levi Beebe, familiarly known as "Beartown Beebe" or "Weather Prophet Beebe of Beartown Mountain." Beebe could foretell the weather, bright or stormy, for weeks ahead, by a peculiar system of his own. He watched the antics of kittens, the gait of caterpillars across a leaf, and whether or not the cattle lay down in the pastures. He also observed the atmosphere, the strata of the clouds, and the diversity of air currents.

Levi Beebe was not a "Berkshire Borner" but a dyspeptic book- binder from New York. When his ailment got the better of him, he left the city and his trade, brought his family to the backwoods of Berkshire, and settled down to the simple life. For many years he communed with Nature and practised his mysterious arts in peace. Lee people liked him, for despite his queer knowledge he was a man of "horse sense." Adopting the vernacular of the hills, he once said to the "Berkshire Tramp," an itinerant news reporter of the day:

I just love this air life I'm livin, for here we are untrammeled as to the conventionalities of fashion or the pride of dress, and we are all away from the temptations of the village—besides we know where the boys and gals are every night. We don't have so much style as some, but we have a comfortable hum . . .

The modern successor to Beebe is Peter Tyer, who lives on the Lee-Lenox town line in Lenoxdale. Tyer has received considerable publicity because of his decoration of a huge stone near the Housatonic. The stone has the sprawling, squat shape of a great frog. Tyer painted it green and added a white mouth and black eyes. For his artistry he has won the title of "The Sage of Frog's Landing." Tyer boasts he was born "the minute General Lee capitulated to General Grant at Appomattox Court House, April 9, 1865." One of the tales he loves to tell concerns the "growing stone" of Darius See, who, while walking along Washington Mountain Road, threw a pebble at a bird. Missing its mark, the pebble lodged in the crotch of a tree. As the tree grew, so grew the stone. In fact, it became an enormous boulder. Peter Tyer will show you the tree to prove his story.

There's another man whom everybody in Lee knows, a kindly lawyer who is said to have more friends to the square mile than any other man in southern Berkshire. "Jim" O'Brien is tall and lanky, with a powerful frame. Lee folks say he reminds them of Abraham Lincoln, and he's as honest as "Old Abe." Mr. O'Brien is always dressed in a low-brimmed black felt hat, long-tailed black coat, black and gray pin-striped trousers, "boiled" shirt, and collar with a shoestring tie. They say "Jim" knows every posy and blade of grass, let alone every man, woman, and child, for miles around, and when you talk about Lee, you don't want to forget Jim O'Brien.

The changes that time brings have not been unkind to Lee. First, farming, then the production of marble and paper supplied the townspeople with a livelihood. Lately a new and fourth industry, the tourist trade, puts butter on the bread. People come both winter and summer for the beauty of the scenery around Lee and the ample recreational facilities. The town has one of the best nine-hole golf courses in Berkshire County, and in Beartown Forest there are ski and snowshoe trails. Lenox and Lee share the great OCTOBER MOUNTAIN STATE FOREST, the largest public recreation territory in Massachusetts. GOOSE POND, reached from East Lee by Goose Pond Road southeast of town, is a favorite spot for fishermen and campers. LAUREL LAKE, shimmering spot of water in the opposite end of town, is famous for rainbow trout. The story of Lee as a recreation center is only in its first chapter. Peter Tyer's frog may become once again merely an old gray stone before the tale of Lee is completely told.

Chapter VIII

LOCKED AMONG THE HILLS

GREAT BARRINGTON—US 7, Mass 23, 41, sett. 1726, alt. 710, pop. 6369.
SHEFFIELD—US 7, sett. 1726, alt. 697, pop. 1810.
Roads—South from Lee on US 20 to East Lee, then west on Mass 102 past Stockbridge to join US 7 going south to Great Barrington and Sheffield.

AN almost complete barrier of hills surrounds *GREAT BARRINGTON*. Monument Mountain on the north; the pine-covered Berkshire Heights on the west; Warner and East Mountains along the eastern sky; and to the south, their heads in the clouds, Race Mountain and Mt. Everett of the Taconic Range. Mountains and hills, brooks and ponds, secluded glens, and the placid Housatonic River make a romantic setting for the valley town. For over half a century rich folk have established their summer homes here. More recently, Great Barrington has become a center for skiing and winter sports. The town has so many modern highways leading into it that the title "Southern Gateway to the Berkshires" seems quite apt. US 7 and Mass 41 bring people from Connecticut and New York; Mass 23 crosses the state from eastern Massachusetts to connect with NY 23.

Great Barrington gives every one a feeling of spaciousness. Wide, shaded streets radiate toward the mountains all around. On Berkshire Heights, in the western part of town, and along Mass 23 toward Egremont, visitors may see mansions built in the architecture of the '90's, alongside of occasional smaller houses whose outward simplicity conceals luxurious interiors—reproductions of eighteenth century farmhouses and Cape Cod cottages many times enlarged and embellished. Hedges are rare and there is little deliberate isolation. Elms arch over streets where tall, cone-shaped Norway spruce, stately white pine, and spreading maple decorate immaculate lawns.

The largest town in southern Berkshire, Great Barrington is the natural trading and business center for a surrounding rural population.

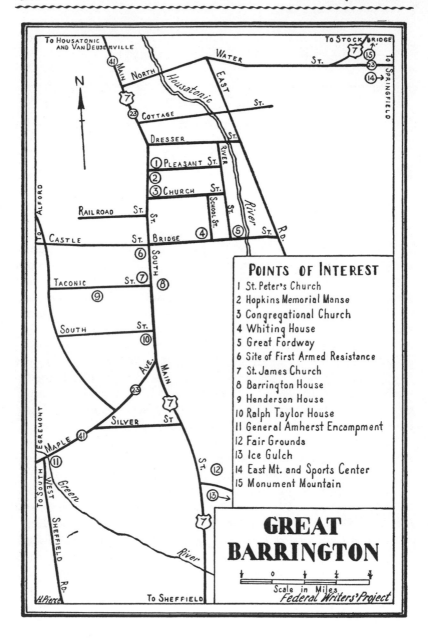

POINTS OF INTEREST

1 St. Peter's Church
2 Hopkins Memorial Manse
3 Congregational Church
4 Whiting House
5 Great Fordway
6 Site of First Armed Resistance
7 St. James Church
8 Barrington House
9 Henderson House
10 Ralph Taylor House
11 General Amherst Encampment
12 Fair Grounds
13 Ice Gulch
14 East Mt. and Sports Center
15 Monument Mountain

GREAT
BARRINGTON

Scale in Miles
Federal Writers' Project

Alford, Egremont, Monterey, and neighboring towns all come here for their shopping, for visits to the dentist, the lawyer, and the bank, to see a movie, and to sell farm produce. In summer the design for life in the town is marked by such little things as news stands piled high with New York, Philadelphia, and other metropolitan papers; instead of the usual movie and murder "thrillers," *Harper's Bazaar, Vogue, Esquire, The Atlantic Monthly,* and *The Nation* occupy places of prominence on the racks. Tradesmen are alert and eager to tell you about their town and its resources, their tongues loosened by frequent conversation with a type of customer not found in the average small town. The wide "Saratoga porch" of the rambling Berkshire Inn is gay with the bright colors of sports clothes; fine homes hang out signs reading "Over Night Guests" or "Luncheon, Tea and Dinner"; sleek motor cars dash about the countryside, and smartly dressed men and women stroll the streets. In season, the Yankee town goes urban.

The fastidious character of the summer trade has led to the passage of careful zoning regulations against garish "improvements." Townspeople have tried to keep gasoline stations and unsightly corners from destroying the charm of the community. Great Barrington has something of the dignity of Stockbridge, but there is a subdued bustle and an unconscious air of sophistication which Stockbridge does not possess. The isolation of the town's factories in outlying Housatonic helps to preserve an appearance of planned beauty.

Almost the whole of the permanent population, except the mill workers of Housatonic, has some contact with the recreation business. The sale, development, and improvement of property employ real estate agents, contractors, carpenters, masons, and plumbers. A retinue of cooks, gardeners, waiters, waitresses, maids, handy-men, caddies, hostelers, and even dog trainers serve the wealthy in summer.

The names of the region seem to have had their origin in a conviction of grandeur. Near the old fordway of the Housatonic River was the Great Wigwam, and the main council fire of the Mahicans. The ford itself was called the Great Fordway, and when the first bridge was thrown across the river it became, of course, the Great Bridge. Then there was the Great Road from Boston to Albany, which in the beginning was only an Indian trail through the forest to Westfield in the Connecticut Valley. Eventually, Great Barrington.

The prosaic probability is, however, that when a name was chosen at the incorporation of the town in 1761, the Berkshire settlement was afraid lest it be confused with the Rhode Island village of Barrington, until 1770 incorporated in Massachusetts. Both towns had been named for a famous apostle of religious tolerance, Viscount Barrington, of a family intimately connected with that of Cromwell, the Puritan liberator. The implications of the epithet are accidental, for, as someone has remarked, "Great Barrington is a name from which the modesty, perhaps, of its people is gradually eliminating the adjective."

White men invaded this valley as early as 1676, when Major John Talcott and his troops came up from Westfield in hot pursuit of a band of Narragansett Indians along the Great Road, then just an Indian trail. Near the Great Fordway the Indians escaped, but not before twenty-five braves had fallen and twenty others had been taken captive.

Almost before Great Barrington had time to get its bearings after separation from Sheffield in 1761, there came the rumblings of revolt against the English crown. General Thomas Gage, commander-in-chief of the royal forces in America, wrote in alarm to his king across the sea, "A flame has sprung up at the extremity of the province . . . the popular rage is very high in Berkshire and makes its way rapidly to the rest." The brand kindled in Great Barrington was passed along throughout the country. In August, 1774, a group of Berkshire men assembled on the village green near the present Town Hall in Great Barrington Center. As a protest against Great Britain's oppressive taxation, they seized the Court House, and even dared to prevent the King's Court from holding sessions. A rough stone marker on the spot relates that:

> Near this spot stood the first Court
> House of Berkshire County, erected 1764.
> Here August 16, 1774 occurred the first
> open resistance to British rule in America.

Like many historic "firsts," this claim has been open to question—though not in Berkshire.

When the Revolution actually broke out in 1775, the town was ready for a leading rôle. The news from Lexington did not arrive until noon on April 20, but by next morning a company of men started off to join the Colonial forces in the east. Despite this outburst of spontaneous patriotism, a number of well-to-do Tories lived in Great Barrington, the best known among them David Ingersoll, a magistrate and one of the leading citizens. He had represented Great Barrington, Sheffield, and Egremont in the General Court in 1770; four years later he was one of the "Addressors" who presented a laudatory tribute to Governor Hutchinson on the eve of His Excellency's departure for England. This courtesy to a royal governor angered Ingersoll's former friends. On more than one occasion he was roughly treated, and ultimately he was seized by a mob of Connecticut men to be imprisoned at Litchfield. By the Massachusetts Banishment Act of 1778 he was exiled, his house and lands were taken over by the Committee of Safety, and he had to borrow money to pay his passage to England.

During the early days of the war, a barbecue and feast were held on a nearby mountain summit, and after the sports of the day were over, the patriots erected a liberty pole. In the dark of the night, some Tories pulled it down. The patriots, infuriated by such audacity, elevated the pole on a treetop, filled the trunk of the tree with spikes, and posted a guard to see that no Tory again disturbed their sacred symbol of liberty.

Tradition has it that General Burgoyne with his Hessians received a welcome in Great Barrington rather unusual for a defeated army in ignominious retreat. The fanciful legend persists that the General and his officers were invited to a ball at the home of Elijah Dwight, and that Burgoyne "fell madly in love" with Peggy Brownlee, a local belle. For what confirmation it may be, a drawing in the town Library depicts Colonel Elijah Dwight in the act of offering the hospitality of his home to the defeated Englishman. Attired in the knee pants of aristocracy and wearing a three-cornered Continental hat, the Colonel is portrayed as a figure in full dignity. Burgoyne looks rather flabbergasted at an invitation to dance upon a polished floor, when he might well have expected to dangle at a rope's end.

Great Barrington's common folk joined Shays' Rebellion against the ruinous tax rate of post-Revolutionary Massachusetts. On one occasion a mob of Shaysites surrounded the court house, captured the judges, and warned them to hold no court until the grievances of the farmers were righted. Insurrectionaries marched on the jail to release the debtors. Bement, the keeper, fled his post to warn the people of Sheffield of the coming attack, while his wife, a bright, black-eyed little woman, attempted to hold the jail single-handed.

"Hand over the keys!" brusquely demanded a farmer of the Shays force. Mrs. Bement produced the keys, motioned the glowering men aside, and as she grimly unlocked the heavy door, sang out:

> Hark from the tombs a doleful sound,
>   My ears attend the cry.
> Ye living men, come view the ground
>   Where you must shortly lie.

Not content with the ominous prediction in poetry, she curtly elucidated in prose, "We will have you all in here before tomorrow!"

Among celebrities associated with Great Barrington was William Cullen Bryant. In 1816, as a young man, he trudged into town afoot, carrying his few possessions in a pack on his back. After seven months in law partnership with George H. Ives, Bryant bought the practice for a trifling sum; his immediate returns, according to old letters and ledgers, were likewise trifling. Four years later he became town clerk. When he decided to marry, his official position required him to post his own banns on the church door. So great was his diffidence in this embarrassing situation that he ran away; but he returned, perhaps a bit shamefaced, in time to stand up with Miss Frances Fairchild in the paneled southeast room of the HENDERSON HOUSE (now an annex of the Berkshire Inn on Main Street) and take his marriage vows.

During their stay in the town, the Bryants occupied various dwellings at one time and another. They first set up housekeeping in rooms in the RALPH TAYLOR HOUSE on South Main Street, and here their daughter Frances was born. Bryant's ledger reveals that items of family expense—"Rent, $30 for a year," and a bill sent by a zealous landlady "for pasturing the cow 28½ weeks at seventeen cents per week"—kept him in a constant state of apprehension. He is said to have been a "fiery young lawyer" with a large practice, but he never liked his profession. "I am plagued," he wrote, "with the disagreeable, disgusting drudgery of the law." His unhappiness in this work is reflected in one of his few poems written in Great Barrington. One summer day he stole away to the banks of the Green River and wrote:

Though forced to drudge for the dregs of men,
And scrawl strange words with the barbarous pen,
And mingle among the jostling crowd,
Where the sons of strife are subtle and loud—
I often come to this quiet place,
To breathe the airs that ruffle thy face,
And gaze upon thee in silent dream,
For in thy lonely and lovely stream,
An image of that calm life appears
That won my heart in my greener years.

During his stay Bryant wrote another poem, "The Death of the
Flowers," a somewhat somber but lyrical work once highly esteemed.

The melancholy days are come, the saddest of the year,
Of wailing winds, and naked woods, and meadows brown and sear.
Heaped in the hollows of the grove, the withered leaves lie dead;
They rustle to the eddying gust, and to the rabbit's tread.

In 1825 the poet forsook the shadow of the elms and the banks
of the Green and Housatonic rivers, and closed his law office forever
to enter the publishing world. He founded the *New York Review,*
and in 1826 became editor of *The New York Evening Post,* a position
he held until his death.

Bryant, whom Walter Prichard Eaton considers "as much a poet
of the Berkshires as Wordsworth of the Lake Country," wrote his
version of the tragedy on MONUMENT MOUNTAIN, the height
north of town. The mountain had been named from a rock cairn
which stood beside an Indian trail. According to the poet, the cairn
commemorates the fearful punishment of an Indian girl who had
fallen in love with her cousin. For such transgression of tribal laws,
the penalty was death, death at the foot of the towering cliffs.

. . . But when the sun grew low
And the hill shadows long, she threw herself
From the steep rock and perished. There was scooped,
Upon the mountain's southern slope, a grave;
And there they laid her, in the very garb
With which the maiden decked herself for death.
With the same withering wild flowers in her hair
And o'er the mound that covered her, the tribe

Built up a simple monument, a cone
Of small loose stones. Thenceforward, all who passed,
Hunter, and dame, and virgin, laid a stone
In silence on the pile. It stands there yet.
And Indians from the distant West, that come
To visit where their fathers' bones are laid,
Yet tell the sorrowful tale, and to this day
The mountain where the hapless maiden died
Is called the Mountain of the Monument.

Another Berkshire celebrity was Franklin Leonard Pope, the electrical genius, born in Great Barrington in 1840. His eventful career included the invention of the first system for the distribution of Wall Street quotations over the Gold and Stock Reporting Telegraph. Later, as a partner of Thomas Edison, he devised the rail circuit for the electric signal system on the railroads, and the Pope and Edison printer, an improvement in telegraph printing instruments. An inventor to the last, he died in the cellar of his Great Barrington home while tinkering with a transformer.

This electrical device had been invented in 1880 by William Stanley, Great Barrington resident who was later to found an industry still thriving in Pittsfield. In 1886 he decided to make a practical test of alternating current by obtaining enough subscribers to install his transformer and provide a lighting system for his home town. Great Barrington was the first town in the world to have an alternating current system in commercial use.

During the "gay nineties" in Berkshire, the town was a lively place. Summer people lavished fortunes on entertainments attended with all the extravagance of theatrical displays. "Fashion has decreed that the seaside sojourn at Newport should be followed ere returning to town by a fall visit to the Berkshire Hills." Ward McAllister, known as "Beau Brummel," joint-creator with Mrs. William Astor of New York's famous list of "Four Hundred," frequently visited the town. McAllister and other sportsmen organized week-long hunts for ruffed grouse and woodcock, plentiful in the neighboring woods. In a single week strings of seven hundred grouse and twelve hundred woodcock were shipped off to friends of the huntsmen—a practice quite within the law of the time.

President Dwight of Yale College, visiting Great Barrington in

1798, had found the village untidy and neglected in appearance: "The houses are, in many instances, decayed; the Episcopal Church is barely decent; the Congregational, ruinous. Few places can boast of a better soil or more delightful situation, yet I suspect few have been less prosperous or less happy. Religion has had here, generally, a doubtful existence." The people, he said, were "very wicked" and without a minister, and devout observers of the Sabbath had to go to other towns for worship while the unregenerate devoted the day to visiting, sitting in taverns, horse racing, and other frivolities.

Today, some 140 years later, churches are among the most striking features of the town. The CONGREGATIONAL CHURCH on Main Street, a beautiful building of blue dolomite erected in 1883, is the successor to many structures since the original parish was organized in 1743. Adjoining the church is the lavish HOPKINS MEMORIAL MANSE built to honor the Rev. Samuel Hopkins, pastor in Great Barrington, 1744-69. Of blue dolomite, it has cloisters to connect it with the church. Baedeker's *Guide to the United States* stars both buildings. The site of the church is approximately that of the Great Council Fire of the Mahican Indians. Beyond the Library is ST. PETER'S ROMAN CATHOLIC CHURCH, of native marble. Adjacent to the Town Hall is ST. JAMES' EPISCOPAL CHURCH, the oldest parish of this denomination in the county. The Episcopal society was established in 1762 to satisfy the Dutch, whose children the local Congregational minister refused to baptize because their parents were "unconverted." Nothing daunted, the Dutch settlers sent to Connecticut for an Episcopalian minister, who established St. James' Church. The first building, facetiously called the "glass house" because of its large windows, was opened in 1764.

In the center of the town is the showplace of the community, BARRINGTON HOUSE, a residence built by Mrs. Edward F. Searles over fifty years ago. A high stone wall and a thick stand of trees conceal it from the passerby. Planned gardens and a small lagoon with a broad stretch of greensward set off the house, in the midst of nearly a hundred acres of meadow and woodland. A chateau of the Renaissance period, it is constructed of blue dolomite, a native stone reputedly quarried right on East Mountain.

Barrington House, now a girls' school, is as interesting inside as out. The Great Hall and the dining room are in the English manor-house style, hand-carved native oak with enormous fireplaces. The atrium off the Great Hall is an adapted copy of the Erectheum, an almost pure example of Greek Ionic architecture. The French reception room, Louis XIV period, was shipped to Great Barrington in sections. No other building in the county, save possibly the Tytus Palace in Tyringham, can compare in pomp and circumstance.

The house, lagoon, and extensive property, though it has now passed to other hands, is a constant reminder of past connections with the Hopkins family. The story goes back to the earliest Hopkins of any fame in the Berkshires, the Reverend Samuel, about whom Harriet Beecher Stowe wrote a novel, *The Minister's Wooing*. Hopkins married a Great Barrington girl and was for twenty-five years the town minister. Always ardent in defense of his beliefs, he is best remembered for his defiance of slave-holding parishioners in Newport, where he went to preach against slavery after his Great Barrington charge. His doctrines, still surviving when Unitarianism made its appearance in New England, were ridiculed by supporters of the new theology as "Hopkinsianism" and as the gospel of the "willing-to-be-damned." In reality, Hopkins' books added little to the harsh severity of Jonathan Edwards. The family lingered on in Great Barrington, and Moses Hopkins, son of Samuel, was long one of its chief citizens. Mark Hopkins, Moses' son, was among those who left the Berkshires; in 1806 he migrated, going first to New York and later to Michigan. It was in Henderson, New York, that his son, Mark Hopkins, junior, the object of this genealogy, was born in 1813.

This offshoot of the Berkshires was destined to play an important rôle in American history. He was only a small merchant up to the age of forty-one. Six years after the first gold rush, he came across Collis P. Huntington in California, and the two went into business selling miners' supplies in Sacramento. Later the partners took in Leland Stanford and Daniel Crocker to form what came to be called "the Big Four." On a mere shoestring of capital and amid cries of "fraud" and "swindle," they built up the railroad system of the West. When Hopkins died in 1878 he left a fortune of twenty million dollars. A few years later his widow, a member of the Sherwood family of Great Barrington, took a second husband, Edward F. Searles. In 1885 Searles, an interior decorator and amateur architect, conceived the idea of the dominating palace-like structure of Barrington House.

After his wife's death in 1891, he lived on in the house, extending his land purchases from time to time until he became almost the feudal baron of the area. But Great Barrington, though priding itself as a "refuge from tax robbers" because its rate of $8.70 compared favorably with Boston's $17.00, tried to assess the Searles mansion at a valuation of six hundred thousand dollars. Despite the cost of Barrington House, estimated at amounts varying from five hundred thousand dollars to two million dollars, the owner was in no mood to contribute taxes for a trolley line (like all others in Berkshire now unused) which passed in front of his property. He built a great stone wall, adorned by turrets, to assure himself of privacy and quiet while he railed at the assessors' affront. He denied that his house was worth the assessed value; in fact he would sell it, he said, for only slightly more than a tenth of that sum. A group of Great Barrington residents, anxious to possess the place for a school, took him at his word and eagerly collected the necessary sixty-five thousand dollars. Huffy over the calling of his hand, Searles sold the property at the price agreed on and withdrew to another castle in Methuen, Massachusetts. After his death, litigation as to who would inherit the railroad millions dragged on for many years until the "Searles Will Case" became a legal classic. Today Barrington House is all that remains in Great Barrington of this strange family saga.

Great Barrington is said to have been built on or near the site of the Indian village, Mahaiwe, a name preserved by the leading bank and a principal street in the town. The Indian word is a corruption of the original "Neh-hai-we," meaning "place down stream." This is the interpretation given by an early minister, the Reverend Jeremiah Slingerland, who based his opinion on a letter written from Indian Town (later Stockbridge), November 8, 1735, in which mention is made of going to Mahaiwe down the river.

Great Barrington's attraction comes in great part from its natural setting on the river whose musical name, Housatonic—"the river beyond the mountains"—was given by the Indians. "Aussatonag," "Ousetonuck," and "Housatunnak," sometimes appear, but students of the Stockbridge Indian tongue maintain that "Hoo-es-ten-nuc" is the spelling which best represents the pronunciation.

A number of tablets mark spots of historic interest. One in the park in front of the Town Hall indicates the SITE OF THE FIRST

ARMED RESISTANCE to the British rule in America, July 16, 1774. On the grounds of the High School on Bridge Street another tablet shows where the Indians battled at the GREAT FORDWAY with Major Talcott and his soldiers in 1676. East of Green River Bridge on Mass 23 toward South Egremont a marker records the temporary ENCAMPMENT OF GENERAL AMHERST and his army in 1758 during the march on Ticonderoga.

The DR. WHITING HOUSE, built over two hundred years ago, was the scene of the surrender of the judges, Whiting among them, to the demand of the Shaysites for a written agreement guaranteeing that court would not sit.

The second oldest house in Great Barrington is the HENDER-SON HOUSE (1759), which once occupied the site of the Berkshire Inn and has been removed to the rear of the hotel. The two-story frame structure with lean-to roof and clapboarded walls, though remodeled in the roof and its "Connecticut entrance" a thing of the past, has some noteworthy interior details, particularly in the southeast corner rooms of the first and second stories. Supplies for the soldiers of the Revolution were stored in the house, which in 1777 served to confine General Burgoyne, then on his way to Boston as a prisoner of war.

Clustered together on the banks of the river a couple of miles north of the village proper are the few farmhouses that make up the hamlet of VAN DEUSENVILLE, one of the two smaller settlements of the town. This was a part of the region deeded by terms of the "sider and rum treaty" signed by Chief Konkapot and twenty other Indians in 1724. The tavern at Van Deusenville was once a stagecoach stop. In the early '40's June and Company used to put on their small circus and menagerie in the rear of the tavern. Among the animals that astounded the natives was a giraffe, advertised as·the camel-leopard and the first ever seen in the county. A minstrel show, like the accompanying circus the first of its kind to visit in Berkshire, was presented from an ordinary baggage wagon fitted up as a stage. The star of the evening was a husky Negro who came out in a fantastic costume to sing "Jump, Jim Crow," before a wide-eyed audience.

A few miles north of Van Deusenville is HOUSATONIC, the industrial section of Great Barrington, Precinct B of the town. Its hydro-electric plant of some three thousand horsepower derives power from the Housatonic River. The Monument Mills, incorporated in 1856, manufacture cotton warps in one of the largest cotton textile factories in New England. In 1870 the mills were combined with the Waubeek Mills, first manufacturers of Marseilles counterpanes. The B. D. Rising Paper Company is successor to a small paper mill erected by the Hurlbuts in 1856 and operated by them until 1862. At various times paper for the United States Government has been made here.

Some five miles north of Great Barrington gleams the white-cliffed wall of Monument Mountain. Its chief prominence, locally known as SQUAW PEAK, lies wholly within the limits of the township. Fragments of the peak have split away on either side, leaving a long, knife-like ridge of pinkish quartzite scarcely fifteen feet wide in some places. From this summit there is a view of the Housatonic, Williams River, Konkapot Brook, and the Green River, winding through the meadows and groves—an outlook as fine as anything in the county. Lake Agawam shimmers in the northwest and Beartown Mountain's long ridge stretches to the north and east. The notch in Warner Mountain, to the southeast, marks the spot where an earthquake long ago opened a wide gulf known as ICE GULCH or "PURGATORY," freezing cold the year round. A few miles south rise the slopes of old East Mountain, and still farther in the southwest is the great rounded dome of Everett, its fire tower outlined against the sky. On Monument Mountain, wrote Bryant, "the lovely and the wild mingled in harmony on Nature's face."

There is another version than his of the

> Tale about these reverend rocks,
> A sad tradition of unhappy love,
> And sorrows borne and ended, long ago.

According to a wilder account than Bryant's plaintive verse, a condemned Indian maiden was hurled from the lofty peak by her tribesmen. She saved herself by catching desperate hold on a long branch of an old pine tree, whose roots had found lodgment in a cleft in the rocks. The branch lowered with her weight but held firm, and as she clung to it, her screams echoed through the mountain stillness. For two days and nights she clung to the old pine until, just before the dawn of the second day, a fierce storm burst forth. Neither driving rain nor howling wind could drown out the girl's renewed shrieks. As the storm lulled a moment, her last plea for mercy rose to her tribesmen gathered on the mountain summit. While they gazed in horror, a bolt of lightning struck the tree and tore it from its anchorage in the cliff. The tree and the maiden spiraled downward in horrifying plunge, disappearing in the darkness. Long the Mahicans searched, but found no trace of tree or maiden. In memory of her whom the Great Father had taken in this weird manner the awe-stricken Indians fashioned a rude cairn. Strangers visiting the spot added their tribute of more stones, gradually forming the crude monument that now gives the mountain its name.

Some people think the cairn is one of many altars in New England erected to an unknown god to whom the Indians brought symbolic offerings. A plausible story is that Konkapot, chief of the Mahicans, declared that a monument should mark the boundary of land agreed upon in a treaty between his tribe and the Mohawks, by which the Mahicans were to have as their hunting grounds all the area within a day's journey of the pile.

Whatever the truth may be, THE CAIRN, a pyramid six or eight feet in diameter at the base, was fashioned before white settlers looked upon the Housatonic Valley. The curious may find it on the trail opposite the Squaw Peak Cabins on US 7.

On the western slope of Monument Mountain once stood the Pelton Farm, whose stone gatepost led to a tragi-comic episode. The wife and mother of the family occupying the house had died; as the funeral cortège was leaving the yard, the conveyance carrying the body hit the post. The force of the collision was so great that the corpse was thrown to the ground and the shock revived the woman, who not only showed signs of life but lived five years before she again passed away. Once more the funeral party started on its way, but this time when the hearse approached the post, the husband suddenly stopped the procession and solemnly warned the driver, "Be careful now, don't hit that post again!"

On South Main Street, away from the center, are the grounds where each fall the HOUSATONIC FAIR is held. On September 28 and 29, 1842, the Housatonic Agricultural Society, representing eleven towns in South Berkshire, opened the fair for the first time, in a field south of the Congregational Church. Until 1864, when the present property was acquired for fair purposes, the entire event went on in the town center—cattle on exhibit near the church, horses on Main Street, household manufactures in Academy Hall, and horse, racing in the street. Visitors came by buggy, in democrat wagons, carryalls, coaches, and even hayracks; those from a distance used the newly opened Housatonic Railroad.

At first the only exhibits were oxen, but gradually horses, sheep, swine, and poultry were added. Plowing contests were included at an early date; witness the proud tone of an 1854 report.

> The boys of Southern Berkshire are not to be beaten. They cannot well beat each other. Direct them to cut a furrow slice of precise width and depth, to lay it flat or oblique, and the direction will be obeyed to a hair. . . . How can a committee discriminate? When all stand upon equal footing, instead of making solemn award in discrimination of merit, the attempt to do which must necessarily be greatly perplexing, the more readier way would be to permit the competitors to "draw cuts!"

Prizes for female horsemanship were introduced about 1856, and an effort was made to foster competition in spading and in wood chopping, but no one seemed interested. Once three competitors appeared for the foot races, two of them Negro boys. The committee "experienced some embarrassment in regard to the first two prizes in view of the Dred Scott decision, the prizes having been taken by a couple of gentlemen who are not legally recognized as citizens, but another consideration overcame this scruple, that it was our duty to encourage the habit of running among a class who earn their freedom only by the best exercise of this power."

To the cattle show were added carnival events—bicycle teams, balloon ascensions, trapeze acts, and baseball games. By 1890 jugglers, contortionists, and strong men were part of the program and soon the Fair had a real midway with barkers, snake charmers, and automobile racers. When pari-mutuel betting was legalized in Massachusetts, gate receipts rose. These "extra added attractions" are sometimes strongly condemned by lovers of the good old-fashioned cattle shows, but the younger men who instituted them feel they have saved the Fair from extinction. The Fair still has its exhibits of field corn, cheese, butter, and home cooking.

Southeastward from Great Barrington, above the broad green valley of the Housatonic, spreads the wooded flank of EAST MOUN-TAIN. In the 1890's, Searles, builder of Barrington House, presented the town with a park here. The mountain is within a State Forest reservation on whose northern edge lies the GREAT BARRINGTON SPORTS CENTER. In the summer of 1938 a Dude Ranch complete with cowboys and rodeo occupied the Sports Center, but it is in winter that real activity appears—nine or ten ski trails and slopes on the side of Warner Mountain. Facilities include a skating rink, a log cabin canteen, and Pixley Tavern, a one-hundred-year-old inn on Mass 23, accommodating forty-five guests. The Center proudly proclaims that it "has everything from food to first-aid, toast to trails."

After weaving its way through miles of farming land to the west, the Green River joins the Housatonic a few miles due south of the village. Near the present bridge over the river on Mass 23 is a spot which inspired young Bryant to write his "Green River," beginning—

> When breezes are soft and skies are fair,
> I steal an hour from study and care,
> And hie me away to the woodland scene,
> Where wanders the stream with waters of green,
> As if the bright fringe of herbs on its brink
> Had given their stain to the waves they drink;
> And they, whose meadows it murmurs through,
> Have named the stream from its own fair hue.

There is an old tale associated with an earlier bridge over the Housatonic. A Mr. Van Rensselaer of Albany, New York, came one evening to the tavern that once stood near here. The night was not merely dark, but profoundly black. The host, previously acquainted with his guest, spoke of the remarkable pall that seemed to have settled over the river and its environs.

"By the way, Van Rensselaer," he said suddenly, "how'd you get over the river? Where'd you come across?"

"Oh, the usual place," answered Van Rensselaer, indifferently; "I came over the bridge, of course."

"But good heavens, man!" Root, the inn-keeper, exclaimed, "there's no bridge to come over! Why, they tore off the flooring today and there's not a plank been laid on it yet to my knowledge!"

"Nonsense! The bridge is there the same as ever. My horse came over it without any hesitation or difficulty. In fact, I gave him the rein, knowing he knew the road as well as I."

Root looked suspiciously at Van Rensselaer, thinking himself the victim of a "tall story." His guest reciprocated with equally questioning scrutiny. The next morning, to satisfy Root, the gentleman from Albany went to look at the bridge. There was not a single piece of planking; only the bare stringers were visible. Van Rensselaer fainted.

Almost directly south over US 7, about four miles from Great Barrington, is *SHEFFIELD*. No one who has ever seen its Main Street can forget the smooth green ribbons of grass that border it, the double row of majestic elms which curve gracefully over the sidewalk, and the long archway of a second double row of elms just beyond. This tree-vaulted avenue is delightful at any season of the year, whether in leaf of spring or in winter's black and ghostly tracery. Snow and ice turn it into a glittering fairyland.

Long before the visitor has entered this green tunneled vault he has seen another glory of the town, five miles to the west, the DOME OF MOUNT EVERETT. The summit (alt.2,624) may be over the line in the hilltop town of Mount Washington, but the great slopes that bolster it up belong to Sheffield. In morning light, or silhouetted against the setting sun, the high peaks form a brilliant background for the little town on the broad meadows of the valley.

A county historian in 1829 described Sheffield as consisting of "four churches, four general stores, one drug store, one hotel, one park, one town hall, and many small cemeteries." This is a bare picture of the village nearly a century after the town was incorporated and named in honor of Edmund Sheffield, Duke of Buckingham.

The first settler in Sheffield, Matthew Noble, was a hardy pioneer if ever there was one, when in 1725 he came alone into the wilderness, made friends of the Indians, cleared some land, and put up a log cabin. He then returned to Westfield for his daughter, and on horseback they made their way through the dense wood to set up the first home in Berkshire territory. Neighbors were slow in coming and often found themselves in legal difficulties when they did arrive. The

Dutch were like the wait-a-bit thorn in New England forests, a constant hindrance to those who would clear land. Under the New York Patent of 1705 the western portion of Sheffield was granted to the New York State Dutch, who were continually contesting priority of title with the English settlers. The grant, however, imposed certain conditions regarding rents, settlements, and improvements to be complied with before the end of a specified term of years. The provisos were not observed and the problem of title eventually straightened itself out.

New settlers then began to stream in, and a solid foundation was laid not only for Sheffield, but for all Berkshire. In 1735 the community considered itself permanent enough to vote that a meetinghouse should be erected. As an incentive to convert Berkshire forest trees into a house of the Lord, they decided to supply "three barrels of good Beare for the raising of the meetinghouse, twenty gallons of Rhumb . . . and twenty pounds of sugar to go with the Rhumb." A fine of ten shillings a day was imposed upon every able-bodied person who did not attend the raising. With these inducements to virtue and penalties for disobedience, the meetinghouse was soon completed on Sheffield Plain, the site of the original settlement, about a mile north of the present village center.

Attendance at church once every three months was compulsory in the early days. Four persons in the parish were not attending Parson Samuel Hopkins' services, and he requested the tithing man to bring them to meeting. Haled before a magistrate after refusal to obey the call to service, they had the choice of paying a fine or being put in the stocks, and the obdurate fellows chose the stocks. Other strict Sunday regulations were in force, as John Pell, one of the earliest lawyers in Sheffield, must have known when he decided to go traveling on the Lord's Day. He was promptly arrested and fined 20 shillings, the fine being equally distributed among the three towns through which he had passed.

Until its disestablishment in 1834, everyone in town was taxed to support Congregationalism. Citizens with other religious preferences had to be "certificated" by a civil officer. It is said that a town official, disgruntled at the growth of a rival to his own sect, once gave a certificate reading: "This is to certify that A.B. has renounced the Christian religion and joined the Episcopal Church."

When Berkshire and Hampden counties were separated in April, 1761, Sheffield was declared "to be for the present the county or shire town." The glory of this distinction was somewhat dimmed two months afterwards when the court house, built in the "North Parish," passed into the possession of Great Barrington. Later the capital of the county was moved again, this time to Lenox.

Although the town was never a large industrial center, there was a time when it manufactured its own cloth, carriages, and silverware. Three sizable tanneries were in operation and a number of iron forges, all long since inactive. For a while tobacco was an important local crop. Most of the manufacturing was carried on in the section known as ASHLEY FALLS, where quarries supplied marble for the Boston Customs House and the Court House in New York City. After the use of blocks of stone had been abandoned in the building trade, the marble was crushed into a fine gravel and shipped away to be cast into composite stone of any desired size or shape. Ground into powder for use as fertilizer, large quantities of Ashley Falls marble dust nourish the potato fields of Aroostook County, Maine. The quarry is easily discernible from US 7, and its presence known long before it is actually seen. The fine, almost snow-white powder films the nearby countryside, giving the small number of Negro quarrymen a curious, ghost-like appearance.

Sheffield is Berkshire's leading agricultural community, its foremost center for poultry raising and dairy farming. In 1935 a population of 1,810 kept 1,615 cows, almost a cow to a person. One of the best of the model dairies is on BALSAM HILL FARM, lying off a country road east of the river, owned by Albert Chapin, descendant of a line that has held the property for a hundred years.

HEWINS STREET, a group of old run-down farmhouses, lies on the same road about a mile and a half south of the Chapin farm. A sense of time retarded hangs like a veil over the scene. It is easy to imagine the unmechanized world of homespun and ox-carts a hundred years ago. Now the old chimneys exist mostly for swifts to nest in, the aged trees for owls and whip-poor-wills to flit through, the gray cliffs for moss to cling upon. In this atmosphere of the past dwells Charles Lindsay, the "water finder," a gentle old soul. His slow voice is awe-inspiring, as if he were gathering deep, earth-felt meanings. Charley knows things long forgotten by his fellow men.

His greatest "gift" is the power to find water with a forked stick. Men come from miles around to seek his skill and to hear him tell of his experiences in the practice of water-finding. He has suffered some defeats, he admits, when men have tried in vain to dig wells where his wand indicated water. Great ledges of rock, he declares, barred the way, else water would have been found.

Most of Sheffield's residents, even to the fifth generation, are descendants of the original settlers. Probably no other town in western Massachusetts has a larger percentage of native stock. The growing summer population, generally from New England, have bought and remodeled many of the old houses.

Despite its size, Sheffield has contributed men of unusual note to the world. Among them was Chester Dewey, famous in the 1830's and '40's as a botanist and mineralogist. His early interest in the plants and minerals of his native town was broadened by four years at Williams College. After graduation he was successively a Congregational minister, a tutor at Williams, founder of Berkshire Gymnasium in Pittsfield, a high school for young men, and finally a professor at Rochester University. In his day he was a leading authority on mineralogy, geology, fauna, and flora. His service to botany is recognized in the name of the *genus Deweya,* an umbelliferous plant of California, and to mineralogy in the name of deweylite, a form of magnesium silicate.

Sheffield was also the birthplace of Frederick Augustus Porter Barnard, son of Robert and Augusta Barnard. After filling various teaching positions, he was elected President of Columbia University in 1864, a position he held until his death. Though he established the School of Mines at Columbia, he is best known for broadening the scope of the university to include instruction for women. Six months after his death in 1889, a college for women was established, appropriately bearing his name.

Though Sheffield sent few soldiers to the Civil War, it did furnish George Francis Root, born here in 1820. At the time of the Civil War he was a member of the publishing house of Root and Cady in Chicago. President Lincoln had just issued his second call for troops. One afternoon Root was resting on a lounge in his brother's home when the words and music of "The Battle Cry of Freedom" came to him, and the next morning it was a finished song. He did not shoulder a musket, but he served his country well by writing her war songs, for after the initial inspiration he went on to write the popular "Tramp, Tramp, Tramp, the Boys Are Marching," "Just Before the Battle, Mother," and "The Vacant Chair."

About a mile below Sheffield village, a dirt road leads west from US 7 to a spot favored by picnickers—the remarkable group of boulders known as BARTHOLOMEW'S COBBLES. They have been described by a long-time resident of the village, Walter Prichard Eaton, as

a limestone formation rising in sharp little cliffs directly out of a sickle-shaped bend in the river, its white promontories picked out with green moss and crowned with pine and cedar.

One of the oldest houses in Berkshire is the ASHLEY HOUSE, in the Ashley Falls section, originally situated about a half mile from its present location. It was built in 1735 by John Ashley, a lawyer who was among the leading residents of Sheffield, as were his descendants after him. The two-story, pitch-roofed frame house has a large center chimney and interesting detail in the front and side entrances; a second floor room has unusual paneling. Ashley, appointed Major General of the Massachusetts militia by Governor Hancock in 1780, was an ardent patriot. Near the close of the Rebellion, when the period of enlistment of his troops had expired, they were preparing to return to their homes. The General was without legal means to compel them to remain in service but he determined to try the effect of his eloquence. After a few words of exhortation to fight on and win the gratitude of their country, he added:

"I am going to see who are the brave men and who are the cowards among you. I wish you to give me your attention. When I give you the word, 'Shoulder arms,' let every brave man bring his musket properly to his shoulder, and let every coward slink back out of ranks." He stopped a moment, then drew his sword, and added with a strong oath, "But remember, that I'll run the first man through the body that leaves the ranks. Attention, fellow soldiers: Shoulder arms." Needless to say, on sight of the sword, every man's musket sprang to his shoulder, and not a soldier broke ranks.

The old RED MILL at Ashley Falls has been in operation continuously for over two hundred years. Visitors are admitted from eight to five o'clock. The ancient millstones still grind out a little grain for local farmers. In the basement are huge, hand-hewn beams, some sixty feet in length, and below the floor may be heard the churning of the dark water. Upstairs, everything has been hand-rubbed to a glass-like smoothness over the span of years. The floor is polished to a lesser degree by the sliding of thousands of bags of grain and flour over it. The building sags in the middle because the timbers have rotted at the bottom where water splashed against them. At the back of the great room are two flour bolters, one still in service, though its silk sieve has not been changed within the memory of man. The smell of age pervades the place. Old cobwebs hang flour-heavy from the ceiling. Now the millstones rarely turn, for little grain is raised in Sheffield. Once in a while, some old-fashioned farmer brings in his oats and barley, along with a little wheat or buckwheat. Then the sluice is opened, the huge millstones begin to turn, and the whole building shakes and trembles, like a feeble old man who has suddenly renewed for a brief hour the activity of his youth.

Sheffield may well take an antiquarian's pride in its rare souvenirs of a century ago, two COVERED WOODEN BRIDGES. One time-worn structure is about a half mile east from the village center and spans the sluggish Housatonic. Traffic still passes over the bridge to the rattling of the floor boards, as it has for a hundred years. The venerable structure is 126 feet long and still has many of the original timbers hewed from the forests that were nearby when it was erected.

On what is now known as the back road from Sheffield Plain to South Egremont is a marble monument marking the LAST BATTLE OF SHAYS' REBELLION in 1787. About a hundred of Shays' men, nearly all from New York State, swept down on Stockbridge one night, and from there set off for Great Barrington to make a jail delivery, stopping long enough to replenish themselves at the tavern. The shorter way to New York State for the rebels would have been the "Knox Trail" through Great Barrington, and on this road the militia concentrated most of their forces. For some reason the Shays men went by the Sheffield back road, only to be overtaken by government troops. After ten minutes of fighting the rebels broke and fled, ending Shays' ill-fated Rebellion.

In the western part of the town of Sheffield and not far from the scene of Shays' last fight, is BOW WOW CEMETERY, a neglected but still interesting burial ground, first used several years before the Revolutionary War. It is the last resting-place of a number of well-known southern Berkshire families. The reason for the name "Bow Wow" has never been ascertained. The oldest grave is that of Simon Willard, who was killed in 1766, at the age of fifty-six years. There is a tradition that Willard was watching the progress of a severe thunderstorm from the doorway of his house, when he was struck by a bolt of lightning. His untimely end is recorded in the tombstone verse:

> Stop here ye gay and ponder what ye doeth,
> Blue Lightnings flew and swiftly seized my Breath.
> A more tremendous flash will fill the skies,
> When I and all that sleep in death shall rise.

Among Berkshire small towns, Sheffield is unique in having two Negro colonies—IN THE SANDS, at Ashley Falls, and NEW GUINEA, a mile west of the center. The 1930 census shows more than five times as many colored people in Sheffield as in the rest of the county. The original members of the colony were doubtless slaves who had escaped from Dutch settlers along the Hudson. Several Negro families live in New Guinea, in tiny houses or in shacks. One member of the colony, Lucius Darling, tells with glee of the only time in his life that he left Sheffield for an extended trip. He had a hankering to visit Georgia and Florida because his ancestors had lived there as slaves. "I was always anxious to see the South," he explains with a chuckle, "so I bummed my way down there on the freights. But oh, boy! Before I saw anything, they had me arrested and put on a chain gang, and I'll never forget it. I can still feel those clamps on my ankles. When I got loose I made tracks for Sheffield in a hurry, let me tell you, and I ain't left it since. Don't intend to, neither."

Chapter IX

IN THE FAR CORNER

ALFORD—Sett. 1740, alt. 960, pop. 210.

EGREMONT—Mass. 23, sett. 1730, alt. 740, pop. 569.

MOUNT WASHINGTON—Sett. 1692, alt. 1670, pop. 64.

Roads—West from Great Barrington, Castle Street runs to join East Road, unnumbered but marked, north to Alford; south of Alford Village West Road turns sharply to join Mass 23 at South Egremont. Going west and south from South Egremont, Mass 41 meets Mount Washington or Reservation Road, a steep and rocky dirt road to the summit of the town.

ALFORD, guarded by Tom Ball range on the east, clings closely to the border mountains between New York and Massachusetts. If you have the leisure to talk fishing, politics, or farming, you will find this smallest of Berkshire towns a friendly place, where a glass of cider drawn from a barrel in a cool cellar will whet your thirst for conversation. The tempo of the town has not changed with the coming of the "summer people" who have built fine new homes and restored old farmhouses that had fallen on lean years. Old-fashioned, easygoing Alford is not so far off the main traveled routes through Berkshire that it is a backwoods village, nor so close as to have taken on the frills of a summer resort.

The scattered houses, white church, and little school are built on a narrow shelf of land extending a quarter of a mile along the eastern side of the platter-shaped valley. To the south is Mt. Everett, one of the highest mountains in Berkshire, 2,624 feet above sea level. The western slopes of the valley are checkered with meadow and woodlots, mounting toward an unbroken line of trees against the sky.

Alford was originally part of the town of Great Barrington. The earliest settlers who came from Connecticut probably established homes in the valley about 1740. In October 1756, they purchased from the Indians the piece of land where Alford Center now stands. The area was called Shawenon, probably from Shauanon, who, with several other Mahican tribesmen, sold the tract for "Twenty Pounds paid to us in hand. . . ."

As early as 1769, the Barretts, Johnsons, Hulberts, Wilcoxes, Bakers, Mungers, and others who had settled here during a period of some twenty years tried unsuccessfully to separate from Great Barrington. On February 16, 1773, they finally obtained legislative consent, and Alford was incorporated. Perhaps the fame of the pious Colonel John Alford of Charlestown, a wealthy merchant who endowed a missionary society for Indians and a chair of theology at Harvard in 1761, had penetrated to the interior of Berkshire.

From the beginning Alford was a small industrial center. In 1763, when the first grist mill was erected, there were 375 people in the town. By the turn of the century, there were six hundred. In 1799, Sanford Fitch from Salisbury, Connecticut, settled in Alford and shortly afterwards discovered a rich deposit of high-grade marble. Investigation revealed several other deposits of equal quality, so that from 1800 to 1850 there were a dozen or more quarries operating in the town. Marble from Alford was used in the construction of the old City Hall in New York City, and in the State House, the Market, and the Law Building in Albany. Blacksmith shops, cooper shops, a reed factory, saw and grist mills, tanneries, and woodenware concerns were thriving. With wealth came community improvements. By 1817, a UNION MEETING HOUSE for the use of the Congregational, Baptist, and Methodist worshipers was under way. It still stands on the main road near the Town Hall and Schoolhouse.

The prospect of a bright future was blotted out when the railroad ignored Alford and laid its ties through other Berkshire quarry towns. Since long hauls over rough land delayed shipments and competition with the "iron horse" was impossible, marble quarries were abandoned, and in their wake small enterprises dwindled and died. Many former residents of Alford migrated across the state line to New York, some moving as far west as Ohio. An early historian of the town dryly records, "Alford is remarkable for changing its inhabitants." Population declined until the village lapsed into the rural calm in which two hundred residents abide today.

Dairying, farming, fruit growing, and catering to "summer people" make up Alford's economic life. For its size, more farming is carried on here than in any other Berkshire town. Acres of the fertile valley are planted to grain, corn, potatoes, and hay, while over the broad hillside pastures run herds of from ten to eighty cows. Alford is more interested in the revival of farming than in getting more summer business. Newcomers are welcome, of course, and many of them are "fine people," according to the townsmen. They show a healthy interest in the community, take part in civic and social affairs, and gradually come to be accepted as "real folks." But few of them cultivate the old farms they buy. They repair the houses, install bathrooms, keep the front lawn mowed, and plant shrubs and flower gardens. The back fields and pastures grow up to tall grass and brush, and the "south meadow" may be turned into a "tennis court, like as not." The summer people certainly dress the old farms up, but when the assessors come around, that's a different story. There is little left to assess. The barns hold motor cars instead of high-bred herds of cattle and stores of grain. Farm machinery has long been sold or discarded, and crop lands have gone to waste.

A few of the summer people have carried on where the old Alford natives left off. Occasionally a family become all-year residents of the town and continue to plant, hoe, and harvest. These are the newcomers Alford folks take to their hearts. They talk with pride of the stranger who came to town several years ago, bought a stock farm on a "shoe string," and went into debt to purchase adequate farm machinery. For five years he struggled to make a go of the place and pay off his obligations. Today he is one of the most successful farmers in the valley and one of the best liked. It takes brains and good farm sense to do a job like that. Alford residents recognize that sort of ability.

The town is looking forward to a program of road building during the next two years. Already plans have been made to construct a twenty-four-foot state highway from the junction of Mass 41 and Mass 23 in South Egremont through a corner of Alford. In another year it will be completed to the New York State Line, connecting US 7 in Great Barrington with NY 22 and US 9 in New York. Alford anticipates these new highways not so much because they will undoubtedly bring more tourists, but because they will provide better facilities for marketing farm products. The farmers sell their produce "down river," that is, down the Hudson River to New York City. As Alford is geographically in the New York milk shed, the efforts of the Massachusetts Milk Control Board to persuade these western Bay Staters to patronize the Boston market have never been successful. The town already has a network of good gravel and oiled county and town roads. There are miles of fine drives through the valley, flanked with open fields, woodlots, and neat, white houses under tall trees. The Alford valley is a joy to the eyes at any season: open stretches banked with winter snow; in the spring, the hillsides covered with pink and white apple blossoms; the fall foliage a mass of scarlet and gold and bronze.

Astride the West Stockbridge-Alford boundary line in the northeastern part of the town rises TOM BALL MOUNTAIN, the highest point of land in the township. On its western slope, just off the West Stockbridge road, is the DEVIL'S DEN, a cavern so wide that a load of hay can be driven into it. Within the den is a stone altar fashioned out of curiously arranged boulders; the stones before it are stained as if with sacrificial blood. The visage of Satan appears on a bank nearby. Water, constantly dripping, adds to the weird atmosphere, reinforcing a popular belief that Indians made sacrifices here. The cavern is on the property of Steve Mosher, who permits sightseers to cross his farmyard to reach the entrance.

You have to pass over a part of the Seekonk Brook on your way to the Den. The Seekonk is a branch of the Green River, and was probably named after an Indian who lived on its banks, although no one definitely knows the origin of the name. Over the West Stockbridge town line, the Seekonk, or Alford Brook, as it is sometimes called, is controlled by an exclusive trout-fishing club. Alford farmers have been roused to action by the restrictions and have posted their own lands along the stream. But if you know how to make friends and can show a little interest in farming, you will probably be able to do some fishing along the Seekonk. There is only one place in Alford where you are definitely warned to keep out. The gate of the old cemetery on East Road is strung with barbed wire. Only they who die in Alford may enter here.

South of Alford, in a narrow valley hemmed in by the Taconic Mountain Range, lies the village of *EGREMONT*. The base of Mt. Everett slopes into the southern corner of the town, thrusting out a bald knob called JUG END. One of the loveliest caves in the Berkshires is little CRYSTAL POOL, sometimes called the "Cave of Beauty," which is one of several on the slope of Jug End. The cavern is lined with stalagmites and stalactites, and shows masses of rockflow. At the end, a tiny grotto holds a pool of clear water, reflecting in its white-bottomed basin the delicate formations along the roof and walls of the cave.

Egremont was incorporated as a town in 1760 and named after Charles Windham, Earl of Egremont, the British Secretary of State during the Revolution. When the first English settlers came into the territory in 1730, they found a colony of Dutchmen, including Andrew and Robert Karner, and Isaac, John, and Jacob Spoor from the Hudson Valley, who had arrived twenty or thirty years earlier, in the belief that the territory was part of the colony of New York.

Egremont was part of the Indian grant made in 1724 by the "sider and rum treaty," signed by Konkapot, chief of the Mahicans, and twenty other Indians. By this compact, Indian Reservation, as it was later known, was set apart for the Mahicans. Previously they had made an agreement for ninety-nine years with Andrew Karner for half the reservation. According to tradition, Karner got possession of the land by a family alliance, allowing his sister to marry John Van Guilder, an Indian brought up by a Dutch settler. Van Guilder, whose name appears on most of the Indian deeds of southwestern Berkshire, is said to have persuaded his tribesmen to sign away their rights that he might have Mary Karner as his wife. Karner's title was contested by new white settlers, who naturally objected to this arrangement, but the General Court of Massachusetts granted the land to him and his heirs forever. The Karners were among the wealthiest settlers in Egremont.

On Karner's death in 1781, his land, rented at the time, was left to the Van Guilder family. When the leases expired in 1832, they attempted to gain possession of their inheritance but, rebuffed by the courts, withdrew entirely from the state. Their name is preserved in Guilder Hollow, Guilder Brook, and Guilder Pond, all except the last in Egremont township.

During the first seventy-five years of its life, Egremont remained a typical New England village, with grist and sawmills, small farms, tavern, meetinghouse, and general store. The stagecoach that followed the turnpike from Albany to Hartford stopped in the town to break the journey over the hills. Water power from the hillsides was abundant, and small manufacturing plants were soon established, producing chairs, leather goods, glue, boots and shoes, harnesses, and gin. Several marble quarries yielded high-grade stone. Egremont was at its most prosperous period in the 1840's, and by the middle of the century the population had mounted to more than a thousand.

When David Dalzell came to Egremont from Hudson, New York, in 1845, he purchased a carriage factory from Major Karner. Dalzell and his two sons worked out novel techniques in the manufacture of case-hardened axle boxes. Forty years later the axle works was the leading enterprise in town. When "horseless buggies" came in, the Dalzells turned to automobile axles and the company proudly boasted that "the King of the Sandwich Islands, the President of the United States, and Henry Ford" were among their patrons. In the early part of the twentieth century the factory was moved to Michigan to be near the center of the automobile industry. The Dalzell plant in Egremont continued to produce axles for carriages and wagons, until the overwhelming popularity of the motor car put an end to the business. Dalzell Brook still runs through South Egremont, but not a trace of the factory is left.

Contemporary with the axle works was a unique establishment for the manufacture of the "Bliss Hoof Cutter," an invention whose object was "to supply a tool for hoof cutting that could cut the hardest and largest feet without the hard labor that has always accompanied this work."

None of the industries humming in Egremont a hundred years ago remains today. Lack of railroad connections and inability to meet the stiff competition of cities with better locations and resources started Egremont on the downgrade. The twentieth century found the little village drifting into shabby decline.

In 1932 along came Olde Egremont, Inc. The corporation was really an ambitious real estate scheme organized to preserve the "antiquity, traditions and architecture of the town." It had an immediate success, and before the first year had passed, the firm owned one-eighth of the assessed valuation of the community. But in the years since then they have seen a lessening of enthusiasm and an increase of financial difficulties. The future of Olde Egremont is uncertain, but the town still hopes it may make a comeback. In its first flush of success, the corporation owned about sixty buildings, including Olde Egremont Tavern, a part of which was built in 1830, the Egremont Inn, built in 1793, the Village Smithy and Garden Shop, Jug End Barn, the Egremont Store, and even the "Ole Swimming Hole." Permanent ownership of Olde Egremont, Inc., and of all real estate within the area was reserved for community development under unified control. Anyone wishing to come to Olde Egremont and build a home had to be admitted to the Olde Egremont Association. If his credentials were acceptable, he purchased stock in the company, to cover part of the expenses of road-building and to provide electricity and water for the colony. He then became a life member of the corporation and the owner of a summer home without the necessity of paying taxes, water, electricity or repair bills.

Berkshire's recreational advantages are always a lure to city dwellers, and a good many accepted Olde Egremont's invitation to sign up for a home where fishing, golfing, riding, tennis, swimming, and other sports were easily available. In the sleepy community, city people nostalgic for the "olden days and olden ways" they had never experienced, were sold the scenery, the sky, the stars, and country food cooked by city chefs. It was the food of their Berkshire forefathers, minus the lumps and the shucks. There is no industry and little farming in Egremont, but "ye olde tavern" and "ye olde spinning wheel" were revived. By a careful spin or two, Olde Egremont experimented with the past in order to make a living.

Although swank Olde Egremont, Inc., is apt to usurp the attention of visitors to the town, there are still some evidences of the time when it was just plain old Egremont. Near the village is the TULLER HOUSE, the first brick structure in the town. It was built in 1761 by John Tuller, one of the early settlers, from bricks baked on his farm. The Masonic emblems, a square and a compass, and the year 1761 are incorporated in the masonry, with the initials "A" for Anna and "JT" for John Tuller, and a heart engraved between to show a happy union.

About the time that Tuller was building his house, the first church in Egremont was organized, and in 1767 the Reverend Eliphalet Steele, the first pastor, came to its pulpit. He seems to have been well liked and respected until the time of Shays' Rebellion. Steele took the side of the government, while most of his parishioners, burdened with debt, sided with Shays. They invaded his house one night, mussed him up a little, wrecked the furniture, and stole his watch and his clothes. When the insurgents were defeated by government troops in Great Barrington in 1788, they fled through South Egremont into New York, the state militia at their heels. Wounded men were cared for by the sympathetic inhabitants of Egremont at the old tavern which stood on the site of the present Egremont Inn.

Churchly and religious matters were events in so small a community. The "Methodist saint," Francis Asbury, traversed all this region shortly after making himself a bishop. His mild preaching on sin and redemption, with the hope of Heaven and fear of Hell, probably reinforced Methodism as the favored denomination of the "far corner." The fiery, long-haired, and otherwise eccentric shouting revivalist, Lorenzo Dow, best-known of the queer circuit riders of the early nineteenth century, also penetrated the fastnesses of Mount Washington and put up, as his diary shows, with a "strongly Methodist brother" in Guilder Hollow.

Of the local clerics the best-remembered was Aaron Kinne, a preacher of the old type, who lived in Egremont in 1803 and for twenty years sermonized in the various towns of southern Berkshire. During a severe drought a special meeting was called that all members of the church might pray for rain. The crops were drying up and the meadows looked as if they had been scorched by fire. Mr. Kinne was asked to lead the meeting, and when the congregation had gathered, he called loud and long upon the Almighty to send rain to the Berkshires, especially to Egremont and the adjoining town of Alford. Then, closing his prayer, he paused and added as an afterthought, "But after all our petitions, O God, we would not presume to dictate, but we would advise."

Not far from the meadow whence Mr. Kinne is said to have sent up his admonition, a curious old marble tombstone was recently uncovered in a pasture lot on FENTON BROOK FARM. The top of the stone had been broken off, but on the spotted surface of the lower section this legend was deeply chiseled:

COGNAC
AND
OLD RYE
ET HOC GENUS OMNE

No one knows why a tombstone should have been erected to cognac, rye, and all of that family, but it looks as if a Berkshire wag, electing to forswear old friends, had literally buried temptation.

In the very far corner of the State, on a mountain-fringed plateau south of Egremont, and two thousand feet above all neighboring towns, is the tiny hamlet of *MOUNT WASHINGTON,* with its sixty-four hardy inhabitants. The only approach to Mount Washington from Massachusetts is a narrow gravel road climbing out of South Egremont along a small shelf of land. From other towns one must go by prolonged detour to get around Mt. Everett. No state highway, no railroad, and no store serve the town; no local post office, for residents get their mail from Copake, New York, by rural delivery. In 1938, no births, no deaths, no marriages.

The approach to Mount Washington from South Egremont is an adventure into real backwoods country. The narrow road clings to the steep mountainside; a rickety wooden fence offers doubtful protection from a long fall into the ravine below. The road leading up to the lookout on Mount Everett is too narrow for two cars. When you round a curve and find someone approaching, one driver has to back to a turnout. Mount Washington is the most isolated and backwoods town in Berkshire. Houses are widely scattered, roads are never wide enough for two cars to pass without slowing up. Yet out here "in the sticks" of Mount Washington, you see luxurious automobiles and liveried chauffeurs unpacking sumptuous lunches for a picnic under the trees.

The center of the town—a little white church and a Town Hall that looks like a woodshed—occupies a lonely clearing at a crossroads. You would never know it was the "center" of a town, unless some native told you so. Yet down the road a mile or so is a smart tea house with a menu and the accoutrements of Fifth Avenue. This is Mount Washington's only condescension to the visitors who invade the town in summer. In winter the town is locked up by narrow, snow-filled roads and slippery hillsides.

For years Mount Washington has attracted summer visitors who "put up" at local farmhouses and boarding houses. The chief of these is the "Penny Royal Arms," run by the Spurr family for over half a century in the shadow of Mount Everett. It's a sprawling old house, set close to the dusty gravel road, with a mixture of dogs, children, and "visitors" sitting or walking over the fields that encroach on the house from every side. The trip to Mount Washington is worth the dusty roads and occasional bumps.

Almost cut off from neighbors by its ring of mountains, Mount Washington has always lived to itself. Even the details of the founding of the town, the names of the first settlers, whence they came and why, are not absolutely known. For years it was believed that a group of men from eastern Massachusetts and Connecticut first penetrated the mountainous region about 1730. A recent discovery seems to indicate that there were settlers in Mount Washington forty years earlier than that. In the 1880's Herbert Keith, a railroad surveyor from Boston, came to Mount Washington to lay out a route for a railroad over the Taconics between Poughkeepsie and Springfield. The railroad was never built, but while it was under consideration Keith became interested in the town and started an investigation into its history. When he died in 1922, he left a wooden box filled with original notes, maps, genealogical tables, and two small pamphlets published by the *Berkshire Courier* of Great Barrington. The box is still in the possession of the selectmen, who believe, as did Keith, that this is the oldest town in Berkshire County. Mr. Keith felt he had proof of the coming of a colony of Dutch farmers from the Hudson River Valley before the close of the seventeenth century. The plateau was close to the Dutch settlements along the Hudson, and would have been an ideal refuge from Indian attack. Keith's principal reason for his contention is a report made to the General Court of Massachusetts in 1752, listing the settlers then living west of Sheffield, and recording the number of years any one person had cultivated his acreage. It indicated that there were six families here at the time, and that the land of one John Hallenbeck had been under cultivation for sixty years. This would certainly place one settler here in 1692, making Keith's claim credible.

Soon after 1730, when settlers from the east had arrived, this little corner of land became involved in difficulties because of the anti-rent wars in Columbia County, New York. The governor of that state had in 1715 given Robert Livingston, one of the large land-owners along the Hudson River, a grant which extended into the present Mount Washington. As no definite boundary between the colonies of Massachusetts and New York had been drawn at the time, there was continual dispute over the border territory. The "mountain men" from Mount Washington preferred that their land belong to Massachusetts, where citizens were "free holders" who owned their acres outright. In New York, land was held by feudal tenure under the grant of some great landowner like Livingston. But Livingston was determined that the "mountain men" should pay him rents, and took to open warfare. Violence ruled the border. In 1755, William Race, a Mount Washington pioneer, was shot to death by members of the Livingston party in a section of town near the present Mt. Race, probably named for the murdered man. Six years later, Livingston's hirelings burned several houses in Mount Washington and drove the settlers to seek aid from Sheffield. In 1753 the despairing inhabitants of the area petitioned the General Court of Massachusetts that

. . . your honors in Your Great Wisdom and in your wonted Goodness, would be Pleased for to settl us in our Possessions, or, if not, to make a Grant of Land to us in a Place to the East of Taghknack and to the west of Sheffield, to wit in the mountain, where there is a valley of Land Lying betwene two Great mountains, and may contain a few famileys, Even to the number as to make a small Parish; but it will cost a Great Deal of time to make a road in to the mountain on both side, or to Deal with your Poor subjects as in your Great Wisdom and wonted Goodness shall think fitt, and we, your poor Petitioners as in Duty bound Shall ever Pray.
    Joseph Loomis, George Robinson, Jan Hollenbeck,
    Jacob Loomis, Joseph Orlcutt, Michael Hollenbeck.

The petition was not granted, and the "mountain men" continued their struggle for existence. The boundary dispute was not finally settled until 1787, although Mount Washington had been incorporated as a town eight years earlier.

At the height of Mount Washington's activity, in the 1840's and 1850's, charcoal from the town furnaces supplied the iron smelters at Mount Riga in Connecticut, the iron works in Copake, New York, and Dalzell's axle factory in Egremont. As elsewhere in Berkshire, industry declined and eventually disappeared when the railroads made some towns prosperous and left others to "stew in their own juice." After 1860 Mount Washington became a farming town, renowned for its potatoes. The soil was fertile along the plateau and not a potato bug disturbed production. But even farming gradually declined in the tiny town until by 1912, so Herbert Keith reported, not a single person was making his whole living off the land. Some people worked in New York, others took in summer boarders, and rumor had it that still others earned an illicit livelihood by distilling "moonshine." Dr. Gilbert Van der Smissen, the personal physician of Raymond L. Ditmars, famed curator of the New York Zoological Park, is now making an attempt to revive potato-raising as a profitable crop.

Dr. Van der Smissen and Dr. Ditmars originally came to Mount Washington to hunt snakes, an old business in the town. The most famous snake hunters were members of the Whitbeck family; Russell Whitbeck, caretaker of the 1200-acre Mt. Everett State Reservation, still hunts them occasionally. The snakes are desired, particularly in universities, for herpetological experiment or observation. Since they live on almost inaccessible rock ledges east and west of the town, tourists rarely encounter them.

When Dr. Van der Smissen's sisters also came to Mount Washington, they lived in the OLD COTTAGE on the main road. This is said to have been at one time the home of Mother Ann Lee, founder of the Shakers in America, and the place where the first Shaker service in New England was held. Near the cottage is MOUNT WASHINGTON CEMETERY, perhaps the oldest burial ground in Berkshire, although the earliest legible stone, that of John Dibble, is dated 1772.

Among other "firsts," the town claims the original Methodist church in the county, organized before Bishop Asbury's visit in 1789. Keith, the town's most recent "booster," has asserted that Mount Washington exercised "far more Christian charity than would be tolerated even now (1912) in many places. From earliest times the funds from the minister's lot were divided among several denominations, differing widely in theological belief." Mount Washington carries on its tradition of tolerance, using Union Church on East Road as the spiritual center for the entire community.

Eighty-five years ago the southwestern part of the township was hardly noted for virtue or piety. This was "Boston Corner," probably so named because it was as far as you could get from Boston and still be in Massachusetts. The nickname was later changed to "A Corner of Hell," and still later, in the nineteenth century, to "Hell's

Acres." There is an old superstition that the soil, underlaid with minerals, is always hot. More likely "Hell's Acres" had reference to the number of horse thieves and counterfeiters who used to make the spot their hide-out in pre-Revolutionary times.

Boston Corner, shut off from the town of Mount Washington by a high mountain, was in the 1850's the scene of an illegal prize-fight. Massachusetts had ceded the spot to New York in 1853; New York did not accept it until 1855. In this No-Man's Land, sporting gentlemen of the "Short Boys" and the Empire Club thought to evade the laws of both states by pulling off the battle. James ("Yankee") Sullivan and Jack Morrissey were the principals. To keep in trim for the bout, Morrissey had walked four miles daily, in shoes that weighed five pounds each. Amounts from $500 to $1500 were wagered on the outcome of the fistic duel. Sullivan ruled the favorite.

The battlers fought thirty-seven rounds with bare fists. One report gave Sullivan the palm in each of the rounds, total fighting time being clocked at fifty-five minutes. There was a row at the end of the thirty-seventh round, after which the Yankee did not "come to time." A gentleman who said he was at the Corners "on business" gave an account of the climax: Morrissey held Sullivan's head under his arm, and had it not been for a knock-out blow from one of Sullivan's seconds, Morrissey would have broken the Yankee's neck. Sullivan, recovering, struck Morrissey while he was still stretched out. "Foul" was called and the umpires pinned the victory on Morrissey.

After the prize-fight, rumor and rage went wild. Morrissey was reported dead on October 15. He was alive October 16. The sporting gang resorted to Philadelphia to settle bets and wipe the slate clean. Sullivan, infuriated by the decision, offered to stake a thousand dollars on another run-in with his rival any time within sixty days. There was indignation everywhere, from the farmer in the dell to the scion of acres on the Hudson. The would-be sports who were not able to horn in on the fun cried out loudly—"Get them!" The appeal was heeded by Governor Seymour of New York, who looked into the matter of his jurisdiction and took measures for haling the pugilists into court. Morrissey sailed for England November 7.

Prizefighter "Yankee" Sullivan put up bail of $1500 on Saturday, said the press of November 15, 1853, and left for New York that night. Mr. James Sullivan, gentleman, took tea with Sheriff Pease of

Lee, before departing for the metropolis. Said the righteous, in bitter criticism, "Sullivan will never show his head in Massachusetts again." Boston Corner returned to its chores.

Along East Road, which winds upward from South Egremont to the base of Mt. Everett, is the site of "SKY FARM," home of the "Apple Blossom Poets," Elaine and Dora Goodale, whose verse was written when they were twelve and fourteen years of age. The Goodales were very much of the Berkshires; their grandfather had been a prosperous farmer and owner of a marble quarry in Egremont. Their farmer father, Henry Sterling Goodale, was also a poet. Between 1870 and 1885 poetry by the sisters and their mother in *St. Nicholas, Harper's, Good Housekeeping,* and other magazines was widely read and admired. A poem in their first volume (1878) gave a title to the book and bestowed an epithet on the young girls. It is a description of their home in apple blossom time:

> The sky is rich in shimmering sheen
>   Of deep, delicious blue;
> The earth is freshly, softly green,
>   Of one translucent hue;
> The choir of birds in wood and field
>   Ring out a happy chime;
> The trees their fairest foliage yield
>   In apple-blossom time.

Also native to the Mount Washington region was the book published two years later, *In Berkshire with the Wild Flowers.* Twenty-nine poems supposedly cover all the local flora—hepatica, anemone, trailing arbutus, mountain laurel, and others. The undistinguished versifying in the early Bryant tradition is now and again relieved by poems as imaginative as the one on the Indian Pipe, beginning

> Death in the wood
> Death, and a scent of decay;
>   Death, and a horror that creeps with the blood,
> And stiffens the limbs to clay;
>   For the rains are heavy and slow,
> And the leaves are shrunken and wan,
>   And the winds are sobbing weary and low
> And the life of the year is gone.

Accessible from the South Egremont road into Mount Washington is the Bash Bish State Forest, pride of Mount Washington, where the famous BASH BISH FALLS make a drop of two hundred feet. When the narrow mountainside road emerges into a clearing the road branches, the right fork going to Bash Bish. From a bridge across Bash Bish Brook, near the New York State Line, a trail leads north through the woods to PROFILE ROCK atop a perpendicular cliff. In June the whole area is thick with azaleas, and the forest floor carpeted with ladyslippers. The rock overlooks a gorge, into which plunge Bash Bish Falls.

In the pool two hundred feet below, according to an Indian legend, is to be seen the "spirit profile" of the beautiful Indian maiden, White Swan, the daughter of a witch who lived beneath the falls. The girl was married to a handsome young brave whom she loved dearly. Because she proved childless, her husband after some years took another wife. White Swan began to pine and brood by the falls, often gazing for hours into the water below. To the despairing maiden came one day the voice of her mother, whom she had never known, calling to her from beneath the cataract. With an answering cry of joy, she plunged over the cliff, to drown just as her husband came through the forest. He leaped after her in a vain attempt at rescue. Next day the brave's body was found, but his bride had disappeared. They say the lovely maiden and her mother still live behind the falls, and on moonlight nights White Swan smiles in the clear pool.

Chapter X

THE BERKSHIRES INVADED

NEW MARLBOROUGH—Sett. 1739, alt. 720, pop. 921.

MONTEREY—Mass 23, sett. 1739, alt. 1200, pop. 325.

TYRINGHAM—Sett. 1735, alt. 900, pop. 243.

SANDISFIELD—Mass 8, sett. 1750, alt. 880, pop. 471.

Roads—About 5 miles east of Great Barrington off Mass 23 is the Lake Buel Road running south to New Marlborough. Monterey is on Mass 23. Off Mass 23 north from West Otis is an improved road to Tyringham. To reach Sandisfield, continue east to Otis on Mass 23 and then south on Mass 8 to New Boston.

Not one of the towns of New Marlborough, Monterey, Tyringham, and Sandisfield, is on the railroad, and only Monterey and Sandisfield are on a main highway. Manufactures and farm produce were exported by wagon and ox team in the old days, but the advent of the railroad through Berkshire in the 1840's diverted all traffic toward towns more fortunately situated. The four sequestered southern Berkshire settlements watched factories move away and saw men grow tired of farming worn-out lands. Slowly the cities drained backwoods Berkshire of its young blood.

The isolation that once crippled these Berkshire villages now may prove their saving grace. Today the region is a haven for summer people in quest of hills, rivers, and the smell of growing things after months of subway jams and city uproar. To the practical Yankees of the villages, the summer army of occupation means a market for farm produce and a season of employment. They would never willingly admit that they rather welcome contact with urban sophistication, and that doings and sayings of the warm-weather transients provide topics of conversation all winter long.

NEW MARLBOROUGH'S first settler, Benjamin Wheeler, built a shack here in 1739. Miles of forest separated him from his home and family in Marlborough, Middlesex County, which had been given a grant of this western territory. A Berkshire annalist, drawing on his pipe, meditated at length about this lonely pioneer: "Picture the fellow, sitting all alone in the forest, thinking of the hills back of hills that cut him off from his folks. There must have been times he felt like running back, but he didn't, and the only thing that ran was the silvery brook near his first rude cabin. They even named the creek Anthony's Brook, after the last Indian to live in the town, and poor old Benjamin Wheeler didn't get so much as a brook named after him, much less a township, like ought to have been done."

Wheeler found the Indians friendly, although they forbade him to fire a gun in the forest because the noise frightened away the game. When he protested, they gave him a bow and arrow, and Ben almost starved that first winter. He was about to kill his horse or dog for food, when settlers from Sheffield, who had heard of his plight, arrived with provisions. This is the "memorable hard winter" recorded in the town annals. He brought his family next year from the older Marlborough and built a permanent home by Anthony's Brook where five generations of Benjamin Wheelers continued to live.

The four townships adjoining New Marlborough had been established along the Great Road between Westfield and Sheffield in 1735. It was hoped that a line of settlements between the Connecticut and Housatonic Valleys would open a shorter route for the Colonial troops to move against the French and their Indian allies.

New Marlborough, organized as a district in 1735 and incorporated in 1759, spreads over shallow valleys through which flow the Konkapot River and its tributaries. Low rolling hills separate it from the Housatonic Valley on the west, and another winding range cuts it off from the Farmington Valley to the east. There are no hotels, no railroad, and no state highway, except for a short stretch that crosses the southwestern corner. But the town is proud of its mileage of well-kept macadam and dirt roads, its trout streams, hills, and meadows. Mass 23, the road to New Marlborough from Great Barrington, forks southeast at the Lake Buel store not far from the Great Barrington-Monterey town line. It runs through the forest, past Lake Buel, into the small settlement of Hartsville on the banks of the Konkapot, famous throughout western Massachusetts for its fishing. Just beyond the center of Hartsville a dirt road runs east to the FEDERAL FISH HATCHERY, which keeps this section of the river stocked with rainbow and brook trout.

The Konkapot, named after the famous chief of the Mahicans, provided water power for industry from 1836 to 1876. Along its banks a dozen or more factories produced paper, textiles, powder, woodenware, and carriages. Today the only survivals of this era are a few ruined dams, half-hidden by brush.

Driving south from Hartsville, you come to NEW MARL-BOROUGH VILLAGE, the oldest corner of the five-sided township. Prim white houses cluster about the Village Green, and very old trees shadow the plot. The little church set apart near the head of the common is crowned with a dome in place of the traditional New England spire. But the town itself is a chip off old New England, and the newcomers who have restored some of its old homes would like to keep it unspoiled.

In times past, the Village was a midway station on the old stage-coach line operating from Hartford to Albany, and could claim taverns, fine houses, and a population of over five hundred, of which only a few scattered families remain. The oldest house in the New Marlborough township is the RICHARDSON HOUSE, built in 1745. In this sturdy, square structure, with low ceilings and enormous fireplaces, was born Mrs. Laura Smith (Catlin) Richardson, who initiated the practice of putting small American flags on the graves of soldiers buried in national cemeteries.

In 1833 the learned blacksmith, Elihu Burritt, operated a smithy here, and the BURRITT STATUE in the Village commemorates the polyglot workingman.

In the OLD BURYING GROUND of New Marlborough, about half a mile from the Village on the road that runs left from the center, black field-stones mark the graves of the early settlers. Much of the lettering is as legible as when it was first carved, though over-grown with lichens and green moss. Here, sheltered by a tall old pine, is the grave of the town's first settler, Benjamin Wheeler. Not far off, on one of the largest stones in the cemetery, is inscribed an unusual tribute to a beloved stepmother:

Sacred to the memory of
Mrs Elisabeth Strong, 2'nd
Wife of the Rev. Thomas
Strong, late of New Marl-
borough deceased, wife departed
this life Dec 21 AD 1775, in
the 55, year of her age.

The Stepchildren of the deceased
remembering with gratitude
her kindness to them, in their
tender years, place this stone.

Ye Step-mothers!
follow her example & ye
shall not lose your reward

Amusing, despite its labored gravity, is the epitaph on the stone erected
to Mrs. Elizabeth Sheldon:

Sacred
to the memory
of Mrs. Elizabeth
Sheldon wife of Mr
Erastus Sheldon
who departed this
life Jan 5th 1809
AE . 24

Oh may you scorn these
cloths of flesh
These fetters and this load
And long for evening to undress
That you may rest with God

New Marlborough was a Whig stronghold until 1832, when the
Democrats were roused to champion Andrew Jackson's cause. As
newspapers were still rare in country towns, those that did reach the
people were believed to print only gospel truth. Taking advantage of
this attitude, the local Jacksonians arranged to have two hundred
copies of the ardently Democratic *New York Evening Post* sent into
New Marlborough each week. They estimated that a month of
Jacksonian newspaper propaganda just before election converted more
than forty Whigs.

Colonel Fitch was the Democratic and Squire Benjamin Sheldon
the Whig candidate for representative. The vote resulted in a tie and

had to be repeated. This time the Whigs were determined to spike their opponents' guns, and set out on a frenzied campaign to collect votes. Since the Democrats proved no less vigorous, the contest became so bitter that even good neighbors lost faith in one another. Two old friends of long standing in the town, Fairbanks, a Whig, and Coles, a Democrat, agreed that neither would vote. As election day approached, the Whigs told Fairbanks that his neighbor had double-crossed him and had already gone to the polls. Fairbanks marched into the hall in a rage and cast his ballot amid loud Whig cheers, while the Democrats proceeded to round up the innocent Mr. Coles and bring him in just in time.

One loyal Democrat, named Aaron Stevens, had been seriously injured some days before, but he was nevertheless propped up in a wagon and carried to the polls. The Whigs retaliated by sending another wagon for a Mr. Woodworth of Mill River, who, in the last stages of tuberculosis, was delivered at the polls in his bed, and died that night. Two minutes before voting ended, one party found a man lying drunk in a woodlot, bundled him off to the polls, and placed a ballot in his hand. When his arm was given a good shake by one of the assistants, he had done his duty. Despite this fantastic competition, the last ballot still showed the election to be undecided.

Two miles to the south of sleepy New Marlborough Village is the more alert community of SOUTHFIELD, praised thirty years ago as a "modern village, spic and span . . . neat and clean looking." The description still fits the large white houses set in lawns and gardens. Labor today is largely concentrated in the only surviving manufacturing plant, the Turner and Cook Shop, which in its prime turned out the largest number of rawhide whip centers of any plant in the United States; now it makes belt pins for industrial machines.

The strip of state highway that runs from Southfield to the Connecticut State Line was won only after some shrewd strategy by residents of the town insistent on a good road laid to their very doors. The State Highway Commission said a traffic census would have to be taken before the award was made. If traffic warranted the construction of a new road, it would be built; if not, it wouldn't. The date of the census leaked out. By strange coincidence the proprietors of the factory nearby made the day a holiday for their employees. It was also suggested that the free time might profitably be spent in driving around the countryside to see the sights. Or was the suggestion a command? Whatever the wording, that day cars whizzed back and forth between Southfield and Canaan from morning to night, producing heavy traffic impressive to the out-of-town census-takers. The road was built.

Near Southfield is TIPPING ROCK, a forty-ton boulder which can be swayed by the pressure of one finger.

EAST INDIA POND, where pickerel and perch are as plentiful as trout in the Konkapot, lies about four and a half miles southeast of Southfield in the middle of a large tract of privately owned forest. A narrow dirt trail, good in dry weather, goes east from the Southfield-Norfolk Road, so that the true adventurer can get through to the Pond on foot, provided he first obtains permission from Mr. Pratt, the caretaker, who lives at the junction of the main road and the Pond trail.

East India Pond is sometimes called Hermit Pond, after the recluse who lived here long ago. Six years before the Revolution, Timothy Leonard, whose spirit had been soured by life and its manifold vanities, built a hut in these parts. He shunned the company of all mankind, and on the subject of women is said to have expressed himself without romantic overtone:

> They say they will and they won't,
> What they promise to do, they don't.

Five miles from Southfield near the road to Norfolk are CAMP-BELL FALLS, which rush over a split rock ledge in a gulch of evergreen woods. Boys of the Civilian Conservation Corps have cleared ground for a parking space and cut out good foot trails. Nearby in a grove of pines are picnic grounds.

The wild Huxley Hill country around the Falls is inhabited by isolated families of hillbillies, descendants of Yankee pioneers who, like the mountain whites of Kentucky, have deteriorated through generations of inbreeding and poverty. They maintain little or no contact with the townspeople, for the land and the forest supply the necessities of their existence. Should you attempt to buy a gallon of their maple syrup, the hillbillies will prove enormously distrustful—that is, if they come out from hiding at all; more likely they'll stay behind a shut door until the stranger goes on his way.

Town Hall in Egremont   *Courtesy of The Society for The
Preservation of New England Antiquities*

Merrell Tavern in South Lee   Courtesy of The Society for
The Preservation of New England Antiquities

Returning from the Falls to the Southfield-Norfolk road, the right turn goes to Norfolk, Connecticut. To reach the largest village in the township, MILL RIVER, the leisurely traveler takes this road, and turning right at the triangle in Norfolk, goes west a few miles to the Whiting River, and turns north up the Canaan Valley road. Turn left again at a small cemetery on the left to CLAYTON, the southernmost settlement in Berkshire. The northern route from this village follows the Konkapot River past some of the richest farming land in New Marlborough. The tourist in a hurry will retrace his route from the Falls back to Southfield and along an unpaved road which goes west into Mill River. South of the village and just off a narrow country road are UMPACHENEE FALLS, a cataract which dashes down a flight of rock stairs for over half a mile.

Mill River was a thriving settlement from 1830 until the 1870's, with a large population of Yankee and Irish mill workers. In 1739 one of the first dams in Berkshire County is said to have been built here, behind the present site of the library. Although at one time the community was a minor paper-making center with a promising future, its bright prospects did not materialize, and the village today is quiet and lonely. In addition to the library, it has a general store, a white town hall, and a dozen or so neat houses.

The MILL RIVER LIBRARY houses a queer-looking contraption that resembles a cheese press. And that is exactly what it was before Marcus Rogers decided he wanted to be a printer. As the cheapest press cost $150, a magnificent sum to a New Marlborough boy, Rogers rigged his mother's dairy implement into what he hoped would be a printing press. With only a matchbox full of type of various points, he proceeded to issue his first newspaper, *The Rising Sun,* which during the years 1854-55 gave townspeople the latest news. Although in the years that followed Rogers became a man of wealth and importance, New Marlborough best remembers him as the editor and owner of *The Sun.* There was nothing dull or imitative about his little journal; he wrote articles on "The Names of the Teeth," "The Female Influence," and "The Doom of the World." As his paper was addressed to all members of the family, news of the latest styles vied for attention with up-to-the-minute political gossip. New Marlborough ladies must have perked up at such items as:

Godey's Lady's Book for May has been received. The illustrations are admirable. "The Motherless Daughter" is a picture of purity and beauty. The Color Fashionplates present figures with the grace of fairies and the beauty of angels. The plate "Cinderella" made us snicker right out. We can get along without a wife, but not without Godey's.

When *The Rising Sun* had become a full-fledged newspaper and acquired a substantial circulation, Rogers went in for "Personals," no slight innovation in those days when the press printed very little local news except accounts of fires, crimes, and accidents. While the owner of the *Berkshire Courier* at Great Barrington, Rogers began the accumulation of a fortune by inventing a machine for folding newspapers. In 1887 he purchased the *Berkshire Eagle* of Pittsfield and almost doubled its circulation. Although he spent much of his later life in travel, Berkshire was Rogers' first love and he retained an ardent interest in anything pertaining to the county. By his efforts the little library in Mill River was built.

Near the center of town is a tiny cemetery where inscriptions, alternately pathetic and amusing, are still legible on the worn stones. One lady, who must have been either rich or beautiful, was:

POLLY RHODES
Being the wife of five husbands

Underneath, the husbands are listed by name as 1st, 2nd, 3rd, *et cetera.*

After you have sauntered around Mill River, visited the general store, or watched the road crew at work, you may hear a few tales about old times in New Marlborough. Perhaps someone will tell you the story Grandfather Sisson used to relate so flourishingly, about a woodchopper he once employed.

Caught in a thunder shower while working in the woods, the man made for a hollow tree and with great difficulty managed to squeeze himself into it. Then lightning struck the tree, stunning the woodchopper; when he came to his senses, he found that the tree had somehow closed about him and he was unable to free himself from its embrace, no matter how much he yelled, shouted, cursed, and prayed. No help arrived; he was deep in the woods and far from any human habitation.

"Mercy! how did the poor fellow get out?" the rapt listener

invariably gasped at this point, for even Grandfather Sisson would have a tough job getting a fellow out of a tree that had wound itself about him.

"Oh, he got out easy enough in the end," Mr. Sisson used to drawl. "He suddenly remembered that he was a d—d Democrat, and it made him feel so small that he just slipped out of a crack."

MONTEREY used to be called "Green Woods," an appropriate name. When the southern part of Tyringham became a separate town during the Mexican War, patriotic selectmen wished to name it in commemoration of General Zachary Taylor's battles in Mexico and Texas, but Palo Alto and Buena Vista were too foreign-sounding. Monterey was musical and not too hard to pronounce, so Monterey it became. That was in 1847, one year before General Taylor was elected President. During the sixteen months he held office, the town felt that it had made a gracious gesture. In later years, when Monterey sounded a little fancy to the younger townspeople, they consoled themselves for not having something more homespun by remembering that eleven other states had towns of the same name and with as little excuse.

Monterey is now largely dependent on the summer people who have built new homes or restored old ones, but seventy years ago it was an industrial center with cotton mills, two rat-trap factories, and a plant for manufacturing paper. Although industry has moved away, some farming and a great deal of trapping are still carried on. Until the steel trap law was passed in 1930, Monterey led all the Berkshire towns in the fur industry; after the repeal of the law four years later, the trapping of mink, skunk, and muskrat was to a large extent resumed. The rocky crags of Mount Hunger in the eastern section of the town are wildcat lairs, and more bounties are paid to Monterey residents than to those of any other Berkshire town. Equally reliable as sources of income to the natives are the hundreds of summer places along the shores of Lake Garfield and Lake Buel, which is shared with New Marlborough. Both lakes are for the most part privately owned, although they have one or two small public beaches.

Among the earliest settlers of Monterey were Tristian Steadman, who settled near the Otis line, Isaac Benedict, who set up the first tavern, and Lieut. Isaac Garfield. LAKE GARFIELD was first called

Twelve Mile Pond, and later Brewer Pond after Capt. John Brewer, who lived on the northern shore. As the original family consisted of thirteen children and subsequent generations equaled or surpassed the initial figure, there were plenty of Brewers around for a good many years. In 1881 Monterey decided to name the lake after President James Garfield, who in his youth had visited relatives in the town. But the actual christening was a sad occasion, for two days before the ceremony the President was shot by an assassin. The lake, famous throughout Berkshire for its fighting black bass and large pickerel, is visible through the thick foliage along Mass 23. On the northern side its waters drop to fifty-foot depths from submerged ledges, but the south and east shores are shallow, with sand bottom and beaches for bathing.

Near the shore is INDIAN CAVE, set back in the woods, where the last Indian seen in Monterey was supposed to have lived. The cave is so small, however, that unless its occupant was an aboriginal pigmy, he must have had to double up to get in and out. When the property was purchased by a new owner a few years ago, a sign with the head of an Indian was put up to show travelers the way to the cave. Too many travelers proved curious, the marker was removed, and now Indian Cave is hidden in the woods. The property where the cave is located is owned today by Henry Ware Eaton of New York, whose pretentious summer home, EATON VILLA, is erected on a sloping ledge and anchored by steel cables to hold it in place.

Monterey's development as a "summer town" commenced in 1894 with the building of several cottages along the southern shore of Lake Garfield. The number of cottages increased, camps for boys and girls were established, and by 1929 the total summer population approached eighteen hundred. The Berkshire Art School, a mile above the lake, was founded by Raymond P. Ensign in 1915 and is open for six weeks during the summer months.

Off Mass 23, leading out of Monterey to Great Barrington, is a road to the right directly into the Headquarters of the supervisor of BEARTOWN STATE FOREST, one of the large reservations in the county. It comprises 7999 acres, the greater part within the limits of Monterey. The ARTHUR WHARTON SWANN STATE FOREST, a tract of almost a thousand acres entirely within town bounds, is also open to lovers of the woods. A section has been set aside for a wild-life preserve where birds and animals may be secure from the guns of sportsmen.

At the present time the State is conducting interesting experiments within Beartown State Forest that may eventually lead to the revival of a sport not practised in New England for the last hundred years—gunning for wild turkey. The thrifty Yankee may soon be taking down his rifle and, at Thanksgiving, with his bone turkey-call handy, going into the forest to pick off the first black turkey he finds roosting in an oak tree. The Commissioner of Conservation has been introducing wild turkey, common in the State up to 1850, into Beartown Forest. In the fall of 1938 as many as twenty of these rare fowl were seen in the forest, survivals of importations started in 1935 by the More Game Birds in America Foundation. As a yearly brood of twelve chicks may be expected from each hen, it should not be long before the birds come out of the sanctuary where they enjoy the soya beans, clover, buckwheat, and millet planted for their special benefit.

The less zestful amusements of picnicking and mountain-climbing will probably have to serve for some time. Beartown Road leads from the Forest Supervisor's Headquarters to BENEDICT POND, fitted with fireplaces and tables for a lunch in the wildwood; from the pond, Mt. Wilcox Road goes off to the right, joining Sky Peak Road into Tyringham. On the summit of Mt. Wilcox looms a great fire tower, rising from a height of over two thousand feet.

Monterey doesn't boast of its green woods, its lakes, its sports. Monterey doesn't boast of anything. People are driven to ask questions about the town, especially about the roads. They can never understand Monterey's attitude toward roads, for the highway between West Otis and Great Barrington, which comes from Springfield, is the only main road in town, and the people of Monterey don't mind. The casual traveler is shocked by such backwardness.

"The town'll stagnate," he urges; "it'll go to seed." A native grins. So does a summer visitor who is listening in.

"Praise God," murmurs the summer visitor.

TYRINGHAM, next door to Monterey, is shut off on three sides by mountains, and by inclination might bar the fourth side as well. It hasn't even a main highway. From West Otis, where an abandoned church and a weatherbeaten old house stand together, an improved road turns left off Mass 23 into the valley of which Richard Watson Gilder wrote:

> Down in the meadow and up on the height
>   The breezes are blowing the billows white.
> In the elms and maples the robins call
> And the great black crow sails over all
>   In Tyringham, Tyringham Valley.

Gilder came from New Jersey by way of Delaware, Barbados, and Kent, England. As editor of *Scribner's,* which later became the *Century Magazine,* he was a power in the literary world from 1870 to his death in 1909. In 1898 he built Four Brooks Farm in Tyringham. Frances Folsom, later the wife of President Cleveland, was a good friend of the Gilders, and both she and the President were guests at the Tyringham retreat. The Berkshire village inspired Gilder's book of poems, *In Tyringham Valley,* and led him also to eulogies in prose:

Tyringham is a state of nature; it is bounded on the north by fountains that never fail, great clouds of laurel and the Great Bear; on the south by Willow Glen, Tyringham River, the ghosts of Mother Ann and her fellow Shakers; the ponderous shadows of Fernside Forest and the high horizon line of the Shaker hills; on the east by the purple dawn on the west by a hundred sunsets.

From Lenox the novelist Edith Wharton was moved to write her "Moonrise over Tyringham," more subjective than Gilder's verse:

> Yet see—night is not: by translucent ways,
>   Up the gray void of autumn afternoon
> Steals a mild crescent, charioted in haze,
>   And all the air is merciful as June.
>
> The lake is a forgotten streak of day
>   That trembles through the hemlock's darkling bars
> And still, my heart, still some divine delay
>   Upon the threshold holds the earliest stars.

In Gilder's wake an unusual group came to the valley: Joseph Jefferson, actor, John Burroughs, naturalist, Daniel Chester French and Augustus Saint-Gaudens, sculptors, Ossip Gabrilowitch, pianist, Cecilia Beaux, artist, and Henry Adams, noted author and medieval scholar. Mark Twain, summering here, presented the local library with a complete set of his books.

Gilder's remark about Mother Ann's ghost brings to mind the Shaker settlement of 1792. From an original group of nine, it grew to over a hundred by 1852, when they had nearly fifteen hundred acres under cultivation. Their views on celibacy made converts rather difficult to obtain, and members occasionally ran away to escape the iron discipline characteristic of the cult everywhere. In vain the Shakers trudged annually up the steep hill behind their workshops to the Shaking Ground, where they "shook off" their sins at the "Devil's Grave"; in vain they prayed in their wholly imaginary tabernacle on the summit of Mt. Horeb. By 1874 there were too few left to work the land; they were compelled to sell their property and migrate to other Shaker communities.

The land was purchased by Joseph Jones of Honesdale, Pennsylvania, who was confident that summer visitors would frequent Tyringham if he provided them with dwelling places. His guess was shrewd and the invasion was on. Summer residents finally cooperated to purchase the colony and restore many of the buildings, though the oldest of the Shaker dwellings, a house erected in 1776, had to be torn down in 1881. Two large houses were combined into a clubhouse where what the Berkshire newspapers called "a galaxy of notables" gathered for diversion. The colony, called FERNSIDE, is southwest of the town center, across the narrow valley of Hop Brook. Although the clubhouse is no longer in use, the surrounding structures continue to be occupied during the summer months by city people. Tyringham lives up to the boast of its historian: "Once a swampy tangle of hops, ivy, and hemlock, now the most beautiful valley in the Berkshire."

One of the leaders in the restoration of the Shaker Colony was Mrs. Robb de Peyster Tytus, wife of the well-known Egyptologist. Mr. and Mrs. Tytus, on their honeymoon in Tyringham, were so attracted by the town that Mr. Tytus purchased an eight-hundred-acre estate. He built a marble mansion called ASHINTULLY, from the Egyptian meaning "Over the Hill." It is locally known as Tytus Folly because of its great size and elaborate design. Some thought it ought to be called Tytus Hoodoo. Ashintully seems enormous, for it dominates the landscape from a mountain shelf at the southeastern end of the town and suggests a king's palace or a state capitol. When Mr. and Mrs. Tytus were alive, the house was filled with rare and priceless objects of art. Henry Adams once spent a restless night in the Flemish tapestry room, emerging heavy-eyed in the morning to insist that the woman in an Italian painting over his bed had kept him awake with her talking. An Egyptian museum contained objects brought back by Mr. Tytus's expedition to Egypt. He had explored the tombs of the Pharaohs, and superstitious people liked to believe that a curse descended upon the family because they had disturbed the sleeping kings of Egypt. Mr. Tytus died two years after Ashintully was completed, and his widow later married John Stewart McLennan, a Canadian senator whom she divorced a year before her death in 1928. Mildred Tytus, a daughter, was killed in an automobile accident in 1934. Daughter and parents are buried in sepulchers hewn from solid rock on the summit of Round Mountain, about a mile and a half from the marble mansion. The path to these graves is so precarious that it can be traveled only on foot.

The town boasts an even more extraordinary structure, the home of Henry Hudson Kitson, sculptor. When Mr. Kitson, an Englishman by birth and an American by adoption, came to Tyringham three decades ago, he erected in the yard of the house he had purchased an edifice faintly resembling a Tahitian chief's hut. The thatched roof of the main building is composed of strips of felt and slate laid on rafters. Behind this hut-like studio stands a cone-shaped tower room. The high fence is constructed of rough brushwood. Huge chunks of rock, irregularly placed, are piled against the walls, leaving only narrow doors with brightly painted lintels as entrance to the odd house. Here Kitson has carved many famous works, including the *Pilgrim Maiden* at Plymouth, the *Continental Soldier* at Washington's headquarters in Newburgh, New York, the *Minute Man* at Lexington, the *Coolidge Portrait-Relief* on South Mountain and, most recently, the *John and Priscilla Alden Memorial*.

Visitors to Tyringham find it hard to imagine that the town was an industrial center in the middle nineteenth century, and that nearly every stream draining into the valley turned a waterwheel. There were lime kilns, textile mills and, in the center, the Turkey Paper Mills, where fine writing paper was manufactured. When the railroad went to Lee, the paper mills followed; gradually other industries either moved away or were abandoned. All that remained to Tyringham, besides a crumbling paper mill near the center of town, was the famous STEADMAN RAKE SHOP. Tyringham has been noted for Steadman rakes ever since Captain Tom, the first of the family, deserted Cape Cod for Berkshire. He settled near Hop Brook, and established a factory still operated by the Steadman family after five generations. The original Rake Shop was moved years ago to its present location near the old dam, and is always open to visitors.

Since Garfield, every President of the United States has testified to the excellence of Steadman handmade wooden rakes. On the Coolidge family farm at Plymouth, Vermont, a Berkshire Congressman delivered two rakes to the President with Mr. Steadman's compliments.

"Handmade of native hickory," said the Congressman. Coolidge took the rakes, and after examining them minutely remarked, "This part is ash."

"Oh, yes, so it is!" responded the emissary.

"So is the handle," added the President.

"Why, I guess it is, at that."

"These are hickory," observed the Vermonter, pointing to the rounded cross-pieces fitted into the tooth bar to strengthen the rakes. "And the teeth are hickory, too."

The Congressman changed the subject.

South of the Rake Shop, at the junction of Jerusalem Road and the main Otis-Lee road, is TINKER'S, another old Tyringham institution. For the past ninety years the only store in town, it is still going strong even though it is "Tinker's" now only by force of habit. Tyringham may be off the main roads, but it is no backwoods village, nor is Tinker's of today the old-fashioned emporium where Mark Twain lounged and swapped yarns during the summer he spent on the Gilder estate. The kerosene lamps and the cracker barrel are gone; today the store has electric lights, and food trucks deliver "bakery" bread, "bakery" pies and cakes. The huge old-fashioned cheese, kept under a glass case so the cat wouldn't sleep on it, has been supplanted by tinfoil packages unadaptable for feline snoozing. The former proprietress of the store was postmistress and reporter for the "city paper up to Pittsfield," also the dispenser of news both official and unofficial. You could hear her at the telephone:

"Yes, schools are closed today and tomorrow. Teachers' convention today. ——had his tonsils taken out at the hospital in Pittsfield, Saturday. No, I don't. Think it's two 'm's in his last name. Yes, I'm sure of it. ——cut his foot with an axe and had the doctor. I'll let you know how bad it is after the doctor leaves. Yes, visiting from New York over the week-end. That's right . . . Oh, not all! Good-bye."

To reach *SANDISFIELD* from Tyringham it is necessary to drive back to West Otis and take Mass 23 to Otis Center, swinging south to join with Mass 8 down through the Farmington River Valley.

If you'd want to locate friends in Sandisfield, inquiries in Otis, the township just to the north, might go something like this:

"I want to find Mr. So-and-So of Sandisfield."

"That so?" the man from Otis would drawl. "Well, now, Sandisfield folks don't trade round here; they all go down into Connecticut, but if you ask the town clerk at New Boston—that's on this same road, just south—he may be able to help you out."

"New Boston?"

"Sure. That's a part of Sandisfield. There's a store with the post office in it. There's an inn there, too, 'n' a schoolhouse 'n' a church."

And it seems there's a West New Boston too, having a postoffice and a town hall, and there's Mountville, with a post office and precious little else, and Sandisfield Center. Anyone in South Sandisfield could easily be found, for there is only one building in the district, the post office, where lives the sole resident of the village. The search might encompass Upper or Lower Spectacle Pond, Silver Brook, Swamp Brook, Clam River, Buck Hill, Town Hill, or Roosterville, where so many cocks were raised in olden days that they were said to have "woke up" everybody for miles around in Berkshire. An Otis native could even track a man down in Skunk's Misery, a part of Sandisfield that many years ago was a stamping ground for this unloved species of wild life.

Between 1840 and 1870 Sandisfield was a prosperous industrial community. Cellar holes, lilac bushes, and an occasional broken millwheel dimly recall the fine houses and factories that stood there during the boom era. Sandisfield once had six taverns and six churches, nine doctors and nine cemeteries, and three lawyers. Its population surpassed that of Pittsfield. When Pittsfield needed money for a Congregational church, Sandisfield made the loan, and when a railroad company surveyed a route through the Farmington River Valley, forty thousand dollars was promptly subscribed by the town's moneyed men for "the Road to Prosperity," as the promoters called it. The railroad embankment, visible for miles as you drive south along Mass 8, is all that ever materialized of the scheme. Sandisfield found itself "holding the bag" for twenty-six thousand dollars and bonded for thousands more. At last the State came to the rescue, refunding twenty-four thousand dollars to the stricken community. The tax rate mounted to meet the remaining debt and property values declined. Today the population of four hundred residents is no match for Pittsfield's fifty thousand. Of three surviving churches, one is the new Jewish synagogue in Montville, and the nine cemeteries are desolations of rank grass. The town's economic life now consists of some dairy farming, work on the ninety miles of dirt roads, sporadic woodcutting jobs, and "summer boarders." The summer business differs from that of other Berkshire communities in that it is monopolized by Jewish settlers from New York City who have, during the past thirty-five years, gradually taken over a part of Sandisfield.

This trend began in 1902 as a back-to-the-land movement. Solomon Polloch, a New York tailor, migrated with thirty-five families. At first Sandisfield Yankees were inclined to resent the newcomers, who seemed none too well-informed on the matter of boundaries. Embarrassing situations arose when Jewish farmers, acting in good faith, tilled Yankee fields and naively gathered fruit from the orchards of their neighbors. Both sides eventually realized that tolerance and understanding would mend the breach, and newcomers and natives now cooperate as neighbors must in an isolated rural community. Farming was rejected as too uncongenial and unremunerative, and at present livelihood comes principally from summer boarders and real-estate enterprises.

The real agriculturists of the town are Russian Cossacks, west of Sandisfield Center. The thirty families of this closely-knit clique are conspicuous in winter by their tall, hairy Cossack hats, exotic sights on the dull New England landscape. Their small farms are well cultivated, and they have little contact with their neighbors. Most of them are naturalized citizens and eligible for work on the town roads, but instead of depending on this they sell their excess crops and dairy products to the Jewish residents of West New Boston and Montville. As the Jews were instrumental in starting the Russian colony, the relationship between the two groups is extremely cordial. In recounting her personal odyssey, one Russian farmer's wife gives an insight into the resources of the Cossack settlement.

Something of a personage in her native land, she came to America and in Hartford married a Russian employed at a New Haven typewriter factory. When her husband became so ill that country air was prescribed as the only cure, a member of the Sandisfield Jewish colony employed him as a handyman, later giving him an old farmhouse. The Russians tore down the house, cut the wood for a new dwelling, had it sawed, and built the house with their own hands, selling the antique molding and fireplaces of the old structure to get money for food over the winter.

"We had hard time, but now we have nice home, and when my son and daughter finish high school, maybe things get better. My son go to high school in Lee. He walks to Montville four miles to take school bus to Lee. Sometime in winter, the snow is up to his hips. Now we got fine house, fine barn. We grow corn, potatoes, cabbage, beets enough for winter. We butcher pig each fall. Smoke hams and shoulder and pickle in brine the rest. We very happy now. We work hard but it worth it."

Within the past few years, because of the opening of the State Forest, a change has taken place in Sandisfield. The Civilian Conservation Corps has improved the road and made accessible miles of forest, a number of stocked streams, and trails for skiing and snowshoeing. New Boston, for half a century one of the main stopping-places on the Hartford-Albany Turnpike, has also felt the stimulus of tourist trade: houses are being restored as summer homes, and the old tavern has been modernized to accommodate summer visitors and winter sports enthusiasts. South of New Boston, on the left, is the steep pitch of SUICIDE HILL, formerly advertised as "America's largest Ski Hill." The hurricane and flood of 1938 destroyed the run.

South of the ski hill, where the Farmington Valley broadens out, a granite crag known as HANGING MOUNTAIN rises almost perpendicularly for some 450 feet above the river. In places the upper ledge overhangs the lower wall—hence its name. At the mountain's base, a granite quarry has been operating for the last year, producing a type of stone for monuments equal to the best from Barre, Vermont. The quarry employs thirty men at present, and hopes to expand.

Sandisfield boasts of a prime story-teller in Jason Sears, the town clerk. One of his favorite tales concerns six young men who about twenty-five years ago went to New York from Sandisfield for a "big time." On a trip to Coney Island, they shot at the clay pigeons and then happened on a weight-lifting machine. One by one they tried their luck, each attracting more onlookers by setting himself a higher record. When the last man, Flanders Denslow, stepped up, he wrenched the machine from its fastenings. Torn between admiration and resentment, the proprietor of the concession could only say in awed tones, "Where the devil do you come from?"

Mr. Sears also recalls the story of Lawyer Ephraim Judson, who was engaged by Eliakin Hull as counsel in a lawsuit in 1807. Hull's dispute was with Squire Canfield, who also sought Lawyer Judson's services. Unable to serve both parties, Judson recommended a colleague of his in Lenox and gave the Squire an introductory letter. Canfield was not a curious man, but as he rode toward Lenox he wondered about the letter in his pocket, thinking that Judson might have tipped off his friend on the matter of fees, or revealed how he thought the case might turn out. Finally, unable to stand the suspense any longer, he opened the letter and devoured the contents. After one glance, color bloomed in his face; he emitted a snort of rage, wheeled his horse about and returned to Sandisfield at top speed, where he reined up at his enemy's door. Without a word he handed the note to Mr. Hull, who read:

"Two fat geese, you pluck one, I'll pluck the other."

Frank Hawley, one of the old-time residents of the town, has a barn at Clam River, named from the "freshwater clams" that used to be washed down from Spectacle Pond. Between the house and the barn a mile below runs a narrow, rocky road along which Farmer Hawley is probably the only one to pass for months at a time. Seventy-five years ago this road was lined with prosperous houses and led to a group of mills situated on the banks of the stream. Mr. Hawley tells of the time when his road was the trunk highway between Hartford and Albany, and a stage stopped daily at a tavern to change horses. His father often recounted the thrills he experienced in his youth when the lighted coach with its four horses rattled along the road into town at nightfall.

Another accomplished raconteur is Frank Bryant of Otis, who tells of starting a trip a few years ago through the woods toward South Sandisfield, driving a team that carried a boiler for a portable sawmill. Until that time, he thought he knew the neighboring town pretty well, although he hadn't been "up in that neck of the woods" for years. "And do you know, I was lost for two days in that bush and never met a single person that could speak English."

Sections of the "back country" give the stranger a cool welcome. On the fringe of the woods or beside a steep mountain trail, he is likely to encounter a bearded man with a shotgun or even a high-powered rifle, in which case he had better be on business he can explain or else keep right on going without asking questions. Sandisfield residents declare that these hillbillies are not natives of the town, but are people who have moved in from somewhere and don't care to mingle. They may be fugitives from *Esquire.*

CHAPTER XI

WHERE PAST AND PRESENT MEET

OTIS—Mass 23, Mass 8, sett. 1735, alt. 1240, pop. 415.

BECKET—Mass 8, US 20, sett. 1740, alt. 1207, pop. 723.

WASHINGTON—Off Mass 8, sett. 1760, alt. 1437, pop. 252.

Roads—Mass 8 goes north from Sandisfield to Otis and Becket; Washington is off this highway to the west on the old Pontoosac Turnpike.

YOU ARE ENTERING GOD'S COUNTRY
DON'T DRIVE THROUGH LIKE HELL

THIS terse, self-confident introduction is painted across a weather-beaten old barn near the Blandford-Otis line. Otis, Becket, and Washington have been invaded by the "moderns," and decline any longer to be considered old-fashioned mountain towns. Elaborate summer camps and fine estates have for their settings lakes, ponds, and woodland stretches. A stream of motor traffic weaves its way along well-laid thoroughfares. But this is only half the picture. A more discerning portrait of the towns would high-light remote farmhouses, old red barns, and tiny settlements of white houses under tall trees. Dense forestland encroaches on field and farm almost as it did when the pioneers first came. In Otis, Becket, and Washington, the eighteenth century still is a visual background for the twentieth.

A century ago these were prosperous communities with tanneries, woodenware factories, and small sawmills, run by waterwheels on swift hillside streams. With the years the little industries, too far off the beaten path, faltered and failed; the forests which had seemed so vast were exhausted; and the prosperity of the towns waned.

Only within recent years have State highways and summer people brought quickening new forces into play. To the nimble-witted natives, strangers have meant a new source of income and a brisk, fresh way of looking at things. Residents of these towns now consider the cultivation of summer business their chief pursuit. Descendants of old-time

Yankees, most of them have lost none of the ingenuity usually associated with the stock. Otis, Becket, and Washington people well demonstrate that once they "get the hang" of city ways they can out-citify city folks. Old houses have been painted and spruced up for "paying guests"; highway tea rooms and rustic gasoline stations use modern wiles to arrest traffic at their doors. From neat roadside stands farmers offer vegetables, chickens, homemade jams, jellies, and friendly aphorisms. Cabin colonies for tourists have been erected in wayside fields and groves. The Civilian Conservation Corps pushes into the forests, fells decayed trees and sets out new ones, builds roads, beautifies picnic grounds, and clears sites for camps. Otis, Becket, and Washington not only acquiesce in modern ways; they even lend a hand in establishing them.

Not all the residents of these towns, to be sure, have accepted the change with equanimity; there remains a small group of firm rejecters, "sot in their ways," who will have nothing to do with new-fangled notions. The advent of speeding cars and girls in halters and shorts has not been a total loss even to this faction, for they have gained an interesting topic to declaim about. Perhaps one of the "sot" ones painted the sign on the barn, but more likely it was a canny farmer seeking to ensnare you for a day, a week, or a lifetime in "God's country." He knows that summer people bear perhaps more than their share of the tax burden in these towns and provide a market for farm produce. Anyhow, advertising brings business, and though the sign on the barn is not exactly glaring with neon lights, it *is* freshly painted every year. Any town bragging that it has the attractions of Paradise is bound to get attention.

OTIS is a composite of two older settlements, Loudon, which at its incorporation in 1773 took the name of Lord Loudon, Commander-in-Chief of the American forces in the French and Indian War of 1756, and Bethlehem, incorporated in 1789. On June 13, 1810, by consent of the General Court, the inhabitants changed the name to Otis in honor of Harrison G. Otis, Speaker of the Massachusetts House of Representatives.

From the 1830's to the 1870's, Otis was a growing place, with sawmills and grist mills and tanneries. Forges in North Otis and Cold Spring turned out pig iron that was hauled all the way to

Circular Stone Barn in Hancock Shaker Village   *Courtesy of The Hancock Shaker Village, Inc.*

Williamstown from Stone Hill   *Courtesy of The Society for*
The Preservation of New England Antiquities

Great Barrington to be made into car wheels. A "right pert" furniture shop in Otis Center made bedsteads, washstands, even coffins. For over 130 years, fine handmade wooden rakes were produced in the OLD RED RAKE SHOP on the Farmington River. Today not one of these industries survives, and even the Old Rake Shop, bowing to competition from larger centers, has become a roadside tea house. Lumbering and poultry raising remain the chief all-year-round occupations of Otis people, though it's work on the roads and the summer trade which really keep the town going.

The zest of Otis for novel ways and manners has even been extended to embrace the only nudist camp in the Berkshires. The NUDIST COLONY was opened in Otis in 1933 by Burgoyne Trail Associates, and offers most of the sports and normal recreational facilities of a regular summer camp. They advocate a healthy outdoor life with good food, pleasant companionship, and instruction in games, sports, and calisthenics—all based on meticulous observance of the nudist creed:

We believe in the essential wholesomeness of the human body and of all nature. We regard the body neither as an object of shame nor as a subject for levity or erotic exploitation. Any attitude or behavior inconsistent with this view is contrary to the whole spirit of the Associates and has no place among us.

Cautiously questioned as to what the natives of Otis thought about the nudists, one thin-lipped, straight-backed spinster gave her opinion: "Fine up-and-comin' people they are. They let us alone and mind their own 'p's' and 'q's,' which is more than you can say for lots of folks. If they want to set in the sun as God made 'em, and *pay* for the privilege, it isn't any of my affair. That's the way I figure it." Another native proved more enigmatic. "Yes, sir," said he, "over in them woods yonder, about a ten-minute walk from here, they go naked and it don't bother them a mite. Set around on logs 'n' rocks as unconcerned as though they had their pants on—but they ain't! . . . Excuse me mister, I've got to go to the store for some bread."

Nothing about prim Otis marks it as a town that would tolerate, let alone welcome, a nudist colony. A cluster of houses, two old churches, the schoolhouse, the Town Hall, a dance hall, a garage, and the general store—that is Otis Center, the civic heart of the town.

The houses are of many designs and in diverse conditions of repair, from well-kept late eighteenth-century dwellings to weather-beaten structures of no particular period or mode. Some crowd close to the narrow highway; others are set far back behind shaggy lawns. The stream of traffic constantly rolling past during the tourist season has small effect on the external placidity of the village. A little chap saunters by, deep in a small boy's thoughts. Along the dusty edges of the highways, a bewhiskered farmer, bright suspenders over checkered shirt, drives his slow-gaited horse. A housewife in fresh gingham dress hangs her washing on lines strung behind old-fashioned flower gardens. It has been this way for years.

The most unusual structure in the center is ST. PAUL'S EPIS-COPAL CHURCH, on the shelf of land above the junction of the two main highways, Mass 23 and Mass 8. Founded in 1828 by Squire Lester Filley, for years a prominent resident of Otis, it is a trim little building, with a squat belfry and long windows made up of 1092 panes of wavy, diamond-shaped glass. The three most visible sides of the church are painted white, but red lead paint, cheaper than white, was good enough for the back. "Why waste good white paint on places no one ever sees?" asks the thrifty "Berkshire Borner." St. Paul's is unique in that the church officers are all women, and all but one are unmarried. They are referred to quite nonchalantly and apparently without disparagement to their status or authority as the "Old Maids."

Next door to St. Paul's stands SQUIRE FILLEY'S HOUSE, a red brick homestead built in 1800. The Squire, a brilliant attorney and ardent Episcopalian, founded not only the church in his home town but also St. George's Episcopal Church in Lee. Members of the Cornwall family, occupants of the house for many years, have kept it in a good state of preservation. One room is decorated with scenes from Italy—the Colosseum in Rome, views of the Mediterranean, and the Carnival in Venice—all in full color on an imported wallpaper almost 150 years old. The house is not officially open to the public, but those interested are usually permitted to go through.

Across the road from Squire Filley's is the CONGREGATIONAL CHURCH, somewhat larger than St. Paul's. Beside the church is the combination Town Hall, Grange Hall and Schoolhouse. Just beyond stands the Otis Firemen's Dance Hall, where natives and summer people gather of an evening for "old-time dancing" under the auspices of the Volunteer Firemen's Association and the town Grange.

The OTIS PUBLIC LIBRARY, on Mass 23 just beyond the center of town, is a ramshackle old building trembling into ruin. Oil lamps and a new square cast-iron chunk stove provide it with light and heat. A standing offer of a modern building to house the library has been made, provided the town will supply the land, but nothing has been done about the offer, since the selection of a site has proved to be too knotty a problem.

Mass 23, which winds through Otis from Monterey to Blandford, follows the route of the "GREAT ROAD," one of the historic highways in the Berkshires. An Indian path through the wilderness existed here long before the coming of the first white men. In 1676 Major John Talcott and members of the Connecticut Militia used the road when in pursuit of a band of Narragansett Indians fleeing from Westfield to the Great Ford on the banks of the Housatonic River. The Otis section of the "Great Road" is called the Knox Trail; it was built in 1759 by General Jeffrey Amherst, British Commander-in-Chief of the North American forces. New settlers heading for southern Berkshire found this the best route up the Farmington River from Connecticut and Rhode Island. As villages were established, the path became the "Great Road from Boston to Albany," a tie that bound the older settlements to the frontier.

Over this road, Continental troops commanded by General Henry Knox brought the fifty-five cannon that saved the day at Dorchester Heights in 1776. Sleighs pulled by 124 pairs of oxen drew the heavy artillery through the drifts of January snow on the narrow, twisting forest road. The wind was sharp and the cold bit through the shabby coats of the soldiers. It was grueling labor for man and beast, every step a victory over snow, wind, and fatigue. The little band trudged up so steep a summit that it seemed to General Knox they "might almost have seen all the mountains of the earth." Daylight had faded when they halted at the Old Inn in Otis, where a greeting of warmth and cheer, a round of flip or toddy, and a mug of New England rum awaited them. They were weary, but they were conquerors on a march of triumph. The rafters of the Old Inn must have rung with the strains—

Fath'r and I went down to camp,
  Along with Captain Goodin',
And there we saw the men and boys,
  As thick as hasty puddin'.

Yankee Doodle, keep it up,
  Yankee Doodle dandy,
Mind the music and the step,
  And with the girls be handy.

The British had made up this song to poke fun at the Yankee rustics whom they thought they could "lick in a trice," but they abandoned the tune when they found that "Yankee Doodle," far from angering the uncouth farmers, sent them into gales of merriment.

A year later, another band of soldiers marched along the same "Great Road." These were part of General Burgoyne's army of Hessians and British, plodding eastward after the grim defeat at Saratoga, prisoners of the Yankees. Like the Colonials, the redcoats had marched miles through snow, wind, and cold, but the Colonials were victors marching through their homeland, while Burgoyne's men were enemies in a foreign country. Dragging themselves wearily up the last long hill, they too stopped for the night at the Old Inn, but this group of slow-moving, heartsick men was far different from the merry host of Colonials; there was no singing or laughter. It was lucky for both Englishmen and Germans that they did not know of the long march ahead of them before they reached Springfield, for some were destined to die along the way in the snow and sleet and cold.

Not the least of those who have since traveled the Great Road was "Jubilee" Jim Fiske, king of Berkshire peddlers. In 1835 he sent out through the Berkshires twenty-five outfits, peddling his goods from door to door. Otis remembers "Jubilee" Jim, not so much for his great wealth and power, as for his famous Paisley shawls. The Paisley shawl technique, as practised by Fiske, was a worthy forerunner of twentiety-century advertising methods. Jim, or one of his partners, would go ahead of the peddler's wagon to a prospective town, seek out a woman of local prestige, and courteously offer her a shawl as a gift. The glib presentation speech usually ended something like this: "If I might suggest it, your friends, no doubt, would be pleased to see you wearing such a beautiful shawl to church next

Sunday." With that seed of vanity planted in fertile soil, the peddler would go blithely on to the next village.

Nine times out of ten, the favored lady would mince down the church aisle the following Sunday with the Paisley shawl draped around her shoulders. The effect on the feminine congregation was devastating:

" 'Lead us not into temptation.' Good heavens, where did she get that shawl? Land! If I take that silver dollar I saved from last birthday, and the quarter for the heathen in the rosewood box—'for Thine is the kingdom and the power, Amen.' "

Otis likes to remember "Jubilee Jim" as the shrewd, suave peddler, rather than as the wealthy and famous Jim Fiske who later departed from Berkshire, acquired the Erie Railroad, beat down the power of his rival Jay Gould, and behind the scenes of State and Federal politics, pulled wires manipulating officials like puppets.

One of Fiske's associates on his treks around Berkshire was Volney Haskell, descendant of the prominent Haskell family of Otis, who traced their ancestry back to three brothers said to have sailed from England to America in a skiff with leather sails. Upon being discharged from his duties in the army at the time of the Revolution, one of them, Philip, bought a barrel of brandy with money received for his military services, traded the beverage for a piece of land in Otis, and established his home there.

Among other characters who have helped to make life interesting in Otis down through the years was Professor Alfred Hazard, inventor of a "perpetual motion" machine that might have startled the world, had it not worked so well that it flew to pieces and could never be put together again. The professor's plan for developing electricity from water power in Otis went so far that poles were set up along the main street for the electric lights which were to illuminate the town. His scheme failed and the only illumination that ever shone from the tops of the poles came from oil lanterns hung there one night by pranksters.

Today Otis is famous not so much for its old-time characters as for a lively modern maestro, Sammy Spring. Sammy is the kind of old-time fiddler octogenarians of our day might never have expected to see or hear again this side of Jordan. He began his career fiddling at dances in the neighboring towns of Berkshire, and since then has played at fashionable resorts in Massachusetts and Connecticut, over the Phillips Lord radio program, at the estates of leading Berkshire socialites, at the Eastern States Exposition in Springfield, and before Mrs. Franklin D. Roosevelt at the Copley Plaza Hotel in Boston. Though he may play for the Four Hundred, Sammy is still a Berkshire farmer, who has no intention of ever permanently leaving the hills and streams of his native Otis.

Hunters and fishermen find these same hills and streams a sportsman's delight, where deer and small game abound and good fishing is taken pretty much for granted. One of the largest bodies of water in Berkshire County is OTIS RESERVOIR (Mass 23 at East Otis). Bass, pickerel, white and yellow perch, pike, and bullheads abound in all the streams of the town. During the trout season, when the dozen miles of public fishing ground along the Farmington River are open, Otis is the angler's Eden. Springtime sees the natives and people from all parts of the district going out with pails, bags, and tubs for the "sucker run." The fish are speared and sometimes caught by hand; those not immediately fried and eaten are either canned or put in brine for use during the winter.

Despite its quiet exterior there have been at times rumblings of a spirit of revolt in Otis; in 1924, for instance, when the road superintendent failed to be reappointed. The people in East Otis where he had lived were enraged. The disappointed office-holder had held the job for several years, and his father before him for half a lifetime. It almost seemed as if the roads would go to rack and ruin if this family were not in charge of construction and repair. East Otis people claimed that they were not getting their share of good roads, and, anyway, the whole business of the ousting seemed just a plot to deprive them of road money.

They were righteously indignant, for the one occupation which survives all depressions in the small Berkshire villages is road work. Regardless of bad financial conditions, citizens sidetrack other appropriations to continue voting "to raise and appropriate the sum of —— dollars for Chapter 81 highways," "—for Chapter 90," "—— dollars for bridge work," and "—— for snow removal."

Local politics center largely around road work, since the selectmen who are the "town fathers" appoint the road superintendent, subject to approval by the State Department of Public Works. This, the highest salaried job in town, naturally is the most coveted. Every year the selectmen receive innumerable applications—from veteran road bosses down to those unable to distinguish a "shoulder" from a "fire broom." The town fathers also determine who shall work on the roads and for what length of time. Consequently a man votes for the selectman who, he thinks, will appoint the road boss who will give him the most work.

As time draws near for the appointment of the road boss, the whole town gets excited. If he is a novice in the field, will "Public Works" accept him? Will they find out that he drinks? Will someone slyly defame his character? Will the selectmen appoint the man they appeared to favor before election, or will they turn traitor and choose someone else? The selectmen also have many an uneasy moment, for, regardless of how great a monarch one may be in a small town, even the most overbearing villager stands in awe of "Public Works." If the selectmen insist upon appointing a superintendent of whom the State Department does not approve, it may mean a complete loss of state funds for the town. Usually a choice is amicably decided upon.

The position of road boss is not without honor. Previously a mere citizen, one of the crowd, suddenly he becomes THE BOSS, the ruler of ninety per cent of the men in town and particularly of his enemies, who are now forced to work for him. He is boss even of the selectmen and other important town officials, and he has control of several thousand dollars. He strides along demanding attention, a note of recently acquired authority in his voice. Before many weeks, however, a haggard, worry-worn look creeps into his eyes. The selectmen hire, but only the superintendent has the inalienable right to fire. This means responsibility, for the road workers are usually heads of the largest families and survivals of the most indebted, rather than the fittest. References, ability, and experience count for little. The work is so divided that married men receive two days' work for each single man's one. The superintendent must do a good job or he is in danger of losing his appointment, yet the townspeople must be fed, clothed, and be enabled to pay taxes and purchase bare necessities. In hard times it is either road work or welfare. The townspeople look with disfavor on a road boss who sends men "back to the welfare." Naturally, the boss's right to fire is little exercised.

The first day of road work is almost like a class reunion, for many who live in one remote part of town haven't seen those who live in other parts for several months. They swap hard-luck stories, local gossip, opinions on current events, hints on farming, and the latest jokes. Tired of months of worry, meager meals, threadbare clothing, and large bills, they view a pick and shovel almost with pleasure and anticipation. What are the backbreaking experiences of former years? Eight hours' work means four dollars pay.

The first road work to be done in the spring is patching improved, tar-surfaced main highways. This work begins immediately after the first frost is out of the ground, usually around the middle of April or the first of May, and lasts only a week or two.

Road improvement, called "Chapter 81 work," starts shortly after the patching is completed, usually around the middle of May. The first operation is scraping the road with a large scraper to remove sod from ditches and shoulders. A second gang follows the first and throws the sod on the banks; a third unit cleans out waterways and ditches with shovels and removes stones the scraper missed. Still another group replaces rotten and rusty culverts with new ones. Brush along the roadside is cut and gravel dumped to fill the mudholes. Any money left over is used to widen sections made dangerous by washouts and floods.

"Chapter 90 work," done usually in August, is entirely devoted to building new roads under state supervision. It is paid for by the joint funds of state, county, and town. First a state survey is made, then the roadbed is smoothed out and covered with a foot of stone fill, which is topped by a layer of poor gravel and then by a layer of good-grade gravel. Culverts are placed wherever necessary for drainage. The road "shoulders" (dirt embankments three to five feet wide between the ditches and roadbed) are "dressed," smoothed, and leveled.

"Chapter 221" calls for resurfacing improved main roads. A tar truck, with spreader attached, drives slowly along the highway, dripping hot tar; men follow behind to dust the tar with sand. Snow work includes erecting snow fences and plowing out roads. In some places, the job is done entirely by the town; in others, the town hires large state plows to keep the main highway open.

Improved methods of performing road operations, the mistakes recent road bosses have made, the need for more and larger road appropriations, who the next road boss will be—these are the main subjects of conversation not only in Otis but in all Berkshire small towns during the winter months.

A story that illustrates the spirit of Otis was told by a former city resident who had lived in the town for only a year. At first not quite sure how to deal with his new country neighbors, he soon was to find out. A chimney fire began to burn inside the inner wall of his dining room. Smoke poured through the joints in the woodwork, billowing out into the room. He was confused, for apartment dwellers rarely have to cope with such situations. His first thought was to rush at once to the doors and windows and fling them open. Before he made another move, however, there came a knock at the door, and in walked the next-door neighbor.

"Havin' some trouble, eh? Fetch me your axe and we'll fix it up." Axe in hand, friend neighbor began chopping the plaster around the pipe hole to expose the smouldering framework.

"Fetch me a bucket of water," he ordered, and then proceeded to douse the wall thoroughly.

When the fire was out, the Otis neighbor departed without a farewell. In a few minutes he was back with a small bag of plaster, a roll of wallpaper, and some chicken wire. He tacked wire over the hole, and laid on plaster. With a curt "I'll be back later to paper it over," he was gone again.

That evening he came back and announced, "Papered this house myself. Got this wallpaper from Montgomery Ward, lucky I saved some, ain't it?"

In ten minutes the paper was on and he was ready to leave. Asked how much the bill was, he gave the city fellow a look of scorn and snapped, "Not a cent. Can't a man be neighborly if he wants to?" With that he slammed the door and departed.

Somewhat stunned by the encounter, the newcomer resolved to be on the lookout for a chance somehow to repay the favor. Considerable window-watching in the direction of the next-door house was finally rewarded one winter day when he saw his neighbor trying in vain to get his car started. Immediately the city man got out his own car, drove into the next yard, and hooked up a tow line. Not a word was said. After the car was going, the city man unhooked the ropes and silently drove away. The following day the Otis native drove into the next yard and came to the door. "How much do I owe you?" was his sharp question.

"Not a cent," was the reply; "can't a man be neighborly if he wants to?"

"Guess so," said the Otis man with a slow smile, and went off. And as the ex-city dweller tells it—"Now we were even, and I had learned a lesson I never knew in the city."

The scenery of *BECKET* is much like that of its southern neighbor, Otis. In the early nineteenth century the Hoosac Range, separating the Connecticut Valley from the Housatonic, was considered too steep for travel; the only road from the east to Becket was from Blandford through Otis. Not until the twentieth century did the high-flung road over the Hoosacs, the famous JACOB'S LADDER, become the direct way from Springfield to Pittsfield.

The Ladder joins Mass 8 at West Becket, where an old stagecoach tavern keeps company with an abandoned school and a tiny hillside cemetery. From this point Mass 8 and US 20 merge to go over the Ladder. JACOB'S DREAM is a little settlement two miles west; during the summer months Ted Shawn's colony of male dancers give public performances near here on Fridays. You will swing up to a height of 2,100 feet. From this elevation a TOWER overlooks the widespread panorama of the Berkshires to the south and east. A few hundred yards below this spot is JACOB'S WELL, a spring whose purity has attracted a roadside stand and a tourist shop.

About 1801 Johnny Appleseed, whose passionate interest in planting apple orchards has been woven into our folklore, is said to have trudged the old Walker Brook trail to the topmost point of the Ladder. Today people still stop here, as Johnny Appleseed did, to view the beauty of the landscape.

The highway continues east down the side of Becket Mountain, making its way toward BONNY RIGG FOUR CORNERS, a well-known stopping place for stagecoaches in the first half of the nineteenth century, now but a crossroads. Mass 8 here turns away again from US 20 to run north to Becket and Becket Center.

Several hamlets make up the town of Becket: West Becket, Charcoal City, Union Mill (also known as Bancroft), and North Becket. WEST BECKET was prosperous from 1800 to 1840. The old tavern, now a private home, is the solitary relic of that era. CHARCOAL CITY, dotted with forges and sawmills during the same period, today is a mere name. UNION MILL is partly in Hampden County, but the paper mill that bears its name is in Becket.

BECKET CENTER is a mile from the Ladder. From 1740, when it was settled, to the 1840's this village thrived. Now the tiny one-story TOWN HALL, the CHURCH OF CHRIST, CONGREGA-TIONAL (1780), a plain white structure, and a white farmhouse are all the sightseer need stop for. A boulder on the sidehill opposite the church was marked in 1936 to commemorate the building of the first meetinghouse, 1762-1764. The present church has hanging in its belfry an old bell thought to be one of Paul Revere's. Copper utensils were donated by residents of the community to be melted into the bell; but on its arrival in town a crack was detected. Back to Boston for recasting went the bell, along with a hundred silver dollars and a committee to make sure that the silver was really added to the metal to give the bell a silvery tone. Behind the church the OLD CEMETERY, chained and padlocked as if to hint that Berkshire's past is Berkshire's own, has its headstones all facing the setting sun. Stone walls surround the little plot, straight and plumb as when the farmers set them up long ago.

During times of war in the colonies there was much traffic over the old Blandford road that passes through the village center. With Burgoyne's captive army went a young Scotsman, David Cairn Cross. At Chester Hill he fell in love with Nancy Mulholland of Chester and married her. After the wedding he joined the Continental Army and today his saber, powder horn, and flintlock pistol, are cherished treasures of the McCormick family, descendants of Nancy and David.

The road to Becket from Becket Center winds through thickly wooded countryside and passes the north end of CENTER POND, encircled by summer camps. About two miles beyond, a dirt road on the left leads to YOKUM POND and the Becket section of October Mountain State Forest. The pond was named for the Indian Chief Yokun (sometimes spelled Yokum), once a mighty land-owner in Becket. Despite his real-estate activities and the wealth which must have been his, he is believed to have drowned himself in the waters of the pond. A mound off the shore is pointed out as his grave.

The village of BECKET is the largest settlement in the town, and through it pass trains of the Boston and Albany Railroad, after making the hard climb from Chester over the top of the Hoosac Range. Often "pusher engines" are needed to get the cars over the range. In 1927, when the Ballou Reservoir burst its earthen bank and poured a twenty-five-foot wall of water down the narrow valley, the railroad embankment was destroyed, roadways were ruined, and the settlement was nearly wiped out. The town's principal industry, a silk mill, was swept away; houses and shops floated downstream with the flotsam and the debris. This disaster marked the end of Becket's era of industrialism. Since then, save for Ballou's basket factory and a gristmill, the town's shops and mills have either closed down or been destroyed.

In the early nineteenth century, when stone and wood were the basic materials for the town's enterprise, there were sawmills and gristmills and quarries in both the western and northern parts of the town. Two or three mills for turning bowls were in operation in "Dish Hollow," the present site of the village of Becket. In North Becket, at the same period, there were two woodworking shops where furniture was made from curly or bird's-eye maple. From two small tanneries in 1800 grew an extensive business, which at one time tanned fifty thousand sides of upper leather a year. Hemlock bark, once plentiful around the village, was essential to this work. Unwisely, the wanton cutting of this species of timber and the failure to plant new trees exhausted the supply. Claflin, one of the tannery owners, meantime had become governor of the state and an academy in Becket, now defunct, had been named in his honor. In 1883, when tanning was no longer profitable, the Claflin factory became a silk mill. This prospered and a new building went up. The flood of 1927 completely destroyed the mill, then operated by an Illinois company.

Long before this, towns with better locations and more generous sources of raw materials began to push Becket out of the industrial picture. Villagers say there is still enough blue granite in the town to pave a road around the world, but, paradoxically enough, all the local curbstones are made of Quincy granite, carted up from tidewater to Becket in the hills. Granite quarries operate today, and the industry is still of local importance. Copper and emery have been vainly sought in the neighborhood.

The sawmills, tanneries, quarries, and other industries that once flourished in Becket were ordinary—nothing exotic, glamorous, or at all exciting about them. But today the little town has an industry, occupation, and art, that is, to say the least, a bit queer.

"Unique? Wa-al now, I dunno 'bout that. But we hev got a lady here in town who raises rabbits," a native will drawl if questioned about the matter. "Yes, sir, regular business o' raising 'em."

"I suppose she sells them to the local butcher," may be the indifferent murmur to prop the conversation. "Importing rabbits when the woods are full of them! Now, if it were the hunting season . . .'"

"Landsakes! You dun't reckon she raises 'em for butchering, do you? Them bunnies is jest like pets, jest like pets, I'm a-tellin' you, stranger. Combed and brushed and put t' bed like babies ev'ry night."

The traveler is on his way again, but he turns for a parting glance. The native cups his hands to shout better. "You'd better go see this woman. She *spins* them bunnies o' hern, stranger. Yes, siree, she puts them bunnies on a spinnin'-wheel 'n spins 'em!"

A visit to Miss Lucille Griffith's Colonial house in Becket bears out all the native said, for these Angora bunnies are truly pampered. The business end of this home industry easily warrants any expenditure of care on behalf of the creatures which supply the delicately fine wool that is put on spinning-wheels and spun. This occupation, now very much alive because of the demand initiated in Hollywood for angora sweaters and boleros, is one of the most unusual of all the small home industries scattered through Berkshire.

WASHINGTON is Becket's neighbor on the northwest. Two reservoirs within the village limits, Ashley Lake and Farnham Reservoir, supply the city of Pittsfield with drinking water. OCTOBER MOUNTAIN STATE FOREST, reached from the Washington town hall by a road going west, is the largest reservation in Massachusetts. Its 14,189 acres of high land are covered with spruce, hemlock and hard-wood forests, and twelve hundred acres are given over for a wild-life sanctuary.

The principal highway, Mass 8, traverses only a corner of the town and entirely avoids the town center, high up on the summit of Washington Mountain. Mass 8 from Becket to Hinsdale runs past Washington Station, the highest point on the railroad between Boston and Albany, but if you want to see the Town Hall, turn left in Becket and go up the steep road behind the white church and the schoolhouse. About two-tenths of a mile up the hill is a junction with a trail that leads across a bridge and part way up a steep bank. Here BECKET FALLS plunge twenty-five feet into a grotesquely worn rock channel.

The road then swings up through thick woods to emerge on a plateau from which there is a broad view of the distant Hoosacs, the little white church in Peru standing out against the sky far off on the horizon. Almost at the summit of the mountain perches ST. ANDREW'S CHAPEL (1899), the gift of George F. Crane, wealthy New Yorker who spent his summers in Washington for many years. The church was dedicated to the Reverend Andrew Oliver, a former minister of the town, and his wife, parents of Mrs. Crane. The Manor House, now the property of the Episcopalian Diocese of Massachusetts, stands nearby. Girls from the Friendly Society of New York are frequently sent here on vacation. Most of the Baptist or Congregationalist residents of Washington have gladly attended St. Andrew's since their own churches were destroyed by fire. The Gothic structure, made of field stone, was built on the site of the home of the first minister who settled in Washington.

On the very top of Washington Mountain stands the windswept OLD TOWN HALL, once the civic center of the town. Now only an old farmhouse keeps it neighbor, and the State Forest encroaches on every side. When Washington was in the golden age of its history, about a hundred years ago, the road from Becket over Washington Mountain was part of the old Pontoosac Turnpike. The route had been surveyed in 1819 but the pike was not ready for use till 1830. It ran through Chester to Pittsfield, providing daily stage travel till 1837. Toll gates were set up to pay the cost of the road. Since Washington Center was one of the stops for rest and fresh horses, the town was then quite a place. It had a thousand inhabitants, and, even in pre-Civil War days, farmers among its hills are said to have been so prosperous that men came from other towns to borrow money. Great flocks of sheep and herds of cattle roamed over the hillsides, charcoal burners sent up their smoke in the woods, and farmers cultivated the sloping fields. Down near the railroad, "The City" hummed with the activity of a dozen sawmills and tanneries.

Washington had its origin in a tract of land called Tukonick by the Indians. One Watson, a Sheffield farmer, owned it up to 1758, when two groups of new settlers from Connecticut purchased the land and named it Greenock. Disputes with the Indians led to a petition in 1762 to grant the proprietors a township. On April 12, 1777, the town was incorporated as Washington.

In 1855, the peak of activity in the town, most of the people made their livelihood either from sawmills, some of which were run by Shakers, or by raising cattle on the available pasture land. The Western Railroad, opened in 1841, which meant hope for some Berkshire communities, ruined the local farmers by making western beef cheaper than native. The timber lands were soon entirely wasted and people began to look for a better living elsewhere. In the 1870's about six hundred were still earning their living hard in Washington; by 1900 only 377; and today most of the 252 residents of Washington either work on the roads or "hire out" to summer people.

The vacation colony was begun in 1896 by a Lenox summer resident, William C. Whitney, Secretary of the Navy under President Cleveland. He purchased about eleven thousand acres of land within the town and began a game preserve on an area about five by seven miles. Whitney spent twenty thousand dollars in building a fine house and stables, and enclosed a hundred acres to be stocked with moose, elk, deer, and buffalo. A herd of eight Wyoming buffalo and five bulls were imported, among them Apache, the king of the herd, said to have been the largest buffalo in the world. Other areas were devoted to angora sheep, to goats, and to Belgian hares; an aviary was stocked with some two thousand pheasants. Whitney's pay roll of twenty-five hundred dollars a month sustained fifty-five game keepers, workmen, and servants. It was by grace of the taxes he paid for so many years that the town was able to have good schools and to be free from debt.

After the death of his wife Mr. Whitney abandoned the preserve, though it had cost him two hundred thousand dollars or more. The animals were shipped to the New York Zoo, a few moose and Virginia deer escaping into the Berkshire hills. Two years ago, according to several reliable witnesses, a moose was seen in central New Marlborough. For some years the estate was a lonely, untenanted place, until a group of Berkshire men pledged twenty-five thousand dollars to enable the state to purchase the area. In 1915 the property, in addition to sections of forest land in Lenox and Lee, was taken over by the state and opened to the public as October Mountain State Forest.

The part of the forest nearest Lenox is known as SCHERMERHORN GORGE after a wealthy Lenox resident of that name who donated the property to the state. Groves with fireplaces, tables for picnicking, and facilities for camping are found at regular intervals throughout the Forest. In the Gorge at an elevation of 1,800 feet is FELTON LAKE, a little body of water surrounded by thick woods. Along the shores of the lake, log cabins, a bathing beach, and additional campsites are now being developed. TORY GLEN, running through the forest, is so named because of a belief that it was a refuge for Tories during the Revolution. ROARING BROOK rushes for a mile and a half through this ravine before it joins the Housatonic River.

Two miles east of the Town Hall is the OLD RED SCHOOL-HOUSE which Edwin D. Morgan, financier and politician, attended when he was a Berkshire boy. Morgan was born in Washington in 1811 but moved with his parents to Windsor, Connecticut, in 1822. In later years he was employed in Hartford by two uncles in the mercantile trade. One shrewd speculation followed another, until Edwin Morgan eventually accumulated a fortune, became governor of New York for two terms, and twice declined the post of Secretary of the Treasury of the United States.

Though it has a similar name, Washington is not to be confused with Mount Washington, in the southwestern corner of the Berkshires. The more easterly village proudly claims to be the first community ever named after the Father of Our Country, and his likeness is on the face of the town seal. The claim is not valid, however, for Washington, North Carolina, takes precedence by a number of years, and New Hampshire's Washington predates the Massachusetts town by one year.

Like all Berkshire towns, Washington has a story or two worth telling. One concerns the Reverend Braman Ayres, possibly the last of the old-time "A-h-men!" Methodist ministers who preached here, a man who mixed wit and ingenuity with religion to the disparagement of neither. One fine spring day he paid a visit to his brother's home. Driving past, he sniffed the smell of his sister-in-law's tasty johnny-cake, and quite designedly he reined his horse into his brother's yard at high noon. Invited to eat dinner with the family, the minister seated himself at the table, apparently oblivious of the dismay on his sister-in-law's face.

"Johnny-cake indeed!" she probably muttered to herself as she deftly slid the cake out of the oven. "If Brother Ayers eats one piece, he'll eat two; and if he eats two, he'll certainly eat three; and if he eats three—"

Silently imploring the Lord to remember her virtues and be as lenient as possible with her transgression, she shoved the fragrant yellow cake out of sight. In its place, wheat bread was set in prominence on the red tablecloth, while the parson's hostess reminded him, in somewhat of a hurry, "Brother, it's time to say grace."

"Oh Lord," began the Reverend, sniffing for direction, "bless this food prepared for our use, and bless the johnny-cake"—sniffing triumphantly—*"under the stove!* A-h-men!"

CHAPTER XII

PAPER, AND THE SMELL OF PINES

HINSDALE—Mass 8 and 143, sett. 1763, alt. 1431, pop. 1144.
DALTON—Mass 8 and 9, sett. 1755, alt. 1199, pop. 4282.
Roads—Mass 8 goes north from Becket to Hinsdale and Dalton.

HINSDALE is a hybrid of the mill town and the backwoods hamlet. A century ago its five woolen mills, cotton factory, tannery, two bedstead factories, and sawmills rivaled the industrial prospect of its northwestern neighbor, Dalton.

The first settlers of Hinsdale in 1763 were the three Miller brothers from Middlebury, who were followed by other "Connecticut Yankees" and by settlers from Rhode Island and the Connecticut River Valley. Hinsdale, originally a district of Peru or Partridgefield, became a separate township in 1804. It was named after the Reverend Theodore Hinsdale, who in 1795 made a start at farming on the Ashuelot Equivalent (now Dalton) after retiring from his home church in Windsor, Connecticut. He soon became involved in the religious affairs of the community, and took part in the direction of the parish for the rest of his life.

No little difficulty attended the erection of the church Mr. Hinsdale served. The raising began with an auction of the pews, and it would seem that some of the congregation became inebriated for the occasion, since bids reached staggering sums before the auction was over. Many of the bidders awoke the next morning to learn that they had promised to pay more than they could scrape together in a lifetime. Some fled the community, leaving heavy obligations upon those who remained, and during the long winter evenings townspeople spun tow and linen by the light of pine knots in an effort to free the parish from debt. A few conscientious individuals parted with their last cow to meet their pledges; one luckless fellow was taxed for over a hundred dollars, although he owned little more than a side saddle and some tools.

The church was built in 1799 on the "schoolhouse hill," opposite the present Shady Villa on Maple Street. As the center of town shifted with the coming of the railroad, churchgoers wanted to be nearer Main Street. In 1857 the church was moved bodily off its foundation to its present site on the village green, near the junction of Mass 8 and Mass 143. Although its interior has been completely remodeled, the edifice remains a plain, square white building without decoration, typical of the sedate New England meetinghouse of more than a century ago.

The auction is an episode in its history Hinsdale would prefer to forget, but an earlier anecdote concerning post-rider Israel Bissell is one they treasure. Bissell spread the news of the Battle of Lexington and Concord through the countryside of Massachusetts and Connecticut to New York and Philadelphia. It is said that he traveled for four days and six hours, leaving the post station in Watertown almost as soon as the encounter began. From 10 o'clock on the morning of April 19 until 5 o'clock on the morning of the 23rd, he stopped only to change horses and permit the copying of the "Call to Arms" he carried. The proclamation is now treasured in the archives of the Historical Society of Pennsylvania.

Some years after this stirring ride, Bissell settled in Hinsdale, where he spent the rest of his life. His grave in the old section of the Maple Street Cemetery is marked by a simple inscription.

The Plunkett Woolen Mills were the most prosperous factories ever operated in Hinsdale. The first one was built about 1831 by Charles H. Plunkett, son of Patrick, who came from Ireland to settle in Lenox in 1795. Charles Plunkett was known as the "Squire" and for years dominated Hinsdale. In 1860 his mills employed 250 hands, a majority of the town's population. He owned over half the houses and operated the Plunkett Mills Store, where his employees were obliged to trade. Workers were paid annually, and when the day of settlement came, often found that after the store accounts and the house rent were deducted, they had no salary in cash at all. If they had overtraded, they had to work overtime to square the account. Little real money changed hands in Hinsdale in those days, and consequently there was a low labor turnover. Men in debt to their employer hadn't the funds to pack up and leave.

The successive owners of the mills for sixty-two years, always

Plunketts, had another scheme for making employees behave. They encouraged workers to invest whatever money they had in the company, rather than deposit it in the banks of Pittsfield. In the '90's, the Plunketts failed and sold out to the Hinsdale Brothers, who already owned one woolen mill. Many employees who had worked all their lives in the mills and had put their little savings back into them found their old age unprovided for; they received less than forty cents on the dollar of the money they had invested.

The limestone deposits which supplied the three lime kilns in the early days proved thin, the forests were rapidly exhausted, and the textile factories found competition with the larger towns of Pittsfield and North Adams a losing battle. In 1880, when the mills were prospering, Hinsdale's population numbered 1,500; today, without a single factory, it has shrunk to 1,100. The town has been able to check further decline only because every year increasing numbers of workers from the Pittsfield and Dalton factories arrive with their families to settle in this suburban area.

The Irish who came to Hinsdale with the Western Railroad in 1842 remained to work in the textile mills. The English acted as wool-sorters or superintendents, but the heavy work was performed by the Irish, or by French-Canadians, lured by factory wages during the '60's and '70's. In time, the Irish rose to positions of importance in the mill, and manual labor was done by Poles and Germans. When the mills were abandoned, the English and Scotch departed to other textile factory towns near at hand, but the Poles and a number of the French-Canadians turned to the land, truck gardening and dairy farming. The largest groups in the town at present are the descendants of Yankees and Irish-Americans.

Far out beyond the Maple Street Cemetery, near the Peru town line, is LAKE ASHMERE, christened by no less a personage than William Cullen Bryant, who stopped one day to admire the native ash trees lining its shores. The lake is almost completely surrounded by summer homes and camps. Because of its clear air and high altitude, the town is an ideal health resort, and at one time three private tuberculosis sanitariums were located here. These closed upon the advent of public institutions for treatment of the disease, but seven summer camps have recently been established in the vicinity. Although widely different in character and background, the camps are dedicated to the common purpose of providing healthy outdoor life for young people.

At the turn of the century, when Hinsdale was gaining prominence as a health resort, stories began to circulate about a rich vein of gold reputedly discovered in the nearby hills. The Hinsdale Mining and Milling Company was organized by Mr. and Mrs. George Page, a mysterious and apparently wealthy couple who displayed gold supposedly refined from local ore. This flourish impressed the townspeople, as did an announcement that the gold assayed $35 to the pound. From 1899 to the mid-winter of 1901, the mine was "worked," largely by means of issuing stock certificates. Mr. Page frequently found it necessary to issue public statements in promotion of his gold mine, once going so far as to publish a lengthy manifesto upbraiding certain doubting Thomases for their lack of faith. When subjected to detailed questioning, he and his lady invariably quoted the "world-famous authorities," "California Jack" O'Brien and "Professor" Sutphen; but by 1901, not even the experienced Pages could keep up the ruse any longer. They abandoned their mine of "fool's gold" and lit out of town, no doubt congratulating themselves upon their narrow escape from a necktie party.

The town has a much keener memory of its native son, R. H. White, who left it for Boston in 1859 and founded the large department store that still bears his name. Nancy Hinsdale went from the town in 1830 to undertake the management of the school that became Emma Willard School at Troy, New York. Of those who traveled further afield the most prominent was Francis E. Warren.

Warren was born here in 1844. During the Civil War he left the town as a soldier of the 49th Regiment. The experience of army years made him too restless for the life of a Berkshire farmer, and by 1868 he had established himself as a sheep-rancher in Wyoming. With the settlement of the western territory, his political power grew, keeping pace with his wool business. He was governor of the territory and also senator from the state for over forty years. Wyoming benefited by his efforts to obtain proper irrigation facilities, and he became known as the "Father of Reclamation." From his long interest in the wool trade as president of the National Woolgrowers Association and as rancher, he was called the "patriarch of sheepmen." Warren was the father-in-law of John J. Pershing, until 1924 Chief of Staff of the Armies of the United States.

Of living residents, the best-known is Thomas A. Frissell, one of Hinsdale's oldest citizens and the leading apostle of temperance in western Massachusetts since the days of Governor Briggs. Born in Peru in 1851, he moved to Hinsdale when he was twenty-five. He conducted the general store and the express office until his son took over for him a few years ago. Mr. Frissell (who swears he never puffed a cigar, pipe, or cigarette and doesn't know the taste of liquor) became one of the leading lights of the Massachusetts Total Abstinence Society. He steadfastly supported the national Prohibition ticket from 1884 to 1920 and has been the Prohibition Party candidate for state treasurer, senator, representative, and county commissioner. Of the many stories about his hatred of alcoholic beverages, one deals with his treatment of a barrel of beer which arrived for some one living only a short distance from the store. Mr. Frissell, as the express agent, disdained to touch the barrel but started kicking it to its destination. The barrel broke and he had to buy the man another. For many years after he started his store he refused even to sell cigarettes or tobacco. Although now retired from business, Mr. Frissell appears at the store every day, takes entire charge of the several houses he owns, is active in the Hinsdale Congregational Church, and is largely credited with the success of "Old Home Sunday" services in Peru every August. His interest in temperance hasn't lessened with the years. Regularly he writes letters to the *Berkshire Eagle* on the subject.

The manufacture of army cloth created a temporary boom in Hinsdale during the World War, but since the 1920's all manufacturing has been abandoned. The town is now without any industries and dependent for livelihood upon farming, the Christmas-tree business, the summer-tourist trade, and employment afforded by neighboring communities. At present Hinsdale is making a strong bid for summer business. Two or three small inns have been opened and tourist signs have been nailed up.

Once the center of diversified industries, Hinsdale now concentrates almost entirely upon the exportation of Christmas trees, ferns, and greenery. The pioneer in this business was Louis B. Brague, a native of the town, who started a modest Christmas-tree export enterprise eighty years ago, doing all the work himself. About one hundred men and women, most of them independent, are now occupied each fall and winter cutting, trimming, and tying evergreen trees for shipment to city markets. In prosperous times an average of thirty thousand trees, thousands of cartons of spruce and balsam boughs, and millions of delicate ferns are shipped annually to Boston, New York, Chicago, Philadelphia, and even as far south as New Orleans.

Overhead expenses are relatively small, for almost everyone who owns land in the hill towns has acres of spruce and balsam growth, taxable whether the trees are felled or left standing. Practically every man in hilltop Berkshire enters the business, either selling his trees directly to wholesalers like the Brague Company or transporting them to market himself.

Early in the summer foresighted cutters are busy making arrangements to get trees from neighboring woodlots. Widows, spinsters, non-resident landowners, and even men with steady jobs sell trees "on the stump" at ten or fifteen cents apiece. Although nearly every acre of spruce and balsam is thinned out annually, the woodlot is never completely cut. The huge trees that throw seed cones are left standing.

The spruce, balsam, and hemlock boughs are used to protect hardy plants during the cold weather, to cover graves made in winter before the sod can be filled in, and for decorative purposes. Boughs cut in three- or four-foot lengths are baled in presses made especially for that purpose and tied with a tar rope. Picking ferns is a tedious, back-breaking job. The ferns are picked in the early fall in bunches of twenty-five and tied with string. As they must be kept cool to preserve their life, they are packed in sphagnum moss and wet newspapers, before shipment to wholesale florist supply houses in the cities. Wreath making is an allied small-town industry, largely carried on by women.

The Christmas-tree busines is a gamble. Retailers at the last minute find themselves in need of an extra carload of trees and have to pay almost any price to meet an order. "Pawing over the bunch," as they call it, costs money in hilltop Berkshire, and anyone who wishes to select one tree from a hundred or more pays for the privilege.

The hill farmers used to peddle their trees on the sidewalks of big cities directly to customers. In the early days of his business, Louis Brague sold trees and evergreens in baskets on the streets of New York and Chicago. For years the corner of Lexington Avenue and Forty-seventh Street, New York, was headquarters for Brague Christmas trees. The passage of laws prohibiting sidewalk displays without special permits has forced farmers and retailers who still go to the metropolis to rent the yard of a gas station or the entranceway of a store for a stand.

The Yule season is a mad rush for even the most easy-going farmers. The children work as hard as their parents, nor is it uncommon to see women, muffled in men's work breeches, mackinaws, four-buckle overshoes, with their heads wrapped in woolen scarfs, helping to tie up trees in the farmyards.

Ice storms stop the work entirely, for the shape and beauty of a tree cannot easily be determined if it is coated with ice. Nor can trees be dragged to the roadside or loaded on trucks with the branches ready to break under a load of icicles. Selection of the trees to be cut depends upon good judgment, experience, and an eye for beauty. Perfect trees are rare. Lopsided, scrawny ones are passed by. Occasionally, however, by cutting and trimming here and there, a tree can be fixed up to present a fair appearance.

The Christmas-tree trade of the larger dealers has of late declined, because of the encroachment of the small hilltop farmer who has gone into the business. Berkshire farmers are sure that this source of income will regain its footing, and Berkshire will be saved by Santa Claus.

On the banks of the Housatonic, rimmed by hills, lies the industrial town of *DALTON*. The original proprietors were forced to do some swapping of land before they obtained the Dalton grant known as the "Ashuelot Equivalent." Colonel Oliver Partridge, Berkshire's first real estate operator, and a company of associates were awarded a large tract of land on the lower Ashuelot River in New Hampshire, but since the boundary line between Massachusetts and New Hampshire was as yet undecided, the territory was claimed by both colonies. The British Privy Council settled the dispute in 1740 by granting the land to New Hampshire, which gave Massachusetts no alternative but to offer Colonel Partridge and his group their choice of an equal allotment from the unappropriated lands in the western part of the colony. Selecting the upland valley of the Housatonic as it expands eastward, they gave it a literal name, the Ashuelot Equivalent. In 1784, the town was incorporated and renamed Dalton after Tristram Dalton, speaker of the State House of Representatives.

Among the proprietors of Ashuelot Equivalent was Colonel Israel Williams, a cousin of the founder of Williams College. Colonel Williams was appointed a "Mandamus Councillor" by the Royal Governor of the colony in 1774, hardly a propitious time to be singled out for any Tory honors. Of all appointments, the office of Mandamus Councillor was the most odious. Williams was especially unfortunate in that the town of Hatfield where he lived was a hotbed of colonial sympathy. A mob of patriots lost no time in abducting him and shutting him up in the schoolhouse, where they proceeded to stuff the chimney and light pitch fires. After a brief but trying inquisitorial session, the Colonel signed a confession repudiating his loyalty to the King. His change of heart inspired the couplet in John Trumbull's poem, "McFingal":

> Have you made Murray less big
> Or smoked old Williams to a Whig?

But evidently "Old Williams" regarded a confession under duress as no confession at all, for a few months later Hatfield learned that he had recommended "drastic measures" against the rebellious Colonists. Once more a mob seized him, and again he was locked up, this time in a regulation jail. The townspeople soon wearied of having so persistent a Tory in their midst, and banished him to Ashuelot Equivalent, where the Pittsfield Committee of Safety and Inspection could keep a watchful eye on his activities.

William Williams, the Colonel's son, left Hatfield of his own accord to join his father in the Equivalent, and became one of the leading men of the town. Year after year he was elected to the chief offices of the local government; yet in 1792 because of Tory sympathies he was among the fifty Dalton citizens accused of treason and banished from the community. The act of banishment was a farce, for as sheriff and selectman it became his duty to warn himself and his friends out of town. Needless to say, not one of the fifty ever stirred from his home in Dalton.

In its early years Dalton had troubles other than the Tories. One scandal not easily laid to rest was the prolonged quarrel over the location of the meetinghouse. The structure was only half completed when each of the several settlements in the town decided that the church should have been situated within its precincts. Unseemly controversy raged despite an attempt by a neutral committee from Lanesborough to arbitrate. Its decision failed to satisfy any of the warring factions and was voted down. A second committee, made up of residents of Williamstown and Peru, was appointed to restore a sense of Christian amity to their stricken neighbors. This body took its responsibility very seriously, measuring the town off in every direction and estimating down to a "T" just how far this corner was from that. The town was in great suspense until the final report was made—that the meetinghouse should remain exactly where it then stood! The decision was accepted.

Industrial Dalton is a community raised by hand, still accepting the system of benevolent paternalism that has persisted from the early nineteenth century. One fourth of the town's population of four thousand is employed in the paper and woolen mills. Skilled workers, most of them English, Irish, and Yankees, live in trim, modest houses along elm-shaded streets. The manors of officials in the paper and wool industries which control the town are flanked by formal gardens and velvety lawns, in neighborly proximity to the homes of employees. The two families who founded the paper industry founded town dynasties. Their descendants, to this day owners and executives of the mills, have a long tradition as townsfolk behind them.

The Dalton "manufactory" for which its owners urged "due encouragement" as a public duty was the first paper mill in that part of Massachusetts west of the Connecticut River, and the beginning of the rise of the Cranes as "fathers" of the community.

Before Zenas Crane and his partners sent out their plea for domestic economy, Berkshire housewives had looked upon the odds and ends of the family wardrobe as useless clutter. Until then, Hepzibah's old aprons, Father's shirts too ragged even for young Johnny's hand-me-downs, the tablecloths that wouldn't stand another patch, and Aunt Hannah's billowing "unmentionables" were good only for scrubbing floors or braiding rugs. The paper makers, the newspaper editors, and the post-riders taught the thrifty ladies of Berkshire that their rags could be as valuable as coin of the country. While they delivered the mail and relayed the latest news, Berkshire post-riders preached the gospel of rag saving.

The story began with a newspaper notice in the *Pittsfield Sun* for February 8, 1801.

Americans !

Encourage your own Manufactories,
and they will Improve.

LADIES, fave your RAGS.

AS the Subfcribers have it in contemplation to erect a PAPER-MILL in *Dalton*, the enfuing fpring; and the bufinefs being very beneficial to the community at large, they flatter themfelves that they fhall meet with due encouragement. And that every woman, who has the good of her country, and the intereft of her own family at heart, will patronize them, by faving her rags, and fending them to their Manufactory, or to the neareft Storekeeper— for which the Subfcribers will give a generous price.

HENRY WISWALL,
ZENAS CRANE,
JOHN WILLARD.
Worcefter, Feb. 8, 1801.

Shaker rags were the choicest, because they were always clean and strong in texture. Homemade linen was an especially desirable fabric, but unfortunately for the paper makers, this material wore like iron. It could be handed down through a whole family without getting threadbare, and Grandmother's nightgowns made good panties and petticoats for the children.

Although the collected rags, variegated in color and fabric, were sorted out in piles by tint and texture, in the early years bleaching was far from thorough. Newspapers of the day presented a diversity of hues, from a dingy gray-white to a dull blue, depending on the predominant color of the rags used. If the sorting was carelessly done, paper came out streaked and shaded. Dyed rags made the cheaper kind of wrapping paper, and those tinted with indigo were saved for tobacco wrappers because the dye was thought to add a pleasant flavor.

In 1777 the founder of the paper industry in Berkshire, Zenas Crane, was born in Canton, Massachusetts. His home was not far from the Milton Mill, the first paper mill in the state, established in 1730. Crane's oldest brother was a partner in the Milton Mill and later established his own factory in Newton; and Zenas, before his arrival in Berkshire at the age of twenty-two, had spent several years in the paper mills of Newton and Worcester. His capital was modest but his experience was sufficient to start a business of his own in the untried territory of western Massachusetts.

At the close of the eighteenth century Dalton was an agricultural town with a population nearing the thousand mark. Shrewd young Crane recognized that the community had all the assets essential to his purpose—abundant water power from the Housatonic River, and numerous hillside springs of the pure water necessary for cleansing rags and preparing pulp. Land was cheap, the surrounding countryside was sufficiently populated to provide an immediate supply of rags as well as a market for the finished product, and surplus paper could be easily transported across the Taconics to Albany, thirty miles away.

Zenas Crane interested two partners in his proposal, and in the spring of 1801, true to the advertised "contemplation" of the associates, the paper mill was erected. So skeptical about the enterprise was Martin Chamberlain, from whom they purchased the land for the sum of $194, that he would not agree to the deed's final delivery until the "thing should be done" and operating successfully. The mill, a small two-story structure, had at first only one vat. Its daily output was 100 to 120 pounds of paper, all made by the slow hand process. This consisted of dipping a square frame covered with a wire screen into the vat of liquid pulp, and shaking down the pulp into a flat sheet. The water drained off through the screen. Sheets were made one at a time.

The partners could figure their pay roll on their fingers. An engineer received three dollars weekly, and a vat man and a coucher (who did the actual work of making the paper) three and a half dollars. The lay boy, or general helper in the mill, was paid sixty cents; one man and two girls who handled the finished paper seventy-five cents each. All workers received board in addition to their wages. Even the proprietors were not overpaid. One became foreman at eight dollars a week and Zenas himself held the title of superintendent and general manager at a salary which, after several years, was nine dollars weekly.

The success of Crane's business after eight years induced competition, and a second paper factory, later known as the Old Red Mill, was erected by David Carson, Joseph Chamberlain, and Henry Wiswall. In the next few years, the Old Red Mill and Zenas Crane's little establishment changed hands several times, and in the end Zenas became owner of the second mill, while Carson acquired the original Crane property. By 1822 Zenas had bought out his partners and was the sole owner of the larger paper mill in Dalton.

A third mill was built in 1824 by Thomas Carson, David's son. Year after year the wooden dams above his structure were washed away during the spring freshets. Carson commissioned a well-known engineer of the day to build a dam "that would stay." The natives, distrusting the ability of the "outsider," predicted the dam wouldn't last through the next spring. "I defy the Devil himself to wash it away!" shouted the engineer. His rash challenge made such a profound sensation in the town that both the dam and the mill were named "Defiance" from that day on. Not a badly chosen name, as it turned out, for the dam weathered the spring floods of forty years and was replaced only when a larger one became necessary.

Until the '80's, natural springs afforded sufficient water for the mills. The growing demand for paper finally made this water supply inadequate if the Dalton concerns were to expand. The use of surface water was too risky. Its cleanliness could never be assured, as even a slight summer shower polluted it with mud and silt, the heartbreak of every paper-mill man. Several attempts were made to provide new sources of water supply by drilling artesian wells. None was very successful until in 1884 Byron Weston, then owner of the Defiance Mill, determined to sink a well that would be deeper than any in the region. He was rewarded with a gusher that flowed at the rate of five hundred gallons a minute and on chemical analysis was found to be of exceptional purity. Clear artesian well water henceforth was a factor of first importance in the town's production of paper.

In 1832 Zenas Crane replaced hand labor by the first paper-making machines and in 1835 cylinder dryers were added to his equipment. About four years later, Crane was one of the first in Massachusetts to use chloride of lime as a bleaching agent for removing dye from rags, and from that time on the production of pure white paper was possible. The Dalton industry has continued to specialize in a high-grade product for which linen and cotton cuttings are the base.

Crane & Co. originated the term "bond" as applied to paper. The president of a New York banknote house ordered a new shipment of "bond paper," using the term literally for paper on which bank bonds might be printed. Zenas Marshall Crane, son of Zenas I, ever on the alert for new notions, adopted the term and ever since "bond" has been used to designate any hard-surfaced, long-fibered paper.

Until the late 1860's, fashionable women in America favored stationery imported from France and England, as the native product was considered only good enough for business purposes, not for polite correspondence. The imported note papers tinted in delicate blues, pinks, and lavenders were more to the feminine taste. Crane & Co. undertook to prove that homemade goods need not be inferior to foreign imports. In 1865 a mill was equipped with special machinery to manufacture note papers so seductive as to eliminate foreign rivals once and for all. By the 1870's they were marketing an average of five thousand pounds a year of their "Ladies' Paper."

In 1847 the second Zenas Crane had developed a special paper for banknotes with linen threads cleverly incorporated in the sheet lengthwise of the note; it was his plan to sell this at a high price to banks and commercial houses. After long controversy over patent and royalty rights with an English inventor, Crane & Co. in 1879 obtained an exclusive contract to furnish the United States Government with paper for its currency and securities. Except that one year the contract was divided, it has since been continuous. In 1938 the government was supplied with thirteen hundred tons of Crane's threaded paper, improved by changes in the color and character of the thread, but otherwise little different from Zenas Crane's first attempts of almost a hundred years ago.

This paper is 25% domestic cotton and 75% linen, made from cuttings imported from England and Ireland. From 1879 to 1891 its distinctive feature was the colored silk threads running lengthwise, but thereafter until 1928 two lines of mixed blue and red cut silk threads occurred in each note. Since 1928, when the bills were reduced in size and a sturdier type of paper substituted, the silk fibers have been scattered throughout the bill instead of being arranged in lines. The Crane Mills supply more than forty countries with specialized papers for their bond issues and currency. Although the Government Mill manufacturing this paper lies over the boundary line in Pittsfield, it is considered a part of the Dalton unit. An American flag flies over the mill and government employees guard the plant day and night to foil thieves and counterfeiters.

The CRANE MUSEUM in Dalton exhibits an old account book originally belonging to the Milton Paper Mill where Stephen Crane, Zenas' oldest brother, worked. One entry of 1776 notes that thirteen reams of paper were sold to Paul Revere for £26 to be used for "money paper." It is only one of numerous museum records and documents tracing the development of the paper industry from the days of Zenas I to the present.

The Museum, originally a wing of the Old Stone Mill built in 1844, is a small one-story building of native field stone set in the midst of green lawns and bright gardens on the bank of the Housatonic River. Opened to the public in October, 1930, it may be visited without charge each weekday afternoon, from 2 to 5 p.m., Saturdays and holidays excepted. To reach it, go west along Main Street (Mass 8 and 9) beyond the Community House. At the little square, turn left on South Street past the Crane & Co. office building and take the first left, Pioneer Street. At the foot of the hill in the yard of the Pioneer Mill is the Museum.

The interior has been restored to resemble the Old Ship Church in Hingham, Massachusetts. The rough-hewn oak beams, old-fashioned chandeliers, many-paned windows, wide oak floor boards fastened with wooden dowels, and plain oak benches go far to reproduce the feeling, if not the exact appearance, of the Hingham Church. Glass cases ranged along the walls contain the exhibits.

Dalton's one large woolen factory, the Sawyer-Regan Company, is the sole survivor of the period from 1820 to 1850, when as many as twelve small textile concerns operated in the town. The Rev. Isaiah Weston, founder of Dalton's second dynasty, established the factory in 1814, but the ideal conditions for paper making, together with the evident prosperity of the paper-mill owners, turned his descendants away from textiles. The factory was sold, and has been operated intermittently ever since by a series of companies. Today it produces fine woolen cloth and employs approximately two hundred workers.

Naturally enough, Dalton's paper kings took a keen interest in the affairs of government. Among the Cranes, Zenas I served several terms in the State Legislature and on the Governor's Council; Zenas II became a State Senator, a member of the Council, and one of the leaders of the Republican party in Massachusetts. Winthrop Murray Crane, the most famous political figure of the family, was Governor of Massachusetts from 1900 to 1903 and a United States Senator from 1904 to 1913. He is best remembered for his singular record in the Senate of never having delivered a speech or made a motion. Three times he refused a cabinet position. Of the Weston family, Byron Weston served as Lieutenant-Governor and other members held minor State positions.

The two ruling clans had a feud at one time. The eastern section of Dalton, known as the Center, was dominated by Weston interests, and the western or "Flat" area by the Cranes. Each was a business unit in itself. When in the '90's a drygoods merchant who had always conducted his business in one of Weston's blocks moved to the Crane fief, it is said the outraged Mr. Weston left no stone unturned until he had filled the vacancy. He offered his new tenant six months' free rent as an inducement, and considered that saving his prestige was cheap at the price. The story gives insight into a rivalry which may once have affected all phases of local life, but is now only an anecdote on the lips of the "oldest inhabitant."

The paternal dynasts of the town are responsible for peculiarly sentimental bonds between employer and employee. The Cranes and Westons have lived in Dalton for so long that they have both status as honored residents and power as economic forces in the town. Profits for the company mean benefits for the community at large; of this principle the town has no doubt. A tradition of philanthropy has grown up in Dalton. The "dynasts" divert a portion of their wealth to public ends, and maintain an almost personal interest in every employee. Both the Crane and Weston companies had a private plan of old-age pensions and sick benefits prior to the Social Security Act, though there has never been any system of profit-sharing or employee management. Educational advancement, medical facilities, and conditions of housing are all responsibilities preempted by Dalton's industrialists.

In 1923 Senator Winthrop Murray Crane gave to Dalton a modern brick COMMUNITY HOUSE. Located in the center of town on Main Street (Mass 8 and 9), it has several community rooms, a gymnasium, a swimming pool, bowling alleys, and sundry facilities for indoor recreation. Just west of the Community House is the combined PUBLIC LIBRARY and TOWN HALL, presented to the town by members of the Crane family in 1892. PINE GROVE PARK, another gift, is the center for outdoor activities; it lies off Main Street north of the Town Hall.

Dalton is well known for the "Dalton Laboratory Plan," tried out as an experimental system of education. The plan preserves grouping by grades, although the pupils work at their own speed and may be quick in some subjects and slow in others without being dropped from their group. Classrooms are called "subject laboratories," and one or more rooms are assigned for every subject taught in the school. Free study time allows children to work at their own gait. The plan attempts to give students a sense of the interrelation of studies. If a child is working on a problem in English which involves carpentering, he is advised to adjourn to the carpentry shop for a while.

First tried out in the Berkshire School for Crippled and Deformed Children, the plan is long since out of use in Dalton, although it has spread to other communities. By 1930 it was in effect in over six hundred American towns. English "board schools" have been particularly attracted by this form of progressive education, and in Australia, too, the "laboratory plan" has been popular.

About three miles east of Dalton Center on Mass 9, a road branches off to the right towards the FALLS OF WAHCONAH BROOK, named after the chieftain's daughter who won her "brave" only after many trials in which the evil spirit played no small role. The memory of the story remains in the verse of Dalton's poetess:

> 'Tis said that an Indian maiden
> Whose love was wooed and won,
> Against her father's wishes,
> By a hostile chieftain's son,
> Had her fortune told in this rushing tide
> That hurries down the mountain side.

So they called the Falls Wahconah,
By the Indian maiden's name,
And I love their picturesque beauty,
Though they never reach to fame,
For they lift the soul from the common clod
To a broader sense of Nature's God.

WIZARD'S GLEN (turn off Mass 9 at the junction of Mass 8 and 9, into High Street and then Gulf Road) has a profusion of giant rocks like a huge, crumpled wall. Indian legend calls the pile the Devil's Altar Stone, and here medicine men and tribal wizards are supposed to have offered human sacrifice to Ho-bo-mo-ko, Spirit of Evil.

Many years ago a local hunter named Chamberlain came to the Glen, carrying the carcass of a deer which he had killed. While he was dressing the animal, a terrific thunderstorm arose and Chamberlain sought shelter under one of the great boulders, placing the deer's body under another. A vivid flash of lightning suddenly illuminated Satan and his Court. Every cranny in the rocky surroundings of the Glen held frightful specters. His Satanic Majesty, a terrifying picture, seemed to resemble the Indian of song and story, his rawboned visage painted in ghastly fashion and blood-dripping scalps hanging in festoons from his body. The phantoms began a wild chant and dance as two of their number dragged a beautiful maiden, robed only in her long, black hair, toward the sacrificial altar. One of the guards placed her on the rock and the Wizard raised his hatchet to strike. The girl, catching sight of Chamberlain in his retreat, gave a piercing shriek of appeal, rousing him from his stupor of fascination. Whipping out his Bible, which he always carried with him, Chamberlain "pronounced the Great Name." With a crash of thunder, the entire scene vanished. Chamberlain, dazed and horrified, thought he must have been dreaming. When he looked for his venison, it had disappeared.

Chapter XIII

WHERE OLD NEW ENGLAND LINGERS

PERU—Mass 143, sett. 1767, alt. 2295, pop. 151.

WINDSOR—Mass 9, sett. 1767, alt. 1944, pop. 412.

SAVOY—Mass 116, sett. 1777, alt. 1880, pop. 299.

Roads—Peru is best reached by Mass 143 east from Hinsdale, Windsor by Mass 9 northeast from Dalton, and Savoy by Mass 116 southeast from Adams. Dirt roads connect the three towns, making it possible to go from Peru to Windsor and Savoy.

TUCKED in among the hills stand three dwindling towns—Peru, Windsor, and Savoy. The early Berkshire pioneers who built them hacked their way along the route now followed by the modern highway. Through virgin forests and over the tops of the Hoosac range, two thousand feet and more in altitude, they slashed a trail to the high peaks, and there they built meetinghouse and school and established their villages.

Fear drove them up from the fertile valleys of the Housatonic and Hoosic Rivers, fear of fever that lurked in the mist creeping through the lowlands at night. No less compelling was their dread of the Indians, who could descend with terrifying suddenness on homes built in the shadow of the hills. On the mountaintops was the Land of Promise.

In their own little way these tiny mountain towns were prosperous. The great forest shadowed their doorstep. Valuable timber was free for the taking. Sawmills sprang up beside brooks, and staunch houses were reared in the wilderness. Pioneers of the mountains forced obedience from an enemy whose weapons were crags and precipices, stiletto peaks, and an almost impenetrable armor of forest. The conquered territory yielded them game and fish, soil rich in leaf mould, and pasturage for their cattle.

As time passed and old superstitions died, new settlements grew up in the once-dreaded valleys. Without fear, settlers established manufacturing communities beside the swift streams whose energies could be harnessed to their will. Lowland industry drew upon the small towns back in the hills. Their population declined.

It's a summer evening in one of these small towns out "in the sticks" of the Berkshires. A Thursday evening, to be exact, and the scene is the old Town Hall. There is an air of tense excitement, an atmosphere of hilarity, though right now the hall is quiet enough. The prim benches are set back close to the walls, the floor speckled over with cornmeal, or it may be wax, the windows swathed carefully with heavy brown paper—or perhaps a cleansing powder has been applied and not wiped away—and the flames of the kerosene bracket lamps sway crazily as they are caught by some current of air.

Seven-thirty. A crowd arrives. Country swains and sweethearts dressed in clothes as up-to-date as those you see on city streets step jauntily into the room, pay their small bit at the door, and begin tapping their feet impatiently.

Then comes the "orchestra." It may be a lone man with an accordion strapped around his neck, or it may be a banjo player and a fiddler. A wild clapping of hands, shouts, and stamping of feet greet the musicians and before they can settle to their tasks and get properly tuned up, some self-appointed prompter leaps up on the platform and, loosening his collar with an experienced finger, booms in the voice of a street-fair fakir.

"Fill up the floor, folks, fill up the floor! Come on, come on! Don't be bashful! Four more couples is all I need now! Three more couples! Two more! . . . How about you, young feller—you and that sweet little gal? . . . What, you're a stranger? Never went t' one of these square dance shindigs before? Well, don't be scairt, the folks 'll all. . . . Too late, there! Sets all full."

The fiddle begins to squeak, the banjo starts strumming, and though the music hasn't the fine synchronism of a first-class jazz orchestra, to the ears of the shy little six-year-old who is being initiated into the charming intricacies of the "Virginia Reel," and to the old granny who is "promenading" for the nth time in her life, heavenly harps will sound no sweeter! Another old-fashioned country square dance is on out "in the sticks." It will last till well past dawn.

The tunes played at these country dances are the old familiars:

"Money Musk," "Pop Goes the Weasel," "Darling Nellie Gray," "Old Dan Tucker," and that priceless classic, "Turkey in the Straw"—

> Went out to milk and I didn't know how,
> I milked the goat instead of the cow.
>
> A monkey sittin' on a pile of straw,
> A-winkin' at his mother-in-law.

And that grand, rollicking chorus:

> Turkey in the straw,
> Turkey in the hay,
> Roll 'em up and twist 'em up
> A high tuck-a-haw,
> And hit 'em up a tune called
> Turkey in the Straw!

The "calls" to the dances, which are usually sung rather than shouted by the prompter, are extremely complicated to outsiders who may come to the Town Hall for the first time, expecting to be entertained by village crudities. These "foreign" delegates soon find that they themselves are the entertainment, unless they are quick steppers and even quicker thinkers. To be a proper participant and not an admiring spectator, a person must be up on such terms as "right and left your corners," "swing your partners" and "swing your corners," "chassez down the hall," "alimand your corner," "do-se-do your partner," "grand right and left," and "promenade her home." He must be an "old-timer" or the following jingle will be Greek in his ears:

> Oh, the first two gents cross over and by that lady stand.
> The next two gents cross over and do it like a man.
> Salute your opposite partner and now salute your Jane.
> Swing your corner lady and promenade the same.

According to unwritten law at these parties, a girl has to dance with whosoever presents himself for her favor, be he old, young, ugly, or handsome, with a springy step or a foot loaded with lead. For unless she wishes to sit forlornly as a wallflower the rest of the evening, she will know better than to refuse more than once. There's no formality among the dancers. There's no need for it. Sometimes a man has only to wiggle his finger at a girl or to raise a careless eyebrow in her direction to signify that he would like to "promenade" with her. If she refuses—well, ten to one he won't ask her again, neither he nor any of his friends. It isn't that these country fellows are so easily discouraged; they just won't be bothered with a girl who's too choosy or high-hat.

"Come 'leven o'clock," refreshments are served and "right good 'n' hungry" everyone is. Sandwiches and hot dogs, doughnuts, cake, or pie are the rule, with coffee and sweet cider to "wet folks' whistles." Sometimes the refreshments serve as admission tickets at the door, or again they may be donated or sold. The total gate receipts—whether from a straight admission price or from refreshments proceeds—often go direct to the orchestra. According as they are large or small, the dance will continue; music till the cock cows if the hall is crowded and plenty of change is loose in ready fingers.

"Spooning" at these old-fashioned dances? There isn't time. No time for casual conversations. No time for anything but to sway and twirl and "promenade." Squealing fiddle, tinkling banjo, gasping accordion carry on triumphantly above the clapping, stamping, laughing, and shouting—sometimes together, now and then in raucous disagreement.

But in March the old Town Hall will see something far more exciting than an old-fashioned dance. Something exciting in a serious way and of such great import to the villagers that only people who have witnessed Town Meeting Day in an isolated Berkshire hill town can appreciate its significance. More often than not, the day is cold and blustery with the wind sweeping in small cyclones over the hills; the roads may be well-nigh impassable, for these hill towns can only afford to keep their main road open for traffic in the wintertime. Some of the town's citizens may be "snowed in"—those who live some six to eight miles back from the center, in sections where fifteen- or twenty-foot drifts are not uncommon and nothing can be done about them until the spring thaw.

Whether a voter is "snowed in" by the elements or "snowed under" by the weight of years, he usually manages to get to the Town Hall in *PERU* on the second Monday in March, the official Town Meeting Day. Not only will he be there personally, on snowshoes, in a sleigh, driving an old tin "Lizzie," or on his own two feet, but his wife, children, and grandchildren (if he has no one with whom to leave them), any relatives who are getting their winter board by "going the rounds" of their families, and possibly a pet dog or cat which can't be left at home alone—even a new baby—they'll all come with him.

How the voters get to the Town Hall is immaterial, but come they must and will, even those citizens who spend the winter months in warmer climes but retain the right to vote as resident landowners. Strangers come from out-of-town to witness the fun—serious business to the townsmen—along with newspapermen on the trail of front-page news for their journals. Meanwhile, the ninety registered voters of the village prepare for a spirited session. Once again they are out to make political history.

Although the highest-paid town officer is usually the tax collector, who receives about sixty-five dollars a year for his services, there is always a lively contest for each office—even for that of tree warden and field driver, for which no salary is paid. The greatest rivalry, however, occurs over the election of the selectmen, because they pick the road boss for the coming year.

Major political parties don't come in for much attention on Town Meeting Day, for it's all a matter of "one side" and the "other side." Personal grievances and vague prejudices are usually the platforms adopted by the "sides." It doesn't take much to make a man change his opinion of things, either. Beneath the calm exterior of these seques-tered villages, dark political undercurrents are at work. Before the eventful day itself arrives, the ardent satellites of the leaders of the two factions are out along the backwoods roads trying to find out, if they can, just how the "land lays," and whether Old Jim has made up his mind to vote for So-and-So this year, or if that blank-blank shyster friend of his has persuaded him over to the "other side." When the power of eloquence fails to change a man's opinion, sometimes the gift of a pig or a good brood hen will do the trick.

Assembled at the Town Hall, the voters take seats according to "sides," which may be a good thing, since frequently neighbors are not speaking to neighbors. Before the Moderator cracks down his old wooden mallet, State Troopers are on hand to relieve the tension if things get too "hot." Bitter controversies are ahead. Feuds which have been gathering animosity since last Town Meeting Day are ready to explode.

Points of law are observed meticulously and the "Fireside Law Books" are much in evidence. Ask a "hill-towner" to recite a certain chapter of Fireside Law and he rolls it glibly off his tongue, letter perfect. If Fireside Law will not take care of a dispute (and frequently it won't), Pittsfield lawyers are resorted to. Who has and who hasn't the voting privilege, needless to say, is of deep concern to the villagers. Why shouldn't it be, when officers are often elected by a margin of one or two votes?

A few years ago, just two weeks before Town Meeting in Peru, one "side" found, to the extreme annoyance of its adherents, that no matter which way things were counted, their "side" would be beaten. They racked their brains to discover some way out. Finally one of the most lively-witted shouted, "I've got it—how about ridding out a few of the other-side voters?—Let's see, now, take 'bout half a dozen of 'em out, 'twould upset their apple-cart, wouldn't it?"

"What d' you mean?" another member spoke up, fearsomely, "—*murder?* I'm not doin' anything like that. T' commit murder's carryin' things too dog-goned fur!"

"Murder nuthin'!" answered the spokesman disgustedly, "all we got t' do is t' prove that half a dozen of the other side ain't legal voters —you know, that they ain't registered fair 'n square-like."

The very next day charges were brought against six members of the opposing faction, challenging their right to vote. That was only the beginning. In a short time, half the residents of the town were accused of having no legal right to exercise the franchise. On the day when the case came up before the district court in Pittsfield, almost the entire population of Peru was sitting in eager expectation in the Court House. But the confusion before the hearing was nothing to what followed when some of the leaders of the fight emerged with no clear conviction as to their legal residence, and one poor fellow found that he had no legal home at all.

For nearly thirty years "Mayor" Frank G. Creamer, who ran the only store in Peru, was leader of one "side" in the town, vying with citizen James Bolger for first honors as chief functionary in the community. "Mayor" Creamer was, without a doubt, one of the most remarkable characters in the history of these old New England hilltop villages. Throughout a busy political career he was elected town clerk and selectman twenty-five times, treasurer and tax collector nineteen times; and intermittently he held the offices of moderator, assessor, pound-keeper, fire and tree warden, library trustee, fence viewer, measurer of wood, bark, and lumber, and overseer of the poor. He was likewise road boss for a good many years, justice of the peace, postmaster for twenty-eight years, auctioneer, noted horse-trader, real-estate dealer, storekeeper, and telephone "central." Whenever he found that the multiplicity of official duties weighed too heavily on his shoulders, Mrs. Creamer obligingly stepped forward and helped out with the burdens of office. Creamer's stove in the general store was the center of his strategy board of advisers; he has been reported conferring in the same locale with W. M. Crane when the latter was Senator from Massachusetts.

In 1902, "Mayor" Creamer was chosen as Representative to the General Court of Massachusetts—one of the few Democrats to go from an overwhelmingly Republican district. In 1927 he went down to defeat before the combined onslaught of two of his opponents. Since that memorable day, town offices in Peru have been more equitably apportioned among the populace.

People living in the "hills behind the hills" of the Berkshires are both "fair-weather Christians" and "fair-weather students." They go to church only from May to November and send their children to school from August to Christmas and from March to June; that is, if traveling will permit such a schedule. During the winter months both church and school are closed.

The "little red schoolhouse" of Berkshire hill towns is generally a little white one, and it is every bit as quaint as the one in the poem:

> Still sits the schoolhouse on the hill,
> A ragged beggar sunning.

The building has but one room and a fair-sized entrance hall where coats can be hung and wood stored. A little heat is a necessity during nearly the whole of the school term, for the wind blows up cool in the hills of the Berkshires even in August or June. Children are of all ages and the grades run from the first through the eighth or ninth. The teacher must be able and patient if she is to "weather" the year and be a success. She must know how to build a fire in a wood stove that accommodates three-foot lengths, for there is not always a big boy living near enough to the school to help her out. She must know how to pump an organ and pitch a tune, bind a bruise, and teach a variety of subjects no one of which may occupy her for more than ten or fifteen minutes at a time. She must administer justice impartially, comfort and often hold on her lap during the later hours of the day some woebegone little tike old enough to learn his A-B-C's, but not sufficiently inured to the hardness of his seat to sit hours on end without relief. She must be physically strong, brave, gentle, and a good disciplinarian. Above all, she must have a vast sense of humor. No easy job, being schoolmistress in a backwoods Berkshire town.

Tourists and visitors, of course, are more or less of a trial to these country teachers. "They mean well enough," sighs the calm-eyed Berkshire schoolmarm; "yes, they mean all right, but the children have such a lot of ground to cover in their studies in such a short time, and they're dreadfully shy before strangers. It's not that we don't *want* to be friendly; it's just that schooling means so much to these farm children. You see, they work twice as hard as city children for their education.

"Many of them have heavy chores to do before they start for school —milking, feeding livestock, chopping wood, washing and rinsing milkpans. Then they have the long ride to school in the none too comfortable school 'buggy,' rattling over back country roads. They eat a cold lunch at noon, which, you'll admit, isn't as stimulating as a hot one; then the ride home again, more chores in the evening, and studying on top of that!—that is, there's studying for those who expect to go to high school in some larger town."

The windswept village of Peru, highest town in Massachusetts, is on the very top of the Washington Mountain Range, 2,295 feet above sea level. Its only paved road is the stretch of state highway, Mass 143, which passes through some of the most beautiful country in Berkshire on its way to Hinsdale. This was once part of the stage line from Boston to Albany, and the coaches stopped at Peru to rest horses and refresh passengers.

Peru Center now consists of a small white church, an even smaller white TOWN HALL, a schoolhouse with "Peru Center School" painted in large letters over the door, and five houses, two of which have no tenant. Along the narrow dirt roads out from the Center, farmhouses are scattered. Here live the rest of Peru's 151 inhabitants. The town is built on an isolated knoll rising above a swampy plateau. Scrub spruce trees, which impede a view of the mountains and valleys, give Peru the wild, somber aspect of a more northern region. The little white church, its steeple visible for miles, is set so exactly on the mountaintop that its ridgepole is said to split a raindrop between the Housatonic and Connecticut watersheds.

Peru was incorporated on July 4, 1771, as Partridgefield, named after Oliver Partridge, one of the original purchasers of the grant. Among the earliest settlers was Charles Ford, who came from New London, Connecticut, in 1799. He brought with him a horse and cart, a yoke of steers, two cows, and one hog. According to legend, the hog became footsore and delayed the party by limping along in the rear. Mr. Ford, who was a shoemaker by trade, had leather and tools with him. He made boots for the hog's feet, and hog-in-boots arrived in Peru none the worse for travel.

When the village was renamed in 1806, townsmen explained, "Like Peru in South America, we are in the mountains, and though there is no gold and silver under the rocks, our town favors hard money and begins with a P." Two years before, the western district of Peru had been set off, and, along with additions of land from neighboring grants, incorporated as the town of Hinsdale.

Peru has always been primarily an agricultural township. At one time several sawmills, a small limestone quarry, and a cheese factory operated here, but they have long since disappeared. Some of the inhabitants now engage in dairy farming and gardening, marketing their produce in Hinsdale, Dalton, and Pittsfield. Since Peru's soil is thin and early frosts cut short the growing season, townsmen supplement their income by working in the mills of Dalton and Pittsfield or on the town roads.

"Mayor" Frank Creamer moved away to Pittsfield after his defeat in 1927, the village store in Peru was closed down, and there is now no post office. Even delivery trucks from Hinsdale and Dalton do not range into the back country where most of the inhabitants live. When the farmers come to town with their produce, they do their week's shopping. Families in the backhills usually stock up a winter's supply in the autumn.

While the Mayor's general store was still doing business, its proprietor often asserted that his emporium could fill any need on an instant's notice. Tired of the boast, a customer once decided to call the bluff, and put in a hurry call for a pair of false teeth and a casket. Both were produced from stock without delay!

After Town Meeting Day, the third Sunday in August is Peru's gala event. This "Old Home Sunday" at the CONGREGATIONAL CHURCH attracts about two hundred people, most of whom are former residents or descendants of the early settlers. The afternoon is spent renewing old friendships and swapping stories of the days when their forefathers came in ox carts to worship in the first little meeting-house. The Congregational Church has always been the only religious organization in Peru. At one time the church was the center of com-munity activity and had eight hundred members, but since 1920 there has been no resident pastor and there are only ten church members.

The road to *WINDSOR* is Mass 143, which leads back from Peru down the western slope to Hinsdale, then up Mass 8 to Dalton and out on Mass 9 (the Berkshire Trail). A dirt road leads cross-country from Peru to East Windsor. It is a short cut through the forest, but danger-ous because of the mud in wet weather.

Windsor's story is like that of its hilltop neighbors, Peru and Savoy. Settled in 1767, it became a prosperous community in its first half-century through agriculture and lumbering. The severe climate and thin, stony soil were better adapted for livestock than for field crops, but enough grain could be raised in the secluded valleys to supply the needs of the community.

In the 1820's the supply of lumber along the swift mountain streams seemed inexhaustible; sawmills, tanneries, shingle and woodenware factories were busy from sun-up until sun-down. The population in-creased and new churches and schools were built. Windsor, Savoy, and Peru seemed certain to become important manufacturing centers.

In a single generation the forest was stripped bare. By 1850 there were no more giant hemlocks, birches or oaks for the sawmills, nor enough hemlock bark to supply the tanneries. With their natural resources exhausted, the Berkshire hill towns began to decline. Wind-sor suffered a death blow when the railroad ran its tracks too far away to provide transportation.

In its heyday in 1830, Windsor had a population of over a thousand; today about four hundred remain. The last industry departed seven years ago—the Old Red Mill which had been grinding out lollipop sticks and butcher skewers. As in Hinsdale, the farmers of Windsor, losing hope for productive crops from the wornout soil of the steep hillsides, have turned to selling Christmas trees. Every winter truckloads of trees and greens are shipped to the railhead, and as fast as one slope is cut over, new seedlings are planted.

In addition to the Christmas-tree trade, Windsor depends on poultry raising and dairy farming. It has no organized summer colony and so must make the most of its large estates. One of these, BROOK-VALE FARM, for many years in the possession of the Crane family of Dalton, was sold in 1937 to a wealthy New Yorker for a summer home. It is three miles from the Dalton-Windsor town line on Mass 9. East from Windsor Center along both sides of the same road stretches the estate of Colonel Budd, retired United States Army officer.

Windsor used to have much the same sort of partisan politics as Peru. One "side" was led by Charles H. Sturtevant, who retired from his carpentry labors in Pittsfield years ago and now operates a combined gas station, bar, and grocery on the Berkshire Trail (Mass 9). To the townspeople and the *Berkshire Eagle,* which occasionally repeats his "sayings," he is the local "Uncle Ezra." They call him "Pop" Sturtevant. He explains his present occupation as quite accidental, for it had been his original intention to erect a hunting lodge on the acre of ground he purchased in Windsor some years ago.

"While I was working at it, folks would stop and ask, 'What are you building, a gas station?' I'd say 'Yes' and they'd go on. I said it so many times I believed it myself, and one day a gas company man stopped, and first thing I knew I'd signed up for some tanks and pumps."

"Big Bill" Estes is leader of the other "side." In true Shakespearian fashion, "Pop's" daughter married Mr. Estes's son, much against the wishes of the respective fathers. "Big Bill" is the real boss in Windsor, but as selectman he runs the village with the aid of the ladies. Women play a large part in local political life; the school committee members are all women; there is a woman town clerk; and until last February Miss Euphemia Drysdale was the only minister in town.

In his *American Notebook* Nathaniel Hawthorne wrote with wonderment about the natural setting of Windsor over a hundred years ago:

> The highest point of our journey was at Windsor, where we could see leagues around over the mountain—a terrible bare, bleak spot, fit for nothing but sheep, and without shelter of woods. We rattled downward, into a warmer region, beholding, as we went, the sun shining on portions of the landscape miles ahead of us, while we were yet in chillness and gloom. It is probable that, during part of the stage the mists around looked like sky clouds to those in the lower regions. Think of riding in a stagecoach through the clouds!

Windsor may yet become a tourist town on the Berkshire Trail. Each year now, more signs read "Tourists accommodated" and roadside stands appear along the stretch of highway. Miles of old wooded roads lie back among the hills, excellent for hiking and riding; there are streams well stocked with fish and open slopes for skiing.

On the summit of Windsor Mountain is WINDSOR CENTER, marked only by the Post Office, flanked by red gasoline pumps and overnight cabins, the Town Hall with the name "Windsor" painted across its roof, the small plain church, and a scattering of neat, inconspicuous houses. Behind the church the old horse and carriage sheds are reminders of days when a chorus of hungry whinneys would prompt a long-winded parson to terminate a two-hour sermon.

THE WINDSOR STATE FOREST, bordering on the town of Cummington, contains 1,500 acres of land, thirty-five acres of which have been equipped for picnics and camping. The Forest is accessible from West Cummington by a marked road into the woods following the East Branch of the Westfield River. The road leads past a swimming pool to a parking space. Three hundred feet further on is the famous WINDSOR JAMBS, where the waters of Boundary Brook flow through a deep gorge in a series of cascades, one of which drops about fifty feet. The cascades may best be seen from the top of the cliffs, reached only by foot trails. From Windsor Center, a dirt road goes north to Savoy and joins Mass 116 running west to Adams.

The town of *SAVOY* was given away to get it started. In 1771 the General Court presented it to the "heirs of Captain Samuel Gallup and Company for services and sufferings rendered and endured in an expedition against Canada during King William's War about 1690."

Abel Lawrence, a Boston landowner, had bid for the tract at £1,350 but never turned over more than a down payment of £20 "as the land was not as good as represented."

Savoy seems once to have been a town of varied accomplishments. In the nineteenth century the township had five villages, six religious bodies, sixteen sawmills, sixteen cemeteries, and a tavern. Two post offices still serve a town of three hundred people—Savoy Hollow and Brier, each receiving its mail from a different route.

Up to 1920 the farmers sold their cordwood at the limekilns in Cheshire and Adams. Recently even this occupation has ceased because three State Forest areas have absorbed much of Savoy's land. Despite the decrease of taxable territory and the increase of non-productive acreage, the thrifty town was free of debt in 1938. Although the State Forests attract more and more visitors yearly, as yet there is small compensation for the loss of the land.

Savoy is an old people's town. Ruddy-faced Yankee farmers and buxom housewives make up the majority of the population. The men are usually "jacks-of-all-trades." They have to be, in a town where there are no regular jobs and where soil is too rocky and thin for good crops. Most of the houses are old and weatherbeaten, with ells and additions denoting the growth of large families down through the years. On Mass 116, coming from Adams, is a typical Savoy house with seven distinct additions. All the children stayed at home and raised more children to live in new wings. They are all probably buried in one or more of the town's sixteen cemeteries.

Just as almost every town on Cape Cod has a sea-serpent story, Berkshire abounds with tales of missing travelers. At every second town, some unfortunate wayfarer has disappeared, never to be seen again. Of all these legends, the most gruesome is the tale of the traveler who haunted the tavern in Savoy.

One black night when the rain poured down the mountains and the thunder sounded like the trumpets of Judgment Day, a lone traveler stopped for the night at the tavern in Savoy Hollow. He was never seen thereafter. The landlord, accused of robbing and murdering his guest, sobbed out an indignant denial. Since there was no proof of death, nothing could be done; but from that day on the tavern was haunted. Travelers fled in terror when they saw bloodstains on the stairs—bloodstains that could not be washed away or even covered. The specter of the murdered man, hollow-eyed and gory, appeared in an upstairs window, mutely warning wayfarers to shun the dubious hospitality of the tavern. To make matters worse, a short time after the traveler vanished, a man working in a hay field nearby mysteriously broke his neck. For years afterward his spirit was said to haunt the vicinity, moaning and groaning mournfully. No tavern could survive the attentions of two spooks like these, and at last it closed its doors. One would not suspect so bloodcurdling a chapter in the annals of Savoy, the peaceful hamlet which never housed a lawyer nor paid the bills of more than one "home" doctor.

Savoy's most remarkable character was a witless wanderer, "Crazy Sue" Dunham, of whom it was said that "no fairer human being ever blossomed out into maidenhood upon these hills than she, or lass more pretty, pert, and quick witted." Sue lost her sanity while still young, either from religious excitement, study, or a tragic love affair. For fifty years, through the storms and heat, ice and snow, Sue traveled the roads of Berkshire, a poor, wild, aimless, and harmless being who recognized no family and no home.

Crazy as she was, Sue was not stupid. She could score on any prankster who sought to make sport of her. At one time when she was visiting at the home of Abel West in Savoy, Abel was awakened at midnight by the smell of fire. Alarmed, he rushed downstairs to find Sue calmly sitting before a blaze roaring so high out of the fireplace that it licked the mantelpiece.

"Sue, Sue, what are you doing?" he cried, hugging his nightshirt close around him with one hand while trying to put out the fire with the other.

"Oh, I heard that Cain had killed Abel," she replied, "and I thought I might as well have Abel's clothes."

She was wearing her host's entire wardrobe—one reason he was in his nightshirt.

Still and all, Savoy did not really get excited over the antics of "Crazy Sue." If she set a fire, someone put it out. If she "swapped" babies, well, mothers usually recognized their own and "swapped" them back again. If she had a verbal battle with a preacher—why, the preacher was always defeated. Did a preacher good to have the wind taken out of his sails occasionally. Savoy folks had felt that way ever since the wild revival of 1810, started by the "Reverend Joseph Smith" (not the Smith who founded the Church of the Latter Day Saints). That, of course, was pretty close to being real excitement, what with this out-of-the-state preacher coming into town so fine and high, stirring folks up to a fearful state of frenzy and jitters, and then topping it all by courting a pretty Savoy lass. But even that soon blew over, with the girl sobbing into her mother's apron and the preacher—who already had a wife—taking infinite pains not to outstay his welcome in Berkshire. In fact, he scooted out of town like a streak of greased lightning at the very first mention of his former marital adventure, without waiting for a hymn or a hallelujah.

Savoy's chief attractions today are its three State Forests. A large portion of both the Savoy and Mohawk Forests are within the town's boundaries, and the northern tip of the Windsor Forest extends into the southeastern section. Not one of these is easily accessible from Savoy. SAVOY STATE FOREST is near Savoy Hollow and the Mohawk area near Brier, but neither road is comfortable to drive over. The best entrance to the Savoy Forest is from the Mohawk Trail, Mass 2. Where the Trail crosses the Cold River bridge in Florida a dirt road turns left over the hill into the reservation. The 10,000-acre forest includes a game preserve and a large picnic and camping ground, as well as Tannery Falls. TANNERY FALLS PARK near the waterfall has been developed by the Civilian Conservation Corps as a picnic place. From the park, trails lead through the woods beside a brook which gurgles along a gorge to plunge one hundred and fifty feet into a clear pool. The same path leads past ROSS FALLS, a miniature of Tannery Falls. In the northeastern corner of Savoy is MOHAWK TRAIL STATE FOREST, named from the Trail which runs through it. Although smaller than the Savoy preserve, it has been better developed for picnicking, camping, and winter sports.

As a special lure Savoy boasts "the best hard cider in New England."

CHAPTER XIV

IN THE VALLEY OF THE HOOSIC

CHESHIRE—Mass 8, sett. 1766, alt. 945, pop. 1660.
ADAMS—Mass 8, 116, sett. 1766, alt. 799, pop. 12,858.
Roads—Mass 116 runs northwest from Savoy to Adams or, after a circle tour ending in Dalton, take Mass 8 west and then north to Cheshire and Adams.

THE towns of Cheshire and Adams lie sheltered in the Hoosic Valley, at the foot of Greylock, king of the Berkshires. Cheshire—clean and prim; Adams—smoky and sprawling.

Visitors reared in the proper literary traditions naturally hope to find cats and cheeses in *CHESHIRE*. The only cats are family pussies, no relation to Alice's grinning feline, but once this little town was renowned throughout the country for its cheeses, and the most famous is actually commemorated. A large SIGNBOARD on the main highway (Mass 8) in the center of Cheshire reads:

NEAR THIS SPOT
WAS   THE
MADE IN   1 8 0 1   GREAT
CHESHIRE CHEESE

Weighing 1235 lbs, One Day's Product of the
Town's Dairies, Moulded in a Cider Press
It was drawn by Oxen to Hudson, N.Y.
And Shipped by water to Washington
It was presented at the White House to President

THOMAS JEFERSON

As a Token of Regard from the Citizens of Cheshire.

"The Great Cheese" symbolized Cheshire's satisfaction with the election of Thomas Jefferson to the Presidency in 1800. The idea of creating this monster among edibles was put forth by a Baptist clergy-man of Cheshire, Elder John Leland. A friend of Jefferson, he thought the town should send the new executive a testimonial of esteem. Most appropriate would naturally be a Cheshire product with-out peer in size or quality—cheese, of course. Elder Leland broached the subject to his congregation one Sunday from his pulpit. On a certain day, he told them, those favorably disposed toward the venture should bring their milk or curds to Brown's cider mill, where a suit-able hoop would be in readiness. When the time came, Democrat farmers from miles around rattled up in wagons generously loaded, and even three Federalists dispensed with their political differences for the occasion. The ultimate masterpiece was carted off to Washington under the personal supervision of Elder Leland. A presentation speech echoed the sentiment of Cheshire's vigorous farmer-Democrats:

We believe the Supreme Ruler of the Universe, who raises up men to achieve great events, has raised up a *Jefferson* at this critical day to defend Republicanism, and to bafflle the arts of aristocracy . . . The cheese was procured by the personal labor of *freeborn farmers* with the voluntary and cheerful aid of their wives and daughters, without the assistance of a single slave. It is not the last stone of the Bastille, nor is it an article of great pecuniary worth, but as a free-will offering, we hope it will be favorably received.

The gargantuan delicacy was eaten by President Jefferson, by mem-bers of his cabinet, and by various foreign and domestic dignitaries; and even though the White House servants got their wedge, after six months cheese was still in evidence. Jefferson insisted on making a cash present; in his diary for 1802 he records, "Gave Rev'd Mr. Leland, bearer of cheese of 1235 lbs. weight, 200d." This is at the rate of sixteen cents a pound, high for the time, particularly since Jefferson returned a goodly slice that the inhabitants of Cheshire might enjoy the product of their own labors.

Twenty-eight years after the presentation of the "Great Cheese" at Washington, Molly Cole and her husband fashioned another, weigh-ing a hundred pounds, for President Andrew Jackson. "Aunt Molly" plied her trade in Berkshire for fifty-two years, and "Cole's Cheshire Cheese" came to be a household byword. "Old Hickory," acknowledg-ing the gift, neatly combined domestic and foreign affairs in his letter, which is preserved in the old COLE HOUSE, opposite the Baptist Church and north of the Cheese sign on Mass 8. It reads:

                                        Washington, May 5, 1829

Sir:

I have rec'd today the large and fine cheese which you and Mrs. Cole have been so kind as to present to me, and I accept it with much satisfaction as a proof of your joint respect for my character. Its value is much enhanced by the consideration that it is an offering from those whose industry and management in this branch of domestic economy deserve the thanks of the Country.

In regard to the naval resources of the United States upon which you express a desire to have my opinion, it gives me pleasure to answer that I have not the least doubt of their sufficiency to place us on a par, at no distant day, with the most powerful nation in the world. This period however and the necessity for the naval power to which you allude must depend upon many considerations which I could not enumerate in this letter. Be pleased to present me respectfully to your lady and believe me your

                                        obliged servant,
                                        ANDREW JACKSON.

The house where the Coles molded their cheese for President Jackson is now a tea room, THE CHESHIRE CAT, operated by a great-granddaughter of the cheese makers, Mrs. Bennett. When she had the house redecorated in 1921, workmen discovered elaborate Masonic emblems under the five layers of wall paper. The symbols, brown on a blue-green background, included the royal arch, the beehive, the anchor, a square and compass, a Bible, a balance, keys, a bugle, and insignia unfamiliar even to Masons today. The Franklin Lodge, according to local tradition organized in 1794 on Stafford Hill, held meetings in this house when it was known as Hall's Tavern. Built in 1804, it was used eight years later as a place of confinement for British soldiers captured during the War of 1812. The front door of the old house has a large double cross on it, traditionally a protection against witches and evil spirits.

STAFFORD HILL was the site of the original settlement of Cheshire. In 1766 Nicholas Cook of Providence and Joseph Bennett of Coventry, Rhode Island, purchased a tract of land at the foot of Greylock and employed Joab Stafford to survey and map the new community. Captain Stafford was a Rhode Island Baptist, as were all the first settlers who built houses on the wind-swept hilltop. Many of them claimed descent from Roger Williams himself.

For more than ten years, New Providence went its way alone. At last, in 1780, despite a protest from Adams, the little colony was annexed as a district of the older town. The arrangement was not satisfactory, for New Providence was too far from Adams. Eventually it occurred to the settlers that they could separate from a town that did not want them, and in cooperation with some neighboring communities could form a new town of their own. There was, for instance, a tract of land in northeast Lanesborough which was separated from the center by a range of hills. A corner of northwest Windsor, adjoining the Lanesborough area on the side of Mount Amos, was remote from the voting district of Windsor. To the northwest, a group of New Ashford families were faced by a high mountain ridge when they headed for the polls in their town. All these communities were in the valley of the Hoosic River. With one accord they joined in demanding to become a new township.

The new town was formed in 1793 and named after the cheese-making county of Cheshire in England. The boundaries, staked off in the peculiar fashion revealed by the map today, appear to have been laid out by a bolt of lightning. When complete, there were twenty-five or more corners with angles of all degrees.

It is a tradition with some basis of truth that this gerrymandering wasn't really necessary, despite the fact that the town was made up of odd corners of older communities. But at that time Cheshire was almost unanimously Baptist, while some of its sister towns, particularly Lanesborough, were Congregational. According to the story, pressure was brought to bear on the surveyors to include the Baptists and leave the Congregationalists out of Cheshire.

Another account of the marking of the town's boundaries takes little stock in the religious element. It states flatly that, "It is quite evident that the line was drawn to follow the summit of the ridges, and . . . until four corners were rounded off some time ago . . . it was the most irregular town in the county." By counting in "several jogs in the bank of the river," Lenox now claims the distinction.

Upon the completion of their meetinghouse on Stafford Hill in 1774, the townspeople sent for the Reverend Peter Werden, who had been their pastor in Coventry, Rhode Island. This "Father of the

Baptist Churches in the Berkshires" ruled his little flock with high conscience during his forty years of service, as one anecdote leaves no room for doubt.

Colonel Samuel Low, one of the first settlers in Cheshire, a prominent and wealthy citizen, lived near the meetinghouse on Stafford Hill. Before coming to Cheshire, he had made his home in Providence, where he had been master of four slaves, parents and two children. He freed the parents but brought the children with him to Berkshire.

When the Colonel applied for membership in the Baptist Church on Stafford Hill, Elder Werden refused him admission unless he freed the two young slaves. The issue developed into a long polemic between the two men on the morality of slaveholding. One letter written by Elder Werden to Colonel Low on March 2, 1792, has been preserved:

Dear Brother:
We received your letter and the brothers hath heard it read. . . . We wish you, my dear brother, to attend to the proposition you mentioned— all men are born free. Therefore our desire is, you liberate him [the slave Anthony] immediately . . . as we think it will dishonor our profession if this is not dun.

Elder Werden won his point.

But it remained for John Leland, the Baptist Elder of Cheshire, to put all clerical rivals in the shade. Leland obtained a Baptist preacher's license in 1774, and was ordained, seemingly in North Carolina, in 1787. When catechized by the ordaining officers, he displayed a stubborn reluctance to admit anything he might find hard to back up afterwards.

"Brother Leland," began the interrogation, "it becomes my duty according to prearrangements to ask you a few questions upon your faith and in reference to your call to the ministry."

Question: "Brother Leland, do you believe that God chose His people in Christ before the foundation of the world?"

Answer: "I know nothing, Brother, about what God was doing before the foundation of the world."

Question: "Brother Leland, do you not believe that God had a people before the foundation of the world?"

Answer: "If he had, Brother, they were not our kind of folks. Christian people were made out of dust, you know, and before the foundation of the world there was no dust to make them out of."

Question: "Well, well, Brother Leland, you believe at least that it is your duty to preach the Gospel to every creature?"

Answer: "No, my Brother, I do not believe it to be my duty to preach to the Dutch, for instance, for I can't do it. When the Lord sent the Apostles to preach to every nation He taught them to talk to all sorts of people, but He never taught me to talk Dutch yet."

Before he moved to Cheshire in 1791, Elder Leland had been a Revolutionary soldier; and, although born in Massachusetts, had become the leader of the large Baptist group in Orange County, Virginia. A forceful speaker and ardent exponent of religious freedom, he was nominated by his followers in 1788 as delegate to the Virginia Convention, where he planned to oppose the adoption of the Federal Constitution. Another candidate for the Convention was James Madison, who discovered to his alarm that one John Leland, a Baptist divine strongly opposed to ratification, had a considerable following and would practically control the voting in his section. Madison was told that Leland was a man of strong mind and iron will. He had sprung from the lower class of society and considered himself "called" from on High to preach the Gospel as well as whatever else came into his head. The people of his district loved and respected him.

In the shade of an oak near the Orange County Court House, Madison and Leland met. They talked long and earnestly, their horses tied to the oak and they themselves pacing up and down the road. Madison was polite, persuasive, and very sure of his facts. The persuasiveness and the certainty at last bore fruit. Elder Leland was convinced that Madison should be elected to the Virginia Convention and that the Constitution must be ratified.

Leland was Elder of Cheshire's Baptist community from 1791 until his death in 1841. One of the many stories about him concerns the habit he had of carrying a favorite hymn book in his coattail pocket. One evening before a large prayer meeting he reached for his hymnal but instead drew out a pack of playing cards, which flew in every direction. For some seconds the Elder stood riveted to his pulpit in speechless horror; finally he turned from his shocked and astonished audience, murmuring in a resigned voice, "My John!"

"My John" was no apostle, but the Elder's own son.

Cheshire must have been proud of its militant pastor Leland, for prior to its incorporation as a town, New Providence soldiers had joined the independent company of Silver Greys who marched to Bennington on August 12, 1777. A MEMORIAL to these patriots has been erected in front of the cemetery just off the highway north of the Cheese sign. A bas-relief, depicting the entrance of the Berkshire volunteers into Bennington, shows Parson Allen of Pittsfield with his Bible under one arm. Colonel Stafford is at the head of the New Providence Greys, and in the lead are friendly Stockbridge Indians, acting as scouts. This tablet, the original of which was erected by the Commonwealth of Massachusetts on the Bennington Battlefield, was dedicated by Eugene Bucklin Bowen, fourteen of whose ancestors are named on the plaque.

Colonel Stafford, the Revolutionary hero, died in 1801, three months after he had lost all his land in Cheshire by quit-claim. He was buried in "God's Acre," the little cemetery built by the first settlers of New Providence, on the westernmost slope of the hill which bore his name. A century and a half later, when a MEMORIAL TOWER was erected on the hill to the memory of "The Pioneers and Patriots of New Providence," Colonel Stafford's remains were removed to a stone crypt beneath the tower. The monument, built of rough field stone, is a replica of the old Stone Mill, commonly called the Norse Mill, which was erected by Governor Benedict Arnold on his Newport estate.

Stafford Hill lies northeast of the present town center. If you have come from Savoy on Mass 116, watch for the sign marked STAFFORD HILL after you cross the Cheshire town line, and if you have driven out from Adams, you will also have to look sharp for the sign. But if you have come into Cheshire along Mass 8, turn east at the Cheese sign, go down into the center of the town, and bear left at the austere Town Hall.

The Stafford Hill settlement has left today only two old farmhouses, a monument in the field, "God's Acre" on the sheltered slope, and its outlook over the countryside. The pioneers who selected hilltops for their homes chose them from motives of sense rather than sentiment, but whether they realized it or not, the Rhode Island Baptists picked for themselves one of the loveliest spots in Berkshire, in full view of majestic Greylock, and overlooking the green Hoosac Valley.

To reach Cheshire Center from Stafford Hill, return to the junction with Mass 116 and turn left on a dirt road to Cheshire's "East Side," disparagingly called SCRABBLETOWN. Although the first settlers here were so poor they had to "scrabble" for a living, and the forbidding name persists, the village today is a neighborhood of small neat houses with trim little gardens. Scrabbletown's peculiar name is by no means unique, for Cheshire has some choice ones—Hell's Kitchen, Pork Lane, Zip Thunder, and Pumpkin Hook.

As you cross the railroad tracks from Scrabbletown you are entering Cheshire's "West Side," the quiet and prosperous section around the TOWN HALL.

In Cheshire Center, as you swing onto Mass 8 at the Cheese sign, look down toward the old CHESHIRE INN, built in 1797. In stagecoach days glass blowers, lime burners, iron miners, and woodsmen stopped here to regale themselves with rum or flip. The inn, known at that time as the Hoosac Valley House, was the favorite meeting place of glass blowers, many of whom lived in Cheshire, the first Berkshire town to take up glass manufacturing as a major occupation. The excellent sandbeds in the vicinity are said by local authorities to have been used in the production of cut glass and later plate glass, but "pressed glass," a specialty of Sandwich industry, was never manufactured in this town. Indeed, the claim is that Cape Cod's famous Sandwich glass was made of an inferior grade of Cheshire sand.

As early as 1812 the Cheshire Crown Glass Company was incorporated by Daniel Brown and three associates. In one year no less than thirteen factories in Pittsburgh were kept going solely with the products of local pits. George W. Gordon, an ex-postmaster of Boston and one-time American minister to Brazil, was among the first to recognize the possibilities of the white quartz sand.

Though the manufacture of blown glass, plate, and window glass all originated in Cheshire before spreading to other Berkshire towns, it survives today only as a quarrying operation in one locality, about a mile out of the village near the south shore of Hoosac Lake. The principal contemporary industry has become the processing of lime for building and allied purposes. Twenty-one limekilns in the southern part of Cheshire, in the section known as Farnams, are now all owned by the United States Gypsum Company. Set up several years before the Civil War, the original limekiln was sold in 1866 to the Farnam brothers, under whose guidance the Farnams Lime Works became one of the largest in Berkshire.

The coating of white dust on the factory roofs of the United States Gypsum Company, on their cupolas and blower stacks, gives the place an arctic look, even in midsummer. A narrow-gauge railroad runs through a long tunnel from the factory to the great quarries. In 1923 and 1924, tenement houses were built near the plant at Farnams for sixty families, most of them Irish, Italian, Polish and Yankee. Others of the hundred-odd employees lived in Cheshire Center or in Berkshire, a section of Lanesborough which lies south and west of Cheshire.

In the nineteenth century, when the products of the glass factories, limekilns and cheese presses were being shipped out of Cheshire in increasing quantities, human freight was being shipped in. Cheshire Harbor was in Abolitionist days an active station on the Underground Railroad. Suitable as a refuge, it lay three miles north of the Center in a secluded ravine just off Mass 8, from which Cheshire Harbor Trail winds up the side of Greylock. One of the last passengers on the Underground system was John Brown of Osawatomie. No one knows who sheltered him, for Harbor people never talked about their guests, but they sent "God's Angry Man" safely on his way to another Berkshire refuge.

There is a tradition that, many years before John Brown, no less a visitor than Captain Kidd came to Cheshire. It is said that he planted a chest of gold and silver beneath the doorstep of Widow Read's house in the Harbor before setting out on a buccaneering adventure. A chance to prove—or rather to disprove—the story went glimmering. A strange gentleman once appeared at the widow's door and asked her permission to make subterranean exploration beneath her home. The privilege was indignantly refused. Dig up her doorstep? The widow guessed not, and told the gentleman so.

Gold in Berkshire! Gold in old Greylock, on its sides and back! Gold in its pockets and piled in masses on its shoulders! Gold in the town of *ADAMS!* GOLD! . . . GOLD! . . . GOLD! Words that have sent more than one man stumbling up the mountain trails, past the ruined hut of the old hermit who lived high up on the moun-

Greylock Mountain and Adams   *Courtesy of The Society for*
The Preservation of New England Antiquities

Quaker Meeting House in Adams   Courtesy of The Society
for The Preservation of New England Antiquities

tainside, back in the 1700's. Whenever he made one of his rare visits to the Adams general store, he paid for his purchases with nuggets and gold dust. When asked where he found the treasure, the old man would wink craftily. Or he would draw the questioner to one side. Then with his withered lips close to an eager ear, he would whisper, "I'll tell you next time. Ha! Ha! Ha!" The old hermit never told. There was a storm, a winter blizzard. After it was over, the old man was found frozen to death.

In the 1700's Greylock was not ready to yield the bright streak in its veins. Nor in the 1800's. The twentieth century finds it still reluctant. Experts have declared their belief in the existence of a mineral belt extending from the north down through New England into the Carolinas and Georgia, and Berkshire County lies directly in its path. But mining engineers unanimously agree that Greylock's gold is present in such small quantities that it would cost more than it is worth to get it out.

Through the years many Berkshire men have hacked into Greylock, and every one has come away disappointed. They left yawning holes in the mountain's sides—holes into which many of them poured their strength, their youth, and their money. There is a twenty-foot pit on the center slope of Greylock, still barely discernible, and higher up, the deep excavation made by the Quakers. There are many others.

The town of Adams owes its expansion to the Quakers. As early as 1738 petition had been made for the land in order that the Dutch from New York might be precluded from settlement. The General Court, to which the petition of Thomas Welles had been directed, generously responded by ordering: "If the land seems accommodable for inhabitants, that they survey and lay out one or more Townships of the Contents of six miles square and return Plats thereof to this Court." A map of the territory later allotted to the towns of Adams, North Adams, and Williamstown was made by Nathan Kellogg in 1739; eight years afterward a party of surveyors under Colonel Oliver Partridge went to "the Province Lands near Hoosuck with a surveyor and chainmen" to "return an account of the distance that said township bears from Fort Massachusetts."

It was more than ten years before the survey was really complete and a territory seven miles long and five miles wide mapped out. All four corners were right angles, so that East Hoosuck became the only unit in the county with a regular geometrical shape. The surveyed land was then sold at auction to the highest bidder.

The pioneer settlers of East Hoosuck, later named Adams in honor of Samuel Adams, the Revolutionary patriot, were Rhode Island Quakers. For many years the Quaker section, in the southern part of the settlement, was the most enterprising, but gradually this "South Adams" was surpassed by North Adams in size. In 1878, the original East Hoosuck area was divided into identical parallelograms, and the southern village called itself just plain Adams.

The Quakers had migrated in 1766 from Rhode Island to establish a colony on better soil where they could perhaps live more prosperously. Devout and industrious, they laid out farms, built saw and grist mills and sought to make their community as self-sufficient as possible. Quite by accident, members of the colony discovered gold high up on the side of Mt. Greylock, but in a vein of ore too narrow and inaccessible to be much worked. Tradition has it that they also found a deposit of copper streaked with silver, but kept their discovery secret; there is no account of it in the early records of Adams.

The Quakers were primarily agriculturists, and after the sporadic attempts at mining they returned to the more prosaic occupation of farming. As time passed and other settlers from New York and Connecticut came into the little town at the foot of Greylock, industry replaced agricultural enterprise. The first mill in Adams was built by William Pollock, whose career began by selling an old horse for a lottery ticket which won the capital prize. The cotton industry was introduced into the town from Rhode Island in 1811; raw cotton was sent up the Hudson from New York City to Troy in river boats and thence was carted by teams to Adams. Along the same overland and water route, the finished cloth was returned to city markets until the Western Railroad extended its line into Berkshire in 1842.

As in Hinsdale, the Plunkett dynasty from Lenox was the real power in Adams' cotton manufacture. General William C. Plunkett, son of Patrick Plunkett from Ireland, was the first of a line which ruled local cotton mills for many years. Although born a poor man, the general had before 1832 acquired the entire stock of the cotton mills then operating under the name of the Adams South Village Cotton and Woolen Manufacturing Company. Until the mid-century manufacture of cloth from native wool was an equally important industry, but farmers discontinued raising sheep with the bitter comment, "Too many dogs in the town."

Paper mills were luckier, being immune to the canine menace. Daniel and William Jenks and their nephew, Levi Brown, began the manufacture of paper in Adams in 1849 under the mark of the L. L. Brown Company. They hold a record of never having used a scrap of colored rags in their products, and are believed to be the only company in the United States using all white clippings in the manufacture of ledger, linen, and bond paper.

On the road to North Adams in the community called Zylonite is jewel-like BLUE LAKE. From Greylock its intense azure catches the eye, distracting it from drab chimneypots and smokestacks. You would imagine yourself in Switzerland. Blue as the heavens when the sun shines over the waters, in a glass it is clear as crystal. The strange phenomenon is caused by lime waste drifting on to the water, for opposite the lake is the New England Lime Company and in the same vicinity the Hoosac Lime Company. The trees, houses and road are powdered with the soft white coating from the floating dust. The town prides itself on this industry and boasts of the tonnage of Adams lime that went into building the Harvard Medical School in Boston.

From one end of town to the other—from Maple Grove, the French village on the south, to Zylonite, the lime town on the north —Adams is dotted with mills. Some of the brick and stone mills are still in operation; others have either been transformed into garages, junk shops and storehouses, or stand vacant with broken windows and sagging doors. Twenty-five years ago, when spindles were flying and every man had a job, new workers and their families crowded into town. But the story is different today. When the mills are "down," as they say in Adams, everyone is hard hit. In the summer of 1938, the cotton mills of the town began production again, after having been shut for months.

Casual visitors to Adams would not easily know when the mills are "down." There might be a number of loungers on street corners or fewer automobiles on the road at weekends; otherwise there would be little indication that Adams was once again on "short time." The uniform brick tenement houses lining the streets would have clean white curtains and an occasional flowerpot to break the monotonous picture. By some extra stamina or heritage of endurance, the sturdy Poles and French-Canadians who make up the larger part of the town's population have contrived to exist and to make a gesture toward gaiety despite "lay-offs" and "short time."

The older Irish and Yankee groups in Adams have long since been outnumbered by the Poles; French-Canadians run second, with Italians and Germans close behind. The influx of Poles began about thirty-five years ago when the Plunkett mills induced a number of families to come directly from the old country. Their section along Summer Street, in the eastern part of town, is known as "Little Poland." The Polish Catholic Church on Wlodyka Square is surrounded by parochial school buildings and parish houses. Stores and business concerns on Summer Street are now owned principally by Poles. Second and third generations seem less content than their fathers with a mill worker's lot; they take to farming, small business enterprises, the professions, or else migrate out of town.

Adams has ten thousand inhabitants either of foreign stock or of mixed parentage, almost eighty-five per cent of the total population. The French and Polish have the strongest tendency to keep their identity and language. Germans, who live largely in Zylonite and on North Summer Street, are of an older immigrant stock and have been assimilated almost completely, though they still keep alive their native culture through their club the *Turnverein,* open to all races and creeds. It provides classes in music, German dramatics, and athletics for young and old. The town, preponderantly Roman Catholic, has an English-speaking congregation of this faith in St. Thomas Church, French in Notre Dame, and Polish in St. Stanislaus.

In 1899 President McKinley paid a visit to William B. Plunkett, and laid the cornerstone of Mill No. 4, at that time the most imposing of the Plunkett buildings. Adams residents admired McKinley, and gave him a rousing reception when he came to town. After his assassination in 1901, a statue was erected to his memory on Park Street (Mass 8), fronting the library, in what has since been named McKINLEY SQUARE.

Although the first Quaker meetinghouse, built in 1781, was destroyed by fire, a second, which dates from 1784, is still standing. To visit it take Maple Street out of McKinley Square and follow the hill past the sign "Thunderbolt Ski Trails," to the crest where the gaunt, weatherbeaten building stands surrounded by a burial ground. The interior is essentially the same as it was a century and a half ago. Each year, on the first Sunday following Labor Day, descendants of Berkshire Quakers gather there for a service. According to old custom, the congregation sat "Quaker fashion," the women on one side of the room and the men on the other, a discontinued practice.

The Society of Friends in Adams seems to have reached its peak of prosperity about 1830, before a schism developed and the Society split into two groups, Orthodox and Hicksites. While one party worshiped in the meetinghouse on Sunday and Wednesday mornings, the other took its turn in the afternoon; but the new wing of the Society gradually declined in numbers, and by the 1850's all but a few had moved into New York State.

One story about this staunch, thrifty sect concerns a Quakeress with a natural antagonism for canines, who was forced to endure the presence of her husband's dog, since he needed the animal to herd his cattle.

"Oh, if thee would only sell or shoot the pesky creature!" she was constantly nagging her spouse. When she returned home from a neighbor's one evening and was greeted by the news that the offending beast had been sold, she was more than delighted.

"What did thee receive for the brute?" she questioned her Quaker mate.

"Ah, good news, good news, Susan," he responded, "I sold the dog for twenty dollars."

"Thee *did*? Then I am happy indeed, for thee made a great profit. The miserable cur was not worth twenty cents," she told him with approval, hastily adding, "Did thee get thy pay?"

"Right I did," replied her husband heartily; "I took two other dogs at ten dollars apiece."

Susan B. Anthony, the pioneer for "woman's rights," probably attended service in the Quaker Meetinghouse. She was born in Adams in 1820 and even before her family moved to New York, when she was six years old, Susan was known for her scholastic brilliance. At the age of three she could read and spell, and at five she gravely requested the village schoolmaster to teach her long division. "Tut, tut, Susan, does thee not know that is a subject only for males?" Susan might not have known at the time, but she was to discover soon enough that a variety of benefits, from long division to the franchise, were denied her sex. Abolitionist and teetotaler, she is best remembered for her efforts in behalf of woman suffrage, to which she devoted her lifetime. In 1899, while a delegate to the International Congress of Women in London, Susan Anthony was presented to Queen Victoria.

The birthplace of this famous suffragist is a shrine to those women who have struggled for political and legal equality. She, more than any other, helped to wipe away the marks of an inferior social status. The house, built by Susan's father in 1810 and now the property of the ADAMS SOCIETY OF FRIENDS' DESCENDANTS, is situated at Bowen's Corners; it is a clapboarded, two-story, cream-colored structure with two end chimneys. To see it, take East Hoosac Street, which runs from McKinley Square between the mills of the Berkshire Cotton Company to the junction with East Road, where you turn right. About two-thirds of a mile beyond, at Bowen's Corner, is the house, marked "SUSAN B. ANTHONY BIRTHPLACE. Feb. 15, 1820."

There is no rational explanation as to why a certain locality in the south part of Adams should in other days have been nicknamed Poordunk. Possibly it was a refuge for the outcasts and bohemians of the time; at any rate, Poordunk is celebrated in a doleful set of verses that came to light in an Adams attic:

> Up in Poordunk where the thistle
>   Blooms, dies and rots;
> Where the winter whirlwinds whistle
>   All around the lots,
>
> Lived the slickest girl you ever
>   Saw in your life,
> Ankle like a blue beech lever,
>   Voice like a fife.
>
> As I sat by her a-courtin',
>   Calm and serene,
> With her apron she was sportin',
>   Checkered and clean;
>
> Mingled was our hands together,
>   All day we sat
> Whisperin' in winter weather,
>   Happy as fat.

Long I stuck to her like teasles,
Summer and fall;
But she went off with the measles,
Ankle and all.

The BROWNE HOMESTEAD on Orchard Street stands with its back to Greylock, a mile and a half from the traffic beacon in Adams Center on Mass 116. Built in 1778 by Eleazar Browne, one of the earliest settlers of the town, it now houses a fine collection of antiques, among them a painting of John Browne, first boy born in Adams.

There is no reason why the Browne Homestead or any other landmark, however hallowed, should turn its back to Greylock, unless Eleazar Browne grew weary of the view. If he did, then history places him in a minority; Hawthorne, Thoreau, Oliver Wendell Holmes, and Washington Gladden, once preacher at North Adams, and scores of others have waxed rhetorical on the subject of Greylock's grandeur. The author of *Walden* has left a rhapsodic account of the spectacle of daybreak seen from the mountain's summit, when he seemed to find himself "in the dazzling halls of Aurora, drifting among the saffron-colored clouds and playing with the rosy fingers of the Dawn."

Thoreau saw this sunrise after a long hiking trip over the Hoosac Mountains by the Mohawk Trail, through North Adams, and up the notch to the peak:

I was up early and I perched upon the top of the tower to see day break. As the light increased I discovered around me an ocean of mist which reached up by chance exactly to the base of the tower, and shut out every vestige of the earth; while I was left floating on this fragment of the wreck of the world, on my carved plank in cloudland, a situation which required no aid from the imagination to render impressive.

As the light in the east steadily increased, it revealed to me more clearly the new world into which I had risen in the night; the new terra firma perhaps of my future life. There was not a crevice left through which the trivial places we name Massachusetts, Vermont and New York could be seen; while I still inhaled the clear atmosphere of a July morning —if it was still July there. All around me was spread for a hundred miles on every side, as far as the eye could reach, an undulating country of clouds, answering in the varied swell of its surface to the terrestrial world it veiled. It was such a country as we might see in dreams with all the delights of Paradise. There were immense snowy pastures, apparently smooth-shaven and firm, and shady vales between the vaporous mountains; and far in the horizon I could see some misty timber jutted into the prairie, and trace the windings of a watercourse, some unimagined Amazon of Orinoco, by the misty trees on its brink.

Nathaniel Hawthorne traveled by stagecoach from Pittsfield to North Adams in 1835, and gave a somewhat more literal description of Greylock in his *American Notebooks*.

. . . I pointed to a hill at some distance before us, and asked what it was. "That, sir," said he, "is a very high hill. It is known by the name of Greylock." He seemed to feel that this was a more poetical epithet than Saddleback, which is a more usual name for it. Greylock, or Saddleback, is quite a respectable mountain; and I suppose the former name has been given to it because it often has a gray cloud, or lock of gray mist, upon its head; it does not ascend into a peak, but heaves up a round ball, and has supporting ridges on each side. Its summit is not bare, like that of Mount Washington, but covered with forests. The driver said that several years since the students of Williams College erected a building for an observatory on the top of this mountain, and employed him to haul the materials for constructing it; and he was the only man who had ever driven an ox-team up Greylock. It was necessary to drive the team round and round, in ascending.

Hawthorne's *Notebooks* contain repeated references to the locality. At another time he records:

August 22nd.—I walked out into what is called the Notch this forenoon, between Saddle Mountain and another. There are good farms in this Notch, although the ground is considerably elevated—this morning, indeed, above the clouds; for I penetrated through one in reaching the higher region, although I found sunshine there. Greylock was hidden in clouds, and the rest of Saddle Mountain had one partially wreathed about it; but it was withdrawn before long. I never saw more beautiful cloud scenery. The clouds lay on the breast of the mountain, dense, white, well-defined clouds, and some of them were in such close vicinity that it seemed as if I could enfold myself in them; while others, belonging to the same fleet of clouds, were floating through the blue sky above . . .

The BEACON, replacing the old wooden tower on Greylock's summit, was erected and dedicated by the Governor of Massachusetts in 1933. The building is cone-shaped, rising from a circular base whose diameter is 421 feet. Within are a marble-lined main room, the Memorial Chamber, and a long flight of stairs leading to window slits at the top, where the view overlooks the states of New York,

Connecticut, Vermont, and Massachusetts. From the western window you look out over the Taconics, and the roads to Bennington and the famous Monument there, and Williamstown and its college lying below. To the northwest the Adirondacks, and to the south the Catskills; directly below to the east in the Hoosac Valley lies Adams, with the Hoosac Mountains beyond. Southward, on the slope of Greylock's sister peak, Saddle Ball (variously called Saddleback and Saddle Bag), is the village of New Ashford, and far to the northeast Mount Monadnock and Mount Washington in New Hampshire. Directly to the north are the Green Mountains of Vermont.

The Beacon Light, blinding by night, has a tremendous flare visible for seventy miles. During the winter of 1937-1938 the stone Summit House, made of Quincy granite from the coast, was kept open for the benefit of hikers and skiing parties. Almost at the foot of the Beacon tower is the take-off of the Thunderbolt Ski Run. This is a great test even for experts; it circles the summit before descending precipitously about a mile and a half to the finish at the Thiel Farm in Adams.

By auto, the summit of Greylock may be reached by the Rockwell Road from Lanesborough and New Ashford, or by the Notch Road from Adams which joins the new Notch Road from North Adams. There are also hiking trails from Adams, North Adams, and Williamstown.

In 1901 the gold fever again rose high and the Greylock Mining and Milling Company was organized. Shares were sold to all comers —ten thousand of them at fifty cents a share. It was proposed that a shaft be sunk in the Notch on Greylock, and the gold in "them thar hills" was promised as a certainty to all investors. Although the futile venture cost shareholders five thousand dollars, undeterred residents dug a thirty-foot hole in 1916.

One seeker after riches found himself left with something far worse than poverty.

"Can you tell me what this is?" the fellow asked a distinguished Boston chemist. He held out a box of mineral specimens.

"Why, yes," replied the chemist lightly, "it's a box of iron pyrites."

"Pyrites? Well, what's it worth?"

"Oh, nothing, nothing at all," said the chemist, amused.

"Nothing!" There was agony in the cry. "Nothing! But, God bless my soul, sir, there's a woman back in my town who owns a whole hill of this stuff!"

"Well, you'd better warn her before she goes trying to mine it for gold. 'Fool's gold' is another name for iron pyrites, my friend," observed the expert.

"Warn *her?*" the man groaned. "Why didn't someone warn *me?* I've gone and married her!"

BERKSHIRE SPORTS, WINTER AND SUMMER

AQUATICS

CAMPING AND PICNICKING

COUNTRY CLUBS

FISHING

HUNTING

ICE SPORTS

OVERNIGHT ACCOMMODATIONS

STATE FORESTS

HIKING AND BRIDLE TRAILS

SKIING

RECREATION IN BERKSHIRE COUNTY

BERKSHIRE COUNTY has excellent facilities for a number of summer and winter sports and at least limited opportunities for the enjoyment of all major outdoor activities. On the following pages, detailed information is arranged by town and alphabetically by subject. Accompanying or near each town, is a map showing the location of the recreation areas and the roads leading to them. Local authorities, county organizations, and state departments were consulted as sources.

The towns themselves follow the order adopted in the narrative section of the book. The combination of two particular recreation areas on one map has in some instances been arbitrarily imposed by the geographical outline of the townships; not every combination can be drawn within the limits of a book page.

AQUATIC SPORTS have been developed on a number of the larger lakes and ponds, generally those in the central and south central sections of the county. In the northern hilly country the ponds, fewer, smaller, and less accessible, have not reached their fullest possibilities. Public water systems, private shore ownership, and industrial practices have prevented public development of otherwise promising bodies of water. Boats can be rented at almost all the ponds, bathing facilities are continually being expanded, and on the larger lakes even yachting is possible.

CAMP AND PICNIC AREAS have been laid out in almost all the State Forests and Reservations and a number of privately owned areas are scattered throughout the county, usually along the main highways. The State Department of Conservation follows a long-range program, each year opening new tent and trailer sites, furnished with adequate water supplies and sewer systems. The Civilian Conservation Corps has cleared brush and built roads to choice camping and picknicking areas in the interior of the forests. Fireplaces and tables are usually found at picnic areas; a few cabins have been built at some of the camping grounds.

279

COUNTRY CLUBS of the finest and most exclusive type, as well as those for general public use, are found in all parts of the county. There are fifteen clubs, most of them self-supporting and on a non-profit basis. In compiling the information listed under the towns, questionnaires were sent to each club; such lack of uniformity as may appear is due to the incompleteness of replies.

FISHING, with almost unlimited facilities, is one of the leading sports of the county. Within its bounds are 122 bodies of fresh water, ranging from small ponds to large lakes. Nearly a thousand brooks course down upland heights to empty into the thirteen rivers that flow east, south, and north out of the county. Almost all can be fished; the important ones are listed under the towns through which they flow.

Fish found in Berkshire waters are Brown Trout, Speckled Trout, Rainbow Trout, Small-mouthed Bass, Large-mouthed Bass, White Perch, Yellow Perch, Pike-Perch, Pickerel, Rock Bass, Crappies (Calico Bass), Blue Gills, Horned Pout, and a few Grayling. Most of these fish are found in all parts of the county. Many ponds and streams are stocked by the State Department of Conservation, which, in this and other matters, cooperates with the seventeen local sportsmen's clubs.

Most of the clubs belong to the Berkshire County League of Sportsmen's Clubs, which in turn holds membership in the Council of Sportsmen's Clubs of Massachusetts, Inc. Some streams are posted by clubs, individuals, or public agencies. Inquiries as to the sections open to public fishing should be made at the clubs or to town officials or game wardens. The State Forests have special restrictions and are under the regulation of the State Department of Conservation.

Fishing licenses and copies of fish and game laws may be obtained from town or city clerks or at the State House in Boston. The fee for a resident sporting license is $3.25, for resident fishing, $2, for resident minors between 15 and 18 and for women, $1.25, for non-resident sporting, $15.25, for non-resident fishing, $5.25, for non-resident minors between 15 and 18, $2.25. A special non-resident license good for three consecutive days between May 30 and Labor Day is issued for $1.50. No license is required for minors under 15 or resident citizens over 70. Minors between 15 and 18 must have written consent of parent or guardian. Onota Lake and the Deerfield River are subject to special regulations, and fishing regulations in general are subject to yearly change.

FISHING REGULATIONS IN GENERAL

Variety of Fish	Open Season	Daily Bag Limit	Min. Length
Yellow Perch	Apr. 15 to Feb. 28	30 in 24 hrs.	none
Trout	Apr. 15 to July 31	15 " " "	6″
Salmon	Apr. 15 to Nov. 30	5 " " "	12″
Pickerel	May 1 to Feb. 28	10 " " "	12″
Pike Perch	May 1 to Feb. 28	5 " " "	12″
White Perch	June 1 to Feb. 28	15 " " "	7″
Horned Pout	Apr. 15 to Feb. 28	30 " " "	none
Black Bass	July 1 to Jan. 31	6 " " "	10″

Note: All Fishing prohibited March 1 to April 14, inclusive.

FISHING REGULATIONS FOR STATE FOREST PONDS

Forest	Pond	Opening Date	Closing Date
Beartown	Benedict	July 1	Sept. 30
October Mt.	Felton	July 1	Sept. 30
Otis	Upper Spectacle	July 1	Sept. 30
Pittsfield	Berry	May 1	July 31
Sandisfield	York	May 1	July 31
Savoy Mt.	North	May 1	July 31

The following rules are also enforced in State Forests. Canoes, boats, or floating devices can be used only on York Pond in the Sandisfield State Forest and South Pond in the Savoy Mountain State Forest. No outboard motors or motor boats are allowed on any of the ponds. The daily bag limit and minimum length of fish is to be the same as in the general laws except for daily bag limits, which are given in the following table:

Trout	5
Horned Pout	10
Crappie	6
Pickerel	5
Small-mouth Black Bass	3

HUNTING is at its best in the less-populated sections of the county, but to some extent can be enjoyed in every town and city. The numerous posted areas must be respected; game sanctuaries and county reservations are closed to hunters. Special regulations are in force in State Forests and permits are required where the Civilian Conservation Corps is working.

Contributing its share toward the preservation of excellent hunting conditions, the Division of Fisheries and Game of the State Department of Conservation has for a number of years maintained a program of wild life protection and propagation within State Forests and on other state-controlled property. The various sportsmen's organizations have also had an extensive interest in game distribution, and as a result of this combined effort, Berkshire holds forth unusual lure to the hunter. Game birds and animals common to the county are: Ruffed Grouse, Pheasant, Woodcock, Rabbit, Raccoon, Wildcat, Fox, Deer, and occasional Canadian Lynx or Bear. There are some Otter and Mink in the southern part of the county.

Hunting licenses and copies of game laws are issued by town and city clerks, or at the State House in Boston. The fee for a resident sporting license is $3.25, for resident hunting, $2, for non-resident sporting, $15.25, for non-resident hunting, $10.25. There is no charge for resident citizens over 70. Some of the important provisions in the game laws are:

(1) Each year the holder of a sporting or hunting license must file a written report of the number and kind of birds or mammals taken during the preceding year.

(2) The wounding or killing of a deer must be reported to the Director of Fish and Game Division of the Department of Conservation within 48 hours.

(3) The open season on deer is one week, beginning the first Monday of December.

(4) Daily closed season is from one-half hour after sunset to one-half hour before sunrise.

(5) The bag limit for a deer is one.

(6) Only shotguns or bows and arrows may be used for deer.

ICE SPORTS are not as fully developed as skiing activities. A number of rinks in the larger towns and cities are cleared by local authorities; the ponds and lakes are likely to be covered with snow.

It is possible to fish through the ice on all bodies of water not posted. Ice boating may be enjoyed when the larger lakes are clear of snow.

OVERNIGHT ACCOMMODATIONS are not a great problem to Berkshire County travelers. The territory is so compact that by automobile the county can be traversed in any direction in little more than an hour. Accommodations ranging from the private dwelling to the swankiest of hostelries offer true Berkshire hospitality. The American Youth Hostel, Inc., has several stations for its members. The Berkshire Hills Conference and the Automobile Club of Berkshire County, both in Pittsfield, and the Southern Berkshire Chamber of Commerce of Great Barrington keep up-to-date lists of summer and winter accommodations. The list appearing under each town was compiled from material supplied by the Berkshire Hills Conference. The asterisk (*) indicates houses open for the summer only; the number in parenthesis refers to the capacity of the houses. American Plan (A) and European Plan (E) are indicated where such information was available. The rates are likely to vary slightly from year to year, or between summer and winter seasons.

STATE FORESTS, sixteen in number in Berkshire County, cover some 66,000 acres and have recreational developments for camping and picnicking, boating and bathing, fishing and hunting, and hiking and horseback riding. Trails to scenic points and waterfalls have been constructed by the State Department of Conservation and the Civilian Conservation Corps. Care must be taken to prevent forest fires, always a hazard in the woods. Each camping and picnic area has posted rules and regulations for guidance of visitors. In part, these regulations are:

Adequate parking spaces, toilet facilities and drinking water have been provided on the principal recreation centers.

Open-air fires allowed only in fireplaces provided for that purpose.

Dogs and cats are prohibited, except that dogs accompanying tenting or trailer parties may be kept on leash.

Lockers are provided in bathhouses for checking of clothing. The state is not responsible for loss or damage.

Use of the above areas for private gain, solicitations, or advertisement is prohibited.

To partially cover the cost of maintenance of the supervised recreational areas, the following fees are charged:

	Week	*48 hr.* *Week-end*	
Three-room log cabins	$20.00	$6.00	
One-room log cabins	$15.00	$5.00	
Tenting and trailer sites	$ 2.50		$ .50 per day
Fireplace and table			.25 2 hrs.
Table without fireplace			.15 2 hrs.
Community fireplace			1.00 2 hrs.

Cabins are not available for a single night's use. These fees are collected by duly appointed agents of the department, who are equipped with identification badges, and who are required to give a receipt for all moneys collected.

Applications for the rental of cabins should be made directly to the supervisor of the forest where the cabins are located.

The HIKING AND BRIDLE TRAILS of Berkshire County are such that no other section of Massachusetts can boast their equal. The hilly terrain, a multitude of old wood roads, and the Appalachian Trail, all lend themselves to walking and horseback riding. There has been active interest among the outdoor-minded citizenry of this western county of Massachusetts in the development of trails. The Civilian Conservation Corps, under the able direction of the National Park Service and the U. S. Forestry Service, has contributed its share of labor and forethought to make the most of the hiking trails for the khaki-clad, knapsack-bearing sportsman.

In the compilation of trail material, reference is given only to the principal or best-known trails. Others come under the classification of walks about town, many of which are picturesque and beautiful, leading through woodland and mossy glen or over the rougher terrain of hillside slopes. All the trails or walks offer the hiker a glimpse of the scenic beauties of Berkshire.

SKIING is fast becoming as important to Berkshire County as summer recreational activities. From the snowy reaches of Mt. Everett to the steep slopes of Mt. Greylock, thousands annually enjoy the fast downhill ski runs and the long cross-country trails. Skiing, snow-shoeing, and tobogganing are available on private and public developments in almost all parts of the county. Overnight accommodations and meals may be had within a short distance of all areas, and transportation from towns is provided to the more important centers. If the weather conditions are favorable, weekly snow trains are run from New York and Boston. State and county highways are kept open to all areas.

The Berkshire Hills Conference and the New England Council publish annual ski bulletins listing new developments. Weekly reports of snow conditions appear in metropolitan papers. The novice skier should remember that one snowfall does not make downhill skiing safe. It only helps form the necessary base indicated in the figures given in the text.

The State Department of Conservation has published regulations governing the use of State Forests for winter sports. A few of these apply in general to all these areas:

Persons using State Forests for winter sports do so at their own risk.

To prevent unnecessary damage to the surface of the snow and to promote safety, persons ascending a ski trail should keep to the side of the trail, giving downhill runners the right of way. After a spill a skier should get out of the way of downcoming runners, and at the cry "Track!" all skiers should move to the side of the trail to give the faster runners sufficient room to pass.

The leaving of clothing or anything else on ski trails is prohibited for the protection of downhill runners

FLORIDA

AQUATICS

North Pond: In SW. corner of town, has a bathing beach on E. side; other developments are planned.

CAMPING AND PICNICKING

The Mohawk Trail State Forest: On Mass 2, near the Florida-Charlemont Town Line, has three picnic grounds with fireplaces and tables and, within a half-mile radius, three camping areas and three log cabins. Rentals at nominal fees may be arranged through the State Forester; cooking utensils and bedding are not provided.

Whitcomb Summit: Adjacent to Mass 2, is a privately owned picnic and tourist area with benches, tables and cabins. Small fees charged.

FISHING

Bog Brook (Brook Trout): Runs from Bog Pond, Savoy, into Cold River near the Town Line.

Carley or Whitcomb Brook (Brook Trout): Flows SE. into the Deer-
field River at Hoosac Tunnel.
Cold River (Brook, Brown, and Rainbow Trout): Flows SE. into Savoy
Mt. State Forest and then N. into Charlemont.

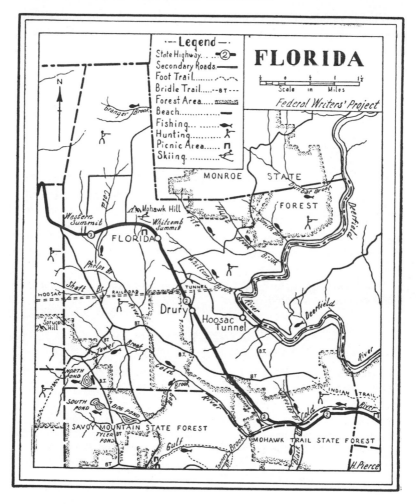

Deerfield River (Brook, Brown, and Rainbow Trout): Forms the E.
boundary of the town and flows in an irregular N. to S. course.
Dunbar Brook (Brook Trout): In the extreme NE. section of town,
flows NE. into Deerfield River.

Fife Brook (Brook Trout): Flows SE. through the town into Deerfield River.

Granger Brook (Part of Dunbar Brook; Brook Trout): In N. section of town flows E. into Monroe.

Hunt Brook (Brook Trout): Flows SE. into Fife Brook.

Manning Brook (Stocked): Flows S. into the Cold River in the Mohawk Trail State Forest.

North Pond (Brook Trout and Pond Fish): In the Savoy Mt. State Forest, SW. corner of town, near the Savoy Line.

Smith Brook (Brook Trout): Flows SE. from the Monroe Town Line into Deerfield River.

Tower or Paddleford Brook (Brook Trout): In SW. section of town flows E. into Cold River.

Wheeler Brook (Brook Trout): Runs S. into Cold River in the Mohawk Trail State Forest.

HUNTING

A splendid game area. Deer, rabbits, and birds in well-stocked covers.

SKIING

Mohawk Trail Hill: Located at Whitcomb Summit (alt. 2000) near the Elk Statue on the Mohawk Trail (Mass 2). *Class,* novice-intermediate. There are no steep slopes. Skiing is often possible when there is none in the valley below.

STATE FORESTS

Mohawk Trail State Forest (5746 acres): Located in the towns of Charlemont, Hawley, Savoy and Florida, along the Mohawk Trail (Mass 2) from which the forest derives its name. Some of the finest scenery in the State is located along that part of the Trail within the State Forest bounds. Five hundred acres have been set aside for recreational purposes, divided into three picnic areas along Cold River. Facilities include 105 tables, 50 fireplaces (on picnic grounds), and 100 tent sites, 6 trailer sites, two 3-room cabins, and two 1-room cabins along Cold River. Both Deerfield and Cold Rivers have been stocked with Brown, Rainbow and Brook Trout.

Monroe State Forest (4237 acres): In Monroe, Rowe, and Florida, is largely undeveloped for recreation. It has excellent panoramic views of the Deerfield River Valley.

Savoy Mountain State Forest (*see Savoy*).

TRAILS

Berkshires to the Capes Bridle Trail: Enters Florida from Savoy near North Pond in Savoy Mt. State Forest. Near the C.C.C. camp the Trail, which follows an old road, turns E. The Trail passes through the village of Drury, crosses Mass 2 and descends sharply to the Deerfield River at the Florida-Rowe Town Line.

N.Y.A. Trails: There are two N.Y.A. Trails, both starting in the Savoy Mountain State Forest W. of North Pond. One runs SW. into Adams, to the end of East Hoosac St.; the other, S. into Savoy, past North and South Ponds, to a junction with Mass 116.

YOUTH HOSTELS

An **American Youth Hostel** is maintained in Drury by Mr. and Mrs. George S. Brown.

CLARKSBURG

AQUATICS

Clarksburg Reservoir: In N. central section of town, near Mass 8 has bathing beach and bath house.

COUNTRY CLUBS

North Adams Country Club (*9 holes, 3000 yds.; green fees: accompanied by member $1, unaccompanied $1.50; 2 tennis courts*). Annual invitation tournament held in August. Invitation by club steward or professional.

FISHING

Beaver Creek or Reservoir Brook (Brook Trout): Flows SE. and then NE. through town into Clarksburg Reservoir.
Clarksburg Reservoir (Pond Fish): In N. central section of town near Mass 8.
Hoosic River, North Branch (Brook, Brown, and Rainbow Trout): Flows S. from the Vermont State Line into North Adams where it joins South Branch Hoosic River.
Hudson Brook (Brook Trout): Runs SE. from Vermont into North Branch of Hoosic River, in North Adams.

HUNTING

Deer, rabbits, partridges, and other game in wooded areas.

STATE FORESTS

Clarksburg State Forest: (2801 acres) Located in western end of town; accessible by foot trail only, no developed recreational areas.

TRAILS

Appalachian Trail: Enters from North Adams (*see North Adams*) at 78.9 m. and passes through the CLARKSBURG STATE FOREST. The PINE COBBLE TRAIL from Williamstown is crossed at 79.4 m. The Trail ascends

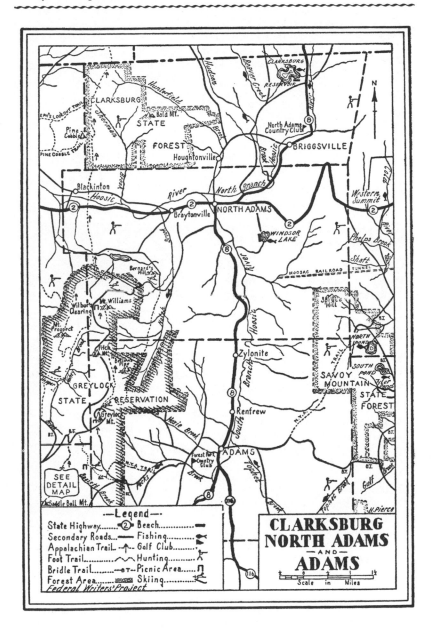

Legend

State Highway	Beach
Secondary Roads	Fishing
Appalachian Trail	Golf Club
Foot Trail	Hunting
Bridle Trail	Picnic Area
Forest Area	Skiing

Federal Writers' Project

CLARKSBURG
NORTH ADAMS
—AND—
ADAMS

Scale in Miles

to the summit of a ridge at **80.2 m.** At **80.7 m.** is EPH's LOOKOUT and the junction (L) with the EPH's LOOKOUT TRAIL of the Williams Outing Club (*see Williamstown*). The Trail proceeds N. to the Vermont State Line, **81.5 m.** where it joins the LONG TRAIL OF VERMONT.

NORTH ADAMS

AQUATICS
Windsor Lake: In the N. central section has bathing beach, diving tower, life guard (during July and August), and boating facilities.

CAMPING AND PICNICKING
Greylock State Reservation (*see Adams*).

COUNTRY CLUBS
North Adams Country Club (*see Clarksburg*).

FISHING
Notch or Cascade Brook (Brook Trout): Flows NE. from the Bellows Pipe, enters Notch Brook Reservoir, and continues over cascades into Hoosic River.
Windsor Lake (Pond Fish): Located E. of Mass 8, about **1 m.** SE. of town.

HUNTING
Excellent game covers in the surrounding hills. Good area for deer, partridge, pheasants, and rabbits. Some bear hunting.

OVERNIGHT ACCOMMODATIONS
Blue Spruce (18): rates (E), $1.
Clum's Tourist Home (15): rates (E.), $1.
Elm Manor (18): 521 West Main St., rates (E), $1.
Gray-Rocks Rest (A-E): Mass 2.
Hairpin Turn Inn (72; E): Mohawk Trail.
Hilltop (10): rates (E), $1.
*****Lefavors Beach:** Windsor Lake, furnished cottages, rates $10-$20 per week.
Maple Shade (18): rates (E), $1.
Richmond Hotel (400): rates (E), $1.50 and up.
The Saxton (15): rates (E), $1.
Wellington Hotel (400): rates (E), $1.50 and up.

SKIING
Bernard's Hill: Located on Bernard's Farm, off Notch Rd., **2.5 m.** SW. of North Adams. All classes; *Len.,* 1800'; *Wid.,* 25'-100'; *V. D.,* 325';

M. G., about 25°; *Exp.*, NE. This hill is maintained by the North Adams Ski Club. It is a semi-open slope with a very wide trail running down the middle.

Greylock State Reservation Trails: (*see Adams*).

Notch Road: Runs from Mass 2, W. of N. Adams to summit of Mt. Greylock. *Class*, novice; *Len.*, 6.9 m.; *Wid.*, *25'-30'*; *V. D.*, *2500'*; *M. G.*, 60°; *Exp.*, NW. and E.

STATE FOREST AND RESERVATIONS

Savoy Mountain State Forest (*see Savoy*).

Greylock State Reservation (*see Adams*).

TRAILS

Appalachian Trail: Enters North Adams from Adams at about **73.6 m.** and ascends to the summit of MT. WILLIAMS (alt. 3000'), **74.4 m.** The Trail descends W. to WILBUR'S CLEARING and a junction with the HONEY BROOK TRAIL (*see Williamstown*). At **75.7 m.** is the junction with the MT. PROSPECT TRAIL which runs L. to the summit of MT. PROSPECT (alt. 2640'). The Trail swings N. with the valley of Paul Brook to the right as the Trail descends and leaves the GREYLOCK STATE RESERVATION at **76.6 m.**

The Trail follows a number of old roads, crosses Mass 2 and the Hoosic River, turns L. on Massachusetts Ave. at **77.8 m.** and R. from Massachusetts Ave. on Wood St. at **78.3 m.** At **78.7 m.** is the village of BLACKINTON. The Trail passes into the woods and enters the town of CLARKSBURG (*see Clarksburg*), **78.9 m.**

Bellows Pipe Trail (Williams Outing Club; marked WOC): This Trail runs from Mt. Greylock (alt. 3505') through the Notch, continuing to Notch Rd. and thence to Mass 2.

WILLIAMSTOWN

CAMPING AND PICNICKING

Taconic Camps (*privately owned; fees charged*): a picnic, camping, and recreation area at western junction of US 7 and Mass 2, near Taconic Park.

COUNTRY CLUBS

Taconic Golf Club (*18 holes, 6600 yds.; green fees, $2 daily; visitors welcome*): On South St., **0.2 m.** S. of Main St. Invitation tournament end of July.

FISHING

Birch Brook (Brook Trout): Flows E. from the NW. section of town into Burton Brook.

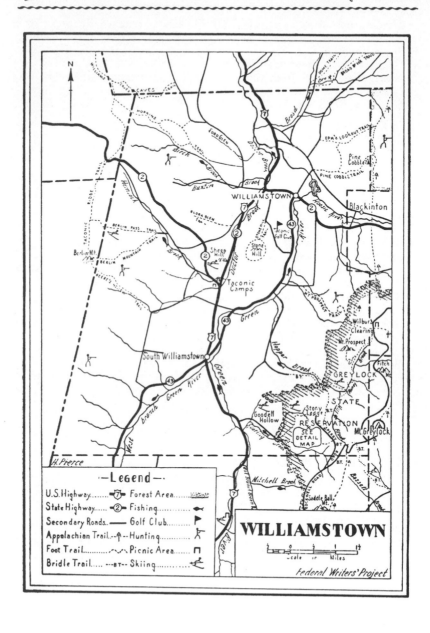

N

CAVES

WILLIAMSTOWN

Blackinton

Berlin Mt.

Sheep Hill

Stone Hill

Taconic Camps

South Williamstown

H. Pierce

Wilbur Clearing
Mt. Prospect
GREYLOCK
STATE
RESERVATION
SEE DETAIL MAP
Mt. Greylock

Goodell Hollow

Mitchell Brook
Saddle Ball Mt.

—Legend—

U.S. Highway......	7	Forest Area......	
State Highway.....	2	Fishing......	
Secondary Roads..		Golf Club......	▶
Appalachian Trail..		Hunting......	⚡
Foot Trail......		Picnic Area.....	⊓
Bridle Trail.....	—BT—	Skiing......	

WILLIAMSTOWN

Scale in Miles

Federal Writers' Project

Broad Brook (Brook Trout): Runs SW. from Vermont through NE. section of town into Hoosic River.

Doctor Brook (Brook Trout): Flows N. from Hemlock Brook to Hoosic River at Ford Glen.

Green River (Brook, Brown, and Rainbow Trout): Flows N. from New Ashford and joints West Branch Green River at South Williamstown.

Green River, West Branch (Brown, Brook, and Rainbow Trout): Flows NE. and N. from Hancock into Green River at South Williamstown. Posted at intervals.

Hemlock Brook (Brook Trout): Begins near the New York State Line in the NW. section of town, flows SE. to Taconic Park Reservoir and then N. into Doctor Brook.

Hopper Brook (Brook Trout): Flows NW. from Greylock State Reservation, then N. into Green River. Posted at intervals.

Roaring Brook (Brook Trout): Flows NW. from Greylock State Reservation into Green River. Posted at intervals.

HUNTING

Good area for partridge, pheasant, rabbits, raccoon, deer, and European hare. Hunting forbidden in the Greylock State Reservation.

OVERNIGHT ACCOMMODATIONS

Green River Inn (A-E): Mass 43.

Haller Inn: rates (A), $4 per day.

Old Brick Homestead (E): Green River Rd.

Taconic Inn (25; E): 28 Hoxsey St.

*****Taconic Trail Tourist Shop** (7 cabins): Mass 2, rates (E), $1 per day.

The Elms Inn (18): 174 Main St., rates (A), $3 per day.

Williams Inn (115): Mass 2, rates (A-E), $6 to $9 per day; $35 per week and up; winter season, $4 per day and up.

The Willows: rates (A), $3 per day.

SKIING

Berlin Pass: Located on Berlin Mt., 4.3 m. W. of town, off Mass 2. *Class,* novice; *Len.,* 18,480', 7920' continuous downhill; *Wid.,* 8'-12'; *V.D.,* 1600'; *M.G.,* 15°; *Exp.,* E. and SE.; *Snow,* 6". A safe run fast enough to be interesting.

Goodell Hollow: Located near the Greylock State Reservation, SW. of Greylock summit and reached by country road off US 7 7 m. S. of town. All classes. A private area open to members and guests of the Mt. Greylock Ski Club.

Sheep Hill: Located on the W. side of Mass 2 and US 7 between the town and the start of the Taconic Trail. All classes; *V.D.,* 500'; *M.G.,* about 30°; *Snow,* 5". One of the best big slopes in the Berkshires. A ski tow, a ski jump for experts (jumps averaging 100' and over), and a practice jump are maintained by the Williams Outing Club. There is another excellent slope directly opposite across Mass 2.

Stony Ledge Ski Trail: Located in the Greylock State Reservation on the SW. shoulder of Mt. Greylock; reached from Sperry Rd. *Class,* intermediate; *Len.,* 8448'; *Wid.,* 15'-50'; *V.D.,* 1405'; *M.G.,* 22°; *Exp.,* W. & SW. (*heavily wooded*); *Snow,* 4". A fine intermediate trail with sporty turns. View from the top, looking toward the summit of Greylock a thousand feet above, and down into the Hopper fifteen hundred feet below, is one of the finest in the East. There is an excellent Adirondack shelter on the Trail. The New Ashford Rd. from US 7 to Mt. Greylock is plowed to the C.C.C. Camp. It is moderately steep and chains should be used.

The Hopper: Located in the Greylock State Reservation, W. of the summit; approached from Mass 43. *Class,* upper section easy grade, novice class; lower section steep, narrow and dangerous, experts only; *Len.,* 20,064'; *Wid.,* 6'-12'; *V.D.,* 2500'; *M.G.,* 20°; *Exp.,* W. Several cross-country trails from the floor of the Hopper.

STATE FORESTS AND RESERVATIONS

Greylock State Reservation in the SW. corner of the town has excellent recreation facilities (*see Adams*).

TRAILS

Appalachian Trail: Enters a corner of town as it ascends MT. GREYLOCK on the Rockwell Rd. (*see Adams*) and passes through another corner as it skirts MT. PROSPECT (*see North Adams*).

Berkshires to the Capes Bridle Trail: Follows Mass 43 S. to junction with the Hopper Trail (*see below*), which it follows to the Sperry Rd. Left on this road to Rockwell Rd. and L. again to the Switchback. From this point the Trail cuts the SE. corner of town and the NE. corner of New Ashford into Cheshire (*see Cheshire*).

Circular and Deer Hill Trails: Begin at the Mt. Greylock C.C.C. Camp on Sperry Rd. These trails extend in a circular direction from the C.C.C. Camp over the New Ashford Town Line and return. A trailside shelter is located along Deer Hill Trail.

Prospect Mt. Trail: Begins at Wilbur's Clearing and follows the Appalachian Trail for a short distance. It then branches off to the SW., continuing in that direction until the summit of Mt. Prospect (alt. 2647), is reached. Proceeding along the razor-backed edge of Mt. Prospect, the trail swings E., joining the Money Brook Trail (*see below*) near the trailside shelter. A branch trail runs E. to Mass 43.

Roaring Brook Trail: Originates at Goodell Hollow (on US 7), near the New Ashford-Williamstown Line. Ascending E. along an old ox road, the trail passes through one of the oldest stands of virgin timber in Massachusetts, ending at the Mt. Greylock C.C.C. Camp.

Williams Outing Club Trails (marked WOC):

Beebe's Hollow Trail: Runs S. from Berlin Mt. and descends the ridge to the valley of Sweet Brook.

Berlin Mt. Trail: Begins near the bottom of the Taconic Trail (Mass 2) about **4.3 m.** W. of town and runs SW. through heavily wooded country to the summit of Berlin Mt. in New York State.

Berlin Pass Trail: Begins at the same place as the Berlin Mt. Trail and runs directly W. to a junction with the Taconic Ridge Trail at the top of the Taconic Range.

Broad Brook Trail: Begins in the White Oaks section of town and runs in a NE. direction following the course of Broad Brook. It ends at the Stamford County Rd. over the State Line in Vermont, a distance of about **4 m.**

Dome Trail: Begins with the Broad Brook Trail, crosses Broad Brook on the main road and then swings NE. through the woods to the Dome (alt. 2754). This Vermont mountain provides an excellent view of the Greylock Range to the south and the Taconic Range to the west.

Eph's Lookout Trail: Runs E. from Clark Trail to the summit of a range on the Clarksburg Town Line in Clarksburg State Forest, joining the Appalachian Trail there.

Flora Glen Trail: Runs through the valley lying between Bee and Sheep hills W. of US 7.

Hopkins Trail: Runs W. from town following the course of Birch Brook and then ascending to the top of the Taconic Range.

Hopper Trail: Originates at the end of the macadamized road off Mass 43 about **2.4 m.** S. of town, at the mouth of the Hopper. The trail follows a steep ascent along the S. bank of Hopper Brook and rises high above it. At the Mt. Greylock C.C.C. Camp, the trail turns E. and ends at the Switchback, there joining with the Rockwell Motor Rd. to the summit of Greylock.

Money Brook Trail: Originates at the beginning of the Hopper Trail (*see above*). The trail ascends E. from Hopper Brook and parallels Money Brook, continuing until it reaches a point about 200 yards beyond the junction of Hopper and Money Brooks. It then veers N. crossing and recrossing Money Brook. Just north of the third crossing, there is a trailside shelter and fireplace. Beyond, the Prospect Mt. Trail (*see above*) enters from the W. Money Brook Trail continues in a northerly direction, veers E., then N., finally ending at the junction with the Appalachian Trail at Wilbur's Clearing. A branch ends at Money Brook Falls.

Pine Cobble Trail: Runs E. from town to the summit of a mountain in the Clarksburg State Forest near the Williamstown-Clarksburg Town Line. This trail joins with the Appalachian Trail. There is an excellent view of Williamstown from Pine Cobble.

Stone Hill Circle Trail: Begins from South St., about **0.5 m.** beyond the Taconic Golf Club. The trail encircles Stone Hill and provides one of the most pleasant walks in town.

Taconic Ridge Trail: Runs N. from the summit of Berlin Mt. along the top of the Taconic Range. The trail passes the Snow Hole and Carter Point which provides an unobstructed view of the Hoosic River Valley, and ends at North Petersburg, N. Y. The Snow Hole is 35′ deep.

Williams Caves Trail: Begins in the NW. section of town near the Vermont State Line and runs W. to Tri-State corner (where Massachusetts, New York, and Vermont meet) and then passes the Williams Caves. The caves can be explored for more than 100′. This trail joins the Taconic Range Trail.

NEW ASHFORD

CAMPING AND PICNICKING

A Picnic Area is adjacent to US 7, about midway between the village and the Williamstown Line.

FISHING

Green River (Brook, Brown and Rainbow Trout): Flows S. to N., adjacent to US 7, to Williamstown.

Green River East Branch (Brook, Brown and Rainbow Trout): Runs N. from S. central section to join the Green River at the N. end of town.

Mitchell Brook (Brown Trout): Flows W. from Saddle Ball Mt. into East Branch Green River.

Thompson Brook (Brook Trout): Flows E. into the East Branch Green River near the Williamstown Line.

HUNTING

Hunting is confined to a limited area of land, the rest is posted. Deer, rabbits, fox, wildcat, raccoons, and game birds abound.

OVERNIGHT ACCOMMODATIONS

Boyce's Tourist Home (15; A).
*****Mill-on-the-Floss** (E).
*****The Springs** (E).
*****Swedish Coffee and Tea Room** (25; E).
Twin Brook Tourist Lodge (E).

SKIING

Mt. Greylock Ski Club Night Hill: Located on US 7, **0.5 m.** N. of the center and directly opposite the New Ashford Rd. to Mt. Greylock.

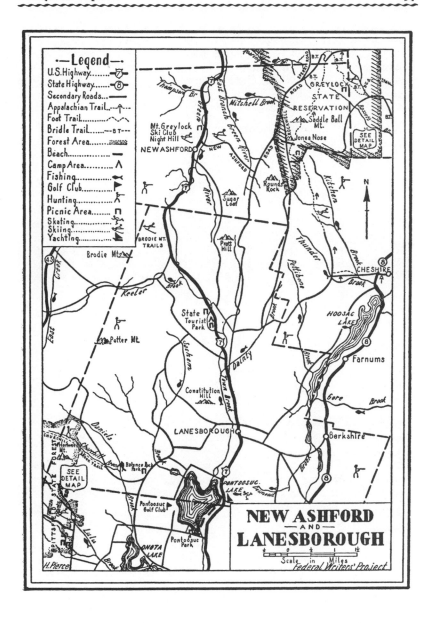

All classes. It is a small slope, steep, yet smooth and well sheltered. The hill is not permanently lighted but can easily be illuminated by automobile headlights or portable lights. There is a small practice jump located above the hill.

Winter Road to Greylock (New Ashford Rd.): Runs E. from US 7, opposite Night Hill, to Rockwell Rd. Used as a ski trail. Open to automobiles (chains necessary).

STATE FORESTS AND RESERVATIONS

Greylock State Reservation (*see Adams*).

TRAILS

Appalachian Trail: Enters from Cheshire (*see Cheshire*) at **68.7 m.** as the Trail tops JONES' NOSE. The Trail continues N., crosses the summit of SADDLE BALL (alt. 3300') at **69.5 m.**, and continues at various elevations over brooks and spruce and fir bogs to ADAMS (*see Adams*) at **71 m.**

Berkshires to the Capes Bridle Trail: This Trail follows the Cheshire Harbor Trail (*see Adams*) and crosses the NE. section of town from Williamstown to Cheshire. There is a trailside shelter near the Cheshire Line.

LANESBOROUGH

AQUATICS

Hoosac Lake (*see Cheshire*).
Pontoosuc Lake (*see Pittsfield*).

CAMPING AND PICNICKING

Balance Rock Park: About **1 m.** W. of US 7. Picnic area, fireplaces; no fees charged.

State Tourist Park: On US 7, **2.5 m.** N. of town center. Fireplaces, benches, tables, small wading pool, and trailer camp site; no charge for use of facilities. Town Brook flows by this area.

FISHING

Dainty Brook (Stocked): Flows W. into Town Brook.
Desmond Brook (Stocked): Runs from a point near the Pittsfield City Line into Hoosac Lake.
Daniels Brook (Stocked): In the SW. section of town; flows SE. into Onota Lake in Pittsfield.
Hoosac Lake (Pond Fish): In the E. section of town, near Mass 8; mostly in Cheshire.
Keeler Brook (Stocked): Flows E. into Town Brook.

Pettibone Brook (Brook Trout): Flows SE. from Cheshire into Hoosac Lake.

Sachem Brook (Stocked): Flows S. then E. into Pontoosuc Lake.

Town Brook or Housatonic River (Stocked with Brook, Rainbow, and Speckled Trout): Flows S., paralleling US 7, into Pontoosuc Lake.

HUNTING

Good game area for deer, rabbits, fox, wildcat, raccoon, pheasant, and grouse.

ICE SPORTS

Ice Boating, Ice Fishing, and Skating (*see Pittsfield*).

OVERNIGHT ACCOMMODATIONS

*Baker Cabins (120): rates (E), $1 per day and up.

Cobblestone Lodge (14): rates (A), $2.50 per day or $18 per week and up.

*Hillcrest Inn (80; A).

*The Iris (8): rates (E), $1 per day.

Josh Billings Place: rates (A), $2.50 per day.

*Lake Shore Tourist Rest (10): On Pontoosuc Lake, rates (A), $16 per week.

Lillie's Tourist Home (E).

Maple Drive (6 rooms; 14 cabins): rates (E), $1 per day and up.

*Mt. Greylock Tourist Home (5 cabins): rates (E), $1 per day.

Rose Bank Cabins (26): rates (E), $1 per day.

Simmon's Cottage (7): rates (E), $1.50 per day.

Wachusett Farm (E).

*West View Cabins (14; E).

SKIING

Brodie Mt. Ski Trails: A private development on E. slope of Brodie Mt. (alt. 2700) off US 7 near the New Ashford Town Line. Small admission fee charged. The trails are smooth and sheltered.

Brodie Mt. Ski Trail: *Class,* novice (except when very fast); *Len.,* 5730'; *Wid.,* 8'-20'; *V.D.,* 930'; *M.G.,* 14°; *Exp.,* E.; *Snow,* 3". A smooth trail with interesting, tricky turns. The racing trail starts 4500' below the tower on the summit; total descent, 1200'.

Diamond Trail: A new, short, fast trail which starts at the finish of the Brodie Trail. There is also a small practice slope.

Gold Ski Trail: Located 0.3 m. N. of Brodie Trail. *Class,* novice (intermediate if steep ending is used); *Len.,* about 1800'; *Wid.,* 15'-25' to open slope; *V.D.,* about 450'; *M.G.,* 20° (30° with optional ending); *Snow,* 2". A smooth trail that joins with the Silver Ski Trail (*see below*) in a small open slope near the finish. Below this are two endings, one very steep, the other moderate.

Silver Ski Trail: Located N. of Brodie Mt. Trail near Gold Ski Trail. *Class,* novice-intermediate; *Len.,* about 2040'; *Wid.,* 15'-30' to open slope; *V.D.,* about 500' (joins Brodie Trail near halfway mark, giving total descent of about 960'); *M.G.,* 20°-24° (30° with optional ending); *Exp.,* E.; *Snow, 2".*

STATE FORESTS

Pittsfield State Forest (*see Pittsfield*).

TRAILS

Churchill Brook Trail: Follows the course of Churchill Brook from town through the Pittsfield State Forest.
Pittsfield State Forest Trails (*see Pittsfield*).

YOUTH HOSTELS

An American Youth Hostel is maintained by Mrs. W. A. Wilbur.

HANCOCK

AQUATICS

Berry Pond: In the central section of the Pittsfield State Forest (*see Pittsfield*).

CAMPING AND PICNICKING

Pittsfield State Forest: In the Berry Pond section are picnic benches, tables, and fireplaces. At S. end of pond is a camping area. Ample parking space. Directions: footpath from town (*see Trails, below*) or auto road from Pittsfield (*see Pittsfield*).

FISHING

Berry Pond (Brown Trout and Pond Fish): In the central section of the Pittsfield State Forest (*see Pittsfield*).
East Creek or Kinderhook (Stocked): Flows S. along Mass 43 then W. to New York State.
Green River, West Branch (Stocked): In the N. section of town, flows N. to join the Green River at S. Williamstown.
Phelps Brook (Stocked): Runs E. from New York State Line into Pittsfield near West St.

HUNTING

Excellent game area: deer, raccoon, rabbits, fox, wildcat, pheasant, and grouse.

OVERNIGHT ACCOMMODATIONS

Friendly Villa (30): rates, $16 to $18 per wk.

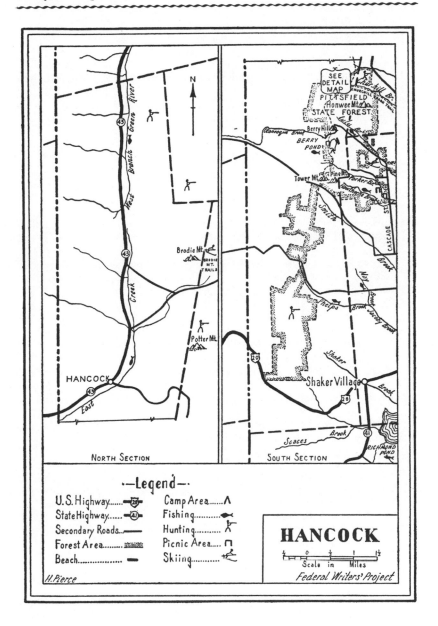

NORTH SECTION

SOUTH SECTION

—Legend—

U.S. Highway......🛑 Camp Area......∧
State Highway......🔵 Fishing..........🐟
Secondary Roads.... Hunting..........🏹
Forest Area......... Picnic Area.....⊓
Beach.............. Skiing...........

HANCOCK

Scale in Miles

H. Pierce   Federal Writers' Project

STATE FORESTS
Pittsfield State Forest (*see Pittsfield*).

TRAILS
Berry Pond Trail: Extends from town to Berry Pond in Pittsfield State Forest.
Tahgonic Skyline Trail: Runs N.-S. over the ridge of mountains separating Hancock and Lanesborough.

PITTSFIELD

AQUATICS
Berry Pond: In the Pittsfield State Forest. Bathing beach.
Onota Lake: West of the center; reached by West St. and Burbank Blvd. Pleasure and fishing boats for rent at Burlingame's, Boynton's and Marcel's.
>   **Burbank Park:** On Burbank Blvd., has bathing beaches (lifeguard), bath house, and lockers.
Pontoosuc Lake: On US 7 on the Lanesborough Town Line. Shell racing ("little three colleges"—Stanley Field Day), yachting (Comet class), and other aquatic features are held here. Fishing boats for hire at South Shore; outboard motor boats at north end of lake.
>   **Lakeview Beach and Lyons Beach:** Bathing; no lockers, lifeguard, or bath house. No fee.
>   **Pontoosuc Park:** Bath house (fee), diving tower, floats, lockers and picnic benches.
>   **Blue Anchor Boat Club:** Boats, bathing, floats, diving tower, canoes. Fees charged.
>   **Y.M.C.A. Boat Club and Camp Merrill:** Boating, bathing, canoeing facilities; cabins, lockers, and floats. Fees charged.

CAMPING AND PICNICKING
Pittsfield State Forest: There are two picnic and camping areas in the State Forest; one with 25 tables and 25 fireplaces is located near the Cascade St. entrance and the other is at Berry Pond. *Directions for reaching:* (*see State Forests, below*).
Pontoosuc Park: On the SE. shore of Pontoosuc Lake, at Hancock Rd., adjacent to US 7; has tables and bench for picnickers.

COUNTRY CLUBS
Berkshire Hills Country Club (*18 holes, 6486 yds.; green fees, $1.50 weekdays; $2 Sat., Sun., and holidays; visitors welcome*): Located on Benedict Rd., **0.5 m.** N. of Tyler St. Tournaments held in August and October.

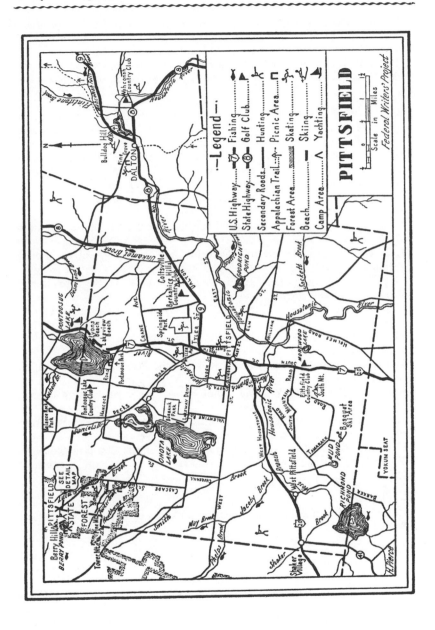

Pittsfield Country Club (*18 holes, 6087 yds.; green fees, $2.50 daily; 3 tennis courts; introduction by member or Treasurer*): On US 7, S. of center. Golf tournaments in July, August, and September.

Pontoosuc Lake Country Club (*18 holes, 6010 yds.; green fees, $1 weekdays; $1.50 Sat., Sun.; visitors welcome*): On Ridge St. off Hancock Rd.

FISHING

Brattle Brook (Stocked): Flows from the Dalton Town Line, in E. central section of city, into the Housatonic River NE. of Goodrich Pond.

Daniels Brook (Trout): Runs SE. from Lanesborough into Onota Lake.

Hawthorne Brook (Brook Trout; lower end open only during summer months, upper end closed year round): In the Pittsfield State Forest; flows from the Hancock Town Line SE. to Parker Brook.

Jacoby Brook (Stocked): Flows SE. from junction of May and Phelps Brooks to West Branch Housatonic River.

Lulu Brook (Stocked): In the Pittsfield State Forest; flows SE. into Onota Lake.

Lulu Pond (Stocked): In the Pittsfield State Forest, W. of the Forest Administration Bldg.

May Brook (Brown Trout): Flows SE. across West St. into Jacoby Brook, near the Hancock Town Line.

Onota Lake: (Rainbow Trout, and Pond Fish): In the NW. section of city.

Phelps Brook (Stocked): Flows SE. from Hancock Town Line into Jacoby Brook.

Pontoosuc Lake (Rainbow and Brook Trout, Pond Fish): In the N. central section of city on Lanesborough Town Line.

Richmond Pond (Brook Trout, Pond Fish): In the SE. section of city, on the Richmond Town Line.

Sackett Brook (Stocked): In the SE. section of city. Flows W. from the Dalton Town Line into the Housatonic River.

Unkamet Brook (Stocked): Flows S. from near the Lanesborough Town Line, parallels Mass 8, and empties into Housatonic River near Coltsville.

HUNTING

Rabbits, grouse, pheasants, and deer on outskirts of city and in Pittsfield State Forest.

ICE SPORTS

Ice Boating: On Pontoosuc Lake.

Ice Fishing: On Onota and Pontoosuc Lakes.

Skating: On city rinks at CLAPP PARK, W. Housatonic St.; THE COMMON, First St.; CRANE SCHOOL WADING POOL, Dalton Ave.; SPRINGSIDE PARK, Springside Ave.; WELLER AVE. PLAYGROUND, Weller Ave., and

WILLIAM PITT PLAYGROUND, Columbus Ave.; on LAKE PONTOOSUC, back of the Ferris Restaurant.

OVERNIGHT ACCOMMODATIONS

Abbott Lodge (15): 48 W. Housatonic St., rates (E), $1 per day.
*Breezy Knoll Inn (125): Pontoosuc Lake, rates (A-E), $25 per week and up.
Brookside (8): 538 South St., rates (E), $1 per day.
*Camp Merrill (140): Pontoosuc Lake, rates (E), $5 per week per room.
Clinton Hall.
The Greymoor (E): 48 Appleton Ave.
Hotel Allen (100): Wendell Ave. Extension, rates (E), $1.50 and up per day per room.
Hotel Berkshire (70): 333 North St., rates (E), $1.50 and up per day per room.
Hotel Wendell (650): South St., rates (E), $2 and up per day per room.
Housatonic Hall (E): 7 W. Housatonic St.
*Liberty Camps (35): US 20, rates (E), $1 per day.
The Linden (8): 501 South St., rates (E), $1 per day.
The Lodge (35): 101 Wendell Ave., rates (A), $3 per day, $16.50 per week.
Miss Mary Clark: 114 Wendell Ave.
Mohawk Tourist Home: 47 W. Housatonic St., rates (E), $1 per day.
Mrs. Rose Cleary (20; E): 16 W. Housatonic St.
Mrs. F. H. Francis (17): 202 South St., rates (E), $1 per day.
Mrs. Elizabeth Johnson (10): 511 South St., rates (E), $1 per day.
Mrs. A. Kaliman (E): 523 South St.
Mrs. A. H. Kilicas (E): 379 South St.
Mrs. W. King (10): 508 South St., rates (E), $1 per day.
Mrs. W. H. Korman (7): 533 South St., rates (E), $1 per day.
Mrs. E. D. McCarthy (E): 19 Taconic St.
Mrs. L. M. Viger (6): 40 George St., rates (E), $1 per day.
*Pontoosuc Inn (E): 1307 North St.
The Red Hen (20): 120 South St., rates (E), $1 per day.
South Street Inn (100): 153 South St., rates (E), $2.50 per day and up.
*Verona Cabins (20): US 20, rates (E), $1 per day.
White Tree Inn (A-E): 41 Wendell Ave.
Yokum Seat Mountain House (19): rates (A), $16 per week and up.

SKIING

Bosquet's Ski Grounds: One of the best developed ski areas in the Berkshires. It is a privately owned enterprise (small adm. fees) on Yokum Seat Mt., 2.5 m. SW. of city. Its facilities include 4 ski tows, 7 trails, and 200 acres of open slopes—one electrically lighted by mercury vapor. *Directions for reaching:* S. from city on US 7 to South Mountain Rd.; E. on South Mountain Rd. to Tamarack Rd.; L. on this road.

Bosquet's Ski Run: *Class,* intermediate-expert (*but safe for all skiers who keep under control*); *Len.,* 2505′; *Wid.,* 40′-75′; *V.D.,* 655′; *M.G.,* 32°; *Exp.,* NE.; *Snow,* 5″ (8″ on upper part). This is an exceptionally fast, sweeping run, steepest near the summit. Novices must keep off when the upper tow is operating.

East Trail: *Class,* novice; *Len.,* 3900′; *Wid.,* 8′-18′; *V.D.,* 570′; *M.G.,* 15°-17°; *Exp.,* N. and NE.; *Snow,* 5″. This trail is long and narrow but easy. From the base of the East Trail a cross-country trail extends for 3 m. to the Pleasant Valley Sanctuary in Lenox.

Goose Neck Trail: *Class,* intermediate-expert; *Len.,* 2800′; *Wid.,* 15′ to open slope; *V.D.,* 600′; *M.G.,* 18°; *Exp.,* N.; *Snow,* 4″-6″. An easy trail except for the last part. Optional endings at top of Russell Slope.

Osceola Trail: *Class,* intermediate; *Len.,* 3800′; *Wid.,* 20′; *V.D.,* 600′; *M.G.,* 26°; *Exp.,* N., NW.; *Snow,* 4″-6″. This trail is fast, steep, and difficult.

Parker Trail: *Class,* intermediate; *Len.,* 4000′; *Wid.,* 20′ to open slopes; *V.D.,* 600′; *M.G.,* 22°; *Exp.,* N., NE.; *Snow,* 6″.

Russell Trail: *Class,* novice; *Len.,* 2385′; *Wid.,* 18′-40′ to open slopes; *V.D.,* 570′; *M.G.,* 23°-25°; *Exp.,* E., N.E.; *Snow,* 5″.

Yokum Trail: *Class,* intermediate; *Len.,* 2715′; *Wid.,* 18′-33′; *V.D.,* 570′; *M.G.,* 20°; *Exp.,* E., NE.; *Snow,* 4″. This is a smooth, fast, and comparatively easy trail. However, it is extremely tricky in places and novices should keep off.

Pittsfield State Forest: One of the leading winter sports areas in the Berkshires. In addition to facilities especially provided for skiing, there are many cross-country trails that have good downhill sections. A new log cabin, used as a warming and refreshment center, is located at the entrance to the Forest. It is available to clubs and large parties. *Directions for reaching:* (*see State Forests, below*).

Cross-Country Trail: Extends from the bottom of Ghost and Shadow Trails to Lulu Slope. The trail is almost level. It is interesting for a beautiful stand of hemlocks, and for the azaleas that fringe the trail. From it may be seen the cascades on Parker Brook. *Len.,* 4224′.

Ghost Trail: Located on the E. slope of Pine Mt. *Class,* intermediate; *Len.,* 2640′; *Wid.,* 25′-40′; *V.D.,* 682′; *M.G.,* 22°; *Exp.,* E., SE.; *Snow,* 4″. A wide, smooth, and exceptionally fast trail. Connects with the Shadow Trail at the top and bottom. Has a shelter at the foot of the run.

Goodrich Hollow Trail: A cross-country trail from Berry Hill (alt. 2200′) to New York State. *Len.,* in forest 3168′; *Exp.,* NW., N.; *Snow,* 12″. This trail is steep and rugged in places.

Hawthorne Trail: A cross-country trail extending from a point near Cascade St., in the SE. section, to junction with Tower Mt. Trail, below Pine Mt. *Len.,* 6336′; *Exp.,* N., NE., E.; *Snow,* 10″. Steep and hilly.

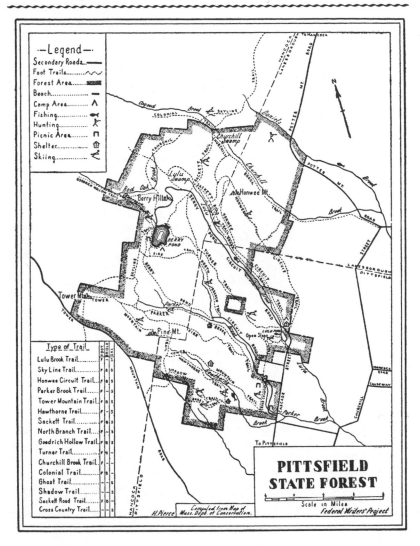

Compiled from Map of Mass. Dept. of Conservation.
H. Pierce.

PITTSFIELD STATE FOREST

Scale in Miles
Federal Writers' Project

Honwee Circuit Trail: A cross-country trail running from the Forest Administration Bldg. to Honwee Mt. (alt. 2450'). *Len.,* 10,032'; *Exp.,* N., NE., S., SE.; *Snow,* 12". Fairly steep.

Lulu Brook Trail: A cross-country trail running N. from Forest Administration Bldg. along Lulu Brook to Lulu Swamp. *Len.,* 8976'; *Exp.,* S., SE.; *Snow,* 8". Easy grade.

Lulu Cascade Open Slope: Located behind the old C.C.C. camp, SW. of Forest Administration Bldg. *Class,* novice; *Len.,* 1584'; *Wid.,* 25'-200'; *V.D.,* 200'; *M.G.,* 18°; *Exp.,* NE.; *Snow,* 4". A new turf slope with a variety of grades suitable for novices.

North Branch Trail: A cross-country trail which runs N. from Berry Pond Circuit Rd. to junction with Fire Trail. *Len.,* 3696'; *Exp.,* NW., N.; *Snow,* 10". Steep and hilly.

Parker Brook Trail: A cross-country trail running between Tilden Swamp and a point near the parking area in SE. section of the forest. *Len.,* 10,032'; *Exp.,* N., NE.; *Snow,* 8". Fairly steep.

Sackett Trail: A cross-country trail which runs in a NE. to SW. direction between Berry Pond and junction with Tahgonic Skyline Trail. *Len.,* 6864'; *Exp.,* N., NE.; *Snow,* 8". Steep in places.

Shadow Trail: Located on the E. slope of Pine Mt. *Class,* intermediate; *Len.,* 2640'; *Wid.,* 12'-35'; *V.D.,* 680'; *M.G.,* 17°; *Exp.,* E., SE.; *Snow,* 6". A winding trail that descends steadily. Meets the Ghost Trail at top and bottom. Both the Shadow and Ghost Trails are usable with the first snowfall. There is a cabin at the foot of the trail.

Skyline Trail: A cross-country trail which runs in a general N.-S. direction through that portion of Hancock in the forest. Typical of most trails in the state forest areas, it is adaptable for snowshoeing, cross-country skiing and hiking. Tower Mt. (alt. 2185'), Berry Pond (the highest body of water in Mass., alt. 2150'), and Berry Hill (alt. 2200'), are all points of interest along the trail.

Tower Mt. Trail: A cross-country trail running between Tower Mt. and junction with Hawthorne Trail, S. of Pine Mt. *Len.,* 12,672'; *Exp.,* N., NE.; *Snow,* 10". Rugged and steep.

STATE FORESTS

Pittsfield State Forest (3850 acres): Located in Pittsfield, Hancock, and Lanesborough. Over 25 acres are devoted to recreation at Berry Pond, at the forest entrance, and at Lulu Cascade. Over 10 bridle and foot trails run through the forest. Many brooks have been stocked with trout. The forest is especially noted for its azalea display. *Directions for reaching:* W. from City Hall Park on West St. at **2.9 m.** is the junction with Churchill St.; R. on Churchill St. to the junction with dirt road, **3.6 m.;** L. on this road to junction with Cascade St., **3.9 m.;** R. on Cascade St. to the forest, **5.2 m.**

TRAILS

Pittsfield State Forest

Burgoyne, Colonial, or Churchill Trail (Foot or bridle trail, steep terrain): Begins in Lanesborough and runs W. through the forest and across the town of Hancock to Stephentown, N. Y.

Goodrich Hollow or Otaneaque Trail (Foot trail, hilly terrain): Begins at the summit of Berry Hill, runs W. through Goodrich Hollow to New York State.

Hawthorne Trail (Foot trail): Extends from a point near Cascade St., SE. corner of forest to junction with Tower Mt. Trail, E. of Pine Mt.

Honwee Circuit Trail (Foot or bridle trail, steep terrain): Runs N. from the Forest Administration Bldg. to Honwee Mt. (alt. 2450) and return.

Lulu Brook Trail (Foot trail, easy terrain): Runs N. from Forest Administration Bldg. along Lulu Brook to Lulu Swamp.

North Branch Trail (Foot trail, steep and hilly): In central section of forest; extends between Berry Pond Circuit Rd. and the Azalea Field.

Parker Brook Trail (Foot trail, fairly steep): Runs between Tilden Swamp, where it joins with the Tower Mt. Trail, and the parking area near the forest entrance. Parallels Parker Brook.

Sackett Trail (Foot or bridle trail, steep in places): Runs in a NE.-SW. direction between Berry Pond and junction with Tahgonic Skyline Trail.

Sackett Road Trail (Foot or bridle trail, level terrain): Runs parallel to Lulu Brook Trail from Lulu Swamp to junction with Honwee Circuit Trail.

Tahgonic Skyline Trail (Foot or bridle trail, steep and hilly): Runs N.-S. through the forest; is part of trail extending from Williamstown to New York State Line in Richmond.

Turner Trail (Foot or bridle trail, fairly steep): Runs from S. end of Berry Pond Circuit Rd. to Berry Pond.

Tower Mountain Trail (Foot or bridle trail, rugged terrain): Runs between Tower Mt. Trail and junction with Hawthorne Trail, S. of Pine Mt.

RICHMOND

AQUATICS

Richmond Pond: Located on the Pittsfield City Line. Has boating facilities on the W. shore.

FISHING

Cone Brook (Brook Trout): Flows S. from central section of town into Shaker Mill Pond, West Stockbridge.

Fairfield Brook (Brook Trout): In E. central section of town. Flows NW., then W. joining with Sleepy Hollow and Cone Brooks.

Furnace Brook (Brook Trout): In the SW. section, flows S. into Mud Pond, West Stockbridge.

Richmond Pond (Pickerel, Perch, and Horned Pout): In the NE. section of town, at the Richmond-Pittsfield boundary.

Richmond Pond Brook (Brook Trout): In N. central section of town, flows E. into Richmond Pond.

Sleepy Hollow Brook (Stocked): Flows SE. from Perry's Peak into Cone Brook.

HUNTING

All small game and deer.

OVERNIGHT ACCOMMODATIONS

*Penrhyn (27): rates (A-E), $25 to $35 per week.

WEST STOCKBRIDGE

AQUATICS

Crane Pond: In N. central section of town, W. of Mass 41; bathing and boating.

Shaker Mill Pond: Located NE. of town; boating at S. end.

FISHING

Alford Brook (Brook Trout): Flows S. into Alford. Posted.

Baldwin Brook (Brook Trout): In NW. section; flows N. to State Line Brook.

Cone Brook (Brook Trout): Flows SW. from Richmond into Shaker Mill Pond.

Cranberry Pond (Pickerel, Perch, and Horned Pout): A private pond on Mass 41, 0.5 m. W. of Shaker Mill Pond.

Crane Pond (Pickerel, Perch, Horned Pout and Trout): In N. central section, W. of Mass 41.

Furnace Brook (Brook Trout): Flows S. from Richmond into Mud Pond.

Mud Pond (Brook Trout, Pickerel, Perch, and Horned Pout): On Richmond Town Line, E. of Mass 41.

Shaker Mill Pond (Brook and Brown Trout): At West Stockbridge Center on Mass 41.

State Line Brook (Brook Trout): In extreme NW. corner of town, flows SE. from New York State into Shaker Mill Pond.

Williams River (Stocked): Flows S. from West Stockbridge Center into Great Barrington.

HUNTING

Good game covers for deer, raccoon, rabbits, fox, and game birds.

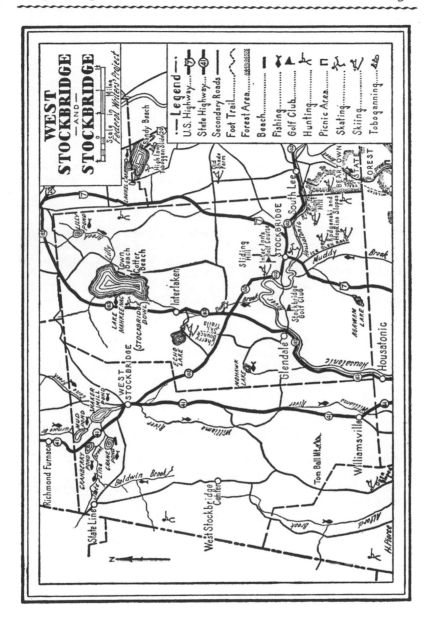

OVERNIGHT ACCOMMODATIONS

Card Lake Hotel (39): rates (A), $18 to $22.50 per week.
*****Hilltop** (14): rates (A), $20 to $22 per week.
Mrs. K. H. Hurley (7): rates (A), $15 per week.

STOCKBRIDGE

AQUATICS

Lake Mahkeenac (Stockbridge Bowl): In N. central section of town; TOWN BEACH on SE. shore; COTTER's BEACH on NE. shore. Annual boat race for summer residents.

COUNTRY CLUBS AND GOLF COURSES

Stockbridge Golf Club (*18 holes, 6140 yds.; green fees, $2 weekdays, $2.50 Sat., Sun., and holidays; 3 tennis courts; introduction by member*): Located in the center of town. The golf tournament held in July is said to be the oldest in the United States.
Inter Inn's Golf Course (*9 holes, 1650 yds.; green fees 75¢ daily; visitors welcome*): In center of town, near Heaton Hall.

FISHING

Duffy Brook (Brook Trout): In central section of town, flows S. from Lake Mahkeenac into Housatonic River.
Lake Mahkeenac (Pickerel, Perch, Crappies, Horned Pout, and Bass): In the N. central section of town off Mass 183. Also called Stockbridge Bowl.
Lilly Brook (Brook Trout): Flows S. from Lilly Pond into Lake Mahkeenac.
Lilly Pond (Pickerel, Perch, and Horned Pout): In NE. corner of town near Lenox Line.
Mohawk Lake (Pickerel, Perch, and Horned Pout): In W. central section of town, near West Stockbridge Line.
Muddy Brook (Brook Trout): Flows N. from Great Barrington into Housatonic River.

HUNTING

Good area for deer, raccoon, rabbits, and game birds.

ICE SPORTS

Ice Boating: On Lake Mahkeenac.
Ice Fishing: On Lake Mahkeenac.
Skating: At Recreation Park on US 7 near the railroad station and on Lake Mahkeenac.

OVERNIGHT ACCOMMODATIONS

The Band Box (8): rates (A), $18 to $20 per week.
Corner House (12): Main St., rates (E), $1 per day.
Cross Roads Lodge (15): rates (A), $4 per day and up.
Denise Roy (7): rates (A), $3.50 per day.
Elm Lodge (10): rates (A), $4 per day, $18 per week.
Elm Street Inn (E).
Harrod's (20): rates (A), $4 per day and up.
*****Heaton Hall** (150): rates (A), $6 per day and up.
Hillcrest Farm (12): Prospect Hill, rates (A), $5 per day.
The Laurel (15): rates (A), $4 per day and up.
The Maples (25): Elm St., rates (A), $15 per week and up.
The Martin (30): Main St., rates (A), $5 per day and up.
*****Oaklawn Inn** (50): rates (A), $5 per day.
Park View Home (30): Park St., rates (A), $18 per week.
*****Red Lion Inn** (100): rates (A), $6 per day and up.
Tracy Inn (6): Main St., rates (A), $4 per day.
Village Tavern (11): rates (A), $4 per day and up.

SKIING

Cherry Bounce Ski Trails: Located about 3 m. NW. of the town center off Mass 102. The trails run N. from Cherry Bounce Lane to Echo Lake (Lake Averic). *Class,* novice; good cross-country trails.
Practice Slope: Located on Inter Inn's Golf Course in front of Heaton Hall, 0.1 m. N. of the center. Excellent hill for novices.
Rodgenski and Hopkins Slopes: Located SE. of the town at the end of Ice Glen Rd. *Class,* novice.
Stockbridge Ski Club Night Hill: Located SE. of the center off Ice Glen Rd. A large, smooth hill that has lighting facilities for night skiing. *M.G.,* 20°; *Exp.,* N., W. Trails connect with Beartown State Forest Trails (*see Lee*).

STATE FORESTS

Beartown State Forest (*see Monterey*).

TRAILS

Foot Trails (marked) lead from the center of town near the high school to Laurel Hill, Beartown State Forest, and Cherry Bounce Lane.

LENOX

AQUATICS

Laurel Lake: On Lee Town Line (*see Lee*).

CAMPING AND PICNICKING

Schermerhorn Gorge: In the October Mt. State Forest (*see Washington*).

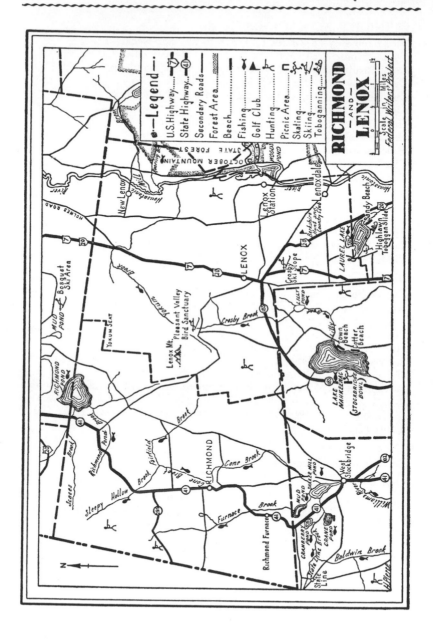

FISHING

Crosby Brook (Brook Trout): Flows S. to Stockbridge and enters Lilly Pond.

Laurel Lake (Rainbow Trout, Pickerel, Perch, and Horned Pout): In the S. section of town on the Lee Town Line.

Roaring Brook (Brook Trout): Flows W. from the October Mt. State Forest to the Housatonic River.

Yokum Brook (Brook Trout): In NE. section of town flows E. into the Housatonic River.

GOLF COURSES

Cranwell School Golf Course, formerly Berkshire Hunt and Country Club (*18 holes, 6410 yds.; green fees, $1 weekdays, $1.50 Sat., Sun., and holidays; 3 tennis courts*): Located on US 20, midway between Lenox and Lee.

HUNTING

All small game and deer.

ICE SPORTS

Laurel Lake: (*see Lee*)

OVERNIGHT ACCOMMODATIONS

*Curtis Hotel (170): rates (A-E), $6 per day and up.
Elm Street Inn: rates (A), $3.50 per day.
Hampton Terrace (8): rates (E), $1.50 per day and up.
Heathercroft.
Mahanna Hotel (A).
Old White House (10; A).
St. Lawrence: rates (A), $4 per day.
Stonewall Lodge (50): rates (A), $3 per day.
Village Inn: rates (A), $4 per day.

SKIING

Crosby Ski Slope: Located E. of the center between US 7 and US 20. *Len.,* 600'; *Wid.,* 300'; *M.G.,* 10°; Ski tow (*small fee*). Illuminated at night.

October Mt. State Forest: A 14,189-acre reservation in Washington, Becket, Lee, and Lenox. Formerly a privately owned game preserve for moose, deer, elk, and buffalo. Several mountain roads good for novices. Several open slopes located near Lenoxdale. Near the New Lenox entrance are warm cabins and open-air fireplaces.

Pleasant Valley Bird Sanctuary: Located on Cliffwood St., W. of US 7 and about 2 m. from town. This 300-acre tract has a network of trails adaptable for cross-country skiing and snowshoeing. An extension of the Skyline Trail connects (N) with Bosquet's Ski Grounds in Pittsfield, and (S) with the Beartown State Forest in S. Lee. Has museum and fireplaces.

STATE FORESTS

October Mt. State Forest: (*see Washington*).

LEE

AQUATICS

Laurel Lake: On US 20 at the Lenox Town Line. Public bathing at Sandy Beach. Boats for rent. There is a private beach connected with the Laurel Lake House.
Goose Pond: (*see Tyringham*).

CAMPING AND PICNICKING

Schermerhorn Gorge: In October Mt. State Forest (*see Washington*), has picnic benches, tables, and fireplaces. A marked road to this area leaves US 20 in East Lee.

COUNTRY CLUBS

Greenock Country Club (*9 holes, 3045 yds.; green fees, $1 daily; 3 tennis courts; introduction by member*): Located on the Stockbridge Rd. **0.5 m.** W. of the center. Members' tournament held in August.

FISHING

Goose Pond (Pickerel, Perch, Horned Pout, and Bass): In SE. section of town on Tyringham Line.
Greenwater Brook (Brook Trout): Flows W. along US 20 into Housatonic River.
Hop Brook (Brook Trout): Flows NW. from Tyringham into Housatonic River.
Laurel Lake (Rainbow Trout, Bass, Pickerel, Perch, and Horned Pout): In NW. section of town on Lenox Line.
Mud Pond Brook (Brook Trout): Flows from Mud Pond into Greenwater Brook.
Upper Goose Pond (Stocked): On the Tyringham Town Line, S. of US 20.
Washington Mountain Brook (Brook Trout at lower end): Flows W. from October Mt. State Forest into Housatonic River.
West Brook (Brook Trout): Flows N. from Beartown State Forest into Housatonic River.

HUNTING

The wooded sections are well stocked with native game.

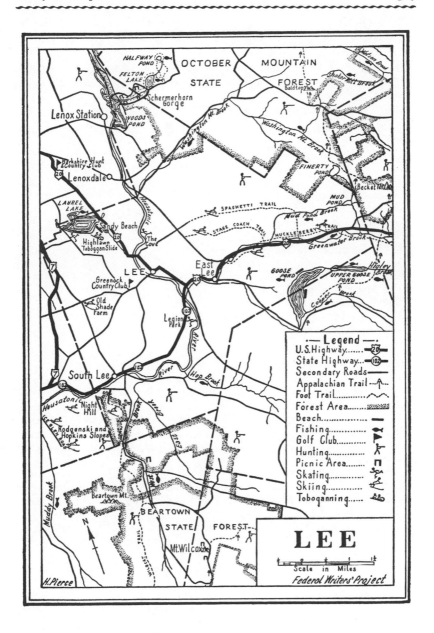

ICE SPORTS

Ice Boating: On Laurel Lake.

Ice Fishing: On Laurel Lake.

Skating: At LEGION PARK, on Mass 102, **1 m.** E. of town; at the COVE, on the Housatonic River, **1 m.** N. of town; and on LAUREL LAKE, on US 20.

OVERNIGHT ACCOMMODATIONS

Auld Wayside Lodge (12): rates (A-E), $2.25 per day, $15 per week and up.

Crow's Nest Lodge (22; A): South Lee.

*****East Lee Inn** (A-E).

Elmore Inn (14): rates $3 per day, $18 per week.

Garfield House (14): rates (A), $3 per day.

Golden Hill Rest (15): rates (A), $2.50 per day, $16 per week.

*****Greenock Inn** (A-E).

*****Greenwater Lodge** (A).

*****Kay's Kamp** (25); Laurel St., for girls only, rates (A), $12 to $15 per week.

*****Laurel Lake House** (30): US 20, rates (A), $20 and up.

The Morgan House (E).

The Red Shutter (A).

*****Teresa Carleton Inn** (15): rates (A), $18 per week.

Willow Brook (20; A).

SKIING

Beartown State Forest: Has many miles of trails suitable for cross-country skiing and snowshoeing. A development designed especially to accommodate snow-train parties is located on Beartown Mt. (alt. 1865) at the S. Lee entrance to the forest. Trails end at the railroad station. Bear Mt. has a N. exposure and is thickly wooded. *Directions for reaching:* US 7 to Stockbridge; E. from Stockbridge on Mass 102 to S. Lee; or W. from US 20 at East Lee on Mass 102 to S. Lee. Parking space near station.

Alternate Polar Trail: Swings to the E. of Polar Trail and provides an ending that eliminates the 24° straightway. Finishes on open slope. *Class,* intermediate; *Len.,* 1000'; *Wid.,* 25'-40'; *M.G.,* 15°; *Exp.,* N.; *Snow,* 4".

Burgoyne Pass Trail: A cross-country trail extending from the bottom of Crow's Nest Trail to Stockbridge. *Len.,* 7920'; *Wid.,* 10'-40'; *M.G.,* 10°; *Diff. elev.,* 500'; *Snow,* 6".

Crow's Nest Trail: *Class,* novice; *Len.,* 2395'; *Wid.,* 25'-50'; *V.D.,* 350'; *M.G.,* 20°; *Exp.,* E.; *Snow,* 6".

Grizzly Trail: *Class,* expert; *Len.,* 2574'; *Wid.,* 10'-40'; *V.D.,* 656'; *M.G.,* 30°; *Exp.,* N.E.; *Snow,* 6". This trail, completely sod-covered, runs parallel to the more difficult Kodiak Trail.

Kodiak Trail: *Class,* expert; *Len.,* 2348′; *Wid.,* 10′-30′; *V.D.,* 608′; *M.G.,* 30°; *Exp.,* NE.; *Snow,* 6″. A steep, difficult trail with a series of right-angle turns.

Mt. Wilcox Rd. (unplowed): Runs from Beartown Rd. to the summit of Mt. Wilcox (alt. 2155). *Len.,* 4 m.; *Wid.,* 20′; *Diff. elev.,* 552′; *M.G.,* 6°; *Snow,* 4″. A good cross-country ski and snowshoe trail.

New Open Slope: Located W. of the Open Slope. *Len.,* 800′; *Wid.,* 300′; *M.G.,* 10°; *Snow,* 4″.

New Semi-Open Slope: Located W. of Open Slope. *Len.,* 400′; *Wid.,* 1000′; *Av. G.,* 8°; *Snow,* 4″.

Open Slope: *Class,* novice; *Len.,* 500′; *Wid.,* 800′ (maximum): *V.D.,* 75′; *M.G.,* 20°; *Exp.,* N.E.; *Snow,* 4″-6″. A sheltered slope.

Polar Trail: *Class,* intermediate; *Len.,* 5407′; *Wid.,* 30′-100′; *V.D.,* 820′; *M.G.,* 24°; *Exp.,* N.E.; *Snow,* 6″. An excellent trail which ends on W. side of open slope. Total length and descent is measured from summit to bottom of short novice trail below the open slope.

Sedgewick Trail: Starts about halfway up Polar Trail and swings W. and N. to an ending near the railroad tracks. *Class,* intermediate; *Len.,* 2000′; *Wid.,* 25′-40′; *V.D.,* 300′; *M.G.,* 15°; *Exp.,* N.; *Snow,* 6″.

Wildcat Trail: A cross-country trail extending from the Beartown Trails to the trails at the East Mt. State Forest (*see Great Barrington*). *Len.,* 11 m.; *Wid.,* 10′-50′; *M.G.,* 25°; *Diff. elev.,* 1200′; *Snow,* 8″. The trail is marked with red ball blazes. A new Adirondack shelter has been built halfway between the C.C.C. camp and Benedict Pond.

Huckleberry Trail: A cross-country trail that begins on US 20 at East Lee and follows the abandoned trolley line over the hills through Becket, Otis, and Blandford into Huntington. Sections of this 30-mile trail are suitable for snowshoeing and cross-country skiing.

Old Shade Farm: Located on the hill road to Stockbridge, 1.5 m. W. of the center. Has 11 miles of forest bridle trails which are good for cross-country skiing and snowshoeing. Horses for ski-joring are available for a nominal fee.

Spaghetti Trail: A cross-country trail running from East St., Lee, to the Here-U-R, a roadside stand on US 20. *Len.,* 3.5 m.

Stagecoach Trail: A cross-country trail running from East St., Lee, to Belden's Tavern, 4 m. E. of town on US 20. *Len.,* 3 m.

STATE FORESTS

Beartown State Forest: Located in Lee, Great Barrington, Monterey and Tyringham. Entered from Mass 102 at South Lee (*see Monterey*).

October Mt. State Forest: Located in Lee, Lenox, Becket, and Washington (*see Washington*).

TOBOGGANING:

The Highlawn Toboggan Slide: A semicircular run, is located on the S. shore of Laurel Lake near US 20.

TRAILS

Schermerhorn Gorge: In the October Mt. State Forest. Has several short foot trails.

GREAT BARRINGTON

AQUATICS

Benedict Pond: In Beartown State Forest on Monterey Town Line. Has bathing facilities.

CAMPING AND PICNICKING

Beartown State Forest: In the NE. section of town (*see Monterey*).
Monument Mt. Reservation: On US 7, near the Stockbridge Line. Has a picnic area with tables and benches.

COUNTRY CLUBS

Wyantenuck Country Club (*18 holes, 6085 yds.; green fees, $2 weekdays, $3 Sat., Sun., and holidays; 3 tennis courts; introduction by member*): Located on W. Sheffield Rd., 2 m. SW. of town. Annual tournaments in golf and tennis held in July and August.

FISHING

Benedict Pond (Pickerel, Perch, and Horned Pout): In the Beartown State Forest on Monterey Town Line.
Green River (Brook Trout): Flows E. from Egremont then SE. into Housatonic River.
Muddy Brook (Stocked): Flows N. through NE. section of town into Housatonic River in Lee.
Roaring Brook (Brook Trout): In S. central section of town flows NW. from Sheffield Line into Housatonic River.
Root Pond (Pickerel, Perch, and Horned Pout): In the SW. section of town.
Thomas and Palmer Brook (Brook Trout): Flows NW. from near Warner Mountain along Mass 23 to Housatonic River.
Williams River (Stocked from W. Stockbridge Line downstream): Flows S. from Stockbridge and then E. into Housatonic River at Van Deusenville.
West Brook (Brook Trout): In Beartown State Forest; flows N. into Housatonic River at South Lee.

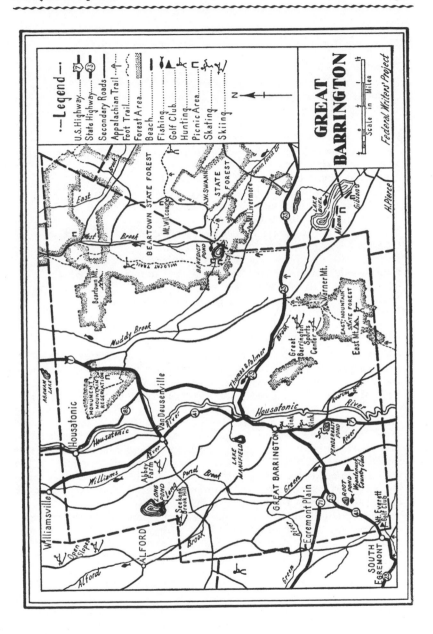

HUNTING

Good area for deer, raccoon, rabbits, fox, and game birds.

ICE SPORTS

Skating: At PENDERGAST POND, opposite Fair Grounds on US 7, **1 m.** S. of town; at TOWN RINKS on Bridge St. near the Great Barrington Manufacturing Co. plant, and at rear of High School.

OVERNIGHT ACCOMMODATIONS

Berkshire Inn (163): rates (A-E), $6 and up; reduced rates in winter.
Berkshire Lodge: rates (A), $18 to $25 per week.
Brookside Lodge (32): rates (A), $3 per day, $16 per week.
*Coach Lamp Inn (50): rates (A), $4.50 per day and up.
Elm Shade Inn (12): rates (A), $18 per week and up.
*Great Barrington Sports Center (75; E): Mass 23.
New Miller Hotel (100): rates (E), $2 per day, $12 per week.
*Oakwood Inn: rates (A), $30-$38 per week.
*Peltonbrook (12): rates (A), $32 per week and up.
Robinwoods Inn (25): rates (A-E), $3 per day, $20 per week.
The Terrace (E): 168 Main St.
Villa Marie (11): rates (A), $3 per day, $20 per week.
*Wayside Inn (E).

SKIING

Abbey Farm: Located off Mass 41, **1.6 m.** N. of the center. Open slopes (lighted at night) ideal for all classes of skiers. Cross-country snowshoe and ski trails run N. and S. *Len.,* about 900'; *Av.G.,* 14°.
East Mountain State Forest and Great Barrington Sports Center: A winter sports area partly on private land on Warner Mt. Reached from Mass 23, **2.5 m.** E. of town center. There are two ski tows (1200' and 1800'; *fee*), enabling skiers to go halfway or to the top of the downhill trails. A canteen, with ski shop, check room, and first-aid facilities, is available at the foot of the trails on private land. There is also an Inn with accommodations for 45 overnight guests. There are toilets, a parking area, and a skating rink at the foot of the trails and an Adirondack shelter and toilets at the top of the trails.

Appalachian Trail: A cross-country trail extending from Beartown Forest (*see Lee*) to the summit of East Mt. is adapted to cross-country skiing and snowshoeing. *Len.,* 11 m.; *Wid.,* 8'-20'; *Diff. Elev.,* 800'; *M.G.,* 10°; *Snow,* 8". Trail is marked with red balls painted on trees.
Bottleneck Slope: A new, wide and safe slope. *Class,* novice; *Len.,* 1500'; *Wid.,* 40'-200'; *V.D.,* 300'; *M.G.,* 15°; *Exp.,* N.; *Snow,* 6".
Forgotten Bridge Trail: *Class,* intermediate; *Len.,* 4000'; *Wid.,* 30'-80'; *V.D.,* 630'; *M.G.,* 22°; *Exp.,* N.; *Snow,* 4".

Open Field: *Class,* novice; *Area,* 8 acres; *V.D.,* 50'; *M.G.,* 10°; *Exp.,* NE.; *Snow,* 4".

Taconic Trail: *Class,* novice and intermediate; *Len.,* 3800'; *Wid.,* 20'-60'; *V.D.,* 630'; *M.G.,* 18°; *Exp.,* N.; *Snow,* 4". Wide, smooth, with many turns.

Warner Open Slope: *Class,* novice; *Len.,* 2500'; *Wid.,* 50'-250'; *V.D.,* 600'; *M.G.,* 15°; *Exp.,* N.; *Snow,* 8".

Warner Road Down Hill Trail: A cross-country trail which follows the Appalachian Trail from the summit of Three-Mile Hill to the top of the ski trails. *Len.,* 5000'; *Av.-Wid.,* 16'; *V.D.,* 1500'; *M.G.,* 8°; *Exp.,* N.; *Snow,* 4".

Wildcat Trail: A cross-country trail (*see Lee*).

Seekonk Brook Hill: Located on the Alford Rd. 3.5 m. from town. *Class,* intermediate; *Len.,* several hundred feet; *Wid.,* 1800'; *M.G.,* about 20°; *Exp.,* E.; *Snow,* 5".

STATE FORESTS AND RESERVATIONS

Beartown State Forest: (*see Monterey*).

East Mt. State Forest (1524 acres): Located off Mass 23 in Great Barrington, New Marlborough and Sheffield; is undeveloped except for skiing and hiking. East Mt. and Warner Mt. are the principal heights.

Monument Mt. Reservation (260 acres): Located W. of US 7 near the Stockbridge Town Line. Has several trails and picnic area. Good view from the ridge to the mountain.

TRAILS

Appalachian Trail: Enters from Sheffield (*see Sheffield*) at about **17 m.** and ascends to the summit of EAST MT. (alt. 1840) at **17.4 m.** At **17.8 m.** on WARNER MT., the Trail follows a ski trail down hill past the Taconic and Forgotten Bridge Ski Trails in the EAST MT. STATE FOREST. Right from the ski trail through fields; L. on the Lake Buel Rd; R. on Mass 23 at **21.2 m.** to **22.3 m.**; L. here through fields to the Blue Hill Rd., **23.3 m.** At **23.4 m.** R. from this road. The Trail enters MONTEREY (*see Monterey*) at about **23.9 m.**

Hickey Trail: From the parking space at the North entrance to Monument Mt. Reservation on US 7, the trail winds in an irregular course to the Pinnacle, **0.8 m.** W. of the summit the trail connects with the Old Woods Rd. South on this road at **1.6 m.** is Indian Monument. The woods road connects with US 7 about **4 m.** N. of Great Barrington.

Wildcat Trail: In Beartown State Forest. It begins at the skiing area at South Lee, runs through the forest past Benedict Pond to East Mt. State Forest. There is a shelter midway on the trail. Length about 11 miles.

SHEFFIELD

FISHING

Conklin Brook (Brook Trout): In S. central section of town. Flows NE. into Housatonic River.
Housatonic River (Bass and Pickerel): Below Ashley Falls only.
Hubbard Brook (Brook Trout): Flows SE. from South Egremont into Mill Pond.
Ironworks Brook (Trout): Flows S. from Three Mile Pond, emptying into Housatonic River about **0.5 m.** S. of town.
Konkapot River (Brook and Rainbow Trout): Flows NW. from Connecticut into Housatonic River at Ashley Falls.
Mill Pond (Pickerel, Perch, Horned Pout, and Bass): NW. of Sheffield and W. of Sheffield Plain.

HUNTING

Excellent area for deer, rabbits, raccoon, fox, and game birds. Ducks usually land on the lower Housatonic during the migrating season.

ICE SPORTS

Skating: On Sheffield Skating Rink, E. of US 7 at Sheffield Plain.

OVERNIGHT ACCOMMODATIONS

Elm Terrace (11): rates (A-E), $2.50 per day, $15 per week.
***Sheffield Inn** (50): US 7, rates (A), $4 and up per day.
***Sheffield Rest Farm** (15): rates (A), $17.50 per week.
Sunset View Farm (65): rates (A), $2.50 per day, $15 per week.
Twin Maples (11): rates (A-E), $3.00 per day, $18 per week.

TRAILS

Appalachian Trail: Enters from Egremont at **12.5 m.** and crosses Hubbard Brook on the Sheffield-South Egremont Rd. At **12.6 m.** is the SHAYS' REBELLION BATTLEFIELD SITE, indicated by a stone marker. Left from the Sheffield Rd. on a dirt road at **13.2 m.** and R. on US 7 at **14.4 m.** At **14.5 m.** L. across the HOUSATONIC RIVER at Upper Bridge to East Rd., **15 m.** Left on East Rd. to **15.4 m.** where the Trail swings R. across fields and woods roads to a road running N.-S. between East and June Mts. Right on this road a short distance and then L. on the Soda Springs Rd. From this road the Trail ascends over a series of ledges and at about **17 m.** enters GREAT BARRINGTON (*see Great Barrington*).
Black Rock Trail (*see Mount Washington*).
Elbow Trail (*see Mount Washington*).
Race Brook Trail (*see Mount Washington*).
Sages Ravine Brook Trail (*see Mount Washington*).
Telephone Trail (*see Mount Washington*).

YOUTH HOSTELS
An **American Youth Hostel** is maintained by Mrs. Wilfred Roys.

ALFORD

FISHING
Alford Brook (Brook Trout): Flows S. into Green River. Partly posted on upper end.
Green River (Brook Trout): In SW. section of the town. Flows from Hillsdale, N. Y., into Egremont.

HUNTING
Splendid area for deer, raccoon, rabbits, fox, wildcat, and **game birds.**

OVERNIGHT ACCOMMODATIONS
Brookside Lodge (40): rates (A), $3 per day, $16 per week.

SKIING
Alford Open Slopes: On the E. side of Alford Valley, **5 m.** NW. of Great Barrington. *Class,* all classes; *Len.,* 2600′; *V.D.,* 300′; *M.G.,* 20°; *Exp.,* W. Some fences. Hills often crusted.

EGREMONT

AQUATICS
Prospect Lake: SW. of N. Egremont. Has a private beach maintained by the Olde Egremont Inc. There is a boat livery.

COUNTRY CLUBS
Mt. Everett Golf Club (*9 holes, 2600 yds.; green fees, $1.50 daily; introduction by member or application to Olde Egremont Inc. required*): On Mass 23, **0.5 m.** E. of South Egremont.

FISHING
Goodale Brook (Brook Trout): Flows N. from Mount Washington, then E. into Hubbard Brook. Posted above dam at W. end of village.
Green River (Brook Trout; parts posted): Flows SE. from Alford into Great Barrington.
Hubbard Brook (Brook Trout): Runs E. through South Egremont into Sheffield.
Prospect Lake (Pickerel, Perch, and Horned Pout): In NW. section of town, **0.8 m.** SW. from North Egremont.

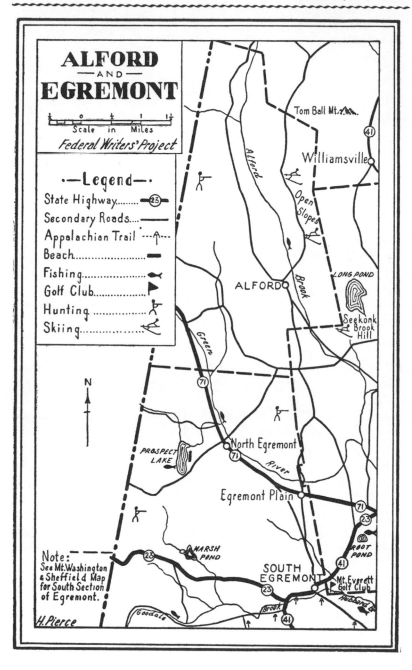

ALFORD
— AND —
EGREMONT

Scale in Miles

Federal Writers' Project

—·Legend·—

State Highway........ ㉓
Secondary Roads....
Appalachian Trail ···↑···
Beach.....................
Fishing.....................
Golf Club...............
Hunting ....
Skiing......................

Note:
See Mt. Washington
& Sheffield Map
for South Section
of Egremont.

H. Pierce

HUNTING

Splendid game area.

OVERNIGHT ACCOMMODATIONS

Elm Court Inn (35): North Egremont, rates (A), $3.50 per day, $20 per week.
*****Egremont Inn** (50): South Egremont, rates (A), $4.50 to $8 per day.
Guilder Hollow Club (60): rates (A), $3 per day, $18 per week.
Jug End Barn (70): South Egremont, rates (A), $3.50 to $4.50 per day.
Lilac Hedge, South Egremont (A-E).
Olde Egremont Tavern (10): South Egremont, rates (A), $5 per day, $30.00 per week.

SKIING

Guilder Hollow Trail: A long cross-country trail with many smooth open slopes at Guilder Hollow. *Class,* novice; *Len.,* 5 m.; *Wid.,* 15′; *V.D.,* 300′; *M.G.,* 10°; *Exp.,* N., NE.; *Snow,* 6″-8″.
Jug End Trail: Located on Mt. Sterling (alt. 1980). *Class,* intermediate; *Len.,* 5280′; *Wid.,* 8′-50′; *V.D.,* 1000′; *M.G.,* 30°; *Exp.,* NE.; *Snow,* 6″-8″.
Mt. Sterling or Skekut Trail: Located on the NW. slope of Jug End Mt. *Class,* novice; *Len.,* 7920′; *Wid.,* 5′-50′; *V.D.,* 750′; *M.G.,* 25°; *Exp.,* NW.; *Snow,* 8″-12″.

TRAILS

Appalachian Trail: Enters from Mount Washington (*see Mount Washington*) at **7.2 m.** on the summit of Mt. Bushnell (alt. 1868). The Trail continues N. along the crest of a ridge, crossing intermediate summits at **7.6 m.** and at **8 m.** before reaching Juc End, **8.5 m.** Descending from the summit the Trail reaches a grassy triangle and a road at **9.5 m.**; R. on this road and L. on next road, **9.6 m.**; at **10 m.** is the junction with another road, R. here to Mass 41, **10.8 m.**; L. on Mass 41 to South Egremont, **11.3 m.** At **12.2 m.** is the junction with the Sheffield Rd. (R). The Trail follows this road and enters Sheffield (*see Sheffield*) at **12.5 m.**

MOUNT WASHINGTON

AQUATICS

Guilder Pond: In Mt. Everett Reservation, has bathing facilities.

CAMPING AND PICNICKING

Mt. Everett Reservation: On Mt. Everett. Has picnic and parking facilities at the summit.

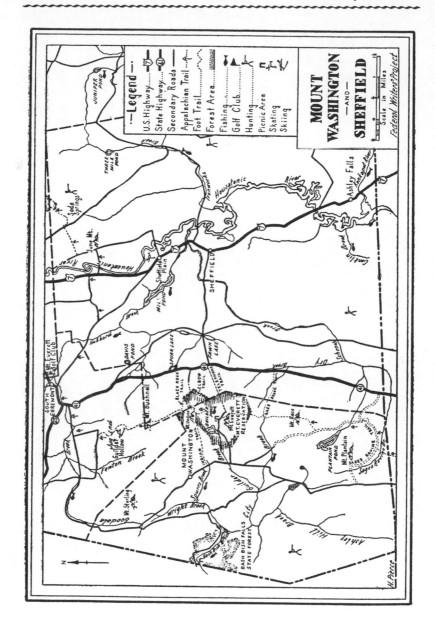

Bash Bish State Forest: On the New York Line. Has a picnic and parking area.

FISHING

Bash Bish Brook (Brook Trout): Flows W. through Bash Bish State Forest into New York State.

City Brook (Brook Trout): Flows SW. from Mt. Everett and W. into Bash Bish Brook.

Goodale Brook (Brook Trout): In NW. section of town, flows N. into Egremont.

Guilder Pond (Pickerel, Perch, and Horned Pout): In the Mt. Everett Reservation between Mt. Undine and Mt. Everett.

Spurrs Brook (Brook Trout): Flows W. into Wright Brook.

HUNTING

Good area for deer, rabbits, fox, raccoon, and wildcat.

STATE FORESTS AND COUNTY RESERVATIONS

Bash Bish Falls State Forest (390 acres): Located on the New York State Line. The most notable feature is Bash Bish Falls. Across the State Line at Copake, N. Y., is an extensive recreational development maintained by the State of New York. The best auto approach to the Forest is through Copake Falls, New York.

Mt. Everett Reservation (1000 acres, County maintained): On Mt. Everett (alt. 2644) and surrounding peaks. There are picnic facilities near the summit, at the end of the auto road, and a number of foot trails. No overnight camping allowed. Fires may be made only in fire pits.

TRAILS

Appalachian Trail: Crosses the Connecticut-Massachusetts State Line at **0 m.** and passes through SAGES RAVINE. The Trail swings N. on an old woods road, which skirts the end of PLANTAIN POND, and then turns R. through the woods to the summit of RACE MT. (alt. 2395), **3 m.** At **4.1 m.** is the junction with RACE BROOK TRAIL (*see below*). The MOUNT EVERETT RESERVATION (*overnight camping and fires prohibited except by permission of the superintendent or Reservation Commissioners*) is entered at **4.4 m.** The Trail ascends through scrub pine and at **4.9 m.** reaches the summit of MT. EVERETT (alt. 2644), the highest peak in southern Berkshire County. Here is the junction with the TELEPHONE TRAIL (*see below*). The Mount Everett Reservation Rd. is crossed at **5.4 m.** and at **5.5 m.** is the junction with a trail (L) to GUILDER POND (alt. 2100). At **6.1 m.** is the junction (R) with the ELBOW TRAIL (*see below*) and (L) with the INDIAN TRAIL (*see below*). The Trail reaches the highest point on MT. UNDINE (2195) at **6.3 m.** and the junction with BLACK ROCK TRAIL (*see below*) at **6.7 m.** Descending the eastern

slope of Mt. Undine, the Trail leaves the Mt. Everett Reservation at
6.8 m., crosses a corner of Sheffield and, as it descends to the summit of
MT. BUSHNELL (alt. 1818), **7.2 m.**, enters the town of EGREMONT (*see Egremont*).

Black Rock Trail: Leads N. then W. from the Berkshire School in
Sheffield, passes the sheer high cliff known as Black Rock, and thence
joins the Appalachian Trail.

Elbow Trail: Starts from the Berkshire School in Sheffield, leads W.
then S. joining the Appalachian Trail near Mt. Undine.

Indian Trail: A continuation of Elbow Trail at the latter's junction
with the Appalachian Trail in the Mt. Everett Reservation. The Trail
runs W. from this junction to the Union Church Rd., about **0.3 m.** N.
of the village of Union Church.

Race Brook Trail: Begins from Mass 41 (Under Mountain Rd.) **3 m.** N.
of the Connecticut State Line. Passing Bear Rock Falls, the Trail proceeds W. and joins with the Appalachian Trail between Mt. Everett and
Race Mountain.

Sages Ravine Brook Trail: Runs W. from Mass 41 in Sheffield **0.2 m.**
N. of the Connecticut State Line and town, parallels Sages Ravine Brook
in its course to a point on Union Church Rd., **0.8 m.** N. of the State
Line.

Telephone Trail: Runs between the motor road atop Mt. Everett to a
point on Mass 41, 800' N. of road to Sheffield Center.

(NOTE: Most of the territory crossed by the above trails is restricted as to fires and
camping. *See instructions under Appalachian Trail.*)

NEW MARLBOROUGH

AQUATICS

Lake Buel: On the Monterey Town Line. There are several private
beaches and boat houses on the SW. side (*see Monterey*).

York Pond: In the Sandisfield State Forest. Bathing beach and bath
house on E. shore.

CAMPING AND PICNICKING

Campbell Falls State Forest (3 acres): On the Connecticut State Line
has 6 tables and 4 fireplaces.

Lake Buel (*see Monterey*).

Sandisfield State Forest (*see Sandisfield*).

FISHING

East India Pond (Pickerel, Perch, and Horned Pout): In SE. section
of town, drains into Whiting River (*permission must be obtained from
Lufkin family*).

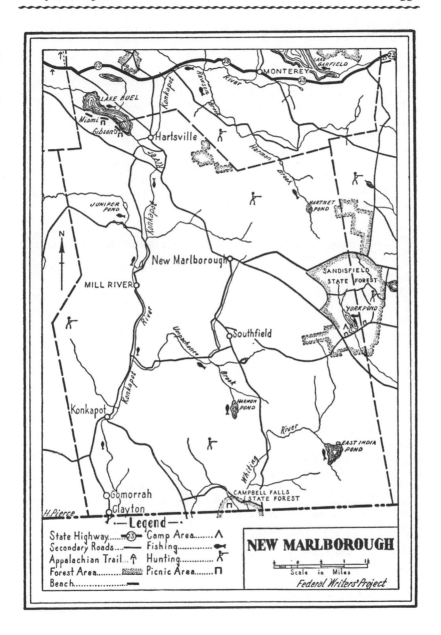

NEW MARLBOROUGH

Legend

State Highway....—23— Camp Area........∧
Secondary Roads....—— Fishing............
Appalachian Trail...↑ Hunting............
Forest Area.......... Picnic Area........⊓
Beach...................

Scale in Miles
Federal Writers' Project

Harmon Brook (Rainbow Trout): In NE. section of town, flows NW. from Hartnet Pond into Rawson Brook in Monterey.

Harmon Pond (Pickerel, Perch, and Horned Pout, and Bass): In S. central section of town.

Juniper Pond (Pickerel, Perch, and Horned Pout): In the NW. section of town, N. of Mill River Village.

Konkapot or **Mill River** (Brown, Brook, and Rainbow Trout): Flows SW. from Monterey into Connecticut. Excellent fishing.

Lake Buel (Bass, Rainbow Trout, and Pond Fish): On the Monterey Line in NW. section of town.

Umpachene Brook (Brook Trout): Flows NW. from Harmon Pond, then SW. and W. into Konkapot River S. of Mill River Village.

York Pond (Brook, Brown, and Rainbow Trout): In Sandisfield State Forest near Sandisfield Town Line.

HUNTING

Excellent game covers in wooded areas. Deer, rabbits, fox, wildcats, and game birds in season.

STATE FORESTS

Campbell Falls State Forest (2.6 acres): On the Connecticut State Line; was acquired to protect Campbell Falls which are 75′ high. There is a small picnic area.

Sandisfield State Forest (*see Sandisfield*).

MONTEREY

AQUATICS

Lake Buel: In SW. section of town on the New Marlborough Line. Has a fine grove and private beaches (*fees charged*).

Miami Beach: Bathing and boating facilities (*small fee*).

Gibson's Grove: Bathing and boating facilities (*small fee*), fishing permitted. Refreshment stands located here, also camp supplies stores.

Lake Garfield: E. of the center on Mass 23. Shore mostly privately owned, a small portion available for swimming; no beach.

CAMPING AND PICNICKING

Beartown State Forest (7990 acres) In Monterey, Great Barrington, Tyringham, and Lee. Has 50 acres devoted to recreation. There are 27 fireplaces and 26 tables at Benedict Pond, on the Great Barrington Town Line, and 13 fireplaces and 14 tables at Mt. Wilcox off Mt. Wilcox Rd. A camp and trailer site is provided. There are other picnic facilities along West Brook.

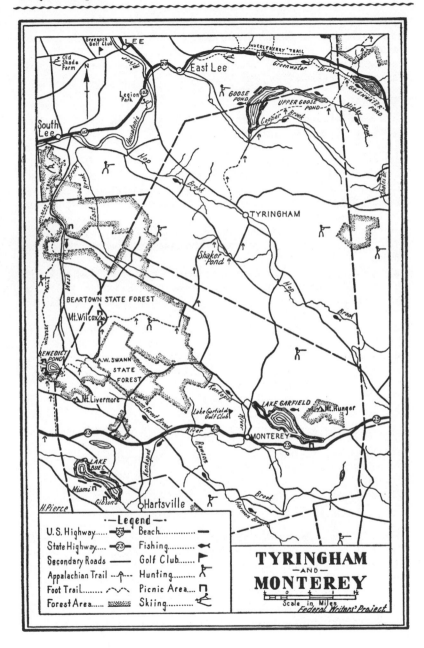

Lake Buel: There are picnic groves and camping facilities on the SE. side of the lake at Miami Beach and Gibson's Grove, both privately owned.

Lake Garfield: The only large picnic and camping area is at Perry Fargo's Grove (*small fee*) on Mass 23.

COUNTRY CLUBS

Lake Garfield Golf Club (*9 holes, introduction by member*): On Mass 23 **0.6 m.** W. of the center.

FISHING

Benedict Pond (Pickerel, Perch, and Horned Pout): In S. central part of Beartown State Forest, on Great Barrington Town Line.

Harmon Brook (Brook Trout): Flows N. from New Marlborough into Rawson Brook.

Konkapot River or **Monterey Brook** (Brook, Brown, and Rainbow Trout): Flows E. then SW. to New Marlborough from Beartown State Forest.

Lake Buel (Rainbow Trout, Bass, Pickerel, Perch, and Horned Pout): On New Marlborough Line in SW. section of the town.

Lake Garfield (Rainbow Trout, Bass, Pickerel, Perch, and Horned Pout): In SE. section of town, E. of center on Mass 23.

Rawson Brook (Brook and Rainbow Trout): In SE. section. Flows NW. then N. from New Marlborough Town Line to Konkapot River.

Swann Forest Brook (Brook Trout): Flows S. from the A. W. Swann State Forest into Konkapot River.

HUNTING

Fine territory for all native game.

OVERNIGHT ACCOMMODATIONS

Brookbend Tavern (60).
The Stone House (12).
*Tyron's.
Willow Glen House.

STATE FORESTS

Arthur Wharton Swann State Forest (987 acres): Located in Monterey. Reached from Mass 23 on Swann Forest Rd. Undeveloped for recreation.

Beartown State Forest (7990 acres): Located in Monterey, Great Barrington, Lee, and Tyringham, and entered from Mass 23 in Monterey or Mass 102 in South Lee. Fifty acres are devoted to recreation at Benedict Pond, Wilcox Mountain, and West Brook. The forest is noted for its fine azalea and laurel displays.

TRAILS

Appalachian Trail: Enters from Great Barrington (*see Great Barrington*), following the same route as the Wildcat Trail (*see Great Barrington*), and reaches the picnic grounds at BENEDICT POND, 23.9 m. The trail turns L. onto Beartown Rd. at 24.4 m. and then R. from the road through the woods to the top of the LEDGES from which there is a fine view (W) of Benedict Pond, Mt. Everett, Mt. Race, and the Catskills in New York. At 25.7 m. the Trail swings R. onto Mt. Wilcox Rd. At 26.6 m. is the junction with a side trail (L) leading to the summit of MOUNT WILCOX (alt. 2155; fire tower). At this point the Trail turns (R) and runs through woods and blueberry barrens to a woods road, 28.4 m., which is followed (L) out of the Beartown State Forest, 29 m. The Trail then follows back roads to TYRINGHAM (*see Tyringham*), 29.5 m.

TYRINGHAM

AQUATICS

Goose Pond: In the N. section of town, on the Lee Line; beaches on N. and S. shore; boats for hire at S. end.
Upper Goose Pond: E. of Goose pond; some bathing, no beach.

FISHING

Cooper Brook (Brook Trout): Flows W. from Becket into Goose Pond.
Goose Pond (Pickerel, Perch, and Horned Pout): On the Lee Town Line.
Higley Brook (Brook Trout): Flows from Becket into Upper Goose Pond.
Hop Brook (Brook Trout): Runs NW. from Otis through town to the Lee Town Line. Has 16 feeders.
Upper Goose Pond (Pickerel, Perch, Horned Pout, and Bass): E. of Goose Pond.

HUNTING

Excellent game covers in the wooded sections; deer, rabbits, raccoon, and various species of game birds.

STATE FORESTS

Beartown State Forest: (*see Monterey*).

TRAILS

Appalachian Trail: Enters from Monterey (*see Monterey*) at 29.5 m. and follows dirt roads through pine, maple, and birch forests and past country estates to TYRINGHAM, 32.2 m. The Trail follows abandoned roads northward to the well-worn Goose Pond Rd. at **34.6 m.** Right on this road to **34.9 m.** and then L. through the woods and across Cooper Brook, **35 m.** The trail ascends the ridge above Goose Pond and then descends to the E. end of Upper Goose Pond, **36.7 m.** At **37.1 m.** the Trail enters Becket (*see Becket*).

SANDISFIELD

AQUATICS

Upper Spectacle Pond: N. part of town in Otis State Forest. Bathing beach and boating.

CAMPING AND PICNICKING

Otis State Forest: On Otis Town Line off Mass 23 (*see Otis*).

Sandisfield State Forest: A picnic area has been developed on the shore of York Pond. There are 20 tables, 12 fireplaces and 6 tent sites.

Tolland State Forest: There is a picnic area along the E. bank of the Farmington River, approached from Mass 8. Facilities include 50 picnic tables, 50 fireplaces, and 10 camp sites.

FISHING

Buck or **Montville River** (Brook and Rainbow Trout): Flows SE. through the central section of town and joins the Farmington River at New Boston.

Clam River (Brook and Rainbow Trout): Flows SE. from West Otis into Buck River at West New Boston.

Farmington River (Brook, Brown, and Rainbow Trout): Flows S. along Mass 8 into Connecticut.

Simon Pond (Pickerel, Perch, and Horned Pout): On the Connecticut State Line **1.2 m.** W. of Mass 8.

Spectacle Pond (Pickerel, Perch, and Horned Pout): In Otis State Forest, S. of Upper Spectacle Pond.

Upper Spectacle Pond (Pickerel, Perch, and Horned Pout): In Otis State Forest on the Otis Town Line near Mass 23.

HUNTING

Considered to be one of the finest game areas of Berkshire County.

OVERNIGHT ACCOMMODATIONS

New Boston Inn.

STATE FORESTS

Otis State Forest (*see Otis*).

Sandisfield State Forest (3895 acres): Located in Sandisfield and New Marlborough. About 10 acres surrounding York Pond have been devel-

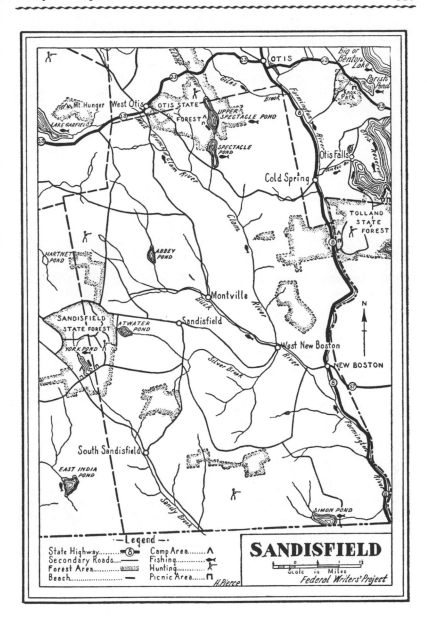

oped for recreational purposes. York Pond (*see New Marlborough*) is an excellent fishing ground.

Tolland State Forest (2940 acres): Located in Tolland and Otis along Mass 8. Twenty-six acres are devoted to recreation, subdivided into two picnic areas, one on the Farmington River and one at Otis Reservoir. There is a camping area at Otis Reservoir. Main entrance from Mass 8 in Sandisfield.

OTIS

AQUATICS

Big or Benton Pond: In the E. central section of town, N. of East Otis. There is a beach on the E. shore.

Otis Reservoir: S. of East Otis. Several beaches, one in the Tolland State Forest; boats available for hire on W. shore.

Parish Pond: In the E. central section of town near Mass 23. Boats for hire at Worden's on the W. shore.

Upper Spectacle Pond: In the Otis State Forest on the Sandisfield Town Line. Bathing.

CAMPING AND PICNICKING

Otis State Forest: S. of Mass 23. Has 18 tables, 10 fireplaces, and 12 tent sites, 6 of which have fireplaces.

Town Picnic Area (Knox Park): On Mass 23, 2.2 m. E. of Otis center.

Tolland State Forest: Camping and picnicking (*see Sandisfield*).

FISHING

Big or Benton Pond (Pond Fish): N. of East Otis.

Clam River, East Branch (Brook Trout): Flows SE. across Mass 23 into Upper Spectacle Pond.

Clam River, West Branch (Pickerel, Perch, and Horned Pout): Flows SE. from West Otis into Clam River in Sandisfield.

Creek Pond (Pickerel, Perch, and Horned Pout): In the NE. section of town, W. of White Lilly Pond.

Dimmock Brook (Stocked): Flows S. from Becket to Mass 23, and turns W., crossing to the S. side of the road and joining the Farmington River S. of the center.

Farmington River (Brook, Speckled and Rainbow Trout): Starts as a spring in cellar of Houston's Inn on US 20. Flows S. along Mass 8.

Giles or Smith Brook (Brook Trout): Flows SE. from Kingsbury Mt., crosses Mass 23 about 1.5 m. W. of the center, and empties into Farmington River S. of Otis Mill Pond.

Hayes Pond (Pickerel, Perch, and Horned Pout): In the W. section of town about 1.5 m. N. of West Otis.

Hop Brook (Brook Trout): Flows W. from Hayes Pond into Tyringham.

Otis Reservoir (Bass and Pond Fish): In SE. corner of town and in Tolland State Forest. Fishing best a month after season opens, and after rainstorms.

Otis Reservoir Brook (Brook Trout): Flows W. from Otis Falls into the Farmington River.

Parish Pond (Pickerel, Perch, and Horned Pout): Near Mass 23, W. of East Otis.

Upper Spectacle Pond (Pickerel, Perch, and Horned Pout): In the Otis State Forest on the Sandisfield Town Line.

Wheeler Brook (Brook, Brown, and Rainbow Trout) Flows W. from Parish Pond into Farmington River.

White Lilly Pond (Pickerel, Perch, and Horned Pout): In the NE. section of town near the Becket Line, W. of Algerie Rd.

HUNTING

One of the best game areas in the county. Famous for deer, raccoon, rabbits, game birds, wildcat, and fox. Canadian lynx have been shot here. Ducks and geese on the town ponds.

ICE SPORTS

Ice Fishing: On BIG POND, OTIS RESERVOIR, PARISH POND, WHITE LILLY POND, and FARMINGTON RIVER at North Otis.

OVERNIGHT ACCOMMODATIONS

East Otis Inn.

Otis Tavern (A).

Rake Shop—Tea Room (16 cabins): North Otis; rates (E), $1 per day.

STATE FORESTS

Otis State Forest (3835 acres): Located in Otis, Becket, Sandisfield, and Tyringham, along Mass 23. There is a 15-acre recreation area at Spectacle Pond. Upper Spectacle Pond, comprising approximately 60 acres, has been well stocked with trout and provides excellent fishing; in addition, there is a bathing beach here.

Tolland State Forest (*see Sandisfield*).

TRAILS

Foot Trails traverse the camping area in the Tolland State Forest (*see Sandisfield*) near Otis Reservoir.

BECKET

AQUATICS

Center Pond: N. of Becket Center; beaches on E. and W. side.

Rudd Pond: NW. of town center. Beach on NW. shore; no lockers or lifeguard.

Shaw Pond: S. of W. Becket; private beaches.

Yokum Pond: In NW. section of town; Camp Yokum, private.

CAMPING AND PICNICKING

There are several picnic areas located along US 20, on privately owned property.

FISHING

Center Pond (Pickerel, Perch, and Horned Pout): In central section of town, W. of Mass 8.

Center Pond Brook (Brook Trout): Flows NE. from Center Pond to the Westfield River.

Greenwater Pond (Pickerel, Perch, and Horned Pout): Adjacent to US 20 near the Lee Town Line.

Higley Brook (Brook Trout): Flows NW. into Upper Goose Pond in Tyringham.

Sawmill Brook (Brook Trout, 1938): Flows N. from Rudd Pond to Yokum Brook.

Shales Brook (Brook Trout): Flows into Shaw Pond, crossing Mass 8 about **0.4 m.** S. of US 20.

Shaw Pond (Pickerel, Perch, and Horned Pout): Adjacent to Mass 8 on the Otis Town Line, about **0.9 m.** S. of US 20.

Stone Brook (Brook Trout): Flows SE. from Washington to Yokum Brook.

Walker Brook (Brook Trout): Runs S. and then E. along US 20 to Chester.

Westfield River, West Branch (Brook, Brown, and Rainbow Trout): Flows E. from its source in Washington, forming part of the N. Boundary of town.

Yokum Pond (Pickerel, Perch, and Horned Pout): In the NW. section of town, W. of Rudd Pond.

Yokum Brook (Brook Trout): Flows E. and N. from Yokum Pond to Westfield River.

HUNTING

Excellent game area.

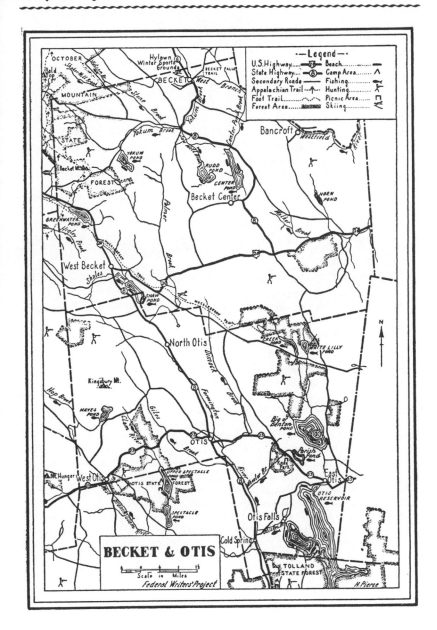

BECKET & OTIS

Scale in Miles

Federal Writers' Project

OVERNIGHT ACCOMMODATIONS

Berkshire Pines (E): Jacob's Ladder (US 20).
Lyttlebrooks (10): rates (A), $18 per week.
***Summit House** (30): Jacob's Ladder (US 20), rates (E), $1 per day.
***Wade Inn** (A-E): Center Pond.

SKIING

Hylawn Winter Sports Grounds: A new development, located on the Washington Town Line, W. of Mass 8 and **0.5 m.** N. of Becket, and formerly known as the Hays Farm Slopes. Several trails for skiing and snow shoeing and a toboggan slide are available. No charge is made; equipment must be brought by patrons. Refreshments are sold in the Wigwam, a warm house.

Hays Hazard Trail: *Class,* novice and intermediate; *Len.,* 4000'; *Wid.,* 20'; *V.D.,* 350'; *M.G.,* 12°; *Exp.,* N.; *Snow,* 6".
50-50 Break Trail: *Class,* novice; *Exp.,* E-W.
The Power Dive Trail: A fast trail with three jumps. *Class,* expert; *Len.,* 2600'; *Wid.,* 10'-30'; *V.D.,* 400'; *M.G.,* 26°; *Exp.,* N.; *Snow,* 6".
Practice Slopes: 140 acres of easy grades. *Snow,* 2".
Snowshoe Trail: A two-mile trail encircling the winter sports area. Begins and ends at the Wigwam.
Toboggan Slide: A natural slide through a wood lane and an open field. *Len.,* about 2000'; *Exp.,* E.
Huckleberry Trail: (*see Lee*).

STATE FOREST

October Mt. State Forest (*see Washington*).

TRAILS

Appalachian Trail: Enters from Tyringham (*see Tyringham*) at **37.7 m.** and descends from the ridge through woods and overgrown clearings. A woods road is followed past the outlet of GREENWATER POND to US 20, which is crossed at **37.7 m.** The trail enters the OCTOBER MT. STATE FOREST and ascends BECKET MT., crossing the first summit (alt. 2200) at **38.9 m.** and the second summit (alt. 2180) at **39.3 m.** The Trail descends through a valley and ascends WALLING MT. (alt. 2272), **39.9 m.** At **40.3 m.**, the Trail enters WASHINGTON (*see Washington*).
Becket Falls Trail: Begins at a point **0.2 m.** E. of Becket and leads across a bridge to a limestone ledge over which Becket Falls plunge into a grotesque rock channel 25' below. At the foot of the cascade is an old swimming hole.

WASHINGTON

AQUATICS

Carl Peer Pond: E. section of town. Has a private beach.

CAMPING AND PICNICKING

October Mt. State Forest: In SCHERMERHORN GORGE there are 25 picnic tables and 25 fireplaces. At WHITNEY TOWER, 2 m. NE. of the Gorge, there are 18 tables and 11 fireplaces.

FISHING

Felton Lake (Bass): In October Mt. State Forest, NE. of Schermerhorn Gorge.

Halfway Pond (Pickerel, Perch, and Horned Pout): NE. of Felton Lake, in the October Mt. State Forest.

Mud Pond (Pickerel, Perch, and Horned Pout): In the center of October Mt. State Forest.

Roaring Brook (Brook Trout): Flows W. from Clapp Pond in October Mt. State Forest into Housatonic River in Lenox.

Shaker Mill Brook (Brook Trout): Flows SE. into Becket.

Washington Mountain Brook (Brook Trout): Flows N. from Becket through October Mt. State Forest, then SW. along Washington Mountain Rd. to Housatonic River in Lee.

Watson Brook (Brook Trout): E. of Shaker Mill Brook, flows SE. into Stone Brook.

Westfield River, West Branch (Brook Trout): Originates in the E. section of town and flows SE. along the Boston & Albany RR. into Becket.

HUNTING

All small game, including wildcat and deer. One of best deer ranges in Berkshire.

OVERNIGHT ACCOMMODATIONS

Colonial Farm (15): rates (A), $15 per week.
Mapleview (50): rates (A), $2.50 per day, $12.50 per week and up.

STATE FORESTS

October Mt. State Forest (14,189 acres): In Washington, Lee, Lenox, and Becket is the largest state forest in Massachusetts. About 100 acres have been developed for recreational purposes. There are excellent fishing streams and ponds and hunting covers. A large wild life sanctuary covers much of the central section of the forest.

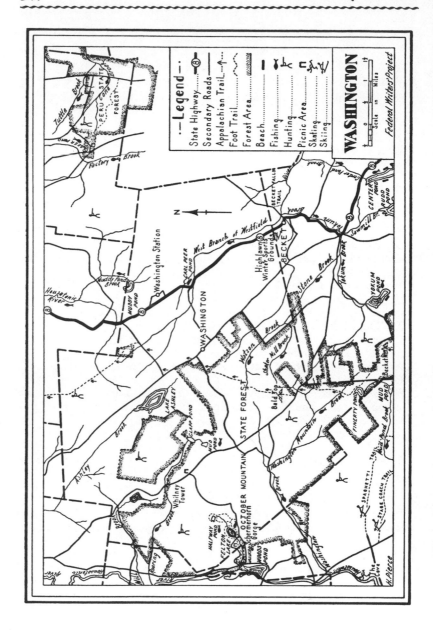

TRAILS

Appalachian Trail: Enters from Becket (*see Becket*) at **40.3 m.** and passes the northern end of Finerty Pond at **40.5 m.** The Trail continues along a woods road and at **41.9 m.** turns L. on an auto road to **42.1 m.** Here the Trail swings R. and ascends to the summit of Bald Top Mt. (alt. 2069), **42.3 m.** The Trail continues N. and leaves the October Mt. State Forest at **44.5 m.** when it turns R. on Washington Rd. Left from Washington Rd., on the Pittsfield-Becket Rd. at Washington, **45.1 m.;** R. from this road on Beach Rd. at Washington, **45.9 m.;** L. from Beach Rd. through the woods at **47 m.** At **49.3 m.** the Trail crosses Blotz Rd. and enters Hinsdale (*see Hinsdale*) at **49.4 m.**

Schermerhorn Gorge: In October Mt. State Forest, is the point of origin for a foot trail that circles Felton Lake and returns to the Gorge.

HINSDALE

AQUATICS

Ashmere Lake: Near the Peru Town Line on Mass 143. Bathing limited because of private ownership of shore property. Boats available for hire on W. shore, on Peru Rd. (Mass 143), and at refreshment stand on the E. shore.

Plunkett Reservoir: In S. central section of town, has a beach and boating facilities.

COUNTRY CLUBS

Hinsdale Golf Club (*9 holes, 2200 yds.; visitors welcome; green fees, 50¢ during July and Aug.; at other times, 25¢ on weekdays, 50¢ Sat., Sun., and holidays; seasonal membership, $10 for men, $5 for women*): On Mass 8, N. of the center. Tournaments held almost every week.

FISHING

Ashmere Lake (stocked): On Mass 143 at Peru Town Line.

Bennett Brook or **Housatonic River, Southeast Branch** (Brook Trout): Runs W. into Housatonic River.

Housatonic River (Stocked): Flows N. from Muddy Pond Brook and parallels Mass 8 into Dalton.

Muddy Pond Brook (Stocked): Flows N. from Muddy Pond on the Washington Town Line, then W. into Housatonic River.

Plunkett Reservoir (Pickerel, Perch, and Horned Pout): In S. central part of town.

Welch Brook (Brook Trout): Flows SE. into Plunkett Reservoir.

Wingtown Brook (Brook and Rainbow Trout): SE. of Plunkett Reservoir, flows NE. into Housatonic River.

HUNTING

Good area for rabbits, grouse, deer, fox, raccoon, and some pheasants.

OVERNIGHT ACCOMMODATIONS

*The Burns Place (20): rates (A), $16 per week.
The Elms (12): rates (A), $15 per week and up.
*Kilfane Lodge (35; E).
The Rath House: rates (A), $15-$28 per week; reduced rates in winter.
The Roy Place (40): rates (A), $18 per week and up.

SKIING AND SNOWSHOEING

Hinsdale Country Club Slopes: Located NE. of Hinsdale Center off Mass 8. The Country Club grounds provide excellent facilities for winter sports, with large open slopes good for skiing, tobogganning. Usable with two-inch base. Hills occasionally illuminated with portable lights.

Mt. Greylock Ski Club Jump: Located on the North slope W. of best ski hill on the Hinsdale Country Club grounds. Jump of 50'-60' possible.

Snowshoeing is popular in several sections of the town. Besides the area about the Country Club, there are WARNER MT. (alt. 2136), in the SW. section of the town off Persip's Rd. and near the Washington Town Line, and the Tulley Mt. Ledge, off Robinson Rd. to the NW.

TRAILS

Appalachian Trail: Enters from Washington (*see Washington*) at **49.4 m.** and ascends WARNER MT. (alt. 2136), **50.1 m.** The Persip's Rd. is crossed at **50.5 m.** and the Trail descends steeply to enter DALTON (*see Dalton*) at **52.3 m.**

DALTON

CAMPING AND PICNICKING

Pine Grove Park: On Curtis St., **0.2 m.** N. of Mass 8. Has tables and benches for picnickers.

COUNTRY CLUBS

Wahconah Country Club (*9 holes, 3225 yds.; green fees, $1.50; introduction by member or application at Club House required*): E. of Dalton between Mass 8 and 9. Open tournament in September.

FISHING

Flintstone Brook (Stocked): Flows S. into Wahconah Falls Brook.
Hinsdale Brook (Stocked): Flows W. from Hinsdale into the Housatonic River.

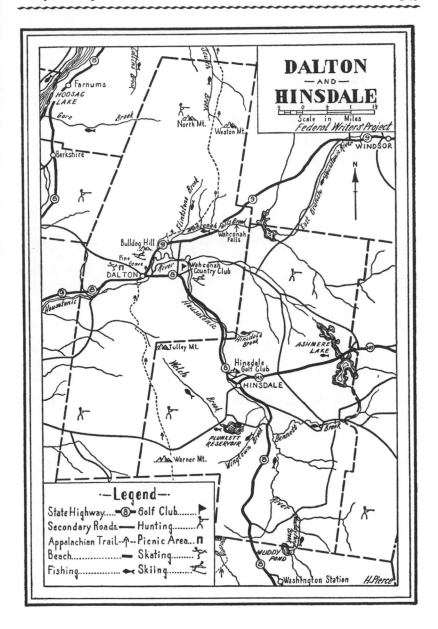

DALTON
—AND—
HINSDALE

Scale in Miles
Federal Writers' Project

Farnums
HOOSAC LAKE
Gore
Brook
Berkshire
North Mt.
Weston Mt.
WINDSOR
N
Flintstone Brook
Wahconah Falls Brook
Wahconah Falls
Bulldog Hill
Pine Grove
River
Wahconah Country Club
DALTON
Housatonic
Housatonic
Housatonic
Tulley Mt.
Hinsdale Brook
ASHMERE LAKE
Welch
Hinsdale Golf Club
HINSDALE
Brook
PLUNKETT RESERVOIR
Wingdawn Brook
Bennett Brook
Warner Mt.
River
Muddy Brook
MUDDY POND
Washington Station
H. Pierce

—Legend—

State Highway......⑧— Golf Club.......▶
Secondary Roads.——— Hunting.........ʎ
Appalachian Trail-↑- Picnic Area...⌂
Beach.................■ Skating.........
Fishing................ Skiing..........

Wahconah Falls Brook or Housatonic River, East Branch (Stocked): Flows W. and then S. from Windsor into Housatonic River.

HUNTING

Grouse, pheasants, rabbits, deer, and raccoon.

ICE SPORTS

Skating: At Pine Grove, **0.5 m.** W. of center.

OVERNIGHT ACCOMMODATIONS

The Irving House (40): rates (A-E), $2 to $3 per day; reduced rates in winter.

SKIING

Bulldog Hill: Located N. of center on Franklin St., off Mass 9. All classes; *Exp.,* N., E., and S.; *M.G.,* 20°. A large acreage of rolling, smooth pasture land. Several slopes are lighted by portables for night skiing.

Wahconah Country Club: Located E. of center on Mass 8 and 9. Several small hills.

TRAILS

Appalachian Trail: Enters from Hinsdale (*see Hinsdale*) at **52.3 m.** and descends through fields and woods to Grange Hall Rd. **53.3 m.,** which is followed L. to **53.8 m.** Here the Trail turns R. and crosses the B & A RR. tracks and Housatonic River and reaches DALTON CENTER at **55.4 m.** Mass 9 is followed R. to **56.4 m.,** where the Trail swings L. to DALTON RESERVOIR, **57.5 m.** The Trail traverses old woods roads and passes through the notch between WESTON (R) and NORTH (L) MTS. at **58.8 m.** The Trail descends the western slope of Weston Mt. and enters CHESHIRE (*see Cheshire*) at **61.2 m.**

PERU

AQUATICS

Lake Ashmere (*see Hinsdale*).

Geer Pond: In the Peru State Forest; has a beach but no lockers or bath house.

CAMPING AND PICNICKING

Peru State Forest: Has a picnic area with 16 fireplaces and 25 tables and a camping area in the NW. section of the forest, on the Hinsdale-Middlefield Rd.

FISHING

Ashmere Lake (Stocked): In E. central section of town on Mass 143 at the Hinsdale Town Line.

Cone Brook (Stocked): In the Peru State Forest; flows E. and joins Tuttle Brook.

Factory Brook (Stocked): Flows S. into Middlefield.

Fuller Brook (Stocked): Flows SE. into Worthington from the N. central section of town.

Geer Pond (Stocked): In the Peru State Forest.

Mongmeadow Brook (Stocked): Flows E. then N. to East Windsor.

Trout Brook (Stocked): In the N. section of town; flows E. into Worthington.

Tuttle Brook (Stocked): Flows E. from the Peru State Forest into Worthington.

HUNTING

An excellent game area. Deer, raccoon, fox, wildcat, rabbits, and game birds in season.

STATE FORESTS

Peru State Forest (2185 acres): In Peru and Middlefield. Three acres have been devoted to recreation areas. There are opportunities for hunting and fishing.

TRAILS

Foot Trail runs E. through the Peru State Forest from a gravel road S. of Geer Pond to a forest truck trail running N. and S. about 2 m. in the interior.

WINDSOR

AQUATICS

Windsor Pond: Extreme NE. section near the Windsor State Forest; bathing beach (life guard), boating, bath house and lockers.

CAMPING AND PICNICKING

Windsor State Forest: Has picnic facilities at Windsor Jambs, at the Clear Brook area, and at the Steep Bank Brook area, all of which provide 42 tables and 38 fireplaces.

FISHING

Clear Brook (Stocked): In E. central section of Windsor State Forest. Flows SE. into Jambs Stream.

Clear Brook Pond (Stocked): In E. central section of Windsor State Forest.

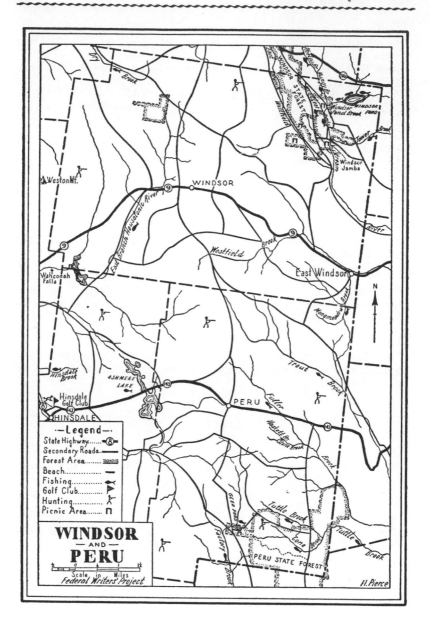

Housatonic River, East Branch or Windsor River (Stocked): Flows from the N. central part of town SW. into Town Supply Reservoir, thence into Hinsdale.

Mongmeadow Brook (Stocked): Flows E., then N. from Peru to East Windsor.

Nungy Brook (Stocked): In NE. section of Windsor, a continuation of Phelps Brook; flows SE. from Savoy into Windsor State Forest.

Quarter-Acre Pond (Stocked): In Windsor State Forest.

Tower Brook (Stocked): Flows W. from Plainfield into Windsor State Forest.

Westfield River, East Branch (Stocked): Flows through the NE. section of town.

Windsor Pond (Brown and Rainbow Trout; Pond Fish): In the extreme NE. corner of town.

Windsor Jambs Stream (Stocked): Runs S. through the Forest into Windsor Jambs, thence into Westfield River.

Windsor Pond Brook (Stocked): Flows from Windsor Pond to Windsor Jambs Stream in Windsor State Forest.

HUNTING

Hunting limited owing to posted land; some open area for rabbits and deer.

STATE FORESTS

Windsor State Forest (1515 acres): Located within the towns of Savoy and Windsor; contains the celebrated Windsor Jambs, one of the scenic attractions of the State. Fifteen acres along the Westfield River and 25 acres at Windsor Jambs are developed for recreation. A bathing pool has been provided at the Westfield River picnic grounds. There is a large Wild Life Preserve. The Forest is best reached from Mass 9 at West Cummington.

TRAILS

Foot Trail: Begins at the parking area near Windsor Jambs and proceeds N. to the Clear Brook Pool and picnic area. At the latter point it turns W. and passes through the Wild Life Area in the center of Windsor State Forest. At about **0.9 m.** from Clear Brook Pool, the Trail turns S., branches out into a series of circular and side-trail by-paths near Middle Rd., and continues on to approach Windsor Jambs from the S.

SAVOY

CAMPING AND PICNICKING

Savoy Mt. State Forest: Has 23 tables and 13 fireplaces at Tannery Falls and Gulf Brook. Twenty tent sites and 6 trailer sites offer adequate facilities for camping.

FISHING

Black Brook (Lower end, Brook Trout; upper end, posted): Runs N. into Cold River, along Black Brook Rd.

Bog Brook (Brook Trout): Flows NE. from Bog Pond into Florida, thence into Cold River. Greater part closed because it is in a Wild Life Area.

Brown Brook (Brook Trout): In Savoy Mt. State Forest. Flows SE. into Carpenter Brook.

Carpenter Brook (Brook Trout): Flows SE. into Chickley River near Hawley Town Line.

Center Brook (Brown, Brook, and Rainbow Trout): Runs in a N. to S. direction between the villages of Savoy Center and Savoy.

Chickley River (Brook and Rainbow Trout): Runs from the SE. section of Savoy Mt. State Forest E. to the Hawley Line.

Drowned Sand Brook (Brook and Rainbow Trout): Flows N. from Windsor to Mass 116 in SW. section.

Gulf Brook (Brook and Rainbow Trout): Flows E. into Cold River.

Horsefords Brook (Brook Trout): In Savoy Mt. State Forest. Flows SE. into Chickley River.

Horton Brook (Brook Trout): In the extreme SE. corner of Savoy Mt. State Forest. Flows N. into Chickley River.

Phelps Brook (Stocked): Flows S. into Windsor.

Savoy Hollow Brook (Brook Trout): In the SW. section of town S. of Center Brook. Flows SE. into Westfield River.

South Pond (Pond Fish): In the NW. section of Savoy Mt. State Forest near the Florida Town Line. Written permit from forest supervisor necessary.

Tannery Pond (Brook and Brown Trout): S. of Tannery Falls, in Savoy Mt. State Forest. Written permit from forest supervisor necessary.

Tilton Brook (Brook Trout): In the SE. section of Savoy Mt. State Forest. Flows E. into Chickley River.

Westfield River (Stocked): S. of Savoy village. Runs SE. into Windsor.

HUNTING

The forests abound in good game covers. Excellent area for deer, rabbits, fox, wildcat, raccoons, and game birds. There is a large Wild Life Area in the Savoy Mt. State Forest.

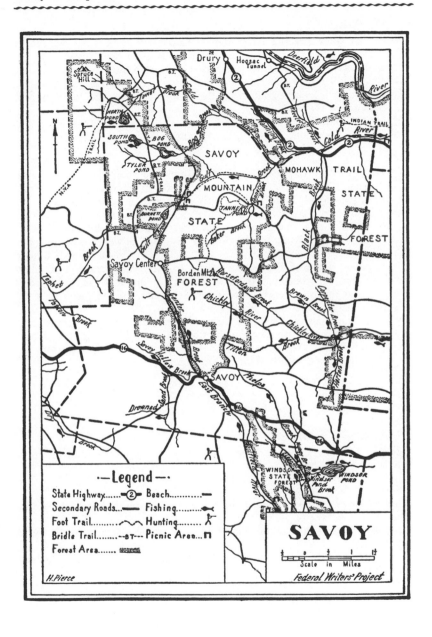

STATE FORESTS

Savoy Mt. State Forest (10,641 acres): Located in Savoy, Adams, North Adams and Florida. The highest elevation is 2500 feet. Thirty-two-acre tract devoted to recreation, subdivided into two picnic areas at Gulf Brook and Tannery Falls. There are good trout ponds and streams; and hunting is permitted outside the wild-life area. The forest is best reached from Mass 2.

Mohawk Trail State Forest (5746 acres): Located on Mass 2 in the towns of Charlemont, Hawley, Savoy, and Florida (*see Florida*).

TRAILS

Berkshires to the Capes Bridle Trail: Enters the Savoy Mt. State Forest from Adams over an old woods road W. of Burnett Pond. The Trail runs N. past South Pond to the Florida Town Line (*see Florida*).

Foot Trails: In the Savoy Mt. State Forest at Tannery Falls and Gulf Brook picnic area, there are several trails, one extending SW. from Balanced Rock, 1.7 m., to the Fire Tower on Savoy Mountain (alt. 2613). A short circular trail begins at the picnic grounds at Tannery Falls, passes Balanced Rock, and returns to the picnic area. Still another trail follows the course of Gulf Brook E. for about 1.4 m., and loops back to the starting point. Another trail leads from the picnic area at Tannery Falls to the Gulf Brook Trail.

N.Y.A. Trails: In the Savoy Mt. State Forest, there are two trails: one running S. from North Pond to a junction with Mass 116; the other, running SW. from the Berkshires to the Capes Bridle Trail about 0.4 m. N. of North Pond to East Hoosac St., Adams (*see Adams*).

CHESHIRE

AQUATICS

Hoosac Lake or Cheshire Reservoir: Bathing and boating; S. of town on Mass 8.

FISHING

Collins Brook (Brook Trout): In S. central section of town; flows N., then W. into Hoosac Lake.

Dry Brook (Brook Trout): Flows NW. from Windsor through town into Adams.

Gore Brook (Brook Trout): In S. section of town; runs W. into Cheshire Reservoir.

Hoosac Lake or **Cheshire Reservoir** (Pond Fish and Bass): Lies adjacent to Mass 8; partly in Lanesborough.

Hoosic River, South Branch (Brook, Brown, and Rainbow Trout): Flows N. from Hoosac Lake through town into Adams.

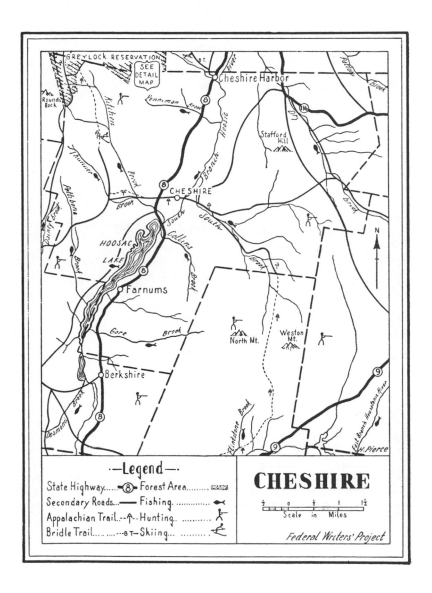

-Legend-

State Highway.....⑧- Forest Area.........
Secondary Roads...— Fishing. ....
Appalachian Trail.--↑--Hunting. ....
Bridle Trail.......-B T-Skiing.. ....

CHESHIRE

Scale in Miles

Federal Writers' Project

Kitchen Brook (Brook Trout): Flows SE. into Hoosic River.
Penniman Brook (Brook Trout): Flows E. into Hoosic River.
Pettibone Brook (Brook Trout): In SW. section of Cheshire; flows SE. into Lanesborough, thence into Hoosac Lake.
South or **Smith Brook** (Brook Trout): Starts in Dalton, flows NW. into Hoosic River.
Thunder Brook (Brook Trout): Flows SE., then E. into Kitchen Brook.

HUNTING

Excellent game covers. Deer, raccoon, rabbits, and game birds.

OVERNIGHT ACCOMMODATIONS

Bickford Farm: rates (A), $2.50 per day.
Broadacres (16): rates (A), $15 per week.
Cheshire Inn: rates (A), $2.50 per day.
Ormesby Farms Inn (12): rates (A), $5 per day and up; special weekly rates.
Mrs. Raymond Wells (10): rates (A), $18 per week.
Shady Lawn Farm: rates (A), $25 per week.

SKIING

Appalachian Trail: That part of the Trail extending from Cheshire to Jones' Nose on Mt. Greylock makes a fine cross-country ski run. It meets the Cheshire Harbor Trail at the Rockwell Motor Rd., near the summit of Greylock.
Cheshire Harbor Trail: (*see Adams*).

STATE FORESTS AND RESERVATIONS

Greylock State Reservation (*see Adams*).

TRAILS

Appalachian Trail: Enters from Dalton (*see Dalton*) at **61.2 m.** and proceeds NW. through a deep gullied road to the STAFFORD TRAIL, **63.7 m.**, which is followed L. to CHESHIRE VILLAGE, **64.2 m.** West Rd. is followed W. from Cheshire to **65.3 m.** where the Trail turns R. and goes through fields and woods, crossing many brooks. KITCHEN BROOK is crossed at **67.9 m.** At **68 m.** the Trail enters the GREYLOCK STATE RESERVATION as it crosses the old Cheshire Harbor Rd., and turns L. to the large rock near the Rockwell Rd. It then turns R. and enters NEW ASHFORD (*see New Ashford*), at **68.7 m.**
Cheshire Harbor Trail: (*see Adams*).

ADAMS

CAMPING AND PICNICKING

Greylock State Reservation: Has a picnic area on the summit of Mt. Greylock, with fireplaces and picnic grounds. Dormitory accommodations and meals are available at the BASCOM LODGE (caretaker on premises; open summer and winter). *Directions for reaching: (see State Forests, page 359).*

COUNTRY CLUBS

Forest Park Country Club (*9-hole course; 2300 yds.; green fees, 50¢ weekdays; $1 week-ends and holidays; 1 tennis court; introduction by member or by applying at club house*). Located on Forest Park Avenue.

FISHING

Dry Brook (Brook Trout): Flows N. from Cheshire into Hoosic River.
Granny or Tophet Brook (Brook Trout): Flows SW. from Savoy Town Line, then NW. into Anthony Creek and Hoosic River.
Notch Brook (Brook Trout): Runs in a northerly direction from the Bellows Pipe on Mt. Greylock, to North Adams.
Pecks Brook (Brook Trout): Flows S., then E. from Mt. Greylock into Hoosic River.

HUNTING

Fine game covers in the thickly wooded hills; partridges, rabbit, and pheasant.

OVERNIGHT ACCOMMODATIONS

Crystal Door Inn (12): rates (E), $1 per day.
Dean Homestead (27): rates (E), $1 per day.
Greylock Hotel (32): rates (E), $1 per day.
Greylock Rest (25): rates (A-E), $1 per day and up.
Mohawk Hotel (40): Pleasant St., rates (E), $1 per day and up.

SKIING

Greylock State Reservation (8660 acres): Has several of the best ski trails in the county and over 25 m. of snowshoe trails. At the summit (alt. 3505) is Bascom Lodge with refreshment facilities and overnight accommodations for 40 people. The New Ashford Rd., from US 7, New Ashford, is plowed to the C.C.C. Camp, about 1.5 m. from the summit. Skiers can also use the Notch Rd. (not plowed in the reservation). The Hopper and Stony Ledge Trails are best reached from Williamstown (*see Williamstown*).

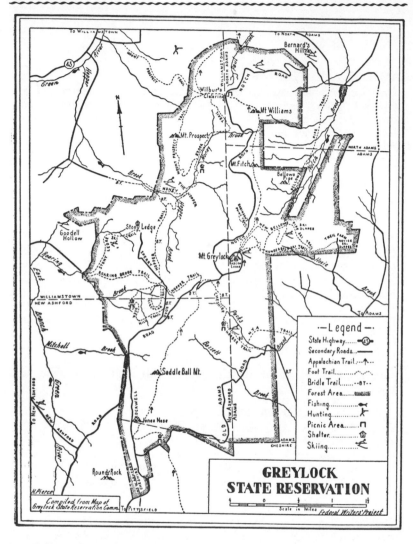

Bellows Pipe Open Slopes: Near Thiel Farm, NE. base of Mt. Grey-lock, end of New Bellows Pipe and Thunderbolt Trails. *Class,* novice. **Cheshire Harbor Trail:** Located partly in Greylock State Reservation on the SE. shoulder of Greylock and descending on to the old Cheshire Harbor Rd. *Class,* novice; *Len.,* 13,200'; *Wid.,* 6'-20'; *V.D.,* 2000'; *M.G.,* 18°; *Exp.,* E., SE. (thickly wooded); *Snow,* 6". This

Trail, one of the very first used for skiing in the Berkshires, is still popular. Advanced skiers will find it sufficiently interesting under fast conditions. The old Adams road, turning off S. part-way up, is an excellent cross-country trail. *Directions for reaching:* W. from Mass 8 at Cheshire Harbor on old state road; R. at first road junction; then L. on to West Mt. Rd.

New Bellows Pipe Ski Trail: Located in the Greylock State Reservation on the NE. slope of Mt. Greylock. The new trail replaces the old Bellows Pipe Trail; it begins and ends with the Thunderbolt (*see below*) but makes a wide swinging course by the upper end of the Notch and then swings SE. across the open slopes. *Class,* intermediate; *Len.,* 7775; *Wid.,* 12'-35'; *V.D.,* 1402'; *M.G.,* 27°; *Exp.,* E. & S.; *Snow,* 5".

Thunderbolt Ski Run: Located in the Greylock State Reservation on the NE. slope of Mt. Greylock. *Class,* expert; *Len.,* 8448' (racing course, 7392'); *Wid.,* 18'-60'; *V.D.,* 2175' (racing trail, 2050'); *M.G.,* 35°; *Exp.,* N., NE., E.; *Snow,* 5" (8" top steep slope). This is one of the steepest and most difficult runs in the East. The annual Massachusetts Downhill Ski Championship races, and the Eastern Downmountain Championship races are usually held here. The lower third of the course has been changed so as to be on Greylock State Reservation property. At the foot of the Thunderbolt Trail, near Thiel Farm, is a huge parking area. *Directions for reaching:* W. on Maple St. from Mass 8 at McKinley Square in Adams to West Rd. **0.4 m.**; L. on West Rd. to road junction, **1.2 m.**; R. on this road to Thiel Farm, **1.9 m.** Chains may be needed on this last part.

STATE FORESTS AND RESERVATIONS

Greylock State Reservation (8660 acres): Located in Adams, North Adams, Williamstown, New Ashford, and Cheshire. Has 25 miles of trails, overnight shelters at vantage points of scenic interest, fireplaces, two swimming pools, and other recreational features. The lodge at the summit is open year round. Best reached by Rockwell Rd. from US 7, Lanesborough, or by Notch Rd. from Mass 2 in North Adams.

Savoy Mt. State Forest (*see Savoy*).

TRAILS

Appalachian Trail: Enters from New Ashford (*see New Ashford*) and reaches Rockwell Rd., **71 m.**, which is followed R. past the cut-off to the Hopper Trail (*see Williamstown*), **71.2 m.**, and the Cheshire Harbor Trail (*see below*), **71.3 m.** Between **71.5 m.** and **71.8 m.**, the Trail leaves the Road and follows the Misery Trail. At **71.9 m.** is the summit of Mt. Greylock (alt. 3505), the highest mountain in Massachusetts. Here is the State War Memorial Beacon and Bascom Lodge (*accommodations for 20 men and 20 women; small charge for food and blankets; open all year*). The Thunderbolt Ski Trail is followed to

72.4 m. The Trail crosses Mt. Fitch (alt. 3220) at **73.2 m.** and enters, North Adams (*see North Adams*) at **73.6 m.**

Bellows Pipe Foot Trail (Williams Outing Club; marked WOC): Extends from the summit of Greylock E. across the Thunderbolt Trail. It reverses its direction at two points on the descent, finally proceeding in a NW. direction to North Adams.

Berkshires to the Capes Bridle Trail: From Mass 8, at junction with the Cheshire Harbor Trail, it extends E. to Savoy Town Line near Burnett Pond.

Cheshire Harbor Trail: From Mass 8, **0.3 m.** S. of the Cheshire Town Line, the Trail leads NW. over a dirt road which parallels Bassett Brook for a short distance. As the road enters the Greylock State Reservation, the Trail goes through the woods and joins the Appalachian Trail and the Rockwell Rd. The Berkshires to the Capes Bridle Trail follows the same route.

N.Y.A. TRAILS: There are three trails: one runs NE. from East Hoosac St. to the Savoy State Forest where it joins the Berkshires to the Capes Bridle Trail; another runs S. from the junction of these trails through Savoy State Forest to Mass 116; the third runs W. from the Dean Farm to Camp Hamblen and then S. to the Cheshire Harbor Trail.

Robinson's Point Trail: This trail branches NW. from the Appalachian Trail at a point **0.4 m.** NE. of the summit of Mt. Greylock. Continuing across the Notch Rd. the Trail leads to a vantage point near the inner Hopper. The view from the latter point is well worth the trip.

Thunderbolt Trail (Williams Outing Club; marked WOC): Primarily a ski trail, it runs NE. from the summit of Mt. Greylock. At about **0.5 m.** the trail turns S., gradually changing to an easterly direction at **0.9 m.**, and ending near Thiel Farm.

YOUTH HOSTELS

An **American Youth Hostel** is maintained by Mrs. Mabel Read Pela, 35 Crandall St.

INDEX

(Abbreviation, *recr.*, indicates recreational section)

Adams, 258, 266-275; *recr.*, 357-360; *map*, 289
Adams, Henry, 198
Adams, Samuel, 268
Adams Society of Friends' Descendants, 272
Alford, 172-175; *recr.*, 325; *map*, 326
Alford Brook, 175
Alford, Col. John, 173
Allen, Jonathan, 82
Allen, Rev. Thomas, 53, 67, 71
Amherst, Gen. Jeffrey, 211
Anthony, Susan B., 271
Appalachian Trail, 288, 291, 294, 298, 322, 323, 324, 327, 329, 335, 342, 345, 346, 348, 356, 359
Appleseed, Johnny, 218
Appleton, Frances, 75
AQUATIC SPORTS, 279; in Becket, 340; Cheshire, 354; Clarksburg, 288; Egremont, 325; Florida, 285; Great Barrington, 320; Hancock, 300; Hinsdale, 345; Lanesborough, 298; Lee, 316; Lenox, 313; Monterey, 332; Mount Washington, 327; New Marlborough, 330; North Adams, 290; Otis, 338; Peru, 348; Pittsfield, 302; Richmond, 309; Sandisfield, 336; Stockbridge, 312; Tyringham, 335; Washington, 343; West Stockbridge, 310; Windsor, 349
Arnold, Benedict, 29, 41
Arnold, Matthew, 117
Arrowhead, 73
Arthur, Pres. Chester A., 128
Asbury, Rev. Francis, 179, 183
Ashintully, 199
Ashley, Col. John, 112, 169
Ashley Falls, 167
"Ashuelot Equivalent," 232
Austin, Nathaniel, 138
Ayers, Rev. Braman, 224
Baker Family, the, 173
Balance Rock Park, 63
Baldwin, Laommi, 1
Barber, William B., 24
Barker, Susan, 62
Barnard, Frederick A. Porter, 168
Barrett Family, the, 173

Barrington House, 157
Barrington, Viscount, 152
Bartholomew's Cobbles, 169
Baruch, Bernard M., 38
Bash Bish Falls, 186
Baxter, James Phinney, III, 39
Beaux, Cecilia, 198
Beaver, 15
Becket, 207, 218-224; *recr.*, 340-342; *map*, 341
Becket Falls, 222, 342
Beebe, Levi, 147
Beecher, Rev. Henry Ward, 132
Beecher Hill, 132
Bellows Pipe, 25
Benedict, Isaac, 195
Bennett, Joseph, 260
Bennett, Mrs., 260
Bennington, Battle of, 7, 53, 68
Berkshire Art School, 196
Berkshire Athenaeum, 72
Berkshire Festival Society, 122
Berkshire Glass Company, 57
Berkshire Medical College, 71
Berkshire Playhouse, 118
Berkshires to the Capes Bridle Trail, 287, 294, 298, 354, 360
Billings, Josh, 47, 57, 58, 60
Bird, Francis, 2
Bishop, Cortlandt Field, 49, 129
Bishop, David W., 129
Bissell, Israel, 227
"Bliss Hoof Cutter," 177
Bolger, James, 248
Boltwood, Edward, 79
Bonny Rigg Four Corners, 218
Bosquets Ski Run, 131
"Boston Corner," 183
Boston Symphony Orchestra, 122
Bow Wow Cemetery, 171
Bowen, Eugene Bucklin, 264
Bradley, Jesse, 136
Bradley, Joshua, 137
Bradley House, 62
Brague, Louis B., 230
Brattle, William, 67
Brewer, Capt. John, 196
Bridle Trails, 284

361